REGION-BUILDING

REGION-BUILDING

Volume II: Regional Integration in the World: Documents

Ludger Kühnhardt

Berghahn Books
New York • Oxford

Published in 2010 by

Berghahn Books

www.berghahnbooks.com

©2010 Ludger Kühnhardt

Library of Congress Cataloging-in-Publication Data

Kühnhardt, Ludger.

Region-building / Ludger Kühnhardt.

p. cm.

Includes bibliographical references and index.

ISBN 978-1-84545-655-9 (hardback : alk. paper)

1. Regionalism (International organization) 2. Globalization. 3. Regionalism—European
Union countries. 4. Regionalism—Europe. I. Title.

JZ5330.K64 2010

341.24—dc22   2010008024

British Library Cataloguing in Publication Data

A catalogue record for this book is available from the British Library

Printed in the United States on acid-free paper

ISBN: 978-1-84545-655-9 Hardback

Contents

Introduction

The Global Proliferation of Region-Building

Ludger Kühnhardt

———⊙———

From Sovereignty-Driven Decolonization to Integration-Oriented Globalization

European integration has, for myriad reasons, gained global interest. Increasingly, European integration is perceived as a source of inspiration for other processes of regional cooperation and integration around the world. To be sure, European integration does not serve as a static model that can be proliferated, as the sources of European integration and its genuine objectives, policies, and institutions cannot simply be duplicated elsewhere in the world. But the global relevance of European integration experiences does not depend on symmetric developments in other parts of the world. Rather, other parts of the world refer increasingly to the European integration experience while their own regional groupings are being reexamined, streamlined, and strengthened. In the course of the twenty-first century this shared experience of region-building will increasingly be linked with the understanding of governance structures, cultural identities, and last but not least, world order–building.

The global proliferation of regional integration coincides with a more assertive global role of the European Union. With its policies, the European Union supports regional integration efforts worldwide. Since the late twentieth century, EU policies and instruments of cooperation with other regions have broadened: from trade to economic integration (EU relations with the Gulf Cooperation Council), from developmental aid to association and political cooperation (EU relations with MERCOSUR, the Andean Community, and the Central American Integration System), from trade to development and governance issues (EU relations with the partner countries of the Cotonou Agreement in Africa, the Caribbean, and the Pacific), from economics to a preferential strategic partnership (EU relations with ASEAN). These developments are not static, nor have they gained a final status. Over time, some processes of biregional cooperation may emerge as more stable, sustainable. and successful than others. Some of the processes of biregional cooperation are a remote echo of colonial and postcolonial memories. Others are a reaction to "globalization" and the global role of the United States. Most relations between the European Union and other regional groupings are asymmetrical, with the EU being more integrated and economically much stronger.

The academic literature about the global proliferation of regionalism is confusing because of its use of various and often ambiguous definitions of regionalism. "Open regionalism," "new regionalism," "regional cooperation," "regional integration," "subregionalism," and "regionalization" are but some of the terms used to characterize trends and processes of different speeds, depths, and structures. Those who compare the European Union with other regional cooperation and integration schemes tend to underestimate the relevance and strength of EU integration. At the same time they tend to maintain a static form of comparison that fails to sufficiently take into account the dynamic and evolving character of region-building outside Europe. They tend also to reduce regional integration to its economic level without recognizing the political and sociocultural dimensions and their implications for world order–building.

So far, no regional grouping outside Europe has reached the EU level of supranationality. However, it would be incorrect to conclude that other regional groupings therefore are doomed to remain flawed and irrelevant. Indeed, the time factor should not be overlooked: it has taken the EU decades to reach its current level of integration, which itself is hardly free of idiosyncrasies and shortcomings. Non-European integration schemes simply need more time to mature, given that most of them launched their serious stage only after the end of the Cold War, as part of the emerging worldwide paradigm of globalization. This turning point for region-building in the early 1990s coincided with the global recognition of European integration as a new and relevant reality in world affairs. It would also be incorrect to compare other regions with the European Union on strictly economic terms, thus concluding, for example, that the EU as an economic giant is incomparable with the Caribbean Community (CARICOM) because of grossly disparate GDP rates. It is instead necessary to broaden the scope of the comparative study of regional integration.

The global proliferation of regional integration will need to be taken seriously in light of a combination of two sets of experiences. On the one hand, it is important to understand regional integration as a process of contingent historical circumstances, specific combinations of challenges and responses, and local actions and consequences. On the other hand, regional integration is always linked to global trends in politics and economics. It is an indigenous response to exogenous challenges as much as it is a local scheme that may echo distant experiences of others. In the years to come, comparative global regionalism will be a source of useful and valuable new research efforts in the social sciences.

Such efforts reflect the growing relevance of processes underway in many regions of the world. Area studies will need to be linked with studies about the relationship between democratic transformation and the evolution of regional stability. Research must also consider regional developments of integration or cooperation in light of specific regional economic, social, cultural, political, and security challenges. The global proliferation of regional integration schemes must be put into its specific historical, cultural, socioeconomic, and political context. It will generate multidimensional approaches of comparative research regarding motivation, structure, function, scope, depth, and deficits of all the regional groupings that exist in the world of the early twenty-first century.

Is there, as Walter Mattli has asked, a logic of integration?[1] Like any other historical determinism, the notion of seemingly inevitable path dependencies must be rejected. There is simply no law of history that unfolds in a global and universally applicable form. By the same token, it would be misleading to assume that regional integration can be molded and made suitable for export and worldwide implementation. Region-building can fail (as happened in East Africa in the mid 1970s). It can also endure divergent modes, patterns, and processes, and it can regain strength after periods of weakness. Since the turn of the century, global proliferation of regional cooperation and integration has begun to re-map the world. With the end of the Cold War and numerous communist dictatorships, the distinction between a first and a second World has dissolved. Manifold transformation experiences in postcommunist countries have substituted geographical and cultural fixations that existed over decades. Realignments such as the inclusion of Central European countries into NATO and the European Union have been experienced, even as Russia has revived its Great Power status as a neo-autocracy in the midst of many Russians' enormous economic impoverishment and Central Asia has reemerged as a geopolitical and, increasingly, also a cultural fact.

In line with transformations in politics, culture, and the economy, the developing world, traditionally labeled the "Third World," has undergone transformations of great magnitude. The global proliferation of regionalism raises questions about the very concept of a seemingly cohesive "Third World." In socioeconomic terms, the distinction between "newly industrialized countries," "threshold countries," and "least developed countries," measured by indicators of human development and criteria for good governance, points to the need for an increasingly differentiated perception. With the global proliferation of regional integration and cooperation on a continental scale, the very term "Third World" must be replaced by a new understanding of the world's continents and specific regions inside these continents. Regional integration brings geography and proximity, but also culture and identity, back to the study of world politics and development issues.

To understand the global proliferation of regional integration, it is useful to distinguish historical periods in the evolution of sovereignty. It is important to reconsider sovereignty outside Europe—as much as inside Europe—in its two fundamental aspects: as state sovereignty and as popular sovereignty.[2] One important perspective links regional integration with the evolution of the sovereign state. To link it with the evolution of popular sovereignty—that is to say, with the relevance of democratic governance and rule of law among the participating members of a regional grouping—is the other important European experience and perspective that needs to be reconsidered by comparative regionalism.

Sovereignty—both as state sovereignty and as popular sovereignty—underwent various stages in its development during the twentieth century. Concepts of integration, region-building, and experiences with region-ness have been transformed. None of these transformations has followed universal patterns. But it is imperative to link the focus of research across stages of time, conceptual reconfigurations, and impacts on regional processes in their complexity. It may be helpful to consider the following description of two distinct stages in the relationship between sovereignty and region-building outside as well as inside Europe.

STAGE ONE

Europe emerged destroyed from the ashes of two World Wars and found itself divided along highly ideological and rigid geopolitical lines. Democratic countries began to rebuild Europe through the mechanism of integration. At the same time, the process of decolonization continued, reflecting the causes and effects of Europe's "de-empowerment" in the twentieth century. Originally, the newly independent countries of the southern hemisphere copied European concepts of state-building based on rigid and proud notions of national sovereignty. In many developing countries, the hope for democratic statehood was challenged in the name of national unity. Notions of state sovereignty and claims to popular sovereignty often clashed in what came to be understood as the "Third World." Attempts at regional cooperation and integration often remained a defensive response to the process of decolonization, if not an element of it. They occurred under conditions of weak sovereignty, in terms of both state structures and governance performance. Weak economies and enormous social pressure due to high poverty levels refocused the priorities of most developing countries. While transnational cooperation and integration were objects of rhetorical invocations, the prime focus was on state-induced socioeconomic development and nation-building. The state was considered to be the promoter of nation-building, and the more its capacities were involved in this process, the more it fell short of engaging in region-building. In the end, many

developing countries achieved neither democracy nor transnational cooperation nor even regional integration.

During the 1960s and 1970s Europe was still perceived as a (post-)colonial
continent; meanwhile, its new reality of democratic integration was still confronted with many internal challenges and backlashes. The 1980s and, more so,
the 1990s brought about two new elements in the relationship between the European integration experience and the evolution of region-building in other parts
of the world. First, European integration gained speed and substance, leading to
the implementation of a Single Market with a common currency and the beginning of political union. Second, the Third World began to undergo enormous
differentiations, with some regions—notably Southeast Asia and parts of Latin
America—improving considerably. These regions began to reconsider national
strategies of import-substitution that had prevailed in much of the Third World
during the 1960s. Export-oriented integration into the world market, linked with
the use of comparative regional advantages, began to prove successful. Most
prominently, ASEAN became a case in point, although ASEAN integration
structures did not aspire to the European degree of supranationality.

Stage Two

Three developments coalesced during the 1990s and into the early twenty-first
century. First, the European integration process intensified, while at the same
time the perception of Europe in the developing world changed from postcolonial suspicion toward an attitude of growing partnership, trust, and interest
in the European integration experience. Second, geopolitical and geo-economic
trends usually characterized as "globalization," coupled with the experience of the
United States as the dominant power of the world system, led to a reconsidera-
tion of both national policies and regional perspectives on all continents. Third,
the fall of communist dictatorships and the Soviet empire brought about a reassessment of the advantage of democratic governance, rule of law, and transborder
cooperation in many developing countries. The conditions for successful development and the resolution of regional conflicts were reevaluated in light of the
European integration experience. This also occurred in Russia and some of the
other successor states of the Soviet Union.

These trends have opened the way to a re-mapping of the world, based on
the characteristics of continents rather than on numerical concepts of a first,
second, and third world. This has led to an increase in regional, continental, and
global cooperation efforts, and to regulatory processes and continental structures
that favor free trade with corresponding arbitration mechanisms (WTO, ASEM,
NAFTA, ALCA, the Euro-Mediterranean Partnership). This development goes
hand in hand with a more assertive European Union encouraging developing
regions and post-conflict regions to pursue integration paths. Finally, these trends

have brought about the reinvention of some older regional groupings in various parts of the world, often coupled with a trend toward deeper political and economic integration.

However, this course of events does not suggest that the economic success of Europe can immediately be copied by other regional arrangements. It does not imply that the European response to the challenge of state-building and nation-building under conditions of democratic integration can be transferred into other regions as if European developments of supranational and intergovernmental integration were an export product. The global proliferation of regional integration does not automatically generate a cohesive multipolar world order. Soft and hard power factors retain their extremely asymmetrical distribution across the world of the early twenty-first century. The state's primacy in defining and providing world order prevails. Yet the global proliferation of regional groupings merits serious consideration. This is also relevant for America's understanding of global trends, although the United States, being a country of continental dimensions, seems largely unaffected by the new surge of interest in and support for regional integration. US interests are generally limited to the concept of free trade and lack sufficient sensitivity to the psychological, cultural (including geographical), and political components of integration patterns elsewhere, including the European integration experience.

New mental maps of world politics and international relations are not the one-dimensional outcome of a single trend, no matter how recurring and strong this trend may be. The global proliferation of regional integration efforts cannot revolutionize notions of sovereignty, international relations, economic power, and patterns of state behavior immediately. Its impact is gradual and long-term. But one can anticipate that in the twenty-first century, most regions of the globe will experience a higher degree of transnational region-building beyond the formation of free trade zones than ever before in human history. To the extent that this follows the European experience with regional integration, it can also be attributed to a revival of Europe's global role. It could be argued that Europe's very success in sharing its integration experiences does not depend upon linear and symmetric copies of the European role model. The most solid and lasting success for Europe might rather occur through indirect and contingent means of "experience transfer": applied local adaptation of European insights into integration will most likely generate highly diverse integration schemes elsewhere. In the process, the European integration experience may be taken as a point of reference, thus recognizing the new global presence of Europe.

This perspective recognizes ongoing differences in economic and social status across the world's regions. European integration might be important for Pacific island nations, even though their collective GDP is below 1 percent of Europe's GDP. Yet one general insight is valid and noteworthy: weak sovereignties will usually generate weak integration schemes. Integration can support but not generate political stability, socioeconomic development, and strengthened sovereignty. Empirical evidence suggests that these conditions can be generated outside Europe under similar circumstances of multilevel governance, shared sovereignty, and multiple identities, as has been the case inside Europe over the past five decades.

TOWARD THE GLOBAL STUDY OF COMPARATIVE REGIONALISM

None of the non-European integration efforts to date has experienced supranationality equivalent to the European Union. In order to do justice to the limited success of regional integration outside Europe, it is imperative to recall the timeline of the global proliferation of regional integration. Hardly any of the efforts outside Europe are "old" enough to allow for final judgments, particularly in regard to their degree of long-term success or failure.

- The Central American Common Market (Mercado Común Centroamericano, MCCA) was founded in 1960 and refounded as the Central American Integration System (Sistema de la Integración Centroamericana, SICA) in 1993;
- The Organization of African Unity (OAU) was founded in 1963 and refounded as the African Union (AU) in 2001;
- The Association of Southeast Asian Nations (ASEAN) was founded in 1967;
- The Pacto Andino was founded in 1969 and refounded as the Andean Community of Nations (Comunidad Andina de Naciones, CAN) in 1997;
- The South Pacific Forum was founded in 1973 and refounded as the Pacific Islands Forum (PIF) in 2005;
- The Caribbean Community (CARICOM) was founded in 1973 and refounded in 2001;
- The Economic Community of West African States (ECOWAS) was founded in 1975;
- The Southern African Development Cooperation Council (SADCC) was founded in 1980 and refounded as the Southern African Development Community (SARC) in 1992;
- The Gulf Cooperation Council (GCC) was founded in 1981;
- The South Asian Association of Regional Cooperation (SAARC) was founded in 1985;
- The Southern Common Market (Mercado Común del Sur, MERCOSUR) was founded in 1991;
- The Commonwealth of Independent States (CIS) was founded in 1991.

The lifespans of these regional groupings are too short to draw final conclusions concerning their relevance and long-term impact. Looking back to the history of five decades of European integration, it would have been unhistorical to judge the European Union's ultimate fate by the stage of development of the European Economic Community in 1970, prior to even fully realizing its primary objective of a customs union. Nobody can project the state of region-building in Central America by 2020, in the Gulf by 2030, in ASEAN by 2040 or in Africa by 2050. Yet some comparative remarks can be made at the end of the first decade of the twenty-first century. On the one hand, one can ask to what degree key features that explain the success of European integration may be found elsewhere, even if only in embryonic form. On the other hand, the current state of regional cooperation and integration outside Europe can be compared by taking into consideration the intrinsic conditions and goals of each non-European region-building effort. Ten preliminary conclusions can be drawn that invite further research on comparative global regionalism.

1. There is no universally applicable theory of regional integration. No law of politics explains inevitable patterns toward region-building. Contingent combinations of motives, context, goals, interests, and potentials define each individual integration process. It evidently is not necessary to begin the path toward integration with supranational elements, and yet it is not impossible to eventually reach this stage of integration. With the Pillar Structure of the Maastricht Treaty, the European Union has shown that intergovernmental cooperation can plant the seed for later supranational integration. The journey in one or another regional grouping outside Europe may take the same course. The pooling of sovereignty over time need not mean starting out with the pooling of sovereignty. One can get there at a later stage. The fact that none of the non-European regional groupings had supranational elements at their beginnings does not necessarily indicate that they will never reach that stage. But it is certain that supranational institutions and decision-making processes clearly distinguish cooperative region-building from economic and/or political integration aimed at gradually binding the fate of partner states and societies together.

2. The assumption that regional integration continues according to consistent patterns of "spillover" is not necessarily valid. The non-European experience with integration suggests that functional integration takes place notwithstanding the original purpose and orientation of integration schemes. It can, in fact, reach out into a new policy field, depending upon the political circumstances in a region and the challenge as defined by regional political leaders (ASEAN, MERCOSUR, SAARC, ECOWAS, GCC, AU). Non-European integration experience suggests that renewed and intensified integration need not necessarily complete a chosen path along the model of European integration. It can leave some integration processes "unfinished" while embarking on a new set of integration policies. It can have unintended consequences of all kinds. Non-European experience attests that integration can fail completely and lead to the dissolution

of a seemingly well-established effort (i.e., the dissolution of the East African Community in 1977). Non-European experience supports the European experience that processes of "deepening" integration, which move from the logic of economic integration to the sphere of foreign policy and security, and initiatives to "widen" the integration community in order to achieve regional membership cohesion (ASEAN, CARICOM, SADC) are not mutually exclusive.

3. Non-European states are basically copying the traditional European notion of state-centered sovereignty (the "Westphalian state system"). Just as European states have encountered the limits of this concept and embarked on the long process of overcoming its constraints and flaws, most non-European states—with the United States as a certain exception—have encountered the limits of their capacity as single states. In fact, they all contribute to our understanding of sovereignty as "organized hypocrisy"—which also contains a lesson for the United States.[3] Most non-European states have concluded that acknowledging the need for, and usefulness of, transnational cooperation and eventual supranational integration is the best possible response to the limits of the Westphalian model. Motives for regional integration differ from country to country, and the approaches to region-building are often highly incoherent. Yet a general experience is evident in non-European efforts of region-building: the search for answers to specific economic, political, or security challenges is increasingly related to regional responses. The formal pooling of sovereignty might come last, but the trend away from rigid state-centered solutions, in order to meet the challenges individual states are encountering, is obvious in all non-European schemes of regional integration–building.

4. The most important insight into non-European experiences with region-building relates to the relevance of symmetric local governance structures for the evolution of the regional process. That is, democratic governance in the member states of a regional grouping is required to turn a regional grouping from functional cooperation to advanced integration and shared sovereignty. The European experience underlines the necessary conditions for embarking on the path toward viable democratic transnational cooperation and supranational integration. Countries are inclined to bind their fate together only if they recognize the political system of their partners as equivalent to their own (GCC, MERCOSUR, SICA). Trust is a key criterion in understanding preconditions for successful region-building. Dictatorships or authoritarian regimes might formally get together with democracies in an intergovernmental organization out of specifically defined common interests, but they will hardly tolerate interference in their domestic affairs (ASEAN, SAARC, AU). As this "interference" is inevitably a consequence of pooled sovereignty, they will remain reluctant to move from rhetorical integration to real integration.

The more the partner countries of a regional integration scheme achieve regime cohesion among themselves, based on democratic governance and rule of law, the more likely it is that the integration process in a particular region can advance toward a better realization of its ambition and potential. Only cohesion between state sovereignty and popular sovereignty can pave the way to transnational trust and supranational pooling of sovereignties, affecting both state systems and the rights of people. As long as bilateral conflicts nurture mistrust in a region that is also divided by different political regimes, progress toward viable integration is unlikely (SAARC, ASEAN, SADC). The seeds of a potential for regional integration may be planted. But region-ness requires democratic governance in the constituent parts of a regional grouping. Only democratic region-building will succeed in becoming an expression of deep integration.

5. The European experience, specifically the Franco-German partnership that advanced the integration process while at the same time overcoming historical resentments and balancing ongoing structural differences between the two countries, has been studied in non-European integration schemes. In some rare cases where such a partnership experience was applied elsewhere—even if only indirectly—it generated effects comparable to the European example of Franco-German cooperation (Argentina-Brazil, Thailand-Vietnam). Widespread in non-European regions is either the presence of one dominating regional power (Saudi Arabia, India, Nigeria, South Africa, Russia) or the absence of a clearly and "naturally" defined "lead couple." Often it is not obvious which countries could play the joint role of a locomotive for regional integration. In the absence of this possibility, region-building remains largely reactive to challenges the whole region can recognize as common concerns. The strong inclination to practice excessively consensual decision making, which is typical in these cases of regional integration, is not conducive to efficient and speedy decision making.

6. The patterns of region-building in non-European settings do not provide particular clarity as far as the choice of priorities is concerned. In some cases, defense considerations have generated regional groupings that nevertheless immediately embarked on economic measures to give substance to the regional interests (GCC, ASEAN). In other cases, unfinished economic integration has not prevented the partners of a regional integration scheme from starting joint foreign and security policy initiatives with their own distinct logic and ramifications (ASEAN, SAARC, ECOWAS, SADC, MERCOSUR). The weaker the national political or economic sovereignty is, the weaker the inclination—or the ability—is to advance toward pooled sovereignty on the regional level. Strengthened national confidence, coupled with recognition of the limits of the state's capacity, can often promote integration efforts. However, strong sovereignty in non-European developing countries, as rarely as it exists, has not been automatically supportive of shared or pooled sovereignty with other partners. This is all the more true if the domestic political system is different or even antagonistic (India, Russia).

7. The discourse on the relationship between integration and identity has not been limited to Europe. Outside Europe too, geographic proximity and traditional patterns of commerce have been identified as "cultural" elements favoring the logic of integration. Obvious cultural cohesion has been invoked in some cases of non-European regional integration, but it is astonishing that this invocation has not generated stronger integrative bonds (SICA, CAN, MERCOSUR, GCC). More surprising still is the realization that enormous cultural differences do not necessarily impede the emergence of regional integration mechanisms (SAARC, ASEAN, CIS). Indeed, they can even encourage arguments favoring regional consciousness, based on geographic proximity and cultural pluralism. Given their own inclination to define culture exclusively, Europeans might believe that multicultural circumstances are unfavorable to region-building. Reality elsewhere proves such European perceptions inaccurate.

8. Most non-European integration efforts—as was the case in Europe—have encountered substantial threats of failure, phases of stagnation, detours, obstacles, and unintended consequences that enforced a change of direction (SICA, CAN, AU). As in Europe, a refocused and ultimately even stronger approach to region-building was usually driven by external challenge and pressure. Integration processes seem to depend somewhat on external pressure. It invariably appears that the integration-building processes can hope for "a second chance" whenever they exhaust their original internal commitment.

9. In Europe as elsewhere, processes of regional integration generate multidimensional integration effects. In Europe, it took several decades for EU member states to thoroughly experience the impact of integration. Since the 1990s, most of them have begun to increasingly view integration as an intrusion into their domestic political structures. Non-European experiences with integration will most likely go through similar stages. In the end, this mechanism could turn out to be more important than a formal transfer of sovereignty. In fact, it may equal a non-overt, informal transfer of sovereignty, leading to pooled sovereignty not by choice, but by implication.

10. The effects of region-building on the global state system and on political theory are only gradually emerging. The European experiment has generated a political form sui generis, followed by a notion of sovereignty sui generis, a notion of multilevel democracy and governance sui generis, multiple identities, and an intuitively multilateral orientation in global affairs.[4] Whether or not these trends will repeat themselves in the context of other regional groupings remains to be seen. The more solidified non-European regional integration becomes, the more it will contribute to the evolution of a multipolar world order, based on the roles of regions and continents with the United States and Canada as the only big Western countries operating primarily outside a regional grouping (Australia and New Zealand are at least orientated toward the Pacific Islands Forum). This trend will also impact our understanding of political theory, most

notably as it pertains to norms of democratic governance, concepts of pooled sovereignty, and notions of multiple identities.

The evolution of regional integration has become a global reality. Even most island countries in Oceania have begun to consider the benefits of regional cooperation, and potentially of regional integration. The Pacific Islands Forum (PIF) group, with fourteen member states, has been evolving recently, driven not least by prospects of a Pacific regional Economic Partnership Agreement with the EU.[5] Interesting, but perhaps not surprising, is the absence of efforts of regional integration-building in the two regions of the world that are at the heart of the most troubling world conflicts and embody the most critical zones of strategic insecurity in the world: the Broader Middle East and Northeast Asia. Both regions echo the mechanisms of outdated European power struggles (Northeast Asia) and unresolved issues of democratic nation- and state-building (Broader Middle East). Both regions are dominated by a balance of suspicion rooted in long-standing conflicts.

In spite of Northeast Asia's share of 25 percent of the global economy, the region lacks a strategic equilibrium based on a common system of cooperative security or on an interdependence-oriented system of economic integration. The Broader Middle East has been "discovered" as a region in the aftermath of the geostrategic implications of Islamic terrorism and the fear of a proliferation of weapons of mass destruction. This regional concept has been framed in response to the absence of democracy and pluralism in the region between "Marrakech and Bangladesh."[6] As in Northeast Asia, in the Broader Middle East there yet exists neither democratic regime cohesion nor shared understanding or interest in the potential benefits of regional cooperation and subsequent integration as a path of overcoming regional insecurity and political antagonisms.

Instead, a balance of mistrust governs the Broader Middle East and Northeast Asia to this day. Yet these parts of the world also are increasingly perceived as regions. Analysts have begun to discuss elements of comparison between the geostrategic stalemate in Northeast Asia and the European integration experience.[7] As for the Broader Middle East, the quest to emulate EU integration experiences in a post-conflict Middle East has already generated remarkable proposals, even as the world is still torn by this ongoing and seemingly irresolvable conflict.[8]

The recent phase of global proliferation has spread the seeds of the process of regional integration to all corners of the globe. Its ultimate result will not be judged merely by the growth in power of any of these integration schemes, although this will always be an important category for the realistic study of world order. The value of regional integration has to be judged through the prism of the peoples and countries involved. No matter what the impact of region-building on global power equations may be, both the peoples and countries involved own, shape, and determine each particular integration process and its effects. It is also in this context that the European integration experience—establishing a union of states that strives to become a union of citizens—has served and will continue to serve as inspiration for other regions around the globe.

THE DOCUMENTS 1957–2007: THE FIRST FIFTY YEARS

Region-building is not simply a political concept. It has put forth legal roots across the world. In the course of developing region-building over more than half a century, the main regional groupings have written, signed, and ratified treaties, conventions, protocols, and declarations to outline their objectives and reassess success and failure. While much may be said and even more ought to be studied in order to better understand region-building, one should first let the actors speak for themselves. The documents assembled in this unique collection give the best available overview of the legal and political evolution of region-building based on the official documents and stated objectives of the actors.

This collection of documents strives to facilitate studies in comparative regionalism. It is based on recognition of the intrinsic conditions, goals, efforts, and achievements of each regional grouping. The documentation facilitates these scholarly efforts by emphasizing the process character of region-building and the dynamics of integration. Far from emerging instantly and overnight, region-ness is a long-term process not sufficiently captured by dry legal documents and political communiqués. But region-building would never succeed if it were not based on reliable agreements among its constituent parts. This is the significance of the documents agreed upon and promulgated across different regional groupings around the world. The main treaties of region-building and their revisions echo turning points in regional developments. They affirm a commitment to region-building and initiate new stages and dimensions of the original ideas and initiatives.

The documents assembled in this volume represent the diversity of regional groupings in the world that have attained a specific degree of region-ness. Reading and studying these documents helps us understand the intrinsic sincerity and ambition with which region-building is conducted around the world. It is not a quick fix. It takes time, maybe even several generations, to achieve viable and reliable "final" results. We do not know the end of the process. We only recognize the growing relevance of region-building around the world. We are aware that it is a new process without precedent. The insights gained by studying the main documents of the regional groupings will lead to more empirical research on each of these regional groupings, as well as to comparative studies on two or more of them and on specific issues—objectives, policies, institutions, effects—that are relevant to more than one regional grouping. The documents collected here ought not to be read with naïve eyes presuming that the written declarations have immediately turned into sparkling realities, for the opposite was true most of the time in practically all of the regional groupings examined. But these documents have always served as a standard for advancing region-building, reinvigorating deadlocks in regional integration, and reacting regionally to a collective challenge.

A study of the documents on region-building underlines the intrinsic links between the economic and political aspects of regionalism. It has never been very helpful or innovative to assume that region-building is only an economic matter. Of course, economic issues are important and often dominate regional groupings—after all, they concern the opportunities for many people and often inspire, legitimize, and advance region-building. But region-building is a multidimensional affair. It includes not only economic and political aspects but also social, cultural, and many other issues, echoing the challenges and opportunities in a region and in its sense of region-ness.

This collection presents excerpts from the most important documents of region-building, which have evolved over the fifty-odd years since the formation of the European Economic Community in 1957. While the process of region-building has become a global one in the past half-century, it remains embryonic or "young" in many areas of the world. The documents chosen for this collection, which are limited to their main parts, tend to follow a pattern and style that is typical for legal and political documents of this nature. In this, they do not differ from other legal texts that constitute international law. At the same time, they differ genuinely from documents of international law as they are united across continents and countries, topics and procedures, by a single idea: they are building blocks in regional integration.

Over time, the documents assembled in this book will be joined by further texts. Future documents in a particular regional grouping may replace some of the texts presented in this collection. This is the normal course of political life. But the documents assembled in this collection, representing the first fifty years of a truly new phenomenon in world affairs, will always remain of historical value. They echo the idealism and the insights of many community leaders across the world, and they have served, and often continue to serve, as sources of inspiration for the management of region-building. They will remain the pillars of a new global architecture.

NOTES

1. Werner Mattli, *The Logic of Integration: Europe and Beyond* (Cambridge and New York: Cambridge University Press 1999); see for worldwide perspectives Ariane Koesler and Martin Zimmek (eds.), *Global Voices on Regional Integration* (Bonn: Center for European Integration Studies, 2007).
2. Ludger Kühnhardt, *Stufen der Souveränität: Staatsverständnis und Selbstbestimmung in der südlichen Hemisphäre* (Bonn and Berlin: Bouvier, 1992).
3. Stephen D. Krasner, *Sovereignty: Organized Hypocrisy* (Princeton: Princeton University Press, 1999).

4. See Ludger Kühnhardt, *Constituting Europe: Identity, Institution-Building and the Search for a Global Role* (Baden-Baden: Nomos, 2003): 225–270.
5. See Martin Holland, *The European Union and the Third World* (Houndmills: Palgrave, 2002).
6. Ronald D. Asmus and Kenneth M. Pollack, "The New Transatlantic Project," *Policy Review* (October 2002), available under: www.hoover.org/publications/policyreview/3459216.html; Ludger Kühnhardt, *System-Opening and Cooperative Transformation of the Greater Middle East: A New Transatlantic Project and a Joint Euro-Atlantic-Arab Task*, EUROMESCO Papers No. 26 (Lisbon: Euro-Mediterranean Study Commission, 2003); Thomas Scheffler, "'Fertile Crescent,' 'Orient,' 'Middle East': The Changing Mental Maps of Southwest Asia," *European Review of History* 10, no. 2 (2003): 253–272.
7. See Christopher M. Dent and David W.F. Huang (eds.), *Northeast Asian Regionalism: Learning from the European Experience* (London: Routledge, 2002).
8. See Amichai Magen and Shlomo Shpiro, *Towards a Comprehensive Security Approach in the Middle East: Lessons from the European Experience in Justice and Home Affairs Cooperation* (Tel Aviv: The Tami Steinmetz Center for Peace Research, 2003).

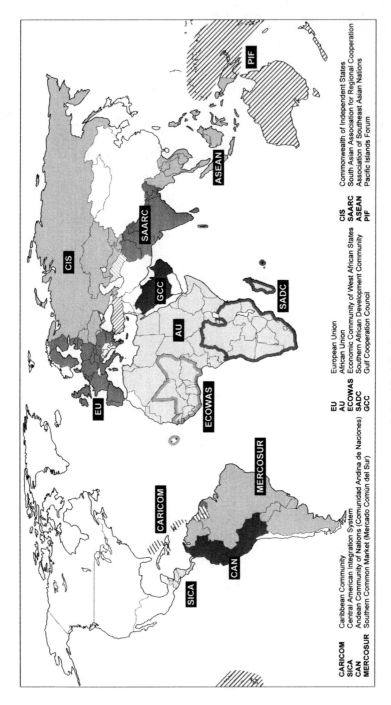

A World of Region-Building

CARICOM Caribbean Community
SICA   Central American Integration System
CAN   Andean Community of Nations (Comunidad Andina de Naciones)
MERCOSUR Southern Common Market (Mercado Común del Sur)

EU   European Union
AU   African Union
ECOWAS   Economic Community of West African States
SADC   Southern African Development Community
GCC   Gulf Cooperation Council

CIS   Commonwealth of Independent States
SAARC   South Asian Association for Regional Cooperation
ASEAN   Association of Southeast Asian Nations
PIF   Pacific Islands Forum

I

REGION-BUILDING IN EUROPE

EUROPEAN UNION (EU)

The European Union is the most advanced regional grouping in the world. In more than five decades of region-building, the European experience with regional integration has undergone several fundamental transformations. It has experienced crises in integration and, sometimes rather dramatically, crises of integration. The European Union has not achieved its "final" expression and remains a continuous process. Main features of the European Union have been established and constitute the backbone of European community-building. The European Union is a union of states and a union of citizens, but first and foremost, the European Union is a community of law. Its member states are defined by democratic regimes and governance structures. Its citizens demand more democracy, transparency, and participation on the level of the European Union. In spite of its flaws, the European Union has developed a multilevel governance system that is unprecedented in the world.

European integration had long been a dream for intellectuals and a series of failed efforts among European politicians when it started with a fundamentally new mechanism in the mid-twentieth century. The European Coal and Steel Community (ECSC) was founded in 1951 as the first attempt in European history to pool the resources of several European countries and arrange for them to share sovereignty over the use of some of their most important natural resources. The High Authority of the European Coal and Steel Community became the model for the European Commission. With the Treaties of Rome, signed on 25 March 1957, France, the Federal Republic of Germany, the Netherlands, Belgium, Luxembourg, and Italy established the European Economic Community (EEC). The European Commission, based in Brussels, was mandated to serve as the protector of the treaties.

Over time, a genuine community law came about, mainly supported and often promoted by the deliberations and decisions of the European Court of Justice.

Crises in European integration could not be avoided. They were mostly reactions to unresolved conflicts among member states over the degree of autarkic sovereignty they were allowed to exercise alone. Coming to recognize the primacy of European law was often a controversial learning process for national political actors, and sometimes remains so. The Luxembourg compromise of 1966 enforced the principle of unanimity in EEC decision making. It was not until the Single European Act of 1986—the first treaty revision since 1957—that the scope for qualified majority voting was extended. Since 1979, the European Parliament has been directly elected by the citizens of the European Community for a five-year period. Over time, the European Council and European Parliament have become co–decision making bodies of European legislation. The institutional balance between European Commission, European Council, and European Parliament is the result of several, often controversial treaty revisions.

The most important one came with the EU Treaty of Maastricht (1992), transforming the European Economic Community into the European Union and the European Community (EC) with its complex three-pillar structure. The Treaty of Maastricht outlined the path toward a single European currency. Before the euro was introduced in 2002, further treaty revisions took place with the Treaty of Amsterdam (1997) and the Treaty of Nice (2001). The Treaty of Nice paved the way for a more visible common foreign and security policy of the European Union. But it, and the Treaty of Amsterdam, also strengthened the veto powers of individual member states, facilitating deadlock in decision making and subsequently increasing disillusionment with the path and direction of European integration.

European integration was a combination of deeper integration and the regular widening of the membership of the EC/EU. Several rounds of enlargement turned the initial European Economic Community of six into the European Union of twenty-seven member states. The enlargements were the result of democratic transformations in Southern Europe and the peaceful revolutions against communism in Central and Eastern Europe, but also the consequence of acceptance of the European acquis communautaire by several traditional democracies in Northern Europe, most notably the United Kingdom. As a result, the European Union has become the embodiment of a unified Europe, overcoming divisions after World War II. Enlargement of the European Union to Southeastern Europe, including Turkey, has not been completed yet.

In order to make the enlarged European Union with its 490 million citizens workable and its decisions stronger, the EU embarked on the project of giving itself a constitution in 2001. After unprecedented public deliberations by the Constitutional Convention, all EU governments signed the first-ever Constitutional Treaty of the EU on 29 October 2004 in Rome. The subsequent, badly prepared ratification process was disrupted when majorities in referendums in France and the Netherlands rejected the Constitutional Treaty in 2005. But by the end of 2006, eighteen EU member states had ratified the text. In 2007, the EU engaged in a process to safeguard the political substance of the Constitutional Treaty. By initiating a new Intergovernmental Conference, the EU resorted to the traditional method of treaty revisions. The Treaty of Lisbon was signed on 13 December 2007 by all twenty-seven EU governments. This so-called Reform Treaty consists of the Treaty Amending the Treaty on European Union and the Treaty Establishing the European Community. The Treaty of Lisbon consolidated the balance between the European Council and the European Parliament as the two equal pillars of EU legislation. A permanent President of the European Council and an EU foreign secretary in all but name are meant to enhance the efficiency of EU policy making. Thus, by the end of 2007, a new basis was reached for more efficient and democratic decision-making in the EU, but the result was less transparent than originally expected. The ratification procedure of the Treaty of Lisbon was not easy. It was left to the national parliaments in twenty-six member states, but failed in a 2008 referendum in Ireland. A second referendum in Ireland in 2009 ended in support of the Treaty of Lisbon. On 1 December 2009 the Treaty of Lisbon ("Reform Treaty") entered into force. The Treaty of Lisbon and its erratic ratification marathon concluded a decade-long search for a new institutional balance in the European Union.

The European Union has developed a global presence with an increasing number of peacekeeping and police operations around the world, a common foreign trade policy, a proactive development aid policy—being the biggest donor of development aid in the world—and several efforts to promote regional integration and negotiate biregional association agreements. The transatlantic partnership with the United States and the EU's neighborhood policies reflect the main concerns of the European Union: to manage world affairs with the US as its most important trading and policy partner, and to stabilize the immediate neighborhood of Europe through policies of constructive engagement with the countries of Northern Africa and Eastern Europe, including Russia. More than ever, the European Union claims to be a community of values, both internally as well as in pursuit of its global role.

TREATY ESTABLISHING THE EUROPEAN
ECONOMIC COMMUNITY (25.03.1957)

. . .

Determined to lay the foundations of an ever closer union among the peoples of Europe,

Resolved to ensure the economic and social progress of their countries by common action to eliminate the barriers which divide Europe,

Affirming as the essential objective of their efforts the constant improvement of the living and working conditions of their peoples,

Recognising that the removal of existing obstacles calls for concerted action in order to guarantee steady expansion, balanced trade and fair competition,

Anxious to strengthen the unity of their economies and to ensure their harmonious development by reducing the differences existing between the various regions and the backwardness of the less favoured regions,

Desiring to contribute, by means of a common commercial policy, to the progressive abolition of restrictions on international trade,

Intending to confirm the solidarity which binds Europe and the overseas countries and desiring to ensure the development of their prosperity, in accordance with the principles of the Charter of the United Nations,

Resolved by thus pooling their resources to preserve and strengthen peace and liberty, and calling upon the other peoples of Europe who share their ideal to join,

. . .

Part One—Principles

Article 1

By this Treaty, the High Contracting Parties establish among themselves a European Economic Community.

Article 2

The Community shall have as its task, by establishing a common market and progressively approximating the economic policies of Member States, to promote throughout the Community a harmonious development of economic activities, a continuous and balanced expansion, an increase in stability, an accelerated raising of the standard of living and closer relations between the States belonging to it.

Article 3

For the purposes set out in Article 2, the activities of the Community shall include, as provided in this Treaty and in accordance with the timetable set out therein:

(a) the elimination, as between Member States, of customs duties and of quantitative restrictions on the import and export of goods, and of all other measures having equivalent effect;

(b) the establishment of a common customs tariff and of a common commercial policy towards third countries;

(c) the abolition, as between Member States, of obstacles to freedom of movement for persons, services and capital;

(d) the adoption of a common policy in the sphere of agriculture;

(e) the adoption of a common policy in the sphere of transport;

(f) the institution of a system ensuring that competition in the common market is not distorted;

(g) the application of procedures by which the economic policies of Member States can be coordinated and disequilibria in their balances of payments remedied;

(h) the approximation of the laws of Member States to the extent required for the proper functioning of the common market;

(i) the creation of a European Social Fund in order to improve employment opportunities for workers and to contribute to the raising of their standard of living;

(j) the establishment of a European Investment Bank to facilitate the economic expansion of the Community by opening up fresh resources;

(k) the association of the overseas countries and territories in order to increase trade and to promote jointly economic and social development.

Article 4

1. The tasks entrusted to the Community shall be carried out by the following institutions:

  – an Assembly,
  – a Council,
  – a Commission,
  – a Court of Justice.

Each institution shall act within the limits of the powers conferred upon it by this Treaty.

2. The Council and the Commission shall be assisted by an Economic and Social Committee acting in an advisory capacity.

Article 5

Member States shall take all appropriate measures, whether general or particular, to ensure fulfilment of the obligations arising out of this Treaty or resulting from action taken by the institutions of the Community. They shall facilitate the achievement of the Community's tasks.

They shall abstain from any measure which could jeopardise the attainment of the obligations arising out of this Treaty.

Article 6

1. Member States shall, in close cooperation with the institutions of the Community, coordinate their respective economic policies to the extent necessary to attain the objectives of this Treaty.
2. The institutions of the Community shall take care not to prejudice the internal and external financial stability of the Member States.

Article 7

Within the scope of application of this Treaty, and without prejudice to any special provisions contained therein, any discrimination on grounds of nationality shall be prohibited.

The Council may, on a proposal from the Commission and after consulting the Assembly, adopt, by a qualified majority, rules designed to prohibit such discrimination.

Article 8

1. The common market shall be progressively established during a transitional period of twelve years. This transitional period shall be divided into three stages of four years each; the length of each stage may be altered in accordance with the provisions set out below.
2. To each stage there shall be assigned a set of actions to be initiated and carried through concurrently.
3. Transition from the first to the second stage shall be conditional upon a finding that the objectives specifically laid down in this Treaty for the first stage have in fact been attained in substance and that, subject to the exceptions and procedures provided for in this Treaty, the obligations have been fulfilled.

This finding shall be made at the end of the fourth year by the Council, acting unanimously on a report from the Commission. A Member State may not, however, prevent unanimity by relying upon the non-fulfilment of its own obligations. Failing unanimity, the first stage shall automatically be extended for one year.

At the end of the fifth year, the Council shall make its finding under the same conditions. Failing unanimity, the first stage shall automatically be extended for a further year.

At the end of the sixth year, the Council shall make its finding, acting by a qualified majority on a report from the Commission.

4. Within one month of the last-mentioned vote any Member State which voted with the minority or, if the required majority was not obtained, any Member State shall be entitled to call upon the Council to appoint an arbitration board whose decision shall be binding upon all Member States and upon the institutions of the Community. The arbitration board shall consist of three members appointed by the Council acting unanimously on a proposal from the Commission.

If the Council has not appointed the members of the arbitration board within one month of being called upon to do so, they shall be appointed by the Court of Justice within a further period of one month.

The arbitration board shall elect its own Chairman.

The board shall make its award within six months of the date of the Council vote referred to in the last subparagraph of paragraph 3.

5. The second and third stages may not be extended or curtailed except by a decision of the Council, acting unanimously on a proposal from the Commission.

6. Nothing in the preceding paragraphs shall cause the transitional period to last more than fifteen years after the entry into force of this Treaty.

7. Save for the exceptions or derogations provided for in this Treaty, the expiry of the transitional period shall constitute the latest date by which all the rules laid down must enter into force and all the measures required for establishing the common market must be implemented.

Part Two—Foundations of the Community

Title 1—Free movement of goods

Article 9

1. The Community shall be based upon a customs union which shall cover all trade in goods and which shall involve the prohibition between Member States of customs duties on im- and exports and of all charges having equivalent

effect, and the adoption of a common customs tariff in their relations with third countries.

2. The provisions of Chapter 1, Section 1, and of Chapter 2 of this Title shall apply to products originating in Member States and to products coming from third countries which are in free circulation in Member States.

. . .

Chapter 1—The Customs Union

Section 1 — Elimination of customs duties between Member States

Article 12

Member States shall refrain from introducing between themselves any new customs duties on imports or exports or any charges having equivalent effect, and from increasing those which they already apply in their trade with each other.

Article 13

1. Customs duties on imports in force between Member States shall be progressively abolished by them during the transitional period in accordance with Articles 14 and 15.

2. Charges having an effect equivalent to customs duties on imports, in force between Member States, shall be progressively abolished by them during the transitional period. The Commission shall determine by means of directives the timetable for such abolition. It shall be guided by the rules contained in Article 14 (2) and (3) and by the directives issued by the Council pursuant to Article 14 (2).

. . .

Title II—Agriculture

. . .

Article 39

1. The objectives of the common agricultural policy shall be:
   (a) to increase agricultural productivity by promoting technical progress and by ensuring the rational development of agricultural production

and the optimum utilisation of the factors of production, in particular labour;

(b thus to ensure a fair standard of living for the agricultural community, in particular by increasing the individual earnings of persons engaged in agriculture;

(c) to stabilise markets;

(d) to assure the availability of supplies;

(e) to ensure that supplies reach consumers at reasonable prices.

2. In working out the common agricultural policy and the special methods for its application, account shall be taken of:

(a) the particular nature of agricultural activity, which results from the social structure of agriculture and frozen structural and natural disparities between the various agricultural regions;

(b) the need to effect the appropriate adjustments by degrees;

(c) the fact that in the Member States agriculture constitutes a sector closely linked with the economy as a whole.

Article 40

1. Member States shall develop the common agricultural policy by degrees during the transitional period and shall bring it into force by the end of that period at the latest.

2. In order to attain the objectives set out in Article 39 a common organisation of agricultural markets shall be established.

This organisation shall take one of the following forms, depending on the product concerned:

(a) common rules on competition;

(b) compulsory coordination of the various national market organisations;

(c) a European market organisation.

3. The common organisation established in accordance with paragraph 2 may include all measures required to attain the objectives set out in Article 39, in particular regulation of prices, aids for the production and marketing of the various products, storage and carry-over arrangements and common machinery for stabilising imports or exports.

The common organisation shall be limited to pursuit of the objectives set out in Article 39 and shall exclude any discrimination between producers or consumers within the Community.

Any common price policy shall be based on common criteria and uniform methods of calculation.

4. In order to enable the common organisation referred to in paragraph 2 to attain its objectives, one or more agricultural guidance and guarantee funds may be set up.

    . . .

Title III—Free movement of persons, services and capital

Chapter 1—Workers

Article 48

1. Freedom of movement for workers shall be secured within the Community by the end of the transitional period.
2. Such freedom of movement shall entail the abolition of any discrimination based on nationality between workers of the Member States as regards employment, remuneration and other conditions of work and employment.
3. It shall entail the right, subject to limitations justified on grounds of public policy, public security or public health:
    (a) to accept offers of employment actually made;
    (b) to move freely within the territory of Member States for this purpose.
    (c) to stay in a Member State for the purpose of employment in accordance with the provisions governing the employment of nationals of that State laid down by law, regulation or administrative action;
    (d) to remain in the territory of a Member State after having been employed in that State, subject to conditions which shall be embodied in implementing regulations to be drawn up by the Commission.
4. The provisions of this Article shall not apply to employment in the public service.

    . . .

Chapter 2—Right of Establishment

Article 52

Within the framework of the provisions set out below, restrictions on the freedom of establishment of nationals of a Member State in the territory of another

Member State shall be abolished by progressive stages in the course of the transitional period. Such progressive abolition shall also apply to restrictions on the setting up of agencies, branches or subsidiaries by nationals of any Member State established in the territory of any Member State.

Freedom of establishment shall include the right to take up and pursue activities as self-employed persons and to set up and manage undertakings, in particular companies or firms within the meaning of the second paragraph of Article 58, under the conditions laid down for its own nationals by the law of the country where such establishment is effected, subject to the provisions of the Chapter relating to capital.

. . .

Chapter 3—Services

Article 59

Within the framework of the provisions set out below, restrictions on freedom to provide services within the Community shall be progressively abolished during the transitional period in respect of nationals of Member States who are established in a State of the Community other than that of the person for whom the services are intended.

The Council may, acting unanimously on a proposal from the Commission, extend the provisions of this Chapter to nationals of a third country who provide services and who are established within the Community.

. . .

Article 61

1. Freedom to provide services in the field of transport shall be governed by the provisions of the Title relating to transport.
2. The liberalisation of banking and insurance services connected with movements of capital shall be effected in step with the progressive liberalisation of movement of capital.

. . .

Chapter 4—Capital

Article 67

1. During the transitional period and to the extent necessary to ensure the proper functioning of the common market, Member States shall

progressively abolish between themselves all restrictions on the movement of capital belonging to persons resident in Member States and any discrimination based on the nationality or on the place of residence of the parties or on the place where such capital is invested.

2. Current payments connected with the movement of capital between Member States shall be freed from all restrictions by the end of the first stage at the latest.

. . .

Article 70

1. The Commission shall propose to the Council measures for the progressive coordination of the exchange policies of Member States in respect of the movement of capital between those States and third countries. For this purpose the Council shall issue directives, acting unanimously. It shall endeavour to attain the highest possible degree of liberalisation.

. . .

Part Four—Association of the Overseas Countries and Territories

Article 131

The Member States agree to associate with the Community the non-European countries and territories which have special relations with Belgium, France, Italy and the Netherlands.

. . .

The purpose of association shall be to promote the economic and social development of the countries and territories and to establish close economic relations between them and the Community as a whole.

In accordance with the principles set out in the Preamble to this Treaty, association shall serve primarily to further the interests and prosperity of the inhabitants of these countries and territories in order to lead them to the economic, social and cultural development to which they aspire.

Article 132

Association shall have the following objectives:

1. Member States shall apply to their trade with the countries and territories the same treatment as they accord each other pursuant to this Treaty.

2. Each country or territory shall apply to its trade with Member States and with the other countries and territories the same treatment as that which it applies to the European State with which it has special relations.

3. The Member States shall contribute to the investments required for the progressive development of these countries and territories.

4. For investments financed by the Community, participation in tenders and supplies shall be open on equal terms to all natural and legal persons who are nationals of a Member State or of one of the countries and territories.

5. In relations between Member States and the countries and territories the right of establishment of nationals and companies or firms shall be regulated in accordance with the provisions and procedures laid down in the Chapter relating to the right of establishment and on a non-discriminatory basis, subject to any special provision laid down pursuant to Article 136.

Article 133

1. Customs duties on imports into the Member States of goods originating in the countries and territories shall be completely abolished in conformity with the progressive abolition of customs duties between Member States in accordance with the provisions of this Treaty.

2. Customs duties on imports into each country or territory from Member States or from the other countries or territories shall be progressively abolished in accordance with the provisions of Articles 12, 13, 14, 15 and 17.

3. The countries and territories may, however, levy customs duties which meet the needs of their development and industrialisation or produce revenue for their budgets.

   The duties referred to in the preceding subparagraph shall nevertheless be progressively reduced to the level of those imposed on imports of products from the Member State with which each country or territory has special relations. The percentages and the timetable of the reductions provided for under this Treaty shall apply to the difference between the duty imposed on a product coming from the Member State which has special relations with the country or territory concerned and the duty imposed on the same product coming from within the Community on entry into the importing country or territory.

4. Paragraph 2 shall not apply to countries and territories which, by reason of the particular international obligations by which they are bound, already apply a non-discriminatory customs tariff when this Treaty enters into force.

5. The introduction of or any change in customs duties imposed on goods imported into the countries and territories shall not, either in law or in fact, give rise to any direct or indirect discrimination between imports from the various Member States.

    . . .

Part Five—Institutions of the Community

Title 1—Provisions Governing the Institutions

Chapter 1—The Institutions

Section 1 — The Assembly

Article 137

The Assembly, which shall consist of representatives of the peoples of the States brought together in the Community, shall exercise the advisory and supervisory powers which are conferred upon it by this Treaty.

Article 138

1. The Assembly shall consist of delegates who shall be designated by the respective Parliaments from among their members in accordance with the procedure laid down by each Member State.
2. The number of these delegates shall be as follows:

Belgium	14
Germany	36
France	36
Italy	36
Luxembourg	6
Netherlands	14

    . . .

Section 2 — The Council

Article 145

To ensure that the objectives set out in this Treaty are attained, the Council shall, in

- ensure coordination of the general economic policies of the Member States;
- have power to take decisions.

Article 146

The Council shall consist of representatives of the Member States. Each government shall delegate to it one of its members.

The office of President shall be held for a term of six months by each member of the Council in turn, in the alphabetical order of the Member States.

Article 147

The Council shall meet when convened by its President on his own initiative or at the request of one of its members or of the Commission.

Article 148

1. Save as otherwise provided in this Treaty, the Council shall act by a majority of its members.
2. Where the Council is required to act by a qualified majority, the votes of its members shall be weighted as follows:

Belgium	2
Germany	4
France	4
Italy	4
Luxembourg	1
Netherlands	2

   For their adoption, acts of the Council shall require at least:
   - twelve votes in favour where this Treaty requires them to be adopted on a proposal from the commission,
   - twelve votes in favour, cast by at least four members, in other cases.
3. Abstentions by members present in person or represented shall not prevent the adoption by the Council of acts which require unanimity.

   . . .

Section 3 — The Commission

Article 155

In order to ensure the proper functioning and development of the common market, the Commission shall:

- ensure that the provisions of this Treaty and the measures taken by the institutions pursuant thereto are applied;
- formulate recommendations or deliver opinions on matters dealt with in this Treaty, if it expressly so provides or if the Commission considers it necessary;
- have its own power of decision and participate in the shaping of measures taken by the Council and by the Assembly in the manner provided for in this Treaty;
- exercise the powers conferred on it by the Council for the implementation of the rules laid down by the latter.

Article 156

The Commission shall publish annually, not later than one month before the opening of the session of the Assembly, a general report on the activities of the Community.

Article 157

1. The Commission shall consist of nine members, who shall be chosen on the grounds of their general competence and whose independence is beyond doubt.

   The number of members of the Commission may be altered by the Council, acting unanimously. Only nationals of Member States may be members of the Commission. The Commission may not include more than two members having the nationality of the same State.

2. The members of the Commission shall, in the general interest of the Community, be completely independent in the performance of their duties.

   In the performance of these duties, they shell neither seek nor take instructions from any Government or from any other body. They shall refrain from any action incompatible with their duties. Each Member State undertakes to respect this principle and not to seek to influence the members of the Commission in the performance of their tasks.

   The members of the Commission may not, during their term of office, engage in any other occupation, whether gainful or not. When entering upon their duties they shall give a solemn undertaking that, both during and after their term of office, they will respect the obligations arising therefrom and in particular their duty to behave with integrity and discretion as regards the acceptance, after they have ceased to hold office, of certain appointments or benefits. In the event of any breach of these obligations, the Court of Justice may, on application by the Council or the Commission, rule that the member concerned be, according to the circumstances, either compulsorily retired in accordance with the provisions of Article 160 or deprived of his right to a pension or other benefits in its stead.

. . .

Section 4 — The Court of Justice

Article 164

The Court of Justice shall ensure that in the interpretation and application of this Treaty the law is observed.

Article 165

The Court of Justice shall consist of seven Judges.

The Court of Justice shall sit in plenary session. It may, however, form chambers, each consisting of three or five Judges, either to undertake certain preparatory inquiries or to adjudicate on particular categories of cases in accordance with rules laid down for these purposes.

Whenever the Court of Justice hears cases brought before it by a Member State or by one of the institutions of the Community or has to give preliminary rulings on questions submitted to it pursuant to Article 177, it shall act in plenary session.

Should the Court of Justice so request, the Council may, acting unanimously, increase the number of Judges and make the necessary adjustments to the second and third paragraphs of this Article and to the second paragraph of Article 167.

Article 166

The Court of Justice shall be assisted by two Advocates-General.

It shall be the duty of the Advocate-General, acting with complete impartiality and independence, to make, in open court, reasoned submissions on cases brought before the Court of Justice, in order to assist the Court in the performance of the task assigned to it in Article 164.

. . .

Article 169

If the Commission considers that a Member State has failed to fulfil an obligation wider this Treaty, it shall deliver a reasoned opinion on the matter after giving the State concerned the opportunity to submit its observations.

If the State concerned does not comply with the opinion within the period laid down by the Commission, the latter may bring the matter before the Court of Justice.

. . .

Article 171

If the Court of Justice finds that a Member State has failed to fulfil an obligation under this Treaty, the State shall be required to take the necessary measures to comply with the judgment of the Court of Justice.

. . .

Article 173

The Court of Justice shall review the legality of acts of the Council and the Commission other than recommendations or opinions. It shall for this purpose have jurisdiction in actions brought by a Member State, the Council or the Commission on grounds of lack of competence, infringement of an essential procedural requirement, infringement of this Treaty or of any rule of law relating to its application, or misuse of powers.

Any natural or legal person may, under the same conditions, institute proceedings against a decision addressed to that person or against a decision which, although in the form of a regulation or a decision addressed to another person, is of direct and individual concern to the former.

The proceedings provided for in this Article shall be instituted within two months of the publication of the measure, or of its notification to the plaintiff, or, in the absence thereof, of the day on which it came to the knowledge of the latter, as the case may be.

. . .

Title II—Financial Provisions

Article 199

All items of revenue and expenditure of the Community, including those relating to the European Social Fund, shall be included in estimates to be drawn up for each financial year and shall be shown in the budget.

The revenue and expenditure shown in the budget shall be in balance.

Article 200

1. The budget revenue shall include, irrespective of any other revenue, financial contributions of Member States on the following scale

Belgium	7.9
Germany	28
France	28
Italy	28
Luxembourg	0.2
Netherlands	7.9

2. The financial contributions of Member States to cover the expenditure of the European Social Fund, however, shall be determined on the following scale:

Belgium	8.8
Germany	32
France	32
Italy	20
Luxembourg	0.2
Netherlands	7

3. The scales may be modified by the Council, acting unanimously.

Article 201

The Commission shall examine the conditions under which the financial contributions of Member States provided for in Article 200 could be replaced by the Community's own resources, in particular by revenue accruing from the common customs tariff when it has been finally introduced.

To this end, the Commission shall submit proposals to the Council. After consulting the Assembly on these proposals the Council may, acting unanimously, lay down the appropriate provisions, which it shall recommend to the Member States for adoption in accordance with their respective constitutional requirements.

. . .

Article 206

The accounts of all revenue and expenditure shown in the budget shall be examined by an Audit Board consisting of auditors whose independence is beyond doubt, one of whom shall be chairman. The Council shall, acting unanimously, determine the number of the auditors. The auditors and the chairman of the Audit Board shall be appointed by the Council, acting unanimously, for a period of five years. Their remuneration shall be determined by the Council, acting by a qualified majority.

. . .

Part Six—General and Final Provisions

Article 210

The Community shall have legal personality.

. . .

SINGLE EUROPEAN ACT (01.07.1987)

. . .

Moved by the will to continue the work undertaken on the basis of the Treaties establishing the European Communities and to transform relations as a whole among their States into a European Union, in accordance with the Solemn Declaration of Stuttgart of 19 June 1983,

Resolved to implement this European Union on the basis, firstly, of the Communities operating in accordance with their own rules and, secondly, of European Cooperation among the Signatory States in the sphere of foreign policy and to invest this union with the necessary means of action,

Determined to work together to promote democracy on the basis of the fundamental rights recognized in the constitutions and laws of the Member States, in the Convention for the Protection of Human Rights and Fundamental Freedoms and the European Social Charter, notably freedom, equality and social justice,

Convinced that the European idea, the results achieved in the fields of economic integration and political cooperation, and the need for new developments correspond to the wishes of the democratic peoples of Europe, for whom the European Parliament, elected by universal suffrage, is an indispensable means of expression,

. . .

Title 1

Common Provisions

. . .

Article 6

1. A cooperation procedure shall be introduced which shall apply to acts based on Articles 7, 49, 54 (2), 56 (2), second sentence, 57 with the exception of the second sentence of paragraph 2 thereof, 100a, 100b, 118a, 130e and 130q (2) of the EEC Treaty.
2. In Article 7, second paragraph of the EEC Treaty the terms "after consulting the Assembly" shall be replaced by "in cooperation with the European Parliament."
3. In Article 49 of the EEC Treaty the terms "the Council shall, acting on a proposal from the Commission and after consulting the Economic and Social Committee," shall be replaced by "the Council shall, acting by a qualified majority on a proposal from the Commission, in cooperation with the European Parliament and after consulting the Economic and Social Committee."
4. In Article 54 (2) of the EEC Treaty the terms "the Council shall, on a proposal from the Commission and after consulting the Economic and Social Committee and the Assembly," shall be replaced by "the Council shall, acting on a proposal from the Commission, in cooperation with the European Parliament and after consulting the Economic and Social Committee."
5. In Article 56 (2) of the EEC Treaty the second sentence is replaced by the following: "After the end of the second stage, however, the Council shall, acting by a qualified majority on a proposal from the Commission and in cooperation with the European Parliament, issue directives for the coordination of such provisions as, in each Member State, are a matter for regulation or administrative action."
6. In Article 57 (1) of the EEC Treaty the terms "and after consulting the Assembly" shall be replaced by "and in cooperation with the European Parliament."
7. In Article 57 (2) of the EEC Treaty, the third sentence shall be replaced by the following:

   "In other cases the Council shall act by a qualified majority, in cooperation with the European Parliament."

Article 7

Article 149 of the EEC Treaty shall be replaced by the following provisions:

Article 149

1. Where, in pursuance of this Treaty, the Council acts on a proposal from the Commission, unanimity shall be required for an act constituting an amendment to that proposal.
2. Where, in pursuance of this Treaty, the Council acts in cooperation with the European Parliament, the following procedure shall apply:

   (a) The Council, acting by a qualified majority under the conditions of paragraph 1, on a proposal from the Commission and after obtaining the Opinion of the European Parliament, shall adopt a common Position.

   (b) The Council's common position shall be communicated to the European Parliament. The Council and the Commission shall inform the European Parliament fully of the reasons which led the Council to adopt its common position and also of the Commission's position.

   If, within three months of such communication, the European Parliament approves this common position or has not taken a decision within that period, the Council shall definitively adopt the act in question in accordance with the common Position.

   (c) The European Parliament may within the period of three months referred to in point (b), by an absolute majority of its component members, propose amendments to the Council's common Position. The European Parliament may also, by the same majority, reject the Council's common Position. The result of the proceedings shall be transmitted to the Council and the Commission.

   If the European Parliament has rejected the Council's common position, unanimity shall be required for the Council to act on a second reading.

   (d) The Commission shall, within a period of one month, re-examine the proposal on the basis of which the Council adopted its common position, by taking into account the amendments proposed by the European Parliament.

   The Commission shall forward to the Council, at the same time as its re-examined proposal, the amendments of the European Parliament which it has not accepted, and shall express its opinion on them. The Council may adopt these amendments unanimously.

(e) The Council, acting by a qualified majority, shall adopt the proposal as re-examined by the Commission.

Unanimity shall be required for the Council to amend the proposal as re-examined by the Commission.

(f) In the cases referred to in points (c), (d) and (e), the Council shall be required to act within a period of three months. If no decision is taken within this period, the Commission proposal shall be deemed not to have been adopted.

(g) The periods referred to in points (b) and (f) may be extended by a maximum of one month by common accord between the Council and the European Parliament.

As long as the Council has not acted, the Commission may alter its proposal at any time during the procedures mentioned in paragraphs 1 and 2.

. . .

Section II

Provisions relating to the foundations and the policy of the Community

Sub-section 1 — Internal market

Article 13

The EEC Treaty shall be supplemented by the following provisions:

Article 8a

The Community shall adopt measures with the aim of progressively establishing the internal market over a period expiring on 31 December 1992, in accordance with the provisions of this Article and of Articles 8b, 8c, 28, 57 (2), 59, 70 (1), 84, 99, 100a and 100b and without prejudice to the other provisions of this Treaty.

The internal market shall comprise an area without internal frontiers in which the free movement of goods, persons, services and capital is ensured in accordance with the provisions of this Treaty.

Article 14

The EEC Treaty shall be supplemented by the following provisions:

Article 8b

The Commission shall report to the Council before 31 December 1988 and again before 31 December 1990 on the progress made towards achieving the internal market within the time limit fixed in Article 8a.

The Council, acting by a qualified majority on a proposal from the Commission, shall determine the guidelines and conditions necessary to ensure balanced progress in all the sectors concerned.

. . .

Sub-section IV — Economic and social cohesion

Article 23

A Title V shall be added to Part Three of the EEC Treaty reading as follows:

Title V
Economic and Social Cohesion

Article 130a

In order to promote its overall harmonious development, the Community shall develop and pursue its actions leading to the strengthening of its economic and social cohesion.

In particular the Community shall aim at reducing disparities between the various regions and the backwardness of the least-favoured regions.

Article 130b

Member States shall conduct their economic policies, and shall coordinate them, in such a way as, in addition, to attain the objectives set out in Article 130a. The implementation of the common policies and of the internal market shall take into account the objectives set out in Article 130a and in Article 130c and shall contribute to their achievement. The Community shall support the achievement of these objectives by the action it takes through the structural Funds (European Agricultural Guidance and Guarantee Fund, Guidance Section, European Social Fund, European Regional Development Fund), the European Investment Bank and the other existing financial instruments.

Article 130c

The European Regional Development Fund is intended to help redress the principal regional imbalances in the Community through participating in the development and structural adjustment of regions whose development is lagging behind and in the conversion of declining industrial regions.

. . .

Title III

Treaty Provisions on European Cooperation in the Sphere of Foreign Policy

Article 30

European Cooperation in the sphere of foreign policy shall be governed by the following provisions:

1. The High Contracting Parties, being members of the European Communities, shall endeavour jointly to formulate and implement a European foreign policy.
2. (a) The High Contracting Parties undertake to inform and consult each other on any foreign policy matters of general interest so as to ensure that their combined influence is exercised as effectively as possible through coordination, the convergence of their positions and the implementation of joint action.

   (b) Consultations shall take place before the High Contracting Parties decide on their final position.

   (c) In adopting its positions and in its national measures each High Contracting Party shall take full account of the positions of the other partners and shall give due consideration to the desirability of adopting and implementing common European positions.

   In order to increase their capacity for joint action in the foreign policy field, the High Contracting Parties shall ensure that common principles and objectives are gradually developed and defined.

   The determination of common positions shall constitute a point of reference for the policies of the High Contracting Parties.

   (d) The High Contracting Parties shall endeavour to avoid any action or position which impairs their effectiveness as a cohesive force in international relations or within international organizations.

3. (a) The Ministers for Foreign Affairs and a member of the Commission shall meet at least four times a year within the framework of European Political Cooperation. They may also discuss foreign policy matters within the framework of Political Cooperation on the occasion of meetings of the Council of the European Communities.

    (b) The Commission shall be fully associated with the proceedings of Political Cooperation.

    (c) In order to ensure the swift adoption of common positions and the implementation of joint action, the High Contracting Parties shall, as far as possible, refrain from impeding the formation of a consensus and the joint action which this could produce.

4. The High Contracting Parties shall ensure that the European Parliament is closely associated with European Political Cooperation. To that end the Presidency shall regularly inform the European Parliament of the foreign policy issues which are being examined within the framework of Political Cooperation and shall ensure that the views of the European Parliament are duly taken into consideration.

5. The external policies of the European Community and the policies agreed in European Political Cooperation must be consistent.

    The Presidency and the Commission, each within its own sphere of competence, shall have special responsibility for ensuring that such consistency is sought and maintained.

6. (a) The High Contracting Parties consider that closer cooperation on questions of European security would contribute in an essential way to the development of a European identity in external policy matters. They are ready to coordinate their positions more closely on the political and economic aspects of security.

    (b) The High Contracting Parties are determined to maintain the technological and industrial conditions necessary for their security. They shall work to that end both at national level and, where appropriate, within the framework of the competent institutions and bodies.

    (c) Nothing in this Title shall impede closer cooperation in the field of security between certain of the High Contracting Parties within the framework of the Western European Union or the Atlantic Alliance.

7. (a) In international institutions and at international conferences which they attend, the High Contracting Parties shall endeavour to adopt common positions on the subjects covered by this Title.

    (b) In international institutions and at international conferences in which not all the High Contracting Parties participate, those who do participate shall take full account of positions agreed in European Political Cooperation.

8. The High Contracting Parties shall organize a political dialogue with third countries and regional groupings whenever they deem it necessary.

9. The High Contracting Parties and the Commission, through mutual assistance and information, shall intensify cooperation between their representations accredited to third countries and to international organizations.

10. (a) The Presidency of European Political Cooperation shall be held by the High Contracting Party which holds the Presidency of the Council of the European Communities.

    (b) The Presidency shall be responsible for initiating action and co-ordinating and representing the positions of the Member States in relations with third countries in respect of European Political Cooperation activities. It shall also be responsible for the management of Political Cooperation and in particular for drawing up the timetable of meetings and for convening and organizing meetings.

    (c) The Political Directors shall meet regularly in the Political Committee in order to give the necessary impetus, maintain the continuity of European Political Cooperation and prepare Ministers' discussions.

    (d) The Political Committee or, if necessary, a ministerial meeting shall convene within 48 hours at the request of at least three Member States.

    (e) The European Correspondents' Group shall be responsible, under the direction of the Political Committee, for monitoring the implementation of European Political Cooperation and for studying general organizational problems.

    (f) Working groups shall meet as directed by the Political Committee.

    (g) A Secretariat based in Brussels shall assist the Presidency in preparing and implementing the activities of European Political Cooperation and in administrative matters. It shall carry out its duties under the authority of the Presidency.

11. As regards privileges and immunities, the members of the European Political Cooperation Secretariat shall be treated in the same way as members of the diplomatic missions of the High Contracting Parties based in the same place as the Secretariat.

12. Five years after the entry into force of this Act the High Contracting Parties shall examine whether any revision of Title III is required.

    . . .

THE TREATY ON EUROPEAN UNION (07.02.1992)

. . .

Title I—Common Provisions

Article A

By this Treaty, the High Contracting Parties establish among themselves a European Union, hereinafter called "the Union."

This Treaty marks a new stage in the process of creating an ever closer union among the peoples of Europe, in which decisions are taken as closely as possible to the citizen.

The Union shall be founded on the European Communities, supplemented by the policies and forms of cooperation established by this Treaty. Its task shall be to organize, in a manner demonstrating consistency and solidarity, relations between the Member States and between their peoples.

Article B

The Union shall set itself the following objectives:

- to promote economic and social progress which is balanced and sustainable, in particular through the creation of an area without internal frontiers, through the strengthening of economic and social cohesion and through the establishment of economic and monetary union, ultimately including a single currency in accordance with the provisions of this Treaty;
- to assert its identity on the international scene, in particular through the implementation of a common foreign and security policy including the eventual framing of a common defence policy, which might in time lead to a common defence;
- to strengthen the protection of the rights and interests of the nationals of its Member States through the introduction of a citizenship of the Union;
- to develop close cooperation on justice and home affairs;
- to maintain in full the acquis communautaire and build on it with a view to considering, through the procedure referred to in Article N(2), to what extent the policies and forms of cooperation introduced by this Treaty may need to be revised with the aim of ensuring the effectiveness of the mechanisms and the institutions of the Community.

The objectives of the Union shall be achieved as provided in this Treaty and in accordance with the conditions and the timetable set out therein while respecting the principle of subsidiarity as defined in Article 3b of the Treaty Establishing the European Community.

Article C

The Union shall be served by a single institutional framework which shall ensure the consistency and the continuity of the activities carried out in order to attain its objectives while respecting and building upon the acquis communautaire.

The Union shall in particular ensure the consistency of its external activities as a whole in the context of its external relations, security, economic and development policies. The Council and the Commission shall be responsible for ensuring such consistency. They shall ensure the implementation of these policies, each in accordance with its respective powers.

Article D

The European Council shall provide the Union with the necessary impetus for its development and shall define the general political guidelines thereof.

The European Council shall bring together the Heads of State or of Government of the Member States and the President of the Commission. They shall be assisted by the Ministers for Foreign Affairs of the Member States and by a Member of the Commission. The European Council shall meet at least twice a year, under the chairmanship of the Head of State or of Government of the Member State which holds the Presidency of the Council.

The European Council shall submit to the European Parliament a report after each of its meetings and a yearly written report on the progress achieved by the Union.

Article E

The European Parliament, the Council, the Commission and the Court of Justice shall exercise their powers under the conditions and for the purposes provided for, on the one hand, by the provisions of the Treaties establishing the European Communities and of the subsequent Treaties and Acts modifying and supplementing them and, on the other hand, by the other provisions of this Treaty.

Article F

1. The Union shall respect the national identities of its Member States, whose systems of government are founded on the principles of democracy.

2. The Union shall respect fundamental rights, as guaranteed by the European Convention for the Protection of Human Rights and Fundamental Freedoms signed in Rome on 4 November 1950 and as they result from the constitutional traditions common to the Member States, as general principles of Community law.

3. The Union shall provide itself with the means necessary to attain its objectives and carry through its policies.

Title II—Provisions Amending the Treaty Establishing the European Economic Community with a View to Establishing the European Community

Article G

The Treaty Establishing the European Economic Community shall be amended in accordance with the provisions of this Article, in order to establish a European Community.

A. Throughout the Treaty:

1) The term "European Economic Community" shall be replaced by the term "European Community."

B. In Part One "Principles":

2) Article 2 shall be replaced by the following:

Article 2

The Community shall have as its task, by establishing a common market and an economic and monetary union and by implementing the common policies or activities referred to in Articles 3 and 3a, to promote throughout the Community a harmonious and balanced development of economic activities, sustainable and non-inflationary growth respecting the environment, a high degree of convergence of economic performance, a high level of employment and of social protection, the raising of the standard of living and quality of life, and economic and social cohesion and solidarity among Member States.

3) Article 3 shall be replaced by the following:

Article 3

For the purposes set out in Article 2, the activities of the Community shall include, as provided in this Treaty and in accordance with the timetable set out therein:

(a)   the elimination, as between Member States, of customs duties and quantitative restrictions on the import and export of goods, and of all other measures having equivalent effect;

(b)   a common commercial policy;

(c)   an internal market characterized by the abolition, as between Member States, of obstacles to the free movement of goods, persons, services and capital;

(d)   measures concerning the entry and movement of persons in the internal market as provided for in Article 100c;

(e)   a common policy in the sphere of agriculture and fisheries;

(f)   a common policy in the sphere of transport;

(g)   a system ensuring that competition in the internal market is not distorted;

(h)   the approximation of the laws of Member States to the extent required for the functioning of the common market;

(i)   a policy in the social sphere comprising a European Social Fund;

(j)   the strengthening of economic and social cohesion;

(k)   a policy in the sphere of the environment;

(l)   the strengthening of the competitiveness of Community industry;

(m) the promotion of research and technological development;

(n)   encouragement for the establishment and development of trans-European networks;

(o)   a contribution to the attainment of a high level of health protection;

(p)   a contribution to education and training of quality and to the flowering of the cultures of the Member States;

(q)   a policy in the sphere of development cooperation;

(r)   the association of the overseas countries and territories in order to increase trade and promote jointly economic and social development;

(s)   a contribution to the strengthening of consumer protection;

(t)   measures in the spheres of energy, civil protection and tourism.

. . .

Article 8

1.   Citizenship of the Union is hereby established.
     Every person holding the nationality of a Member State shall be a citizen of the Union.

2.   Citizens of the Union shall enjoy the rights conferred by this Treaty and shall be subject to the duties imposed thereby.

Article 8a

1.   Every citizen of the Union shall have the right to move and reside freely within the territory of the Member States, subject to the limitations and

conditions laid down in this Treaty and by the measures adopted to give it effect.

2. The Council may adopt provisions with a view to facilitating the exercise of the rights referred to in paragraph 1; save as otherwise provided in this Treaty, the Council shall act unanimously on a proposal from the Commission and after obtaining the assent of the European Parliament.

Article 8b

1. Every citizen of the Union residing in a Member State of which he is not a national shall have the right to vote and to stand as a candidate at municipal elections in the Member State in which he resides, under the same conditions as nationals of that State. This right shall be exercised subject to detailed arrangements to be adopted before 31 December 1994 by the Council, acting unanimously on a proposal from the Commission and after consulting the European Parliament; these arrangements may provide for derogations where warranted by problems specific to a Member State.

2. Without prejudice to Article 138(3) and to the provisions adopted for its implementation, every citizen of the Union residing in a Member State of which he is not a national shall have the right to vote and to stand as a candidate in elections to the European Parliament in the Member State in which he resides, under the same conditions as nationals of that State. This right shall be exercised subject to detailed arrangements to be adopted before 31 December 1993 by the Council, acting unanimously on a proposal from the Commission and after consulting the European Parliament; these arrangements may provide for derogations where warranted by problems specific to a Member State.

   . . .

Article 73h

Until 1 January 1994, the following provisions shall be applicable:

1. Each Member State undertakes to authorize, in the currency of the Member State in which the creditor or the beneficiary resides, any payments connected with the movement of goods, services or capital, and any transfers of capital and earnings, to the extent that the movement of goods, services, capital and persons between Member States has been liberalized pursuant to this Treaty.

   The Member States declare their readiness to undertake the liberalization of payments beyond the extent provided in the preceding subparagraph, in so far as their economic situation in general and the state of their balance of payments in particular so permit.

. . .

Article 105

1. The primary objective of the ESCB shall be to maintain price stability. Without prejudice to the objective of price stability, the ESCB shall support the general economic policies in the Community with a view to contributing to the achievement of the objectives of the Community as laid down in Article 2. The ESCB shall act in accordance with the principle of an open market economy with free competition, favouring an efficient allocation of resources, and in compliance with the principles set out in Article 3a.

2. The basic tasks to be carried out through the ESCB shall be:
   - to define and implement the monetary policy of the Community;
   - to conduct foreign exchange operations consistent with the provisions of Article 109;
   - to hold and manage the official foreign reserves of the Member States;
   - o promote the smooth operation of payment systems.

3. The third indent of paragraph 2 shall be without prejudice to the holding and management by the governments of Member States of foreign exchange working balances.

4. The ECB shall be consulted:
   - on any proposed Community act in its fields of competence;
   - by national authorities regarding any draft legislative provision in its fields of competence, but within the limits and under the conditions set out by the Council in accordance with the procedure laid down in Article 106(6).

   The ECB may submit opinions to the appropriate Community institutions or bodies or to national authorities on matters in its fields of competence.

5. The ESCB shall contribute to the smooth conduct of policies pursued by the competent authorities relating to the prudential supervision of credit institutions and the stability of the financial system.

6. The Council may, acting unanimously on a proposal from the Commission and after consulting the ECB and after receiving the assent of the European Parliament, confer upon the ECB specific tasks concerning policies relating to the prudential supervision of credit institutions and other financial institutions with the exception of insurance undertakings.

Article 105a

1. The ECB shall have the exclusive right to authorize the issue of bank notes within the Community. The ECB and the national central banks may issue such notes. The bank notes issued by the ECB and the national central banks shall be the only such notes to have the status of legal tender within the Community.
2. Member States may issue coins subject to approval by the ECB of the volume of the issue. The Council may, acting in accordance with the procedure referred to in Article 189c and after consulting the ECB, adopt measures to harmonize the denominations and technical specifications of all coins intended for circulation to the extent necessary to permit their smooth circulation within the Community.

Article 106

1. The ESCB shall be composed of the ECB and of the national central banks.
2. The ECB shall have legal personality.
3. The ESCB shall be governed by the decision-making bodies of the ECB, which shall be the Governing Council and the Executive Board.
   . . .

Article 109e

1. The second stage for achieving economic and monetary union shall begin on 1 January 1994.
2. Before that date
   (a) each Member State shall:
      – adopt, where necessary, appropriate measures to comply with the prohibitions laid down in Article 73b, without prejudice to Article 73e, and in Articles 104 and 104a(1);
      – adopt, if necessary, with a view to permitting the assessment provided for in subparagraph (b), multiannual programmes intended to ensure the lasting convergence necessary for the achievement of economic and monetary union, in particular with regard to price stability and sound public finances;
   (b) the Council shall, on the basis of a report from the Commission, assess the progress made with regard to economic and monetary convergence, in particular with regard to price stability and sound public finances, and the progress made with the implementation of Community law concerning the internal market.
      . . .

Article 109f

1. At the start of the second stage, a European Monetary Institute (here-inafter referred to as "EMI") shall be established and take up its duties; it shall have legal personality and be directed and managed by a Coun-cil, consisting of a President and the Governors of the national central banks, one of whom shall be Vice-President.

   The President shall be appointed by common accord of the Govern-ments of the Member States at the level of Heads of State or of Govern-ment, on a recommendation from, as the case may be, the Committee of Governors of the central banks of the Member States (hereinafter re-ferred to as "Committee of Governors") or the Council of the EMI, and after consulting the European Parliament and the Council. The Presi-dent shall be selected from among persons of recognized standing and professional experience in monetary or banking matters. Only nationals of Member States may be President of the EMI. The Council of the EMI shall appoint the Vice-President.

   . . .

Article 109m

1. Until the beginning of the third stage, each Member State shall treat its exchange rate policy as a matter of common interest. In so doing, Mem-ber States shall take account of the experience acquired in cooperation within the framework of the European Monetary System (EMS) and in developing the ECU, and shall respect existing powers in this field.
2. From the beginning of the third stage and for as long as a Member State has a derogation, paragraph 1 shall apply by analogy to the exchange rate policy of that Member State.

   . . .

Title IX—Culture

Article 128

1. The Community shall contribute to the flowering of the cultures of the Member States, while respecting their national and regional diversity and at the same time bringing the common cultural heritage to the fore.
2. Action by the Community shall be aimed at encouraging cooperation between Member States and, if necessary, supporting and supplement-ing their action in the following areas:

- improvement of the knowledge and dissemination of the culture and history of the European peoples;
- conservation and safeguarding of cultural heritage of European significance;
- non-commercial cultural exchanges;
- artistic and literary creation, including in the audiovisual sector.

3. The Community and the Member States shall foster cooperation with third countries and the competent international organizations in the sphere of culture, in particular the Council of Europe.

4. The Community shall take cultural aspects into account in its action under other provisions of this Treaty.

. . .

Title XII—Trans-European Networks

Article 129b

1. To help achieve the objectives referred to in Articles 7a and 130a and to enable citizens of the Union, economic operators and regional and local communities to derive full benefit from the setting up of an area without internal frontiers, the Community shall contribute to the establishment and development of trans-European networks in the areas of transport, telecommunications and energy infrastructures.

2. Within the framework of a system of open and competitive markets, action by the Community shall aim at promoting the interconnection and inter-operability of national networks as well as access to such networks. It shall take account in particular of the need to link island, landlocked and peripheral regions with the central regions of the Community.

. . .

Industry

Article 130

1. The Community and the Member States shall ensure that the conditions necessary for the competitiveness of the Community's industry exist.

   For that purpose, in accordance with a system of open and competitive markets, their action shall be aimed at:
   - speeding up the adjustment of industry to structural changes;

- encouraging an environment favourable to initiative and to the development of undertakings throughout the Community, particularly small and medium-sized undertakings;
- encouraging an environment favourable to cooperation between undertakings;
- fostering better exploitation of the industrial potential of policies of innovation, research and technological development.

2. The Member States shall consult each other in liaison with the Commission and, where necessary, shall coordinate their action. The Commission may take any useful initiative to promote such coordination.

3. The Community shall contribute to the achievement of the objectives set out in paragraph 1 through the policies and activities it pursues under other provisions of this Treaty. The Council, acting unanimously on a proposal from the Commission, after consulting the European Parliament and the Economic and Social Committee, may decide on specific measures in support of action taken in the Member States to achieve the objectives set out in paragraph 1.

This Title shall not provide a basis for the introduction by the Community of any measure which could lead to a distortion of competition.

Title XIV—Economic and Social Cohesion

Article 130a

In order to promote its overall harmonious development, the Community shall develop and pursue its actions leading to the strengthening of its economic and social cohesion.

In particular, the Community shall aim at reducing disparities between the levels of development of the various regions and the backwardness of the least-favoured regions, including rural areas.

Article 130b

Member States shall conduct their economic policies and shall coordinate them in such a way as, in addition, to attain the objectives set out in Article 130a. The formulation and implementation of the Community's policies and actions and the implementation of the internal market shall take into account the objectives set out in Article 130a and shall contribute to their achievement. The Community shall also support the achievement of these objectives by the action it takes through the Structural Funds (European Agricultural Guidance and Guarantee

Fund, Guidance Section; European Social Fund; European Regional Development Fund), the European Investment Bank and the other existing financial instruments.

The Commission shall submit a report to the European Parliament, the Council, the Economic and Social Committee and the Committee of the Regions every three years on the progress made towards achieving economic and social cohesion and on the manner in which the various means provided for in this Article have contributed to it. This report shall, if necessary, be accompanied by appropriate proposals.

If specific actions prove necessary outside the Funds and without prejudice to the measures decided upon within the framework of the other Community policies, such actions may be adopted by the Council acting unanimously on a proposal from the Commission and after consulting the European Parliament, the Economic and Social Committee and the Committee of the Regions.

Article 130c

The European Regional Development Fund is intended to help to redress the main regional imbalances in the Community through participation in the development and structural adjustment of regions whose development is lagging behind and in the conversion of declining industrial regions.

. . .

Development Cooperation

Article 130u

1. Community policy in the sphere of development cooperation, which shall be complementary to the policies pursued by the Member States, shall foster:

   – the sustainable economic and social development of the developing countries, and more particularly the most disadvantaged among them;
   – the smooth and gradual integration of the developing countries into the world economy;
   – the campaign against poverty in the developing countries.

2. Community policy in this area shall contribute to the general objective of developing and consolidating democracy and the rule of law, and to that of respecting human rights and fundamental freedoms.

3. The Community and the Member States shall comply with the commitments and take account of the objectives they have approved in

the context of the United Nations and other competent international organizations.

Article 130v

The Community shall take account of the objectives referred to in Article 130u in the policies that it implements which are likely to affect developing countries.

Article 130w

1. Without prejudice to the other provisions of this Treaty the Council, acting in accordance with the procedure referred to in Article 189c, shall adopt the measures necessary to further the objectives referred to in Article 130u. Such measures may take the form of multiannual programmes.
2. The European Investment Bank shall contribute, under the terms laid down in its Statute, to the implementation of the measures referred to in paragraph 1.
3. The provisions of this Article shall not affect cooperation with the African, Caribbean and Pacific countries in the framework of the ACP-EEC Convention.

E. In Part Five "Institutions of the Community"

39) Article 137 shall be replaced by the following:

Article 137

The European Parliament, which shall consist of representatives of the peoples of the States brought together in the Community, shall exercise the powers conferred upon it by this Treaty.

40) Paragraph 3 of Article 138 shall be replaced by the following:

3. The European Parliament shall draw up proposals for elections by direct universal suffrage in accordance with a uniform procedure in all Member States.

. . .

Article 138a

Political parties at European level are important as a factor for integration within the Union. They contribute to forming a European awareness and to expressing the political will of the citizens of the Union.

Article 138b

In so far as provided in this Treaty, the European Parliament shall participate in the process leading up to the adoption of Community acts by exercising its powers under the procedures laid down in Articles 189b and 189c and by giving its assent or delivering advisory opinions.

The European Parliament may, acting by a majority of its members, request the Commission to submit any appropriate proposal on matters on which it considers that a Community act is required for the purpose of implementing this Treaty.

. . .

Article 146

The Council shall consist of a representative of each Member State at ministerial level, authorized to commit the government of that Member State.

The office of President shall be held in turn by each Member State in the Council for a term of six months, in the following order of Member States:

- for a first cycle of six years: Belgium, Denmark, Germany, Greece, Spain, France, Ireland, Italy, Luxembourg, Netherlands, Portugal, United Kingdom;
- for the following cycle of six years: Denmark, Belgium, Greece, Germany, France, Spain, Italy, Ireland, Netherlands, Luxembourg, United Kingdom, Portugal.

44) The following Article shall be inserted:

Article 147

The Council shall meet when convened by its President on his own initiative or at the request of one of its members or of the Commission.

45) Article 149 shall be repealed.
46) The following Article shall be inserted:

Article 151

1. A committee consisting of the Permanent Representatives of the Member States shall be responsible for preparing the work of the Council and for carrying out the tasks assigned to it by the Council.
2. The Council shall be assisted by a General Secretariat, under the direction of a Secretary-General. The Secretary-General shall be appointed by the Council acting unanimously.
   The Council shall decide on the organization of the General Secretariat.

3.   The Council shall adopt its rules of procedure.

The number of members of the Commission may be altered by the Council, acting unanimously.

Only nationals of Member States may be members of the Commission.

The Commission must include at least one national of each of the Member States, but may not include more than two members having the nationality of the same State.

4.   The members of the Commission shall, in the general interest of the Community, be completely independent in the performance of their duties.

In the performance of these duties, they shall neither seek nor take instructions from any government or from any other body. They shall refrain from any action incompatible with their duties. Each Member State undertakes to respect this principle and not to seek to influence the members of the Commission in the performance of their tasks.

The members of the Commission may not, during their term of office, engage in any other occupation, whether gainful or not. When entering upon their duties they shall give a solemn undertaking that, both during and after their term of office, they will respect the obligations arising there from and in particular their duty to behave with integrity and discretion as regards the acceptance, after they have ceased to hold office, of certain appointments or benefits. In the event of any breach of these obligations, the Court of Justice may, on application by the Council or the Commission, rule that the member concerned be, according to the circumstances, either compulsorily retired in accordance with Article 160 or deprived of his right to a pension or other benefits in its stead.

. . .

Article 158

1.   The members of the Commission shall be appointed, in accordance with the procedure referred to in paragraph 2, for a period of five years, subject, if need be, to Article 144.

Their term of office shall be renewable.

2.   The governments of the Member States shall nominate by common accord, after consulting the European Parliament, the person they intend to appoint as President of the Commission.

The governments of the Member States shall, in consultation with the nominee for President, nominate the other persons whom they intend to appoint as members of the Commission.

The President and the other members of the Commission thus nominated shall be subject as a body to a vote of approval by the European Parliament. After approval by the European Parliament, the President and the other members of the Commission shall be appointed by common accord of the governments of the Member States.

. . .

Article 162

1. The Council and the Commission shall consult each other and shall settle by common accord their methods of cooperation.

. . .

Article 175

Should the European Parliament, the Council or the Commission, in infringement of this Treaty, fail to act, the Member States and the other institutions of the Community may bring an action before the Court of Justice to have the infringement established.

The action shall be admissible only if the institution concerned has first been called upon to act. If, within two months of being so called upon, the institution concerned has not defined its position, the action may be brought within a further period of two months.

Any natural or legal person may, under the conditions laid down in the preceding paragraphs, complain to the Court of Justice that an institution of the Community has failed to address to that person any act other than a recommendation or an opinion.

The Court of Justice shall have jurisdiction, under the same conditions, in actions or proceedings brought by the ECB in the areas falling within the latter's field of competence and in actions or proceedings brought against the latter.

. . .

Article 189a

1. Where, in pursuance of this Treaty, the Council acts on a proposal from the Commission, unanimity shall be required for an act constituting an amendment to that proposal, subject to Article 189b(4) and (5).
2. As long as the Council has not acted, the Commission may alter its proposal at any time during the procedures leading to the adoption of a Community act.

Article 189b

1. Where reference is made in this Treaty to this Article for the adoption of an act, the following procedure shall apply.

2. The Commission shall submit a proposal to the European Parliament and the Council.

   The Council, acting by a qualified majority after obtaining the opinion of the European Parliament, shall adopt a common position. The common position shall be communicated to the European Parliament. The Council shall inform the European Parliament fully of the reasons which led it to adopt its common position. The Commission shall inform the European Parliament fully of its position.

   If, within three months of such communication, the European Parliament:

   (a) approves the common position, the Council shall definitively adopt the act in question in accordance with that common position;

   (b) has not taken a decision, the Council shall adopt the act in question in accordance with its common position;

   (c) indicates, by an absolute majority of its component members, that it intends to reject the common position, it shall immediately inform the Council. The Council may convene a meeting of the Conciliation Committee referred to in paragraph 4 to explain further its position. The European Parliament shall thereafter either confirm, by an absolute majority of its component members, its rejection of the common position, in which event the proposed act shall be deemed not to have been adopted, or propose amendments in accordance with subparagraph (d) of this paragraph;

   (d) proposes amendments to the common position by an absolute majority of its component members, the amended text shall be forwarded to the Council and to the Commission, which shall deliver an opinion on those amendments.

3. If, within three months of the matter being referred to it, the Council, acting by a qualified majority, approves all the amendments of the European Parliament, it shall amend its common position accordingly and adopt the act in question; however, the Council shall act unanimously on the amendments on which the Commission has delivered a negative opinion. If the Council does not approve the act in question, the President of the Council, in agreement with the President of the European Parliament, shall forthwith convene a meeting of the Conciliation Committee.

4. The Conciliation Committee, which shall be composed of the members of the Council or their representatives and an equal number of representatives of the European Parliament, shall have the task of reaching agreement on a joint text, by a qualified majority of the members of the

Council or their representatives and by a majority of the representatives of the European Parliament. The Commission shall take part in the Conciliation Committee's proceedings and shall take all the necessary initiatives with a view to reconciling the positions of the European Parliament and the Council.

5. If, within six weeks of its being convened, the Conciliation Committee approves a joint text, the European Parliament, acting by an absolute majority of the votes cast, and the Council, acting by a qualified majority, shall have a period of six weeks from that approval in which to adopt the act in question in accordance with the joint text. If one of the two institutions fails to approve the proposed act, it shall be deemed not to have been adopted.

6. Where the Conciliation Committee does not approve a joint text, the proposed act shall be deemed not to have been adopted unless the Council, acting by a qualified majority within six weeks of expiry of the period granted to the Conciliation Committee, confirms the common position to which it agreed before the conciliation procedure was initiated, possibly with amendments proposed by the European Parliament. In this case, the act in question shall be finally adopted unless the European Parliament, within six weeks of the date of confirmation by the Council, rejects the text by an absolute majority of its component members, in which case the proposed act shall be deemed not to have been adopted.

7. The periods of three months and six weeks referred to in this Article may be extended by a maximum of one month and two weeks respectively by common accord of the European Parliament and the Council. The period of three months referred to in paragraph 2 shall be automatically extended by two months where paragraph 2(c) applies.

8. The scope of the procedure under this Article may be widened, in accordance with the procedure provided for in Article N(2) of the Treaty on European Union, on the basis of a report to be submitted to the Council by the Commission by 1996 at the latest.

Article 189c

Where reference is made in this Treaty to this Article for the adoption of an act, the following procedure shall apply:

(a) The Council, acting by a qualified majority on a proposal from the Commission and after obtaining the opinion of the European Parliament, shall adopt a common position.

(b) The Council's common position shall be communicated to the European Parliament. The Council and the Commission shall inform the European Parliament fully of the reasons which led the Council to adopt its common position and also of the Commission's position.

If, within three months of such communication, the European Parliament approves this common position or has not taken a decision within that period, the Council shall definitively adopt the act in question in accordance with the common position.

(c) The European Parliament may, within the period of three months referred to in point (b), by an absolute majority of its component members, propose amendments to the Council's common position. The European Parliament may also, by the same majority, reject the Council's common position. The result of the proceedings shall be transmitted to the Council and the Commission.

If the European Parliament has rejected the Council's common position, unanimity shall be required for the Council to act on a second reading.

(d) The Commission shall, within a period of one month, re-examine the proposal on the basis of which the Council adopted its common position, by taking into account the amendments proposed by the European Parliament.

The Commission shall forward to the Council, at the same time as its re-examined proposal, the amendments of the European Parliament which it has not accepted, and shall express its opinion on them. The Council may adopt these amendments unanimously.

(e) The Council, acting by a qualified majority, shall adopt the proposal as re-examined by the Commission.

Unanimity shall be required for the Council to amend the proposal as re-examined by the Commission.

(f) In the cases referred to in points (c), (d) and (e), the Council shall be required to act within a period of three months. If no decision is taken within this period, the Commission proposal shall be deemed not to have been adopted.

(g) The periods referred to in points (b) and (f) may be extended by a maximum of one month by common accord between the Council and the European Parliament.

. . .

TREATY OF LISBON AMENDING THE TREATY ON EUROPEAN UNION AND THE TREATY ESTABLISHING THE EUROPEAN COMMUNITY (13.12.2007)

. . .

Amendments to the Treaty on European Union and to the Treaty Establishing the European Community

Article 1

The Treaty on European Union shall be amended in accordance with the provisions of this Article.

Preamble

. . .

Drawing inspiration from the cultural, religious and humanist inheritance of Europe, from which have developed the universal values of the inviolable and inalienable rights of the human person, freedom, democracy, equality and the rule of law;

. . .

General Provisions

. . .

Article 1a

The Union is founded on the values of respect for human dignity, freedom, democracy, equality, the rule of law and respect for human rights, including the rights of persons belonging to minorities. These values are common to the Member States in a society in which pluralism, non-discrimination, tolerance, justice, solidarity and equality between women and men prevail.

. . .

Article 2

1. The Union's aim is to promote peace, its values and the well-being of its peoples.

2. The Union shall offer its citizens an area of freedom, security and justice without internal frontiers, in which the free movement of persons is ensured in conjunction with appropriate measures with respect to external border controls, asylum, immigration and the prevention and combating of crime.

3. The Union shall establish an internal market. It shall work for the sustainable development of Europe based on balanced economic growth and price stability, a highly competitive social market economy, aiming at full employment and social progress, and a high level of protection and improvement of the quality of the environment. It shall promote scientific and technological advance.

   It shall combat social exclusion and discrimination, and shall promote social justice and protection, equality between women and men, solidarity between generations and protection of the rights of the child.

   It shall promote economic, social and territorial cohesion, and solidarity among Member States.

   It shall respect its rich cultural and linguistic diversity, and shall ensure that Europe's cultural heritage is safeguarded and enhanced.

4. The Union shall establish an economic and monetary union whose currency is the euro.

5. In its relations with the wider world, the Union shall uphold and promote its values and interests and contribute to the protection of its citizens. It shall contribute to peace, security, the sustainable development of the Earth, solidarity and mutual respect among peoples, free and fair trade, eradication of poverty and the protection of human rights, in particular the rights of the child, as well as to the strict observance and the development of international law, including respect for the principles of the United Nations Charter.

6. The Union shall pursue its objectives by appropriate means commensurate with the competences which are conferred upon it in the Treaties.

   . . .

Article 3b

1. The limits of Union competences are governed by the principle of conferral. The use of Union competences is governed by the principles of subsidiarity and proportionality.

2. Under the principle of conferral, the Union shall act only within the limits of the competences conferred upon it by the Member States in the Treaties to attain the objectives set out therein. Competences not conferred upon the Union in the Treaties remain with the Member States.

3. Under the principle of subsidiarity, in areas which do not fall within its exclusive competence, the Union shall act only if and insofar as the

objectives of the proposed action cannot be sufficiently achieved by the Member States, either at central level or at regional and local level, but can rather, by reason of the scale or effects of the proposed action, be better achieved at Union level.

The institutions of the Union shall apply the principle of subsidiarity as laid down in the Protocol on the application of the principles of subsidiarity and proportionality. National Parliaments ensure compliance with the principle of subsidiarity in accordance with the procedure set out in that Protocol.

4. Under the principle of proportionality, the content and form of Union action shall not exceed what is necessary to achieve the objectives of the Treaties.

The institutions of the Union shall apply the principle of proportionality as laid down in the Protocol on the application of the principles of subsidiarity and proportionality.

. . .

Article 6

1. The Union recognises the rights, freedoms and principles set out in the Charter of Fundamental Rights of the European Union of 7 December 2000, as adapted at Strasbourg, on 12 December 2007, which shall have the same legal value as the Treaties.

. . .

2. The Union shall accede to the European Convention for the Protection of Human Rights and Fundamental Freedoms. Such accession shall not affect the Union's competences as defined in the Treaties.

3. Fundamental rights, as guaranteed by the European Convention for the Protection of Human Rights and Fundamental Freedoms and as they result from the constitutional traditions common to the Member States, shall constitute general principles of the Union's law.

Democratic Principles

Title II—Provisions on Democratic Principles

Article 8A

1. The functioning of the Union shall be founded on representative democracy.

2. Citizens are directly represented at Union level in the European Parliament. Member States are represented in the European Council by their Heads of State or Government and in the Council by their governments, themselves democratically accountable either to their national Parliaments, or to their citizens.

3. Every citizen shall have the right to participate in the democratic life of the Union. Decisions shall be taken as openly and as closely as possible to the citizen.

4. Political parties at European level contribute to forming European political awareness and to expressing the will of citizens of the Union.

Article 8B

1. The institutions shall, by appropriate means, give citizens and representative associations the opportunity to make known and publicly exchange their views in all areas of Union action.

2. The institutions shall maintain an open, transparent and regular dialogue with representative associations and civil society.

3. The European Commission shall carry out broad consultations with parties concerned in order to ensure that the Union's actions are coherent and transparent.

4. Not less than one million citizens who are nationals of a significant number of Member States may take the initiative of inviting the European Commission, within the framework of its powers, to submit any appropriate proposal on matters where citizens consider that a legal act of the Union is required for the purpose of implementing the Treaties.

   . . .

Article 8C

National Parliaments contribute actively to the good functioning of the Union:

(a) through being informed by the institutions of the Union and having draft legislative acts of the Union forwarded to them in accordance with the Protocol on the role of national Parliaments in the European Union;

(b) by seeing to it that the principle of subsidiarity is respected in accordance with the procedures provided for in the Protocol on the application of the principles of subsidiarity and proportionality;

(c) by taking part, within the framework of the area of freedom, security and justice, in the evaluation mechanisms for the implementation of the Union policies in that area,

. . .

Institutions

. . .

Title III—Provisions on the Institutions

. . .

Article 9

1. The Union shall have an institutional framework which shall aim to promote its values, advance its objectives, serve its interests, those of its citizens and those of the Member States, and ensure the consistency, effectiveness and continuity of its policies and actions.

   The Union's institutions shall be:
   - the European Parliament,
   - the European Council,
   - the Council,
   - the European Commission (hereinafter referred to as "the Commission"),
   - the Court of Justice of the European Union,
   - the European Central Bank,
   - the Court of Auditors.

2. Each institution shall act within the limits of the powers conferred on it in the Treaties, and in conformity with the procedures, conditions and objectives set out in them. The institutions shall practice mutual sincere cooperation.

3. The provisions relating to the European Central Bank and the Court of Auditors and detailed provisions on the other institutions are set out in the Treaty on the Functioning of the European Union.

4. The European Parliament, the Council and the Commission shall be assisted by an Economic and Social Committee and a Committee of the Regions acting in an advisory capacity.

   . . .

Article 9A

1. The European Parliament shall, jointly with the Council, exercise legislative and budgetary functions. It shall exercise functions of political control and consultation as laid down in the Treaties. It shall elect the President of the Commission.

2. The European Parliament shall be composed of representatives of the Union's citizens. They shall not exceed seven hundred and fifty in number, plus the President. Representation of citizens shall be degressively proportional, with a minimum threshold of six members per Member State. No Member State shall be allocated more than ninety-six seats.

    The European Council shall adopt by unanimity, on the initiative of the European Parliament and with its consent, a decision establishing the composition of the European Parliament, respecting the principles referred to in the first subparagraph.

3. The members of the European Parliament shall be elected for a term of five years by direct universal suffrage in a free and secret ballot.

4. The European Parliament shall elect its President and its officers from among its members.

    . . .

Article 9B

1. The European Council shall provide the Union with the necessary impetus for its development and shall define the general political directions and priorities thereof. It shall not exercise legislative functions.

2. The European Council shall consist of the Heads of State or Government of the Member States, together with its President and the President of the Commission. The High Representative of the Union for Foreign Affairs and Security Policy shall take part in its work.

3. The European Council shall meet twice every six months, convened by its President. When the agenda so requires, the members of the European Council may decide each to be assisted by a minister and, in the case of the President of the Commission, by a member of the Commission. When the situation so requires, the President shall convene a special meeting of the European Council.

4. Except where the Treaties provide otherwise, decisions of the European Council shall be taken by consensus.

5. The European Council shall elect its President, by a qualified majority, for a term of two and a half years, renewable once. In the event of an impediment or serious misconduct, the European Council can end the President's term of office in accordance with the same procedure.

6. The President of the European Council:
   (a) shall chair it and drive forward its work;
   (b) shall ensure the preparation and continuity of the work of the European Council in cooperation with the President of the Commission, and on the basis of the work of the General Affairs Council;
   (c) shall endeavour to facilitate cohesion and consensus within the European Council;
   (d) shall present a report to the European Parliament after each of the meetings of the European Council.

   The President of the European Council shall, at his level and in that capacity, ensure the external representation of the Union on issues concerning its common foreign and security

   policy, without prejudice to the powers of the High Representative of the Union for Foreign Affairs and Security Policy.

   The President of the European Council shall not hold a national office.

   . . .

Article 9C

1. The Council shall, jointly with the European Parliament, exercise legislative and budgetary functions. It shall carry out policy-making and coordinating functions as laid down in the Treaties.
2. The Council shall consist of a representative of each Member State at ministerial level, who may commit the government of the Member State in question and cast its vote.
3. The Council shall act by a qualified majority except where the Treaties provide otherwise.
4. As from 1 November 2014, a qualified majority shall be defined as at least 55 % of the members of the Council, comprising at least fifteen of them and representing Member States comprising at least 65 % of the population of the Union.

   A blocking minority must include at least four Council members, failing which the qualified majority shall be deemed attained.

   . . .
6. The Council shall meet in different configurations, the list of which shall be adopted in accordance with Article 201b of the Treaty on the Functioning of the European Union.

   The General Affairs Council shall ensure consistency in the work of the different Council configurations. It shall prepare and ensure the follow-up to meetings of the European Council, in liaison with the President of the European Council and the Commission.

The Foreign Affairs Council shall elaborate the Union's external action on the basis of strategic guidelines laid down by the European Council and ensure that the Union's action is consistent.

7. A Committee of Permanent Representatives of the Governments of the Member States shall be responsible for preparing the work of the Council.

8. The Council shall meet in public when it deliberates and votes on a draft legislative act. To this end, each Council meeting shall be divided into two parts, dealing respectively with deliberations on Union legislative acts and non-legislative activities.

9. The Presidency of Council configurations, other than that of Foreign Affairs, shall be held by Member State representatives in the Council on the basis of equal rotation, in accordance with the conditions established in accordance with Article 201b of the Treaty on the Functioning of the European Union.

    . . .

Article 9D

1. The Commission shall promote the general interest of the Union and take appropriate initiatives to that end. It shall ensure the application of the Treaties, and of measures adopted by the institutions pursuant to them. It shall oversee the application of Union law under the control of the Court of Justice of the European Union. It shall execute the budget and manage programmes. It shall exercise coordinating, executive and management functions, as laid down in the Treaties. With the exception of the common foreign and security policy, and other cases provided for in the Treaties, it shall ensure the Union's external representation. It shall initiate the Union's annual and multiannual programming with a view to achieving interinstitutional agreements.

2. Union legislative acts may only be adopted on the basis of a Commission proposal, except where the Treaties provide otherwise. Other acts shall be adopted on the basis of a Commission proposal where the Treaties so provide.

3. The Commission's term of office shall be five years.

    The members of the Commission shall be chosen on the ground of their general competence and European commitment from persons whose independence is beyond doubt.

    . . .

5. As from 1 November 2014, the Commission shall consist of a number of members, including its President and the High Representative of the Union for Foreign Affairs and Security Policy, corresponding to two thirds of the number of Member States, unless the European Council, acting unanimously, decides to alter this number.

   . . .

   A member of the Commission shall resign if the President so requests.

   . . .

7. Taking into account the elections to the European Parliament and after having held the appropriate consultations, the European Council, acting by a qualified majority, shall propose to the European Parliament a candidate for President of the Commission. This candidate shall be elected by the European Parliament by a majority of its component members. If he does not obtain the required majority, the European Council, acting by a qualified majority, shall within one month propose a new candidate who shall be elected by the European Parliament following the same procedure.

   The Council, by common accord with the President-elect, shall adopt the list of the other persons whom it proposes for appointment as members of the Commission. They shall be selected, on the basis of the suggestions made by Member States, in accordance with the criteria set out in paragraph 3, second subparagraph, and paragraph 5, second subparagraph.

   The President, the High Representative of the Union for Foreign Affairs and Security Policy and the other members of the Commission shall be subject as a body to a vote of consent by the European Parliament. On the basis of this consent the Commission shall be appointed by the European Council, acting by a qualified majority.

   . . .

Article 9E

1. The European Council, acting by a qualified majority, with the agreement of the President of the Commission, shall appoint the High Representative of the Union for Foreign Affairs and Security Policy. The European Council may end his term of office by the same procedure.

2. The High Representative shall conduct the Union's common foreign and security policy. He shall contribute by his proposals to the development of that policy, which he shall carry out as mandated by the

Council. The same shall apply to the common security and defence policy.

3. The High Representative shall preside over the Foreign Affairs Council.
4. The High Representative shall be one of the Vice-Presidents of the Commission. He shall ensure the consistency of the Union's external action. He shall be responsible within the Commission for responsibilities incumbent on it in external relations and for coordinating other aspects of the Union's external action.

. . .

Article 9F

1. The Court of Justice of the European Union shall include the Court of Justice, the General Court and specialised courts. It shall ensure that in the interpretation and application of the Treaties the law is observed.

   Member States shall provide remedies sufficient to ensure effective legal protection in the fields covered by Union law.

2. The Court of Justice shall consist of one judge from each Member State. It shall be assisted by Advocates-General.

   The General Court shall include at least one judge per Member State.

. . .

Enhanced Cooperation

. . .

General Provisions on the Union's External Action

Chapter 1—General Provisions on the Union's External Action

Article 10A

1. The Union's action on the international scene shall be guided by the principles which have inspired its own creation, development and enlargement, and which it seeks to advance in the wider world: democracy, the rule of law, the universality and indivisibility of human rights and fundamental freedoms, respect for human dignity, the

principles of equality and solidarity, and respect for the principles of the United Nations Charter and international law.

The Union shall seek to develop relations and build partnerships with third countries, and international, regional or global organisations which share the principles referred to in the first subparagraph. It shall promote multilateral solutions to common problems, in particular in the framework of the United Nations.

2.   The Union shall define and pursue common policies and actions, and shall work for a high degree of cooperation in all fields of international relations, in order to:

(a) safeguard its values, fundamental interests, security, independence and integrity;

(b) consolidate and support democracy, the rule of law, human rights and the principles of international law;

(c) preserve peace, prevent conflicts and strengthen international security, in accordance with the purposes and principles of the United Nations Charter, with the principles of the Helsinki Final Act and with the aims of the Charter of Paris, including those relating to external borders;

(d) foster the sustainable economic, social and environmental development of developing countries, with the primary aim of eradicating poverty;

(e) encourage the integration of all countries into the world economy, including through the progressive abolition of restrictions on international trade;

(f) help develop international measures to preserve and improve the quality of the environment and the sustainable management of global natural resources, in order to ensure sustainable development;

(g) assist populations, countries and regions confronting natural or man-made disasters; and

(h) promote an international system based on stronger multilateral cooperation and good global governance.

. . .

Article 10B

1.   On the basis of the principles and objectives set out in Article 10A, the European Council shall identify the strategic interests and objectives of the Union.

Decisions of the European Council on the strategic interests and objectives of the Union shall relate to the common foreign and security policy and to other areas of the external action of the Union. Such decisions may concern the relations of the Union with a specific country or region or may be thematic in approach. They shall define their duration, and the means to be made available by the Union and the Member States.

. . .

The European Council shall act unanimously on a recommendation from the Council, adopted by the latter under the arrangements laid down for each area. Decisions of the European Council shall be implemented in accordance with the procedures provided for in the Treaties.

2. The High Representative of the Union for Foreign Affairs and Security Policy, for the area of common foreign and security policy, and the Commission, for other areas of external action, may submit joint proposals to the Council.

. . .

The Common Foreign and Security Policy

Chapter 2—Specific Provisions on the Common Foreign and Security Policy

Section 1 — Common Provisions

. . .

Article 13a

1. The High Representative of the Union for Foreign Affairs and Security Policy, who shall chair the Foreign Affairs Council, shall contribute through his proposals towards the preparation of the common foreign and security policy and shall ensure implementation of the decisions adopted by the European Council and the Council.

2. The High Representative shall represent the Union for matters relating to the common foreign and security policy. He shall conduct political dialogue with third parties on the Union's behalf and shall express the Union's position in international organisations and at international conferences.

3. In fulfilling his mandate, the High Representative shall be assisted by a European External Action Service. This service shall work in cooperation with the diplomatic services of the Member States and

shall comprise officials from relevant departments of the General Secretariat of the Council and of the Commission as well as staff seconded from national diplomatic services of the Member States. The organisation and functioning of the European External Action Service shall be established by a decision of the Council. The Council shall act on a proposal from the High Representative after consulting the European Parliament and after obtaining the consent of the Commission.

. . .

The Common Security and Defence Policy

. . .

Final Provisions

. . .

Article 46A

The Union shall have legal personality.

. . .

Article 48

1. The Treaties may be amended in accordance with an ordinary revision procedure. They may also be amended in accordance with simplified revision procedures.

Ordinary revision procedure

2. The Government of any Member State, the European Parliament or the Commission may submit to the Council proposals for the amendment of the Treaties. These proposals may, inter alia, serve either to increase or to reduce the competences conferred on the Union in the Treaties. These proposals shall be submitted to the European Council by the Council and the national Parliaments shall be notified.
3. If the European Council, after consulting the European Parliament and the Commission, adopts by a simple majority a decision in favour of examining the proposed amendments, the President of the

European Council shall convene a Convention composed of representatives of the national Parliaments, of the Heads of State or Government of the Member States, of the European Parliament and of the Commission. The European Central Bank shall also be consulted in the case of institutional changes in the monetary area. The Convention shall examine the proposals for amendments and shall adopt by consensus a recommendation to a conference of representatives of the governments of the Member States as provided for in paragraph 4.

The European Council may decide by a simple majority, after obtaining the consent of the European Parliament, not to convene a Convention should this not be justified by the extent of the proposed amendments. In the latter case, the European Council shall define the terms of reference for a conference of representatives of the governments of the Member States.

4. A conference of representatives of the governments of the Member States shall be convened by the President of the Council for the purpose of determining by common accord the amendments to be made to the Treaties.

The amendments shall enter into force after being ratified by all the Member States in accordance with their respective constitutional requirements.

5. If, two years after the signature of a treaty amending the Treaties, four fifths of the Member States have ratified it and one or more Member States have encountered difficulties in proceeding with ratification, the matter shall be referred to the European Council.

Simplified revision procedures

6. The Government of any Member State, the European Parliament or the Commission may submit to the European Council proposals for revising all or part of the provisions of Part Three of the Treaty on the Functioning of the European Union relating to the internal policies and action of the Union.

The European Council may adopt a decision amending all or part of the provisions of Part Three of the Treaty on the Functioning of the European Union. The European Council shall act by unanimity after consulting the European Parliament and the Commission, and the European Central Bank in the case of institutional changes in the monetary area. That decision shall not enter into force until it is approved by the Member States in accordance with their respective constitutional requirements.

The decision referred to in the second subparagraph shall not increase the competences conferred on the Union in the Treaties.

7. Where the Treaty on the Functioning of the European Union or Title V of this Treaty provides for the Council to act by unanimity in a given area or case, the European Council may adopt a decision authorising the Council to act by a qualified majority in that area or in that case. This subparagraph shall not apply to decisions with military implications or those in the area of defence.

Where the Treaty on the Functioning of the European Union provides for legislative acts to be adopted by the Council in accordance with a special legislative procedure, the European Council may adopt a decision allowing for the adoption of such acts in accordance with the ordinary legislative procedure.

Any initiative taken by the European Council on the basis of the first or the second subparagraph shall be notified to the national Parliaments. If a national Parliament makes known its opposition within six months of the date of such notification, the decision referred to in the first or the second subparagraph shall not be adopted. In the absence of opposition, the European Council may adopt the decision.

For the adoption of the decisions referred to in the first and second subparagraphs, the European Council shall act by unanimity after obtaining the consent of the European Parliament, which shall be given by a majority of its component members.

. . .

Article 49A

1. Any Member State may decide to withdraw from the Union in accordance with its own constitutional requirements.
2. A Member State which decides to withdraw shall notify the European Council of its intention. In the light of the guidelines provided by the European Council, the Union shall negotiate and conclude an agreement with that State, setting out the arrangements for its withdrawal, taking account of the framework for its future relationship with the Union.

. . .

Article 2

The Treaty Establishing the European Community shall be amended in accordance with the provisions of this Article.

. . .

1. The title of the Treaty shall be replaced by "Treaty on the Functioning of the European Union."

A. Horizontal Amendments

. . .

2. Throughout the Treaty
   (a) the words "Community" and "European Community" shall be replaced by "Union" and any necessary grammatical changes shall be made, the words "European Communities" shall be replaced by "European Union"

   . . .

   (g) the words "common market" shall be replaced by "internal market"
   . . .

B. Specific Amendments

. . .

Categories and Areas of Competence

. . .

Title 1—Categories and Areas of Union Competence

Article 2A

1. When the Treaties confer on the Union exclusive competence in a specific area, only the Union may legislate and adopt legally binding acts, the Member States being able to do so themselves only if so empowered by the Union or for the implementation of Union acts.
2. When the Treaties confer on the Union a competence shared with the Member States in a specific area, the Union and the Member States may legislate and adopt legally binding acts in that area. The Member States shall exercise their competence to the extent that the Union has not exercised its competence. The Member States shall again exercise their competence to the extent that the Union has decided to cease exercising its competence.

3. The Member States shall coordinate their economic and employment policies within arrangements as determined by this Treaty, which the Union shall have competence to provide.

4. The Union shall have competence, in accordance with the provisions of the Treaty on European Union, to define and implement a common foreign and security policy, including the progressive framing of a common defence policy.

5. In certain areas and under the conditions laid down in the Treaties, the Union shall have competence to carry out actions to support, coordinate or supplement the actions of the Member States, without thereby superseding their competence in these areas.

    Legally binding acts of the Union adopted on the basis of the provisions of the Treaties relating to these areas shall not entail harmonisation of Member States' laws or regulations.

6. The scope of and arrangements for exercising the Union's competences shall be determined by the provisions of the Treaties relating to each area.

Article 2B

1. The Union shall have exclusive competence in the following areas:
    (a) customs union;
    (b) the establishing of the competition rules necessary for the functioning of the internal market;
    (c) monetary policy for the Member States whose currency is the euro;
    (d) the conservation of marine biological resources under the common fisheries policy;
    (e) common commercial policy.

2. The Union shall also have exclusive competence for the conclusion of an international agreement when its conclusion is provided for in a legislative act of the Union or is necessary to enable the Union to exercise its internal competence, or insofar as its conclusion may affect common rules or alter their scope.

Article 2C

1. The Union shall share competence with the Member States where the Treaties confer on it a competence which does not relate to the areas referred to in Articles 2 B and 2 E.

2. Shared competence between the Union and the Member States applies in the following principal areas:

    (a) internal market;

    (b) social policy, for the aspects defined in this Treaty;

    (c) economic, social and territorial cohesion;

    (d) agriculture and fisheries, excluding the conservation of marine biological resources;

    (e) environment;

    (f) consumer protection;

    (g) transport;

    (h) trans-European networks;

    (i) energy;

    (j) area of freedom, security and justice;

    (k) common safety concerns in public health matters, for the aspects defined in this Treaty.

3.   In the areas of research, technological development and space, the Union shall have competence to carry out activities, in particular to define and implement programmes; however, the exercise of that competence shall not result in Member States being prevented from exercising theirs.

4.   In the areas of development cooperation and humanitarian aid, the Union shall have competence to carry out activities and conduct a common policy; however, the exercise of that competence shall not result in Member States being prevented from exercising theirs.

Article 2D

1.   The Member States shall coordinate their economic policies within the Union. To this end, the Council shall adopt measures, in particular broad guidelines for these policies. Specific provisions shall apply to those Member States whose currency is the euro.

2.   The Union shall take measures to ensure coordination of the employment policies of the Member States, in particular by defining guidelines for these policies.

3.   The Union may take initiatives to ensure coordination of Member States' social policies.

Article 2E

The Union shall have competence to carry out actions to support, coordinate or supplement the actions of the Member States. The areas of such action shall, at European level, be:

    (a) protection and improvement of human health;

    (b) industry;

(c) culture;
(d) tourism;
(e) education, vocational training, youth and sport;
(f) civil protection;
(g) administrative cooperation.

. . .

Region-Building in Latin America and the Caribbean

―――◦◉◦―――

Central American Integration System (SICA)

Central America has the longest experience with regional integration efforts apart from Europe. Dating back to the early 1950s, the creation of the Committee of Economic Integration in Central America (CCE) in 1951 and subsequently the Organization of Central American Countries (ODECA)—with the membership of Costa Rica, El Salvador, Guatemala, Honduras, and Nicaragua—predated the creation of the European Economic Community in 1957. Inspired by the Spaak Report and the reflection on economic integration concepts in Europe during the early 1950s, but also in view of the fact that Central America had undergone fourteen failed efforts at regional integration since its independence from Spain in 1821, CCE and ODECA laid the groundwork for a successful phase of regional economic cooperation and integration that nevertheless failed in the end.

With the General Treaty on Central American Economic Integration, signed in 1960 in Managua, the five Central American countries embraced the goal of forming a common market (Mercado Común Centroamericano, MCCA), intended to grow into a full-fledged customs union with a Secretariat for Central American Economic Integration (Secretaria de Integración Económica Centroamericana, SIECA) at its institutional helm. Intra-regional trade increased from $6 million (US) in 1963 to $1.8 billion at the end of the 1970s. Sector-specific free trade, the introduction of a common customs procedure leading to a common customs zone, and a joint procedure for dealing with external goods were completed and supported by the creation of a Central American Bank for Economic Integration (CABEI) in 1975. Around 5,000 kilometers of road were built in order to ensure the necessary infrastructure.

The Golden Age of Central American integration, with attendant growth and modernization, came to a halt as a consequence of deep sociological changes and subsequent cleavages that escalated from the "Football War" between El Salvador and Honduras in 1969 into bloody civil wars during the 1980s, primarily in El Salvador, Guatemala, and Nicaragua. As part of the pacification process for the region, the European Community initiated the San Jose Dialogue in 1984 with a Declaration, jointly signed by the then nine EC member states, the acceding countries Spain and Portugal, and six states of Central America—now including Panama—in the presence of representatives of the UN, the Contadora Group, and the Organization of American States (OAS). This ministerial meeting is considered the foundation of EC/EU relations with Central America. Political support of the EC went hand in hand with renewed socioeconomic cooperation in the region. In 1989, the Peace Treaties of Esquipulas ended the most dramatic period in the modern history of Central America.

In 1993, new efforts for regional integration began. As per capita income had decreased by almost 70 percent since the early 1970s and poverty had sharply increased (25 percent of citizens in Costa Rica and 70 percent in Guatemala still live below the poverty line), the pressure of "neoliberal globalization" and the perspective of the North American Free Trade Zone NAFTA (emerging since 1990 between the US, Canada, and Mexico) forced Central America into new efforts of regional cooperation and subsequently integration. The Tegucigalpa Protocol to the Charter of the Organization of Central American States, signed in 1991, established new institutional mechanisms for regional integration. It was followed by the Guatemala Protocol to the General Treaty on Central American Economic Integration, signed by Guatemala, El Salvador, Honduras, Nicaragua, Costa Rica, and Panama on 10 February 1993, marking a new beginning for Central American economic integration as the Central American Integration System (Sistema de la Integración Centroamericana, SICA).

Institutional arrangements to support Central American integration have improved. The SICA Council of Ministers of Economic Integration, composed of ministers for economic affairs and the presidents of the Central Banks of SICA member states, is the highest body of the Central American Integration System. The SICA General Secretariat is based in El Salvador. The Constitutional Court in Nicaragua has begun to work again after years of being practically closed. The Parliamentary Assembly (PARLACEN), based in Guatemala, and the Central American Bank for Economic Integration, with branch offices in all five member states of SICA, have been charged with new tasks. A whole set of interregional specialized agencies have been established or streamlined, including an academic structure. As the Central American Integration System does not contain truly supranational elements, it has been criticized for remaining too weak to have a lasting impact on the integration of the region. Only 60 percent of the 450 decisions taken by the heads of state between 1990 and 1999 were actually implemented.

Nevertheless, certain progress is noteworthy, all the more so in light of the long and persistent history of crisis and conflict in the region. In 1995, the members of the reinvented integration system agreed upon common customs tariffs as the first important step toward a customs union. In 1996, Guatemala and El Salvador agreed to establish full customs union, a proposition joined by Honduras and Nicaragua in 2000 and by Costa Rica in 2002. While the target date of 2004 for the full completion of the Central American customs union was missed, the trend seems to be more promising than ever before in the history of the region. This especially encouraging in view of the magnitude of obstacles to regional integration: poverty levels, lack of infrastructure, and strong dependency on the US, with which 40 percent of all trade of the Central American countries is conducted.

The European Union supports regional integration in Central America with about 60 percent of all EU funds that are granted to the region. Its economic stake in the region—Central America represents 0.4 percent of the total external trade of the EU—alone cannot explain this commitment. For political reasons, the EU genuinely encourages Central America to take further steps along the long road toward substantial regional integration. Compared to where the EU might stand after more than a decade of civil wars and refugee movements, it seems fair to judge Central American integration by the path that began anew after 1991. The Framework Treaty on Democratic Security in Central America, signed in 1995, indicates the awareness of an intrinsic link between democratic stability and regional integration. In recognizing SICA's efforts, the European Union agreed in 2006 to begin negotiations for a biregional association agreement with SICA.

GENERAL TREATY ON CENTRAL AMERICAN
ECONOMIC INTEGRATION (13.12.1960)

. . .

Mindful of the need to expedite the integration of their economies, consolidate the results so far achieved and lay down the principles on which it should be based in the future.

. . .

Chapter I—Central American Common Market

Article I

The Contracting States agree to establish among themselves a common market which shall be brought into full operation within a period of not more than five years from the date on which the present Treaty enters into force. They further agree to create a customs union in respect of their territories.

Article II

For the purposes of the previous article the Contracting Parties undertake to bring a Central American free-trade area into full operation within a period of five years and to adopt a standard Central American tariff as provided for in the Central American Agreement on the Equalization of Import Duties and Charges.

Chapter II—Trade Regime

Article III

The Signatory States shall grant each other free-trade treatment in respect of all products originating in their respective territories, save only for the limitations contained in the special regimes referred to in Annex A of the present Treaty.

Consequently, the natural products of the Contracting States and the products manufactured therein shall be exempt from import and export duties, including consular fees, and all other taxes, dues and charges levied on imports and exports or charged in respect thereof, whether they be of a national, municipal or any other nature.

The exemptions provided for in this article shall not include charges or fees for lighterage, wharfage, warehousing or handling of goods, or any other charges which may legally be incurred for port, storage or transport services; nor shall they include exchange differentials resulting from the existence of two or more rates of exchange or from other exchange arrangements in any of the Contracting States.

Goods originating in the territory of any of the Signatory States shall be accorded national treatment in all of them and shall be exempt from all quantitative or other restrictions or measures, except for such measures as may be legally applicable in the territories of the Contracting States for reasons of health, security or police control.

Article IV

The Contracting Parties establish special interim regimes in respect of specific products exempting them from the immediate free-trade treatment referred to in article III hereof. These products shall be automatically incorporated into the free-trade regime not later than the end of the fifth year in which the present Treaty is in force, except as specifically provided in Annex A.

The products to which special regimes apply are listed in Annex A and trade in them shall be carried on in conformity with the measures and conditions therein specified. These measures and conditions shall not be amended except by multilateral negotiation in the Executive Council. Annex A is an integral part of this Treaty.

The Signatory States agree that the Protocol on the Central American Preferential Tariff, appended to the Central American Agreement on the Equalization of Import Duties and Charges, shall not apply to trade in the products referred to in the present article for which special regimes are provided.

Article V

Goods enjoying the advantages stipulated in this Treaty shall be designated as such on a customs form, signed by the exporter and containing a declaration of origin. This form shall be produced for checking by the customs officers of the countries of origin and destination, in conformity with Annex B of this Treaty.

If there is doubt as to the origin of an article and the matter has not been settled by bilateral negotiation, any of the Parties affected may request the intervention of the Executive Council to verify the origin of the article concerned. The Council shall not consider goods as originating in one of the Contracting States if they originate or are manufactured in a third country and are only simply assembled, wrapped, packed, cut or diluted in the exporting country.

In the cases mentioned in the previous paragraph, importation of the goods concerned shall not be prohibited provided that a guaranty is given to the importing country in respect of payment of the import duties and other charges to which the goods may be liable. The guaranty shall be either forfeited or refunded, as the case may be, when the matter is finally settled.

The Executive Council shall lay down regulations governing the procedure to be followed in determining the origin of goods.

Article VI

If the goods traded are liable to internal taxes, charges or duties of any kind levied on production, sale, distribution or consumption in any of the signatory countries, the country concerned may levy an equivalent amount on similar goods imported from the other Contracting State, in which case it must also levy at least an equivalent amount for the same respective purposes on similar imports from third countries.

The Contracting Parties agree that the following conditions shall apply to the establishment of internal taxes on consumption:

(a) Such taxes may be established in the amount deemed necessary when there is domestic production of the article in question, or when the article is not produced in any of the Signatory States;

(b) When the article is not produced in one Signatory State but is produced in any of the others, the former State may not establish taxes on consumption of the article concerned unless the Executive Council so authorizes;

(c) If a Contracting Party has established a domestic tax on consumption, and production of the article so taxed is subsequently begun in any of the other Signatory States, but the article is not produced in the State that established the tax, the Executive Council shall, if the State concerned so requests, deal with the case and decide whether the tax is compatible with free trade. The States undertake to abolish these taxes on consumption, in accordance with their legal procedures, on receipt of notification to this effect from the Executive Council.

Article VII

No Signatory State shall establish or maintain regulations on the distribution or retailing of goods originating in another Signatory State when such regulations place, or tend to place the said goods in an unfavourable position in relation to similar goods of domestic origin or imported from any other country.

Article VIII

Items which, by virtue of the domestic legislation of the Contracting Parties, constitute State monopolies on the date of entry into force of the present Treaty, shall remain subject to the relevant legislation of each country and, if applicable, to the provisions of Annex A of the present Treaty.

Should new monopolies be created or the regime of existing monopolies be changed, the Parties shall enter into consultations for the purpose of placing Central American trade in the items concerned under a special regime.

. . .

Chapter IV—Transit and Transport

Article XV

Each of the Contracting States shall ensure full freedom of transit through its territory for goods proceeding to or from the other Signatory States as well as for the vehicles transporting these goods.

Such transit shall not be subject to any deduction, discrimination or quantitative restriction. In the event of traffic congestion or other instances of force majeure, each Signatory State shall treat the mobilization of consignments intended for its own population and those in transit to the other States on an equitable basis.

Transit operations shall be carried out by the routes prescribed by law for that purpose and shall be subject to the customs and transit laws and regulations applicable in the territory of transit.

Goods in transit shall be exempt from all duties, taxes and other charges of a fiscal, municipal or any other character levied on transit, irrespective of their destination, but may be liable to the charges usually applied for services rendered which shall in no case exceed the cost thereof and thus constitute de facto import duties or taxes.

. . .

Chapter VI—Industrial Integration

Article XVII

The Contracting Parties hereby endorse all the provisions of the Agreement on the Regime for Central American Integration Industries, and, in order to ensure implementation among themselves as soon as possible, undertake to sign, within a period of not more than six months from the date of entry into force of the present Treaty, additional protocols specifying the industrial plants initially to be covered by the Agreement, the free-trade regime applicable to their products and the other conditions provided for in article III of the Agreement.

Chapter VII—Central American Bank for Economic Integration

Article XVIII

The Signatory States agree to establish the Central American Bank for Economic Integration which shall be a juridical person. The Bank shall act as an instrument for the financing and promotion of a regionally balanced, integrated economic growth. To that end they shall sign the agreement constituting the Bank, which shall remain open for the signature or accession of any other Central American State which may wish to become a member of the Bank.

. . .

Chapter VIII— Tax Incentives to Industrial Development

Article XIX

The Contracting States, with a view to establishing uniform tax incentives to industrial development, agree to ensure as soon as possible a reasonable equalization of the relevant laws and regulations in force. To that end they shall, within a period of six months from the date of entry into force of the present Treaty, sign a special protocol specifying the amount and type of exceptions, the time limits thereof, the conditions under which they shall be granted, the systems of industrial classification and the principles and procedures governing their application. The Executive council shall be responsible for coordinating the application of the tax incentives of Industrial development.

Chapter IX—Organs

Article XX

The Central American Economic Council, composed of the Ministers of Economic Affairs of the several Contracting Parties, is hereby established for the purpose of integrating the Central American economies and coordinating the economic policy of the Contracting States.

The Central American Economic Council shall meet as often as required or at the request of any of the Contracting Parties. It shall examine the work of the

Executive Council and adopt such resolutions as it may deem appropriate. The Central American Economic Council shall be the organ responsible for facilitating implementation of the resolutions on economic integration adopted by the Central American Economic Cooperation Committee. It may seek the advice of Central American and international technical organs.

. . .

Article XXIII

A Permanent Secretariat is hereby instituted, as a juridical person, and shall act as such both for the Central American Economic Council and the Executive Council established under this Treaty.

The Secretariat shall have its seat and headquarters in Guatemala City, capital of the Republic of Guatemala, and shall be headed by a Secretary-General appointed for a period of three years by the Central American Economic Council. The Secretariat shall establish such departments and sections as may be necessary for the performance of its functions. Its expenses shall be governed by a general budget adopted annually by the Central American Economic Council and each Contracting Party shall contribute annually to its support an amount equivalent to not less than fifty thousand United States dollars (US$50,000), payable in the respective currencies of the Signatory States.

Members of the Secretariat shall enjoy diplomatic immunity. Other diplomatic privileges shall be granted only to the Secretariat and to the Secretary-General.

. . .

TEGUCIGALPA PROTOCOL TO THE CHARTER OF THE ORGANIZATION OF CENTRAL AMERICAN STATES (13.12.1991)

. . .

Nature, objectives, principles and ends

Article l

Costa Rica, El Salvador, Guatemala, Honduras, Nicaragua and Panama constitute an economic and political community, which seeks to promote the integration of Central America. To that end the Central American Integration System is hereby constituted, comprising the original Member States of ODECA, and Panama, which is joining as a Member State.

Article 2

The Central American Integration System shall provide the institutional framework for the regional integration of Central America.

Article 3

The fundamental objective of the Central American Integration System is to bring about the integration of Central America as a region of peace, freedom, democracy and development.

To that end, the following objectives are hereby reaffirmed:

(a) To consolidate democracy and strengthen its institutions on the basis of the existence of Governments elected by universal and free suffrage with secret ballot, and of unrestricted respect for human rights;

(b) To define a new regional security model based on a reasonable balance of forces, the strengthening of civilian government, the elimination of extreme poverty, the promotion of sustained development, protection of the environment, and the eradication of violence, corruption, terrorism, and trafficking in drugs and arms;

(c) To promote a comprehensive system of freedom that will ensure the full and harmonious development of the individual and of society as a whole;

(d) To achieve a regional System of well-being and economic and social justice for the peoples of Central America;

(e) To achieve an economic union and strengthen the financial System of Central America;

(f) To strengthen the region as an economic bloc to provide for its successful participation in the international economy;

(g) To reaffirm and consolidate Central America's self-determination in terms of its external relations by means of a unified strategy to strengthen and broaden participation by the region as a whole in the international sphere;

(h) To promote, in a harmonious and balanced manner, the sustained economic, social, cultural and political development of the Member States and of the region as a whole;

(i) To carry out concerted action to protect the environment through respect for and harmony with nature, while ensuring balanced development and the rational exploitation of the natural resources of the area, with a view to establishing a new ecological order in the region;

(j) To establish the Central American Integration System on the basis of an institutional and legal order and mutual respect between Member States.

Article 4

In order to attain the above objectives, the Central American Integration System and its Members shall proceed in accordance with the following fundamental principles:

    (a) The protection of, respect for and promotion of human rights shall constitute the fundamental basis of the Central American Integration System;

    (b) Peace, democracy, development and freedom constitute a harmonious and indivisible whole which shall guide the acts of the States Members of the Central American Integration System;

    (c) Central American identity as an active manifestation of regional interests and of the will to participate in consolidating the Integration of the region;

    (d) Central American solidarity as an expression of its profound interdependence, origins and common destiny;

    (e) The phased, specific and progressive nature of the process of economic Integration, based on harmonious and balanced regional development, with special treatment for relatively less developed Member States, and on equity and reciprocity, and the Central American Exception Clause;

    (f) The comprehensive nature of the Integration process and the democratic participation therein of every social sector;

    (g) Legal certainty with respect to relations between the Member States and the peaceful settlement of their disputes;

    (h) Good faith on the part of the Member States in the discharge of their obligations; Member States shall abstain from establishing, agreeing to or adopting any measure that contravenes the provisions of this Instrument or that impedes compliance with the fundamental principles of the Central American Integration System or the attainment of its objectives;

    (i) Respect for the principles and norms of the Charters of the United Nations and the Organisation of American States (OAS) and the Declarations issued at the Meetings of Presidents of Central America since May 1986.

    . . .

Institutional Structure

Article 8

This Protocol amends the Central American institutional structure, previously regulated under the framework of ODECA, to which are hereby linked the organs and institutions which relate to integration, and which shall enjoy functional autonomy within the framework of the requisite overall intersectoral coordination to ensure the efficient implementation of and ongoing follow-up to decisions issued at the Meetings of Presidents.

The functioning of the institutional structure shall guarantee the balanced and harmonious development of the economic, social, cultural and political sectors.

Article 9

The organs and institutions of the Central American Integration System shall be guided by the objectives and principles set forth in this Protocol and shall have regard to such objectives and principles in their decisions, studies and analyses as well as in the preparation of all meetings.

Article 10

The organs and institutions of the Central American Integration System shall contribute to effective compliance with and implementation of the objectives and principles of this Protocol. This obligation shall take overriding precedence in all supplementary or subordinate legislation, which shall guarantee in all cases that decisions shall be made public and that proceedings shall be open to those individuals concerned in accordance with the nature of each organ and Institution and the matters in question.

Article 11

The Central American Integration System shall ensure the efficiency and effectiveness of the functioning of its organs and institutions by ensuring unity and coherence in intraregional activities and in relations with third States, groups of States and international organizations.

Organs

Article 12

For the purposes of attaining the ends of the Central American Integration System, the following organs are hereby established:

(a) The Meeting of Presidents;
(b) The Council of Ministers;
(c) The Executive Committee;
(d) The General Secretariat.

The following shall constitute part of this System:

The Meeting of Vice-Presidents and Officials of the Office of the President of the Republic, which will act as an advisory and consultancy organ. The Meeting shall normally be held every six months and, exceptionally, at the request of the Vice-Presidents. Its decisions shall be adopted by consensus.

Without prejudice to the provisions of article 4 of the Transitional Provisions, the Central American Parliament shall act as an organ for exposition, analysis and recommendation; its functions and attributes shall be those provided for under its Constituent Treaty and Protocols currently in force.

The Central American Court of Justice, which shall guarantee respect for the law in the interpretation and implementation of this Protocol and its supplementary instruments and acts pursuant to it. The Integration, functioning and attributions of the Central American Court of Justice shall be regulated in the Statute of the Court, which shall be negotiated and signed by the Member States within 90 days of the entry into force of this Protocol.

The Consultative Committee shall comprise representatives of business, labour, the academic sector and other community leaders within Central America representing the economic, social and cultural sectors and committed to the endeavour to attain the integration of Central America.

The role of the Committee shall be to advise the General Secretariat with regard to the Organization's policies in the development of the programmes being executed.

Meeting of Presidents

Article 13

The Meeting of Presidents shall be the supreme organ of the Central American Integration System.

Article 14

The Meeting of Presidents shall consist of the constitutional Presidents of the Member States and shall meet in ordinary session every six months and in extraordinary session by decision of the Presidents. Its decisions shall be adopted by consensus. The country hosting the Meeting of Presidents shall speak on behalf of Central America during the six months following the holding of the Meeting.

Article 15

The Meeting of Presidents shall address regional questions on which it is required to take decisions, with regard to democracy, development, freedom, peace and security.

The Meeting of Presidents shall be required in particular to:

(a) Define and direct Central American policy by establishing guidelines for the Integration of the region, as well as the provisions necessary to ensure the coordination and harmonization of the activities of the bodies and institutions of the region, and the verification, monitoring and follow-up of its mandates and decisions;

(b) Harmonize the foreign policies of its States;

(c) Strengthen regional identity as part of the ongoing process of consolidating a united Central America;

(d) Approve, where appropriate, amendments to this Protocol submitted pursuant to article 37 thereof;

(e) Ensure fulfilment of the obligations contained in the present Protocol and in the other agreements, conventions and protocols which constitute the legal order of the Central American Integration System;

(f) Decide on the admission of new members to the Central American Integration System.

Council of Ministers

Article 16

The Council of Ministers shall be composed of the Ministers holding the relevant portfolios, or exceptionally, duly authorized vice-ministers. They competent minister of the Member State speaking on behalf of Central America pursuant to article 14 of this Protocol shall act as President of the respective Council of Ministers during the relevant six-month term.

The Council of Ministers shall be required to provide the necessary follow-up to ensure the effective implementation of the decisions adopted by the Meeting of Presidents in the sector in which it is competent, and to prepare the topics for possible discussion by the Meeting.

Depending on the nature of the subjects to be considered, the Ministers may hold intersectoral meetings.

The Council of Ministers for Foreign Affairs shall be the main coordinating body.

Article 17

The Council of Ministers for Foreign Affairs shall be responsible for matters relating to the process of democratisation, peacemaking, regional security and other political matters, as well as the coordination and follow-up in respect of political decisions and measures in the economic, social and cultural sectors which may have international repercussions. It shall also be responsible for approving the budget of the central organization, drawing up the agenda and making preparations for the Meetings of Presidents, representing the region vis-à-vis the international community, implementing the decisions of the Presidents in the field of regional international policy, issuing recommendations concerning the accession of new members to the Central American Integration System and deciding on the admission of observers to the System.

The Council of Ministers for Foreign Affairs shall take cognizance of the proposals of the various ministerial forums so that it may bring them to the attention of the Meeting of Presidents, together with its comments and recommendations.

Article 18

The Council of Ministers responsible for economic Integration and regional development shall be responsible for implementing the decisions of the Meeting of Presidents concerning economic integration, and fostering economic policies geared towards regional integration.

Article 19

The Council of Ministers responsible for other sectors shall be responsible for dealing with matters falling within their respective terms of reference.

Article 20

The intersectoral meeting of Ministers for Foreign Affairs and Ministers responsible for economic integration and regional development shall be responsible for analysing, discussing and proposing to the Presidents the regional strategy for the active participation of the region in the international economic System, and for implementing that strategy jointly.

Article 21

In order to be quorate, meetings of the Council of Ministers must be attended by all the respective ministers, or, exceptionally, by duly authorized vice-ministers.

Each Member State shall have a single vote within the Council of Ministers. Decisions on matters of substance must be adopted by consensus. If there is doubt as to whether a decision concerns substance or procedure, the question shall be settled by a majority vote.

The various ordinary, sectoral or intersectoral meetings of the Council of Ministers shall be convened as often as necessary or at the request of one of the members or of the Meeting of Presidents.

Article 22

Without prejudice to the provisions of article 10, the decisions of the Council of Ministers shall be binding on all Member States and only provisions of a legal nature may serve to prevent their application. In such cases, the Council shall give further consideration to the matter by means of appropriate technical Studies and, if necessary, shall adapt its decision to the needs of the legal System in question.

However, such decisions may be applied by those Member States which have not objected to them.

Article 23

The Executive Committee and the General Secretariat shall be the permanent organs of the Central American Integration System.

Executive Committee

Article 24

The Executive Committee shall be composed of one representative of each Member State. Such representatives shall be appointed by the respective Presidents through the Ministers for Foreign Affairs.

The Executive Committee shall be chaired by the representative of the State which hosted the most recent ordinary Meeting of Presidents. The Committee shall meet in ordinary Session once a week and in extraordinary session when convened by its Chairman.

The tasks of the Executive Committee shall be to:

(a) by the Meetings of Presidents;
(b) Ensure compliance with the provisions of the present Protocol and Instruments additional thereto or emanating therefrom;
(c) Establish sectoral policies and, through its chairman, submit to the Council of Ministers for Foreign Affairs the proposals necessary to comply with the general guidelines issued by the Meetings of Presidents;

(d) Through its Chairman, submit to the Council of Ministers for Foreign Affairs the draft budget of the central Organisation of the Central American Integration System;

(e) Propose to the Council of Ministers for Foreign Affairs the establishment of such secretariats and subsidiary bodies as it may deem necessary for the effective fulfilment of the objectives of the Central American Integration System, particularly in order to permit the participation of all the sectors involved in the comprehensive development of the region and the global Integration process;

(f) Approve the regulations or instruments drawn up by the secretariats or other bodies or secretariats of the Central American Integration System;

(g) Review the half-yearly progress reports of the General Secretariat and other secretariats and transmit them, together with the comments and recommendations of the respective Councils of Ministers, to the Council of Ministers for Foreign Affairs at least one month prior to its last meeting before the Meeting of Presidents, so that the Council of Ministers for Foreign Affairs may bring those comments and recommendations to the attention of the Meeting;

(h) Undertake any other tasks specified in the present Protocol and Instruments additional thereto or emanating therefrom.

General Secretariat

Article 25

The General Secretariat shall be headed by a Secretary-General who shall be appointed by the Meeting of Presidents for a period of four years.

Article 26

The Secretary-General shall be the chief administrative officer of the Central American Integration System and the legal representative of the System.

The Secretary-General must be a national of any Member State and shall have a demonstrated commitment to the integration process, a high degree of impartiality, independent judgement and integrity.

The Secretary-General shall be required to:

(a) Represent the Central American Integration System in the international arena in accordance with the provisions of this Protocol and when called upon to do so by the Council of Ministers;

(b) Execute or coordinate the execution of mandates emanating from the Meeting of Presidents, the Council of Ministers and the Executive Committee;

(c) Prepare the administrative regulations and other instruments of the General Secretariat and transmit them for consideration by the Executive Committee;

(d) Negotiate and sign, with the approval of the relevant Council of Ministers, international instruments which fall within their spheres of competence, in accordance with the principles and purposes of this Protocol;

(e) Ensure financial and technical cooperation among States, groups of States, organizations and other international bodies as required for the smooth functioning of the Central American Integration System and the attainment of Central American objectives, and, to that end, sign contracts and agreements and accept donations and other extraordinary contributions;

(f) Prepare a programme of work, an annual progress report and the budget estimate, and submit them to the Executive Committee;

(g) Participate as a full member in all bodies of the Central American Integration System and head the permanent Secretariat of the Meeting of Presidents, providing secretariat services and other necessary technical and administrative services;

(h) Monitor the implementation of the provisions of this Protocol and of Instruments emanating therefrom or additional thereto, and the implementation by all regional integration bodies and institutions of decisions of the Meeting of Presidents and the Council of Ministers. To that end, the Secretary-General may meet with such bodies and institutions whenever he deems it appropriate or is directed to do so by the Executive Committee;

(i) Ensure that Member States make their assessed contributions and extraordinary contributions, if any, to the regular budget;

. . .

CONVENTION ON THE STATUTE OF THE CENTRAL AMERICAN COURT OF JUSTICE (10.12.1992)

. . .

A jurisdictional power for the Central American States

The creation of the Central American Court of Justice has been the strong and lasting desire of the Central American countries. It has also become the organ of the Central American Integration System that can prescribe a sentence of a unifying legal character for the resolution of regional conflicts.

Thus the Central American Court of Justice views itself as a regional tribunal, with exclusive jurisdiction over the states of the Isthmus.

The court has absolute competence which excludes every other Tribunal. In addition to hearing conflicts between states, the Court may also hear conflicts between natural or legal persons resident in the area and the governments or organisms of the Central American Integration System.

Organization of the Court

The Court's basic organization is set forth in the Statute and shall be further developed in the Court's own rules. Notwithstanding the above, the Court's minimum number of members and the qualifications and requisites that each member must meet are indicated. These qualifications are equal to those required for the exercise of the highest judicial functions in the member's respective countries.

The election of magistrates to the Court is established by the respective organs or judicial authorities. Once elected, the Magistrates shall exercise their functions with absolute and complete independence for a period of ten years, with the possibility of being reelected. In addition, they shall enjoy the immunities and privileges accorded to the heads of diplomatic missions and at no time shall be permitted to exercise public or administrative duties, other than academic functions.

Although the Court's headquarters are designated in the Statute, the Court may agree to meet and function temporarily in any other place in Central America.

The Court shall exist indefinitely. Its members and Secretary shall be required to reside in the country where the court is headquartered. The Court shall have a President and a vice-president who will exercise their functions for one year. The Presidency shall be held in succession according to the alphabetical order of the names of the Member States; and the Vice-Presidency may not be held, for any reason, by a Magistrate of the same nationality as the President.

The court's budget shall be apportioned in equal parts to the Member States.

Competence

The Court shall have mandatory jurisdiction over disputes and voluntary jurisdiction over questions of law and fact.

As has been noted, the Court shall have competence over a wide range of subject matter. One of its areas of competence shall be as an International Regional

Tribunal. In that capacity it shall hear by petitions as court of sole resort the controversies presented by the states.

Another area of competence shall encompass conflicts that arise between natural or legal persons and a state of an organism of Central American Integration System.

It must be emphasized that the Court's competence includes the authority to try, at the request of a party, conflicts that may arise between the powers of the states, and in cases where judicial verdicts are not respected.

In addition to the competencies already mentioned, the Court is attributed the role of Organ of Permanent Consultation to the Central American courts of Justice. In that role it shall hear the questions presented and shall issue recommendations that facilitate the passage of uniform laws.

At any point in time, the respective chanceries may solicit a compromise among the states.

Conclusions

The creation of the Central American Court of Justice is of critical importance given the politicized period in which the Central American countries find themselves.

It is believed that in order to achieve lasting and durable peace in the Isthmus, a form of jurisdictional control must exist to prevent the states from unjustly asserting rights that they do not have, or becoming arbitrary powers that negate all justice.

The Court's grant of exclusive jurisdiction shall result in the creation of a supranational organ that will permit the resolution of problems of the Central American Integration System in a peaceful and civilized manner.

The Member States' Submission to the Court's jurisdiction will limit their sovereignty. This implies that the states must respect the Court's decisions.

The Court's independence and autonomy stem from the delegation of powers by the Member States. In the exercise of its jurisdictional functions the Court examines and controls, through the judicial process, the acts executed by the Member States and by the organs of the Central American Integration System that affect the covenants and the treaties in force among them.

Natural and legal persons whose rights have been affected by the acts of states or organs of the Central American Integration System also have access to the Court.

The supervisory powers conferred upon the "Central American Judicial Council" during the phase prior to the formation and establishment of the Court must be noted in that the Council is granted powers to apply, interpret and execute the provisions of the Statute, and may undertake all necessary efforts to ensure the prompt establishment and functioning of the Court.

The Statute does nothing more than continue the Protocol of Tegucigalpa's recognition of the Council and its participation in the process of Central American judicial integration as evidenced by its work in the area.

Finally, it is worth emphasizing the content of Article 6 of the Statute, which adopts what was established by the Central American Court of Justice, or the Court of Cartago of 1907, and enriches what was established by declaring the Central American Court of Justice the representative of the national conscience of Central America and the depositary of values that constitute the Central American nationality. Article 6 thereby incorporates into the new rules of Central American coexistence the values that will shape the future generations of our Central American fatherland.

. . .

Chapter II—Competence and Authority

Article 22

The Court's competence includes the following:

(a) To hear, at the request of any of the Member States, the controversies that arise among them. Excepted are frontier, territorial or maritime controversies, which may not be heard without the consent of all parties concerned.

Prior to commencement of trial, the respective chanceries must seek to obtain an agreement on the issues, but may also attempt to obtain an agreement during a later stage in the proceedings.

(b) To hear actions that relate to the nullification or non-fulfilment of the agreements of the organisms of the Central American Integration System.

(c) To hear, at the request of any interested party, any matter related to the legal, regulatory or administrative provisions or any other type of rules prescribed by a state, when such provisions or rules affect the conventions, treaties or any other norm of the Law of Central American Integration, or the agreements or resolutions of its organs or organisms;

(cII) To hear and issue verdicts, if it so decides, relating to matters which the parties have requested the Court to hear as a competent tribunal. The

Court may also hear, decide, and resolve disputes ex aequo et bono, if the interested parties so agree;

(d) To act as Tribunal of Permanent Consultation to the supreme courts of justice of the Member States;

(e) To act as a consultant to the organs and organisms of the Central American Integration System in the interpretation and application of the Protocol of Tegucigalpa of Reforms to the Charter of the Organization of Central American States (ODECA) and of the complementary instruments and acts derived from the same;

(f) To hear and resolve, at the request of aggrieved parties, conflicts that may arise among the fundamental powers or organs of the Member States, and disputes which may arise when judicial verdicts are not respected;

(g) To hear matters that are submitted directly by individuals who are affected by the agreements of the organs or organisms of the Central American Integration System;

(h) To hear controversies or questions that may arise between a Central American state and another non-Central American state when such controversies are submitted to the Court by mutual agreement;

(i) To undertake comparative studies of Central American legislation in order to achieve the harmonization of laws and to complete drafts of uniform laws so as to achieve the legal integration of Central America.

This task shall be performed either directly or by means of a specialized institute or organism such as the Central American Judicial Council or the Central American Institute of the Law of Integration;

(j) To hear on appeal, as court of last resort, the administrative resolutions prescribed by the organs or organisms of the Central American Integration System which directly affect a member of the staff of the same whose reinstatement has been denied.

(k) To resolve all pre-judicial consultations as requested by any judge or judicial tribunal which is hearing a pending case or which wants to obtain a uniform application or interpretation of the norms that conform to the legal principles of the Central American Integration System created by the Protocol of Tegucigalpa, its complementary instruments or acts derived from the same.

Article 23

The Member States shall be permitted to formulate and propose questions to the Court which relate to the interpretation of any treaty or international convention in force, or to conflicts between treaties, or between treaties and the national laws of each Member State.

Article 24

Questions decided by the Court pursuant to this Statute, rules or regulations which involve the Central American Integration System, shall be binding on all the states that comprise the system.

Article 25

The Court's competence does not extend to the area of human rights which falls under the exclusive jurisdiction of the Inter-American Court of Human Rights.

Article 26

The Member States are obligated to grant to the Court all necessary facilities for the adequate performance of its functions.

Article 27

The Court and its Magistrates shall enjoy in all the Member States the immunities recognized by international custom and by the Vienna Convention on Diplomatic Relations with respect to the inviolability of its archives and official correspondence and with respect to all that relates to its jurisdiction, both civil and penal.

Article 28

The Court shall possess a legal personality and shall enjoy, in all the Member States, the privileges and immunities that it is due as an organ of the Central American Integration System. These privileges and immunities shall ensure the independent exercise of the Court's functions and the realization of the objectives for which it was created. The Magistrates, the Secretary General of the Court and the officials designated by the Court as international employees shall enjoy the immunities and privileges due to their posts. To that end, the Magistrates shall possess a rank equivalent to that of Ambassadors and the other officials shall possess a rank as established by mutual agreement of the Court and the Government of the country where the Court is headquartered.

Article 29

The Magistrates shall be immune from all responsibility associated with the execution of acts and the issuance of opinions in the fulfilment of their official functions and shall continue to enjoy such immunity after having ceased performing these functions.

Article 30

Consistent with the norms heretofore established, the Court possesses the authority to determine its competence in each case by interpreting the treaties and conventions pertinent to the matter at hand and by applying the principles of both the Law of Integration and International Law.

Article 31

The Court shall be authorized to prescribe pre-trial or protective measures which it considers advisable to safeguard the rights of the parties from the moment that a claim is made against one or more states, organs or organisms of the Central American Integration System until a definitive verdict is issued. This authority shall permit the Court to stabilize the situation in which the contending parties are to remain, so as not to aggravate the harm and so as to maintain matters in the same state pending resolution.

Article 32

The rules of evidence will be established in the Court's rules. The court shall be able to request or accept evidence which it considers useful to define, establish or uphold the rights that the parties hold or claim.

Article 33

In the area of the admission and use of evidence, the orders issued by the Court shall not require ratification or approval prior to their execution, and must be executed by the Court's officials, judicial or administrative authorities, or by whomever receives an order from the Court.

Article 34

The documents from any country, regardless of their form, which are presented as evidence in trials, need only be authenticated in the place of origin by competent officials of that country or by a notary in the exercise of his or her functions.

The rules of evidence to be observed in any one of the territories of the Member States shall comply with the rules prescribed by the Court.

Chapter III—The Verdict and its Execution

Article 35

The Court shall evaluate the evidence as a whole, using its judgment as the evaluating criteria.

Article 36

All of the Court's decisions and those of its Tribunals and Chambers shall be reached by a vote of at least an absolute majority of the members of the relevant decision-making body. The dissenting or concurring Magistrate or Magistrates shall have the right to have their opinion set apart in writing.

The resolution shall set forth the grounds on which it is based, shall mention the names of the Magistrates who have taken part in it and shall contain their signatures in the absence of justification for not including their signatures.

Article 37

The judgment shall resolve every point in dispute. However, the judgment shall only be binding upon the parties to the dispute.

Article 38

The judgement shall be definitive and shall not be appealable; nevertheless, the Court may, either on its own initiative or at the request of a party, clarify or expand the reasoning of the decision within thirty days following the decision.

Article 39

The interlocutory decisions and definitive sentences prescribed by the Court shall not be appealable. All such decisions are binding upon the Member States and upon the organs or organisms of the Central American Integration System and upon natural and legal persons, and shall be executed as would a resolution, award or sentence of a national court. Moreover, the certification issued by the Secretary General of the Court shall suffice for such execution.

In the event that the Court's judgments or resolutions are not enforced by a Member State, the Court shall inform the other Member States, so that they may ensure the execution through appropriate means.

Article 40

In cases submitted to the jurisdictional ambit of the Court, the Court may not avoid passing judgment by alleging silence or uncertainty in the Convention or Treaties alleged to be applicable.

. . .

FRAMEWORK TREATY ON DEMOCRATIC SECURITY IN CENTRAL AMERICA (15.12.1995)

. . .

That the sustainable development of Central America can only be achieved by establishing a regional legal community that will protect, ensure and promote human rights and guarantee security under law, and will ensure peaceful relations and integration among the countries of the region;

. . .

Title I—Government of laws

Article 1

The Central American Democratic Security Model is based on democracy and the strengthening of its institutions and a government of laws; on governments elected by universal, free and secret suffrage and unconditional respect for human rights in the countries of the Central American region.

The Central American Democratic Security Model has its raison d'être in respect for, promotion of and safeguarding of all human rights, so that its provisions ensure the security of the Central American countries and their inhabitants, by creating conditions that permit their personal, family and social development in peace, freedom and democracy. It is based on strengthening civil power, political pluralism, economic freedom, the elimination of poverty and extreme poverty, the promotion of sustainable development, the protection of the consumer, the environment and the cultural heritage; the elimination of violence, corruption, impunity, terrorism, drug trafficking, and arms trafficking; the establishment of a reasonable balance of forces that will take into consideration the domestic situation of each country and need for cooperation among all Central American countries to ensure their security.

Article 2

The Central American Democratic Security Model shall be governed by the following principles relating to this topic:

   (a) A government of law, which includes the supremacy of the rule of law, the existence of security under the law, and the effective exercise of civil liberties;
   (b) Strengthening and ongoing improvement of democratic institutions in each country, for mutual consolidation of them within their own sphere of action

and responsibility, through a continuous and sustained process of consolidation and strengthening of civil power, limiting the role of the armed forces and of the public security forces to the authority given them constitutionally, and the promotion of a culture of peace, dialogue, understanding and tolerance based on the democratic values that the countries have in common;

(c) The principle of subordination of the armed forces, the police and the public security forces to constitutionally established civil authorities chosen in free, honest and pluralistic elections; and

(d) Maintenance of a flexible and active dialogue and mutual collaboration on security issues in the broad sense of the term in order to ensure that democracy in the region is irreversible.

Article 3

To ensure the security of the individual, the Parties undertake to see to it that all actions taken by the public authorities are consistent with their legal system and fully respect international human rights instruments.

Article 4

Each of the Parties shall establish and maintain at all times effective control over their military and public security forces by their constitutionally established civil authorities; shall see to it that those authorities fulfil their responsibilities within this framework and shall clearly define the doctrine, missions and functions of those forces and their obligation to act solely in this context.

Article 5

Public and private corruption is a threat to democracy and the security of the people and of the countries of the Central American region. The Parties undertake to make every effort to eliminate all forms of it at all levels.

In this connection, the meeting of the State comptroller entities of each Party shall assist the Security Commission in the design, establishment and implementation of regional programs and projects to modernize and harmonize legislative, investigative, educational and corruption preventive measures.

Article 6

The Parties shall make every effort to eliminate the impunity of criminals. The Security Commission shall make contact with the institutions and officials connected with this problem in order to help develop programs to harmonize and modernize the criminal justice systems of Central America.

. . .

Article 8

To strengthen democracy, the Parties reaffirm their obligation to refrain from providing political, military, financial or any other support to individuals, groups, irregular forces or armed bands that threaten the unity and order of the State or that advocate the overthrow or destabilization of the democratically elected government of any other of the Parties.

Moreover, they reiterate their obligation to prevent the use of their territory for organizing or conducting military actions, acts of sabotage, kidnapping or criminal activities in the territory of another country.

. . .

Title II—Security of Persons and their Property

Article 10

The Central American Democratic Security Model shall be governed by the following principles in connection with this Title:

(a) Democratic security is integral and indivisible. The solution of problems of security of persons in the region shall therefore be based on a comprehensive and interrelated view of all aspects of sustainable development in Central America, in their political, economic, social, cultural and ecological expressions;

(b) Democratic security is inseparable from human considerations. Respect for the essential dignity of human beings, improvement of the quality of life and the full development of human potential are required for all aspects of security;

(c) Supportive humanitarian aid in the event of emergencies, threats and natural disasters; and

(d) Poverty and extreme poverty are regarded as threats to the security of the people and to the democratic stability of Central American societies.

Article 11

To contribute to the consolidation of Central America as a region of peace, freedom, democracy and development, the following objectives are established:

(a) To guarantee for all persons security conditions that will enable them to participate and benefit from national and regional sustainable development strategies, through the impetus of a market economy that will make economic growth with equity possible;

(b) Establish and strengthen mechanisms for operational coordination of the competent institutions, to make more effective at the national and regional level the struggle against crime and all threats against democratic security that require the use of military, security or police forces, such as terrorism, unlawful trafficking in arms, drug trafficking and organized crime;

(c) Strengthen cooperation, coordination, harmonization and convergence of policies on the security of persons, as well as border cooperation and furtherance of social and cultural ties among the peoples; and

(d) Promote cooperation among the countries to ensure security under law for the property of persons.

Article 12

The General Secretariat of the Central American Integration System shall be in charge of organizing and managing a Central American Security Index and shall from time to time make progress reports on it to the governments concerned, through the Security Commission of Central America.

Article 13

The Parties undertake to:

(a) Help spur regional promotion of all human rights and the culture of peace, democracy and integration among the peoples of Central America;

(b) Promote the contribution of the mass media in the Parties to achieving the objectives set forth in the preceding subparagraph; and

(c) Promote projects to integrate border development, in a spirit of Central American solidarity and democratic participation of the people.

Article 14

The Parties undertake to promote ongoing professional training and modernization of their public security forces to enable them to conduct the broadest and most effective campaign against criminal activity and protect the rights embodied in the domestic laws of each country.

Also, they undertake to put into operation the Central American Institute of Advanced Police Studies.

Article 15

The Parties recognize that poverty and extreme poverty damage human dignity and are a threat to the security of the people and to the democratic stability of the societies of Central America, and to that end, they undertake to give priority to efforts to overcome the structural causes of poverty and improve the quality of life of the people.

Article 16

Tailoring the national budgets to the reality in each country shall be aimed at benefiting the social sector in health, education and other fields that help to improve the quality of life of the people, particularly the most deprived classes of society.

Article 17

The Parties undertake to cooperate in eradicating drug trafficking and the unlawful trade in precursors and related crimes, pursuant to international, regional and subregional agreements to which they are Parties or any agreements they have concluded on these topics, particularly the Agreement Establishing the Permanent Central American Commission for the Eradication, Production, Trafficking in, Consumption and Illicit Use of Narcotics and Psychotropic Substances. To this end, they shall set up streamlined and effective mechanisms for communication and cooperation among officials responsible for this work.

Article 18

The Parties undertake to prevent and combat every kind of criminal activity having regional or international impact, without any exception, such as terrorism, sabotage, and organized crime, and to prevent by every means the planning, preparation and conduct of such activities within their territory.

To that end, they shall strengthen cooperation and shall promote the exchange of information among the agencies responsible for migration control, the police and other competent officials.

Article 19

The Parties shall endeavor, if they have not already done so, to initiate the necessary proceedings to approve, ratify or accede to the following international agreements:

(a) Convention for the Suppression of Unlawful Seizure of Aircraft, 1963;

    (b) Convention to Prevent and Punish Acts of Terrorism Involved in Offenses Against Persons and Any Related Extortion when such crimes are of International Transcendence, 1971;

    (c) Convention for the Suppression of Unlawful Acts Against the Safety of Civil Aviation, 1971;

    (d) Convention on Prevention and Punishment of Crimes against Persons who are Internationally Protected, including Diplomatic Agents, 1973; and

    (e) International Convention against the Taking of Hostages, 1979.

Article 20

The Parties undertake to take steps to combat the activities of organized gangs trafficking in persons when such crimes are of international transcendence in the region, in order to seek comprehensive solutions to this problem.

Article 21

The Parties undertake to make every effort to promote cooperation to ensure protection of the consumer, the environment, and the cultural heritage of Central America, pursuant to any international and regional agreements to which they are Parties or any they have signed on these topics, particularly the Agreement Establishing the Central American Commission on the Environment and Development. To that end, they shall establish streamlined and effective mechanisms for communication and cooperation among officials working in these areas.

Article 22

The Parties recognize that for effective cooperation in these areas, it is essential, in the event this has not yet been done, to initiate the necessary proceedings to approve, ratify or accede to international and regional agreements on protection of the environment and the cultural heritage.

Article 23

The Parties reaffirm their resolve to appropriately reintegrate into society refugees, displaced persons and uprooted persons who return voluntarily and peacefully to their territories, so that such persons can enjoy all of their rights and improve their quality of life on an equal footing with others, taking into consideration the domestic situation prevailing in each country.

Article 24

The Parties undertake to take positions and adopt joint strategies for defending their nationals abroad who face repatriation or expulsion.

Article 25

The Security Commission, based on any proposals it receives from the competent regional organs and in coordination with them, shall formulate and forward to the sectoral or intersectoral councils concerned recommendations on the following topics, among others:

(a) Strengthen internal controls of borders, ports, airports, air space and territorial seas to detect the following: unlawful trafficking of cultural artifacts and facilitate their recovery; unlawful trade in wood, plant and animal species; trafficking in and handling toxic wastes and hazardous substances; drug trafficking and related crimes, particularly the unlawful trade in precursors, money laundering and other activities; theft of vehicles, boats and aircraft, without affecting any regional mechanisms they may agree upon to prevent and punish such crimes;

(b) Define criminal activities and harmonize and modernize their laws on protecting consumers, the environment, the cultural heritage and any other topics that require such action, with a view to establishing a common standard of security;

(c) Conclude agreements on the topics included under this heading; and

(d) Promote cooperation and coordination between entities having jurisdiction and the public ministries of the Parties with a view to streamlining their activities aimed at strengthening the fight against crime.

Title III—Regional Security

Article 26

The Central American Democratic Security Model shall be governed by the following principles, in connection with this heading:

(a) Equal sovereignty of States and enforcement of the law and stability of legal institutions in their relations with each other;

(b) Peaceful settlement of disputes, renouncing the threat or use of force as a means of settling their differences. The countries shall refrain from any act that might worsen conflicts or hamper the settlement of any disputes by peaceful means;

(c) Renunciation of the threat or the use of force against the sovereignty, territorial integrity and political independence of any country in the region that is a signatory of this Treaty;

(d) Self-determination of Central America, by which the signatory states to this Treaty define their own regional strategy for sustainable development and international coordination;

(e) Solidarity and security of the peoples and governments of Central America in the prevention and joint settlement of common problems on this topic;

(f) Prohibiting the use of their territory to invade other countries, to serve as a refuge for irregular forces, or to establish organized crime;

(g) The democratic security of each of the countries signing this Treaty is closely connected with the security of the region. Accordingly, no country shall strengthen its own security at the expense of the security of other countries;

(h) Collective defense and solidarity in the event of armed attack by a country outside the region against the territorial integrity, sovereignty, and independence of a Central American country, in accordance with the constitutional provisions of the latter country and of the international treaties in force;

(i) The national unity and territorial integrity of the countries in the framework of Central American integration; and

(j) Respect for the goals and principles of the Charter of the United Nations (UN) and the Charter of the Organization of American States (OAS).

Article 27

The following are additional goals of the Model regarding this topic:

(a) Establish an early warning system to prevent threats against the security of any of the Model's categories and an ongoing confidence-building program among the countries of Central America;

(b) Continue efforts to establish a reasonable balance between military and public security forces, in accordance with the internal and external situation of each State Party, conditions in Central America, and the decisions of the civil authorities of the democratically elected governments of the Parties;

(c) Establish a Central American Mechanism for Security Information and Communication;

(d) Establish and strengthen Central American mechanisms for the peaceful settlement of disputes, pursuant to the provisions of this Treaty;

(e) Coordinate in the region ways to cooperate with international efforts in maintaining and reestablishing international peace and security; and

(f) Promote law enforcement on the borders of the countries signing this Treaty, through delimitations, demarcations, and settlement of pending territorial disputes, where appropriate, and ensure the joint defense of the territorial, cultural and ecological heritage of Central America, in accordance with the machinery of international law.

Article 28

Without prejudice to the Annual Program of Confidence Building Activities, which the Security Commission should prepare and carry out, the Parties, pursuant to any treaties to which they are Parties, undertake to:

(a) Notify the other Parties in writing, through diplomatic channels, no less than thirty days beforehand, about any land, air or naval maneuver, movement of forces, or military exercise conducted under such conditions as may be determined by the Security Commission, as regards: number of troops, location with respect to the border, nature and quantity of equipment that will be employed, among other things, and

(b) Invite the other Parties to witness the above mentioned activities. The Parties shall accord such observers the same immunity from civil and penal jurisdiction as is accorded to diplomatic agents under the Vienna Convention on Diplomatic Relations, during the duration of their mission and for any acts carried out in the performance of their duties.

Article 29

In the event of unforeseen military operations to deal with immediate security threats, the State that undertakes such operations must report on them as soon as possible, pursuant to the provisions of the previous article.

Article 30

The Parties undertake to combat unlawful trafficking in military weapons, materiel and equipment, as well as small arms for personal protection. To that end, they undertake also to establish specific, modern and standardized regulations within their national jurisdictions.

Article 31

When a situation of unlawful weapons trafficking cannot be resolved within the framework of national legal procedures, the State or States involved shall endeavor to solve the problem by means of communication and cooperation among their competent officials.

Article 32

The Parties undertake to continue their efforts to limit and control armaments, by means of a reasonable balance of forces, in accordance with the internal and external situation in each country.

Article 33

The reasonable balance and the adjustment of military forces and budgets to achieve it shall take into consideration the constitutional provisions of each Party and their defense needs, in light of such basic factors as relevant geographic conditions and borders, and the presence of foreign military forces or advisers, among others.

Article 34

The Parties undertake to refrain from acquiring, maintaining or permitting the stationing in or transit through their territories of weapons of indiscriminate mass destruction, including chemical, radiological and bacteriological weapons. The Parties likewise undertake not to construct or to allow anyone to construct in their territories, facilities to manufacture or store such weapons.

The Parties recognize the effectiveness of the Treaty on the Permanent Neutrality of the Panama Canal and on the operation of the Canal, as States acceding to the Protocol of the Treaty, which guarantees at all times peaceful and uninterrupted transit of the ships of all countries through the Canal.

Article 35

In order to achieve effective control of armaments, the Parties undertake the following:

(a) To submit to the Security Commission, as often as the Council of Ministers of Foreign Affairs determines, a report on the makeup of their military and public security institutions, and the organization, facilities, armaments, materiel and equipment of those institutions, aside from any aspects that by their nature are reserved to the constitution of each State;

The report, which is classified as confidential for the State and region, shall be drawn up according to the format and inventory content the Security Commission may decide and shall include all naval, air,

land and public security data needed to make the information provided complete, transparent and verifiable, solely and exclusively by the
decision-making bodies of the Model established in Article 47 of this
Treaty or by whomever those bodies may designate;

(b) To provide information to the Security Commission on their respective military and public security expenditures approved in their budgets
for the fiscal year, using as a frame of reference the "Instrument for the
Standardized International Presentation of Reports on Military Expenditures," adopted by the United Nations on December 12, 1990, pursuant to Article 52k of the present Treaty; and

(c) To organize the system for Central American registry of weapons and
their transfer, pursuant to such proposals as the Security Commission
may draw up.

Article 36

Regarding any information requested pursuant to the previous Article, each Party
may request in the Security Commission from any other Party such explanations
as it deems necessary, for sixty days following submission of such information.
The Parties undertake to provide the explanations requested, within sixty days
following the date of such requests.

Article 37

The Security Commission shall set up a standardized registry for weapons, explosives and equipments used solely by the armed forces or the public security
forces; this registry must be updated with information the Parties undertake to
provide continually.

Article 38

The Parties undertake to submit, to each other and pursuant to any Treaties to
which they may be parties, in the Security Commission in the first half of each
year, a report on any foreign military personnel and advisers that take part in
military or public security activities in their territory. Likewise, they shall keep
a registry of such advisers as perform technical duties connected with training
or installation and maintenance of military equipment, and they shall provide
a copy of such registry to the Security Commission.

The registry shall be kept in accordance with any regulations the Security
Commission decides upon, which may also set reasonable limits on the number of
advisers of all military public and security categories and specialties, taking into
account the internal situations and requirements of each Party.

Article 39

If any military incidents occur between two or more of the Parties, the ministers of foreign affairs must immediately establish contact to review the situation, avoid any increase in tensions, cease any military activity, and prevent further incidents.

Article 40

In the event that direct channels of communication are not sufficient to achieve the objectives described in the preceding article, any of the Parties may ask that a meeting of the Security Commission or of the Council of Foreign Ministers be called, if deemed necessary. If so, the Chair of the Council of Ministers shall make the necessary consultations with member countries and may call a meeting of the Security Commission beforehand to obtain its recommendations.

Article 41

The Meeting of Presidents, the Council of Ministers of Foreign Affairs and the Security Commission shall reach decisions by consensus on all matters concerning the peace and security of the region.

Article 42

Any armed aggression, or threat of armed aggression, by a state outside the region against the territorial integrity, sovereignty or independence of a Central American state shall be considered an act of aggression against the other Central American states.

In any event, the Central American countries, at the request of the state attacked, shall act jointly and in solidarity to ensure in international fora and agencies the legal political defense, through diplomatic channels, of the Central American state attacked.

Article 43

In the event of armed aggression, after exhausting all avenues of reconciliation and peaceful settlement of disputes, the Central American states, shall, if possible, undertake, at the request of the attacked state, to ensure, through such measures and procedures as may be decided upon by the Council of Ministers of Foreign Affairs, in accordance with the constitutional provisions of the states concerned, the United Nations Charter, the Charter of the Organization of American States, and any treaties to which the states concerned may be parties.

The Council of Ministers shall set up an ad hoc operational organization to plan and coordinate in compliance with the commitments contained in this article, as well as operational support in the area of solidary cooperation to deal with emergencies, threats and disasters.

. . .

Title IV—Organization and Institutionalization

Article 47

The following are the decision-making bodies of the Democratic Security Model in Central America:

(a) The Meeting of Presidents;
(b) The Council of Ministers of Foreign Affairs; and
(c) The Security Commission.

The sectoral and intersectoral Councils shall establish the necessary coordination with the Council of Ministers of Foreign Affairs, to which they shall report on all of their agreements and resolutions on security matters.

In this context, the ministers of defense and security or their equivalents, shall advise and assist the Council of Ministers of Foreign Affairs, on topics relating to the Council's operation, within the areas of their competence.

The Advisory Committee established by the Tegucigalpa Protocol may transmit, through the General Secretariat of the Central American Integration System, its opinions to the Security Commission on matters covered in this Treaty, concerning the security of persons and their property.

Article 48

The Meeting of Presidents is the highest decision-making body of this Model and is responsible for dealing with regional and international security matters that might require its decisions pursuant to the provisions of the Tegucigalpa Protocol.

Article 49

The Council of Foreign Ministers is the decision-making body responsible for all matters concerning regional and international security, in its capacity as the principal coordinating organ of the Central American Integration System.

Article 50

The Security Commission is a subsidiary decision-making body for execution, coordination, evaluation and follow-up, and for drafting proposals and recommendations on early warning, and where appropriate, taking prompt action, and is subordinate to the Meeting of Presidents and to the Council of Ministers of Foreign Affairs.

Article 51

The Security Commission is composed of delegations of the Central American States whose members are Vice Ministers of Foreign Affairs and Vice Ministers or the responsible officials in the areas of Defense and Public Security. The Vice Ministers of Foreign Affairs shall head the delegations of each state.

Article 52

The Security Commission shall have the following responsibilities or duties:

(a) Implement decisions on security matters entrusted to it by the Meeting of Presidents or the Council of Ministers of Foreign Affairs and any decisions that it makes itself in the area of its competence;

(b) Evaluate compliance with Central American agreements on security matters;

(c) Review security problems in the region that require concerted action and draft proposals to deal with them effectively. Such studies and recommendations shall be submitted to the Council of Ministers of Foreign Affairs for consideration and approval;

(d) Establish the necessary communication and coordination, through the General Secretariat of the Central American Integration System, with the agencies, institutions and secretariats of the regional integration subsystems, whose assistance is deemed necessary to deal comprehensively with security problems;

(e) Strengthen the mechanisms for coordinating operations in the areas of defense, public security, and human rights cooperation when faced with emergencies, threats and natural disasters;

(f) Draft proposals for coordination and regional support with international agencies and bodies devoted to maintaining international peace and security and the fight against threats to the security of persons and their property, which proposals shall be submitted beforehand to the Council of Ministers of Foreign Affairs for approval;

(g) Organize the Central American Mechanism on Information and Communication for Security;

(h) Draft activities for an ongoing annual confidence building program, which will involve the participation of the armed forces and the security forces in the region, together with the civil societies in Central America;

(i) Develop a system of periodic reports and a system for registry of weapons and transfer of them, seeing to it that the information provided is complete, transparent, and easily verifiable, and make proposals for gradually establishing a reasonable balance of forces in the region;

(j) Review the information provided by the Parties on foreign military personnel and advisers and other foreign personnel who might take part in military or public security activities in their territory, pursuant to Article 38 of this Treaty;

(k) Review the information provided by the governments on their military security budgets for the fiscal year and draft joint proposals for possible updating of future budgets, taking into consideration the internal situation in each country;

(l) Establish contact with the Central American organizations that group together other branches or organs of the state, in order to reach agreement on standardizing and modernizing laws concerning the subject and on training programs for court and police officials;

(m) Draft their rules of procedure, which shall be submitted to the Executive Committee of the Central American Integration System for information;

(n) Provide all protection measures necessary for the security and confidentiality of information received from the various Central American States; and

(o) Monitor compliance with the provisions of this Treaty and perform any other duties given it herein.

. . .

Article 57

The Council of Ministers of Foreign Affairs, in its capacity as the principal coordinating organ of the Central American Integration System, shall be responsible for adopting and recommending to the Meeting of Presidents any measures on prevention, crisis management, or dispute settlement it deems necessary to deal with situations of any kind that, in the judgment of the governments or the competent organs of the Central American Security System, constitute a potential threat to the security of the states and their people.

Article 58

The governments, through their ministries of foreign affairs, shall submit the situations indicated in the previous article to the Security Commission for review. They may also submit them directly to the Council of the Ministers of Foreign Affairs.

The organs, institutions and secretariats of the Central American Integration System shall, through its General Secretariat, call the attention of the Council of Ministers of Foreign Affairs to any situation indicated in the previous article.

Article 59

Without affecting the Annual Program of Confidence-Building Activities, which the Security Commission is to draft and implement, the Parties undertake to:

(a) Establish and strengthen mechanisms for direct and prompt communication among border officials; and

(b) Promote the exchange of military and public security views and information, consultations, and periodic visits among defense and public security and similar institutions, as well as to award scholarships reciprocally in their military and police academies.

Article 60

The Central American Mechanism on Information and Communication for Security shall be composed of:

(a) The Central American Security Index, organized and managed by the General Secretariat of the Central American Integration System, with the support of the Central American Integration Secretariats and Institutions and of any international agencies it deems appropriate; and

(b) The standing communication mechanism the Parties undertake to establish and put into operation to facilitate sure, effective and prompt contact among their competent civil, military and public security officials, with each other and with the Security Commission, to prevent incidents, respond to alerts and facilitate attainment of the goals and obligations set forth in this Treaty.

Article 61

The Council of Ministers of Foreign Affairs shall see to the enforcement of provisions and the compliance with the obligations set forth in this Treaty.

For these purposes, the Security Commission shall inform the Council of Ministers of Foreign Affairs about the following items in particular:

(a) Compliance by the Parties with the physical actions provided for in this Treaty, such as timely submittal of the required reports;
(b) Compliance by the Parties with any weapons ceilings that may be set, taking into account the internal and external situation of each Party and the conditions prevailing in the region;
(c) Compliance by the Parties with the obligation not to introduce any weapons that are banned in Article 34 of this Treaty or that may be banned in the future;
(d) Compliance by the Parties with the obligations to provide notification of military activities or maneuvers, as well as any other notifications specified in this Treaty; and
(e) The findings of investigations undertaken on their own initiative or mandated by the Council of Ministers of Foreign Affairs, regarding complaints of violation of the obligations set forth in this Treaty.

Article 62

The investigations shall be conducted by the Security Commission or by any ad hoc collegiate body of experts that it may designate and deem the most appropriate for the purpose. The investigations shall be conducted through on site inspections, collection of data, conduct of laboratory technical tests, and any other procedure that it deems necessary for objective verification of the facts.

Article 63

The Council of Ministers of Foreign Affairs shall be the organ charged with coordinating the efforts of the region as a whole with initiatives undertaken in the struggle against threats to democratic security in the Hemisphere and elsewhere in the world, and to that end, shall be the organ responsible for preparing positions and concluding cooperation agreements or conventions with institutions or bodies charged with maintaining international peace and security, except for any pre-established commitments of each State Party with the international community.

Title V—Final Provisions

Article 64

The Central American Democratic Security Model is part of the Central American Integration System, and its content complements the provisions of the Tegucigalpa Protocol, to which this Treaty is subordinated.

. . .

ANDEAN COMMUNITY OF NATIONS (CAN)

Integration efforts in the Andean region started with the Cartagena Agreement of 1969, creating the Pacto Andino. The Cartagena Agreement marked the beginning of almost thirty years of rather unsuccessful integration. Its intention ran counter to national political strategies. Individually, Bolivia, Ecuador, Peru, Colombia, Chile, and Venezuela tried to pursue policies designed by "dependencia"-theories about center-periphery relations in the capitalist world order. Pointing to the fact that American, European, and Japanese capital controlled many industrial investments in Latin America, dependencia-theorists argued in favor of strict control of foreign investment and import-substitution as elements of a strategy to gain stronger national independence and hence strengthen national sovereignty. This approach was neither cohesive nor successful while it paralyzed the hope for regional integration. Furthermore, the geopolitical climate was as unfavorable to sustainable regional integration in Latin America as the recurrent threat of democracy by neo-authoritarian military dictatorships in the region.

The Pacto Andino failed its historic test. Yet aspirations to regional integration in the Andean region reverberated in a new and different global context. With the rise of neoliberal economics and the return to democratic governance in most of Latin America during the late 1980s and early 1990s, the logic of regional integration as a tool for enhancing economic well-being and ultimately generating a stronger political voice spread anew. After four years of intermission, the presidents of the Andean countries met again in 1995 and approved a new strategy of increased regional integration as a response to the challenges and opportunities of globalization. The Trujillo Act of 1996 created a new Andean Integration System, transforming the original Pacto Andino into the Andean Community of Nations (Communidad Andina de Naciones, CAN). The Andean Presidential Council, composed of the Presidents of CAN, became the highest body. In addition to the Andean Community Foreign Ministers Council, the Commission of the Andean Community was established, composed of ministers of trade and industry. The General Secretariat was based in Lima, the Andean Parliament as a deliberative body in Bogotá, and the Court of Justice of the Andean Community in Quito. A whole array of institutions was established, covering social partners, banking, investment, and academic life in the Andean Community.

This reinvigorated Andean Community of Nations included Peru, Bolivia, Ecuador, Colombia, and Venezuela. It encountered its biggest crisis in May 2006, when Venezuela left the Andean Community. Immediately, the four remaining CAN member states invited Chile to join. In the past, Chile had remained absent from the Andean Community, preferring bilateral free-trade agreements with the US and the European Union as well as bilateral relations with the leading Latin American economies. In 2007, Chile accepted associated membership in CAN. Another troubling burden for CAN's development has been the low-profile civil war in Colombia. Also, infrastructure across the region has remained weak, posing a huge obstacle to intensified interregional trade given the difficult geography of the Andean mountain region.

The European Union has continuously supported the development of CAN, up to the point that it at some stage contributed to the salaries in the Lima-based Secretariat. The EU's policy toward CAN is geared to strengthen integration with the ultimate goal of introducing supranational structures. This commitment might come as a surprise, given CAN's limited economic relevance for the EU. Exports from CAN represent 0.9 percent of total EU imports, while EU exports to CAN represent 0.7 percent of the EU's total global exports. It should not be underestimated that the EU is the largest investor in CAN—as it is in the whole of Latin America, except for Central America. Nevertheless, the main driving force for the EU policy toward the Andean Community was never primarily an immediate economic interest in a community with 98 million inhabitants. The rationale of EU policy toward CAN and other regional integration efforts is grounded in the EU's understanding of sustainable and "real" regional integration as a basis for successful development in the context of democratic governance and a new global order in the twenty-first century. In light of the crisis over Venezuela's withdrawal from CAN, the European Union's decision to begin biregional negotiations aimed at achieving a Biregional Association Agreement with CAN was postponed until 2007. Since 2003, the political dialogue between the EU and CAN has added yet another element to the European Union's proactive policy of in favor of regional integration and biregional association. Negotiations on a biregional agreement between the EU and CAN began in 2007.

In spite of the Sucre Protocol of 1997 and the Quirama Declaration of 2003, supranational orientation is still missing in CAN, although the discussion about its usefulness has grown during the initial years of the twenty-first century. Following the EU model, discussions have begun inside CAN about the possible path toward monetary union, a directly elected community parliament, and the creation of Andean citizenship. Since the new beginning of Andean integration in the 1990s, progress has been made toward complementary economic structures, although it remains incremental and slow. While Venezuela, Colombia, Ecuador, and Bolivia agreed on common external tariffs as the cornerstone of a common free trade zone, Peru preferred to remain absent. The less developed economies of Bolivia and Ecuador received temporary exemptions from complete liberalization of their markets. CAN's goal to achieve a free trade zone by 2005 and the subsequent realization of a common market was not implemented by the deadline. Yet the path toward free trade and a common market has received more serious consideration during one decade of CAN than during three decades of the Pacto Andino. The Andean Community Commitment to Democracy of 1998 signals awareness about the link between democratic stability and successful region-building.

One interesting feature of this development is the effect of increased trade between CAN and the Southern Common Market (Mercado Común del Sur, MERCOSUR), established in 1991 in the Southern Cone of Latin America. CAN exporters account for 8.5 percent of MERCOSUR imports, while 10.8 percent of CAN imports originate in MERCOSUR. Both regional integration schemes are contemplating ways toward a bilateral free trade agreement. Visionaries have even talked about the fusion of both processes under the label MERCOCAN. Such plans have met with skepticism among poorer CAN countries afraid of opening up their markets to Brazil, the dominant economy of the Latin American continent. In 1991, the US had proposed the completion of a free trade area for the Americas by 2005, a project whose implementation began in 1994 but has not come to fruition yet. The GDP of the US alone is close to 73 percent of the combined GDP of all the other countries on the American continent, including Canada, Mexico, and Brazil.

Andean Subregional Integration Agreement (Cartagena Agreement) (26.05.1969)

Resolved to strengthen the union of their peoples and to lay the foundations for advancing toward the formation of an Andean subregional community;

Aware that integration constitutes a historical, political, economic, social, and cultural mandate for their countries, in order to preserve their sovereignty and independence;

. . .

Chapter I—Objectives and mechanisms

Article 1

The objectives of this Agreement are to promote the balanced and harmonious development of the Member Countries under equitable conditions, through integration and economic and social cooperation; to accelerate their growth and the rate of creation of employment; and to facilitate their participation in the regional integration process, looking ahead toward the gradual formation of a Latin American common market.

This Agreement also seeks to reduce external vulnerability and to improve the positioning of the Member Countries within the international economic context; to strengthen subregional solidarity, and to reduce existing differences in levels of development among the Member Countries.

These objectives are aimed at bringing about an enduring improvement in the standard of living of the subregion's population.

Article 2

Balanced and harmonious development shall lead to a fair distribution among the Member Countries of the benefits deriving from integration, so that the existing differences among them are reduced. The results of that process shall be evaluated periodically, bearing in mind, among other elements, its effects on the growth of each country's total exports, the performance of its balance of trade with the subregion, the evolution of its gross domestic product, the creation of new jobs, and capital formation.

Article 3

The following mechanisms and measures shall be used, among others, to fulfil the objectives of this Agreement:

   (a) The integration with other economic blocs in the region will be intensified and political, social and economic-trade relations will be established with extra-regional systems.
   (b) Economic and social policies will be gradually harmonized and national laws with regard to pertinent matters will be aligned;
   (c) Joint programming will be instituted, subregional industrialization will be intensified, industrial programs will be implemented, and other means of industrial integration will be applied;
   (d) A more advanced schedule of trade liberalization than the commitments derived from the 1980 Treaty of Montevideo will be instituted;
   (e) A Common External Tariff will be adopted;
   (f) Programs will be carried out to accelerate the development of the agricultural and agroindustrial sectors;
   (g) Resources will be channeled from in and outside the Subregion to finance the investments needed by the integration process;
   (h) Programs will be conducted in the areas of services and the liberalization of intra-subregional trade in services;
   (i) Physical integration will be pursued; and

(j)   Bolivia and Ecuador will receive preferential treatment.

In addition to the mechanisms set out above, the following economic and social cooperation programs and aims shall be carried out in a concerted effort:

(a)   Programs to promote scientific and technological development;
(b)   Border integration measures;
(c)   Programs in the area of tourism;
(d)   Activities for the use and preservation of natural resources and the environment;
(e)   Social development programs: and
(f)   Efforts in the field of social communications.

Article 4

To carry out this Agreement in the best way possible, Member Countries shall make the necessary efforts to seek adequate solutions to the problems stemming from Bolivia's landlocked condition.

Chapter II—On the Andean Community and the Andean Integration System

Article 5

The Andean Community is hereby created, composed of the sovereign States of Bolivia, Colombia, Ecuador, Peru, and Venezuela, and of the bodies and institutions of the Andean Integration System, and is established by this Agreement.

Article 6

The Andean Integration System is made up of the following bodies and institutions:

- The Andean Presidential Council;
- The Andean Council of Foreign Ministers;
- The Andean Community Commission;
- The Andean Community General Secretariat;
- The Andean Community Court of Justice;
- The Andean Parliament;
- The Business Advisory Council;

- The Labor Advisory Council;
- The Andean Development Corporation;
- The Latin American Reserve Fund;
- The Simón Rodríguez Convention, the Social Conventions that join the Andean Integration System, and those that are created within its framework;
- The Simón Bolívar Andean University;
- The Advisory Councils established by the Commission; and,
- All other bodies and institutions that are created within the framework of Andean subregional integration.

Article 7

The purpose of the System is to allow for effective coordination among its component bodies and institutions, in order to deepen Andean subregional integration, promote its external influence and consolidate and strengthen actions related to the integration process.

Article 8

The bodies and institutions of the Andean Integration System are governed by this Agreement and by their respective establishing treaties and amending protocols.

Article 9

In order to achieve the best possible coordination within the Andean Integration System, the Chairman of the Andean Council of Foreign Ministers will call and chair the Meetings of Representatives of the institutions that comprise the System.

The main tasks of the Meeting shall be:

(a) To exchange information about the actions taken by the respective institutions to carry out the Guidelines issued by the Andean Presidential Council;

(b) To study the possibility and desirability of arranging, among all or some of the institutions, to carry out coordinated actions that will contribute to the achievement of the objectives of the Andean Integration System; and,

(c) To present to the Andean Council of Foreign Ministers meeting in enlarged session, reports about the actions carried out in fulfilment of the Guidelines that have been received.

Article 10

The Representatives of the institutions comprising the Andean Integration System shall meet in regular session at least once a year and in special session whenever requested to do so by any of the member institutions, at the site agreed upon before the meeting is called.

The Andean Community General Secretariat shall act as the Secretariat for the Meeting.

. . .

Chapter IV—Harmonization of Economic
Policies and Coordination of Development Plans

Article 53

The Member Countries shall progressively adopt a strategy to achieve the subregional development objectives envisaged in this Agreement.

Article 54

The Member Countries shall coordinate their development plans in specific sectors and shall gradually harmonize their economic and social policies, with a view to achieving the integrated development of the area through planned actions.

This process shall be carried out simultaneously and in coordination with the creation of the subregional market, by means of the following mechanisms, among others:

- (a) Industrial Development Programs;
- (b) Agricultural and Agroindustrial Development Programs;
- (c) Physical Infrastructure Development Programs;
- (d) Intra-subregional Programs for the Liberalization of Services;
- (e) Harmonization of foreign exchange, monetary, financial, and fiscal policies, including the treatment of subregional or foreign capital;
- (f) A common trade policy in relation to third countries; and
- (g) Harmonization of planning methods and techniques.

Article 55

The Andean Community shall have a common system for the treatment of foreign capital and on trademarks, patents, licenses, and royalties, among other things.

Article 56

The Andean Community shall have a uniform regime that Andean multinational enterprises must abide by.

Article 57

The Commission, at the General Secretariat's proposal, shall establish the necessary permanent procedures and mechanisms for achieving the coordination and harmonization referred to in Article 54.

Article 58

The Commission, at the General Secretariat's proposal and taking into account the progress and needs of the subregional integration process, as well as the balanced compliance with the mechanisms of the Agreement, shall approve provisions and define timeframes for the progressive harmonization of economic legislation and the instruments and mechanisms for regulating and promoting the Member Countries' foreign trade that affect the mechanisms provided for in this Agreement for the creation of the subregional market.

Article 59

The Member Countries shall provide in their national development plans and in the formulation of their economic policies for the necessary measures to ensure compliance with the preceding Articles.

. . .

Chapter V—Industrial Development Programs

Article 60

The Member Countries bind themselves to promote a joint industrial development process in order to attain the following objectives, among others:

   (a) Expansion, specialization, diversification, and promotion of industrial activity;
   (b) Profitable use of economies of scale;

   (c) Optimum utilization of the resources available in the area, particularly by industrializing the natural resources;

   (d) Improvement in productivity;

   (e) Closer relations, interlinkage and complementarity among the sub region's industrial enterprises;

   (f) Equitable distribution of benefits; and

   (g) Better international participation by subregional industry.

Article 61

For purposes of the previous Article, the following shall constitute modes of industrial integration:

   (a) Industrial Integration Programs;

   (b) Industrial Complementarity Agreements; and

   (c) Industrial Integration Projects.

     . . .

Chapter VII—Intra-Subregional Trade in Services

Article 79

The Andean Community Commission, at the proposal of the General Secretariat, shall approve a general framework of principles and provisions for liberalizing the intra-subregional trade in services.

Article 80

The general framework provided for in the previous article shall be applied to the trade in services provided in the following ways:

   (a) From the territory of one Member Country to the territory of another Member Country;

   (b) Within the territory of a Member Country to a consumer from another Member Country;

   (c) Through the commercial presence of service enterprises of one Member Country in the territory of another Member Country; and,

   (d) By individuals from one Member Country in the territory of another Member Country.

Chapter VIII—Common External Tariff

Article 81

The Member Countries commit themselves to put a Common External Tariff into effect within the timeframes and according to the modes the Commission may establish.

Article 82

The Commission, at the General Secretariat's proposal, shall approve the Common External Tariff, which must provide for adequate levels of protection for subregional products, considering the Agreement objective of gradually harmonizing the different economic policies of the Member Countries.

On the date indicated by the Commission, Colombia, Peru, and Venezuela shall begin the process of aligning the customs duties that are applicable under their national tariff schedules to the importation of products that did not originate in the subregion, with the Common External Tariff in an annual, automatic, and linear way.

. . .

Article 85

The General Secretariat may propose to the Commission the measures it considers essential to ensure normal supply conditions in the subregion.

. . .

TRUJILLO ACT (10.03.1996)

. . .

Presidential Guidelines—Protocol of Amendment Establishing the Andean Community and the Andean Integration System

The Presidents have decided to establish the Andean Community and the Andean Integration System, to which end they have adopted the Protocol Amending the Andean Subregional Integration Agreement (Cartagena Agreement), which is annexed hereto and forms an integral part of this Act.

They urge their legislatures to expedite the ratification of that Protocol of Amendment to ensure that the procedure is concluded, in so far as possible, within 60 days of the adoption of this Act.

They direct the Andean Council of Ministers for Foreign Affairs to take immediate steps to prepare and adopt the rules of procedure, and instruct the Commission of the Cartagena Agreement to adjust its own rules of procedure accordingly and to prepare new ones for the general secretariat, which will be submitted for consideration to the Andean Council of Ministers for Foreign Affairs.

They also instruct the Andean Council of Ministers for Foreign Affairs to meet, immediately following the entry into force of the Protocol Amending the Andean Subregional Integration Agreement (Cartagena Agreement), to elect a Secretary-General of the Andean Community.

Court of Justice of the Andean Community

The Andean Presidents have decided that the Chairman of the Council of Ministers for Foreign Affairs shall convene, as soon as possible, a meeting of the plenipotentiaries for the purpose of reconciling the draft Protocol Modifying the Court of Justice with the institutional reforms introduced into the Cartagena Agreement by the Protocol of Amendment annexed to this Act. In convening that meeting, the Chairman shall provide the participants with the working paper on the legal order of the Cartagena Agreement which was considered by the high-level working group for the structuring of the Andean Integration System.

Andean Parliament

The Andean Presidents support the strengthening of the Andean Parliament and urge that representatives to that body be elected, by universal and direct ballot, within the next five years.

Andean Development Corporation

The Andean Presidents take note of the sustained and financially sound growth of the Andean Development Corporation in the international sphere, to the point where it has become the primary source of financing for the Andean countries, supporting physical integration projects, private-sector development, increased trade and the procurement of resources in capital markets.

They also note with satisfaction the incorporation of new countries of the region as series "C" shareholders, which opens up new opportunities for financing projects and activities of mutual interest to the Andean Group and to those countries.

In that regard, they express their support for the effective management practices of the entity's current administration.

Social Agreements

The Andean Presidents stress the importance of updating the objectives and strengthening the implementation of the Andrés Bello, Hipólito Unanue and Simón Rodríguez Conventions and the José Celestino Mutis Programme to adapt them to the goals and purposes of the Andean Integration System. To that end, they invite the non-Andean countries parties to those conventions to join that effort.

Democracy and Human Rights

Considering that democracy is the political system that best guarantees the rule of law, citizen participation, respect for human rights and the preservation of cultural diversity, the Andean Presidents agree to continue to strengthen democratic institutions to achieve stability, peace and development for their peoples.

Combating Corruption

The Andean Presidents reaffirm that combating corruption is a basic responsibility of every State, which must be complemented by joint action through international cooperation and mutual assistance. The Andean Presidents express their renewed willingness and commitment to fight corruption in order to consolidate a democratic society that fosters social and economic justice. To that end, they strongly support the convening of the Specialized Conference on the Draft Inter-American Convention against Corruption, to be held in Caracas this month.

Drug Trafficking

The Andean Presidents reaffirm their unshakable conviction, born of the sovereign will of the Andean societies and Governments, that drug trafficking and related crimes must be fought head-on. In this regard, they endorse the commitment made at the seventh meeting of the Andean Presidential Council to strengthen existing ties of cooperation with a view to developing common policies and actions to promote closer cooperation with other countries and regional groupings in order to pursue a concerted, comprehensive effort to combat all of the crimes related to the phenomenon of drugs and illicit substances, including their production, distribution and consumption; money-laundering; the diversion of chemical precursors; and illegal trade in light arms.

. . .

Andean trade preferences

The Andean Presidents are pleased at the momentum gained by the process of dialogue and cooperation between the Andean Community and the European Union with respect to drugs and related crimes, as exemplified by the agreement on the control of precursors and psychotropic substances, signed in December 1995 in Madrid, Spain, as well as the first meeting of high-level experts on the fight against drugs, which will take place in Rome this month.

They also welcome the progress made in modifying the European Union's Generalized System of Preferences in the areas of agriculture and fishing, in the context of cooperation in the fight against drug trafficking.

. . .

Free trade area in the Americas

The Andean Presidents support the development of a free trade area in the Americas, in the belief that the progressive liberalization of trade in goods and services will help achieve growth levels commensurate with the development expectations of all the peoples in the hemisphere. Taking into account the varying circumstances of the countries participating in the free trade area, the Presidents consider that progress in its implementation should give priority to the extension and convergence of existing subregional agreements. This belief is renewed in view of the forthcoming second ministerial meeting on trade and business forum of the Americas, to be held in Cartagena, Colombia, in March 1996.

European Union

The Andean Presidents are pleased that the President of the European Council welcomed, at the Madrid Summit of December 1995, the call to strengthen relations between the Andean Community and the European Union. In that regard, they instruct the Andean Council of Ministers for Foreign Affairs when they meet in April with their European counterparts, in Cochabamba, Bolivia, to take specific measures to deepen interregional relations and to strengthen ties of inter-institutional cooperation between the European Union and the bodies and institutions of the Andean Integration System. Furthermore, they acknowledge the support provided by the Commission of the European Union for the institutional development of that System.

. . .

Physical integration

The Andean Presidents underscore the importance of improving the road networks, ports, and airports in the Andean Community, and take note of the efforts being made in the field of infrastructure and transport services to build roads linking the Andean countries to the
other countries of the region.

. . .

Cultural cooperation

The Andean Presidents encourage ongoing coordination among the member countries to facilitate and carry out cultural exchange policies and programmes. They agree to promote closer relations among their respective national agencies in order to foster specific actions to promote closer ties among their peoples and a better understanding of their cultural values and forms of expression.

They also agree to adopt effective measures to protect their peoples' cultural heritage and to preserve the material evidence of their history, the roots of which are common to all of them, through coordination among the respective national sectors in charge of this area.

They instruct the Andean Council of Ministers for Foreign Affairs to convene a meeting of ministers or other cultural affairs authorities of the member countries to consider specific measures to meet the aforesaid objectives.

. . .

Inclusion of Panama

The Andean Presidents wish to place on record that they would be pleased to have Panama formally join the Andean Community. They appreciate the Panamanian President's offer to provide an area in his country for the installation of a centre for comprehensive action to fight drug trafficking.

. . .

Treaty Creating the Court of Justice of the Cartagena Agreement (10.03.1996)

. . .

First

The Treaty Creating the Court of Justice of the Cartagena Agreement is hereby amended in accordance with the following text:

Chapter I—On The Legal System Of The Cartagena Agreement

Article 1

The legal system of the Cartagena Agreement consists of:
  (a) The Cartagena Agreement, its Protocols and additional instruments;
  (b) This Treaty and its Amending Protocols;
  (c) The Decisions of the Andean Council of Foreign Ministers and of the Commission of the Andean Community;
  (d) The Resolutions of the General Secretariat of the Andean Community; and
  (e) The Industrial Complementarity Agreements and any such other agreements as the Member Countries may adopt among themselves within the context of the Andean subregional integration process.

Article 2

Decisions become binding for Member Countries as of the date they are approved by the Andean Council of Foreign Ministers or the Commission of the Andean Community.

Article 3

Decisions of the Andean Council of Foreign Ministers or of the Commission and Resolutions of the General Secretariat shall be directly applicable in Member Countries as of the date they are published in the Official Gazette of the Agreement, unless they indicate a later date.

When their text so stipulates, decisions must be incorporated into national law through an express act stipulating the date they will enter into effect in each Member Country.

Article 4

Member Countries are under the obligation to take such measures as may be necessary to ensure compliance with the provisions comprising the legal system of the Andean Community.

They further agree to refrain from adopting or employing any such measure as may be contrary to those provisions or that may in any way restrict their application.

Chapter II—On the Creation and Organization of the Court

Article 5

The Court of Justice of the Andean Community is hereby created as its jurisdictional body, with the organization and jurisdiction established in this Treaty and its Amending Protocols.

The Court shall have its headquarters in the city of Quito, Ecuador.

Article 6

The Court shall consist of five judges who must be nationals of the Member Countries, enjoy a good moral reputation, and fulfil the necessary conditions for exercising the highest judicial functions in their respective countries or be highly competent jurists.

The judges shall enjoy full independence in the exercise of their duties. They may not perform other professional activities, either paid or free of charge, except for teaching; they shall also refrain from any act that is incompatible with the nature of their position.

The Andean Council of Foreign Ministers, in consultation with the Court, may alter the number of judges and create the position of Advocate General, to such number and with such powers as may be established for that purpose in the Organization Law referred to in Article 13.

Article 7

The judges shall be appointed by unanimous decision of the Plenipotentiary Representatives accredited for that purpose, from slates of three candidates each submitted by each Member Country. The government of the host country shall summon the Plenipotentiary Representatives.

Article 8

Judges shall be appointed for a six-year term; they shall be renewed in part every three years and may be re-elected only once.

Article 9

Judges shall each have a first and second alternate to replace them, in that order, in the event of their definitive or temporary absence or their impediment or refusal, as provided for in the Court's Organization Law.

Alternates must fulfil the same qualifications as the principals. They shall be appointed on the same date, in the same manner and for the same period as the principal.

Article 10

Judges may be removed from office at the request of the Government of a Member Country, in accordance with the procedure established in the Court's Organization Law, only if in the exercise of their duties they commit a serious violation provided for in that Organization Law. To this end, the Governments of Member Countries shall appoint Plenipotentiary representatives who, upon being summoned by the host country, shall decide the case by unanimous vote, at a special meeting.

. . .

Chapter III—On the Court's Spheres of Jurisdiction

Section One—On the Nullity Action

Article 17

It is the responsibility of the Court to declare the nullity of Decisions of the Andean Council of Foreign Ministers and the Andean Community Commission, Resolutions of the General Secretariat, and the Agreements referred to in Article 1, paragraph (e), if enacted or agreed upon in violation of the provisions comprising the legal system of the Andean Community, and even for the deviation of power, when requested by a Member Country, the Andean Council of Foreign Ministers, the Commission of the Andean Community, the General Secretariat, or natural or artificial persons whose rights or interests are affected as provided for in Article 19 of this Treaty.

Article 18

Member Countries may bring a nullity action only in cases of Decisions or Agreements that were approved without their affirmative vote.

Article 19

Natural or artificial persons may bring a nullity action against the Decisions taken by the Andean Council of Foreign Ministers or the Andean Community Commission, General Secretariat Resolutions, or Agreements that affect their subjective rights or their legitimate interests.

Article 20

Any nullity action must be brought before the Court within a period of two years following the date of the Decision of the Andean Council of Foreign Ministers or of the Andean Community Commission, the General Secretariat's Resolution, or the Agreement in question becomes effective.

Even if the period provided for in the previous paragraph has expired, either of the parties to a litigation brought before national judges or courts could petition those judges or courts to declare that the Decision or Resolution is inapplicable to the specific case, provided that the said case is related to the application of that provision and that its validity is open to question, in accordance with the stipulation of article 17.

Upon the filing of the petition to declare inapplicability, the national judge shall submit an inquiry to the Court of Justice of the Andean Community regarding the legality of the Decision, Resolution, or Agreement; it shall then suspend the process until receipt of the Court's decision, which the national judge must apply in his/her sentence.

Article 21

The filing of a nullity action shall not affect the effectiveness or validity of the provision or the Agreement being challenged.

The Court may, however, at the request of the petitioning party and after guaranteeing that obligation should it deem this necessary, through its final verdict, order the temporary suspension of the execution of the Decision, Resolution or Agreement being challenged or other cautionary measures, if such were to cause or could cause the petitioner damage that is irreparable or difficult to repair.

Article 22

When the Court declares the total or partial nullity of the challenged Decision, Resolution, or Agreement, it shall indicate the effects of the judgement over time.

The body of the Andean Community whose act was annulled shall adopt the required provisions in order to ensure that the judgement is effectively fulfilled within the period set by the Court.

. . .

Article 40

The Court is competent to hear such labor disputes as may arise within the bodies and institutions of the Andean Integration System.

. . .

SUCRE PROTOCOL (25.06.1997)

. . .

Article 3

The following mechanisms and measures, among others, shall be used to achieve the objectives of this Agreement:

(a) The intensification of integration with the other regional economic blocs and of political, social, economic, and commercial relations with extra-regional systems;

(b) The gradual harmonization of economic and social policies and dovetailing of national laws on pertinent matters;

(c) Joint programming, the intensification of subregional industrialization and the execution of industrial programs and other forms of industrial integration;

(d) A more advanced trade liberalization schedule than the commitments arising out of the 1980 Treaty of Montevideo;

(e) A Common External Tariff;

(f) Programs to accelerate the development of the agricultural and agribusiness sectors;

(g) The channeling of internal and external resources to the Subregion to finance the investments that are needed for the integration process;

(h) Programs in the field of services and of the deregulation of intra-subregional trade in services;

(i) Physical integration; and

(j) Preferential treatment for Bolivia and Ecuador.

The following economic and social cooperation programs and actions shall be carried out in coordination to complement the above-cited mechanisms:

(a) Programs designed to expedite scientific and technological development;

(b) Actions in the field of border integration;

(c) Tourism programs;

(d) Actions for the use and conservation of natural resources and the environment;

(e) Social development programs; and

(f) Actions in the field of social communication.

. . .

Article 4

The Andean Council of Foreign Ministers shall formulate the Common Foreign Policy on matters of subregional interest. To that end, the Council shall coordinate joint political positions that will enable the Community to participate effectively in international political forums and organizations.

The Andean Council of Foreign Ministers and the Andean Community Commission shall define and launch a Community strategy aimed at intensifying its integration with the other regional economic blocs and its political, social, economic, and trade relations with extra-regional systems.

To accomplish the aim cited in this Chapter, the Andean Council of Foreign Ministers and the Andean Community Commission shall take the following measures, among others:

(a) Strengthen Community participation in international, multilateral, hemispheric, and regional economic and trade forums;

(b) Coordinate joint Andean Community negotiations with other integration blocs or with third countries or groups of countries; and

(c) Charge the General Secretariat with carrying out research, studies and actions that will enable the Community to achieve the cited objective and take the measures stipulated in this Chapter.

. . .

Article 6

Replace Article 52 by the following text: "Article 52—The Andean Community shall possess a common regime for the treatment of foreign capital and on trademarks, patents, licenses and royalties, among other things."

. . .

Article 11

Replace present Article 71 by the following text: "Article 72—The Program for Liberalizing the trade in goods is intended to eliminate all levies and restrictions of all kinds that affect the importation of products originating in the territory of any Member Country."

. . .

Article 20

Substitute the following text for present Article 141: "Article 141—For purposes of the stipulation of the foregoing article, the Andean Council of Foreign Ministers and the Commission shall, within their respective spheres of competence, adopt programs to orient the joint external actions of the Member Countries, especially with regard to their negotiations with third countries and groups of countries in the political, social, and economic and trade spheres, as well as their participation in specialized international economic forums and organizations."

. . .

ADDITIONAL PROTOCOL TO THE TREATY ESTABLISHING THE ANDEAN PARLIAMENT (23.04.1997)

The Andean Community Countries,

Convinced that the peoples' participation is necessary to ensure the consolidation and future projection of the global integration of the countries of the Andean Subregion;

Conscious that it is essential to create a means of common action for affirming the principles, values and objectives that are identified with the effective exercise of democracy;

. . .

Chapter I—On the Creation, Composition and Headquarters of the Parliament, the Common Deliberating Body

Article 1

The Andean Parliament is hereby created as the common deliberating body of the Andean Integration System, with the composition, organization, purposes and functions established by this Treaty.

Comprised of Representatives

Article 2

The Andean Parliament is the deliberating body of the Andean Integration System. Its nature is that of a Community body; it represents the nations of the Andean Community and shall be comprised of Representatives elected by Universal and Direct Vote in accordance with the procedure to be adopted through an Additional Protocol that shall include appropriate criteria for national representation.

Until the Additional Protocol instituting Direct Elections is signed, the Andean Parliament shall be comprised of five Representatives of each National Congress, chosen in keeping with its internal regulations and the General Regulations of the Andean Parliament.

The Andean Parliament shall have its permanent headquarters in the city of Bogotá, Colombia.

Common Objectives

Article 3

The Andean Parliament and the Representatives shall act in accordance with the common objectives and interests of the Contracting Parties.

Annual Meetings

Article 4

The Andean Parliament shall hold two Regular Meetings a year with no need for prior summons.

The place, date and duration of the annual meetings shall be determined at the previous year's session, using a system of rotation among the countries.

The Andean Parliament may meet on a special basis to take cognizance of urgent and specific matters when requested to do so by at least one-third of the Representatives.

Chapter II—On the Organization of the Parliament

Period of Representation

Article 5

Representatives shall be elected for a two-year period and may be re-elected. Representatives shall continue to be members of the Andean Parliament until they have been legally replaced pursuant to article 2 of this Treaty.

Representative and Alternates

Article 6

Each Representative shall have a first and second alternate, who shall replace him/her, in that order, when absent temporarily or permanently.

Alternates shall be elected on the same dates, in the same way, and for the same period as the Titular Representatives.

Officers

Article 7

The Andean Parliament shall elect, from among its Members, its President and such Vice-Presidents as its Regulations stipulate, for a two-year term of office.

Secretariat

Article 8

The Andean Parliament shall have a General Secretariat, whose composition and functions shall be defined in the Regulations.

International Legal Status

Article 9

The Andean Parliament shall have an international legal status and the capacity to exercise it.

Diplomatic Immunity

Article 10

The Members of the Andean Parliament, as part of the Andean Integration System, shall enjoy such privileges and immunities within the territories of each Member Country as they need to fulfil their objectives. Its international Representatives and officials shall likewise enjoy the privileges and immunities they require to perform their functions in connection with this Treaty with independence. Its premises are inviolable and its property and assets shall be immune from all judicial proceeding, unless this immunity is expressly waived. Notwithstanding, such a waiver shall not apply to any judicial executory measure.

Chapter III—On the Objectives and Functions of the Parliament

Objectives

Article 11

The Andean Parliament has the following objectives:

  (a) To contribute to the promotion and orientation of the Andean Community integration process;
  (b) To uphold, within the Andean Subregion, the full rule of freedom, social justice and democracy in its broadest participatory exercise;
  (c) To ensure respect for Human Rights for all Contracting Parties, within the context of the international instruments existing in that area;
  (d) To promote the involvement of the nations as actors in the Andean integration process;
  (e) To promote the development of an Andean Community consciousness and the integration of the Latin American Community;
  (f) To promote among the nations of the Andean Subregion an awareness and the broadest possible dissemination of the principles and provisions that guide the establishment of a new international order; and

(g) To contribute to the strengthening of the democratic system, international peace and justice, and the right of nations to free self-determination.

Functions

Article 12

The functions of the Andean Parliament are:

(a) To take part in promoting and orienting the Andean Subregional Integration process with a view toward consolidating Latin American integration;

(b) To examine the progress of Andean Subregional Integration and the fulfilment of its objectives by requesting periodic information for that purpose from the bodies and institutions of the Andean Integration System;

(c) To formulate recommendations on the Draft Annual Budgets of the bodies and institutions of the Andean Integration System that are financed through the direct contributions of the Member Countries;

(d) To suggest to the bodies and institutions of the Andean Integration System, actions or decisions that have as their goal or effect, the adoption of amendments, adjustments or new general guidelines in relation to the programmed objectives and the institutional structure of the Andean Integration System;

(e) To participate in law-making for the process by suggesting, to the bodies of the Andean Integration System, Draft Provisions on matters of common interest, for incorporation into the legal system of the Andean Community;

(f) To promote the harmonization of Member Country legislation; and

(g) To foster cooperation and coordination among the Parliaments of the Member Countries, the Bodies and Institutions of the Andean Integration System, and the Parliamentary Bodies for Integration or Cooperation with Third Countries.

. . .

Additional Protocol to the Treaty creating the Andean Parliament, regarding the direct and universal election of its representatives

Article 1

This Protocol establishes the procedures that will be adopted in the Andean Parliament Member Countries for the Election of their Representatives by Universal, Direct and secret vote.

The election of the Representatives to the Andean Parliament by Universal and Direct Vote should be held within a period of no more than five (5) years.

Article 2

The permanent headquarters of the Andean Parliament shall be located in Bogotá, Colombia.

Article 3

Five (5) titular Representatives to the Andean Parliament shall be elected in each Member Country. Each Representative shall have a first and second alternate, who shall replace him/her in that order, in the case of temporary or permanent absence. Alternates shall be elected on the same date, in the same way, and for the same period as Titular Representatives.

Article 4

Until a Uniform Electoral System has been established, the System for Electing the Titular Representatives to the Andean Parliament, as well as their alternates, shall be governed by the national legislation of each Member Country.

Article 5

Representatives to the Andean Parliament shall be elected in each Member Country on the date of the Legislative or other general election, including special elections, in accordance with its own national laws.

Article 6

Representatives to the Andean Parliament shall enjoy full autonomy in the exercise of their functions and are not subject to any imperative mandate. They shall vote on a personal and individual basis and shall act in accordance with Community objectives and interests. Andean Parliamentarians are not responsible to any authority or jurisdictional body whatsoever for the votes they cast or the opinions they express on matters connected with their position. Representatives to the Parliament shall all enjoy, in addition to the immunities stipulated in article 10 of the Treaty Establishing the Andean Parliament, Parliamentary immunity in the same way and to the same extent as the Legislators of their respective Member Country.

Article 7

National Legislators of Member Countries may be Representatives to the Andean Parliament at the same time, although this in no way constitutes a requirement for eligibility.

Article 8

The impediments to the exercise of the function of Representative to the Andean Parliament, in addition to those established in the national legislation of each Member Country, are the following:

(a) Performing public functions in the service of a Member Country, except for legislative duties.

Being a Representative, official or employee of any other Andean Integration System body.

Being an official or employee of any Andean Community Institution or of the Specialized Bodies connected with them.

(b) Furthermore, until the Uniform Electoral System enters into effect, each Member Country may enact national provisions regarding other incompatibilities.

Representatives who, after having assumed their mandate, demonstrate any of the incompatibilities stipulated in this article, shall cease their functions and shall be replaced by their respective alternates, so long as those incompatibilities exist.

Article 9

Until the Uniform Electoral System enters into effect, the Member Countries shall report the official results of the election of their Representatives to the Andean Parliament. The latter shall also duly receive and verify the credentials of those persons elected.

Article 10

The annual budget approved for the operation of the Andean Parliament shall be covered by resources contributed by each Member Country, in keeping with the regulatory provisions that are issued for that purpose.

Their respective Congresses shall pay the fees and other remunerations to which Andean Parliamentarians elected by the people are entitled, in proportions equal to those paid from the General Congressional Budgets to each country's Legislators.

Article 11

This Protocol may not be signed with reservations, nor shall these be acceptable at the time of ratification or accession. Only Member States of the Andean Community, or those that become such, may be parties to this Protocol.

Article 12

In order for this Protocol to enter into force, all of the Andean Community Member Countries must first deposit their instruments of ratification.

The Protocol shall become effective on the day after the last instrument of ratification has been deposited at the Andean Community General Secretariat and shall remain in force for the entire period of effectiveness of the Cartagena Agreement and the Treaty Establishing the Andean Parliament and may not be denounced independently of those instruments.

Article 13

The Andean Parliament shall be responsible for the organic, structural and functional regulation of this Protocol.

Transitional Provision

The current system of Indirect Election under the responsibility of the respective National Legislative Bodies shall remain in effect until the Universal and Direct Elections provided for in article 1 of this instrument have been held.

. . .

ADDITIONAL PROTOCOL TO THE CARTAGENA AGREEMENT — ANDEAN COMMUNITY COMMITMENT TO DEMOCRACY (27.10.1998)

. . .

Article 1

Democratic institutions and a constitutional state that are fully effective are essential to the political cooperation and the process of economic, social, and cultural integration carried out within the framework of the Cartagena Agreement and of other instruments of the Andean Integration System.

Article 2

The provisions of this Protocol shall be applicable if the democratic order is disrupted in any of the Member Countries

Article 3

In the event of developments that could be considered a disruption of the democratic order in any Member Country, the other Andean Community Member Countries shall consult with each other and, if possible, with the country involved in order to examine the nature of those developments

Article 4

If the consultations cited in the previous Article so establish it, the Council of Foreign Ministers shall be convened to ascertain whether the developments in question constitute a disruption of the democratic order, in which case appropriate measures shall be adopted for its prompt reestablishment

These measures specifically concern the relations and commitments deriving from the Andean integration process. They shall be taken in accordance with the seriousness and the evolution of political developments in the country in question and shall include:

(a) Suspension of the Member Country's participation in any of the bodies of the Andean Integration System;
(b) Suspension of its participation in the international cooperation projects carried out by the Member Countries;
(c) Extension of the suspension to other System bodies, including its disqualification by Andean financial institutions from obtaining access to facilities or loans;
(d) Suspension of rights to which it is entitled under the Cartagena Agreement and of the right to coordinate external action in other spheres; and
(e) Other measures and actions that are deemed pertinent under International Law.

Article 5

The measures cited in the previous article shall be adopted by the Andean Council of Foreign Ministers through a Decision, without the participation of the Member Country involved. That Decision shall become effective on the date of its approval and the country in question shall be notified immediately thereof.

Article 6

Without prejudice to the foregoing, the Governments of the Member Countries shall continue to take diplomatic steps to bring about the reestablishment of democratic order in the Member Country in question.

Article 7

Measures adopted pursuant to Article 4 shall cease through a Decision once the Andean Council of Foreign Ministers ascertains that democratic order has been re-established in the Member Country in question.

Article 8

The Andean Community shall seek to incorporate a democratic clause in the agreements it signs with third parties, in accordance with the criteria set out in this Protocol.

Article 9

This Protocol shall enter into force when all of the Member Countries have deposited their respective instruments of ratification with the General Secretariat of the Andean Community.

. . .

QUIRAMA DECLARATION (28.06.2003)

. . .

Reaffirming their conviction that the deepening of the Community integration process requires the adoption of new and efficient strategy lines within the context of a multidimensional agenda that will enable them to achieve their countries' balanced, harmonious and shared economic development, with a view toward strengthening their individual and collective capacity for fighting poverty and social exclusion.

Considering that the progress made in the Subregional integration process places the Andean Community in the position of being able to assume a role as an important and participating player in the international community, confronting the challenges imposed by present world dynamics.

Conscious that in order to strengthen and deepen the process of Andean integration in all of its dimensions, it is necessary to translate our high political will into specific and sustained efforts, particularly in regard to the application of the Andean legal provisions.

   . . .

A. Political Dimension

Reinforce cooperation on issues of essential importance, such as the struggle against poverty and social exclusion; the strengthening of democracy; democratic governance; the defense and protection of human rights; security and confidence-building; the war against terrorism in all its forms and expressions; the crimes that undermine our countries' economic stability, social welfare and public equity; the fight to control the worldwide drug problem and related offenses; the war on corruption and organized crime; the environment and sustainable development.

Boost the Common Foreign Policy, while safeguarding and enhancing our Community wealth to ensure that we secure a world position that will favor the Subregion's interests and priorities, give it a better presence in international forums and organizations, and reinforce our political, economic and cooperative relations with third countries and other regional groups, giving preference to concerted South American, Latin American and Caribbean efforts and integration.

B. Social and Cultural Dimension

Give maximum priority to the design, coordination and harmonization of social policies that will lead to the development of specific coordinated strategies for social cohesion and the struggle against poverty and marginality, which will help to consolidate democracy and reinforce governance in the Andean Community, as well as open up broader spaces for the participation of social actors and organizations.

Make the approval of the Integrated Social Development Plan, as a complement to national development plans, and the creation of innovative financial mechanisms for reinforcing democratic governance and facing up to poverty, among the first issues to be addressed.

Back the advances made in Subregional negotiations to reduce the price of medicines, the Andean Health Plan and the implementation of the Andean Health Card in which the Health Body—the Hipólito Unanue Convention—is engaged.

Affirm the need for the Andean Community to make itself stronger by building and giving enhanced value to a common cultural vehicle that will take education, science and technology into account.

Reinforce the links of cultural exchange and cooperation among the Andean countries by establishing alliances among public and private institutions concerned with preserving and promoting Andean cultural diversity and safeguarding our countries' cultural heritage.

Give preference to actions aimed at deepening the Andean economic space by developing instruments for policy conciliation in areas such as labor migrations, social security and safety and health at work, as well as the recognition of professional licenses and degrees.

C. Economic Dimension

Reaffirm the principles of the Cartagena Agreement as an instrument for promoting the growth and development of the region's production systems and their competitiveness, the diversification of Andean exports and the complementary nature of the Andean economies.

Review the instances of noncompliance and prepare a comprehensive proposal to turn around the situation, with an established timetable, through the joint efforts of the Member Countries.

Acknowledge the importance of creating a favorable environment for the development and growth of trade, tourist and investment flows in the Andean Community.

Boost tourism as one of the basic driving forces for development and integration. Work to foster the interconnection of airline routes and integrated tourist circuits between the Subregional and South American countries. In keeping with these aims, we firmly support the initiative being fostered by the South American Ministers of Tourism, "Discovering South America for the South Americans."

Strive to ensure that the exchange policies adopted by the Member Countries will contribute to the stability and growth of trade flows in an effort that the competent authorities should undertake.

Andean Common Market

Recognize the advances made in the free trade zone and in consolidating the customs union and the current status of the common external tariff and the price stabilization mechanism.

As a result, and with a view to creating the common market, we ratify that the latter is an effective instrument for making the most of the trade among and development of the Community Member Countries that will guarantee the unhampered movement of goods, services, capital and people within the

Community territory, and for efficiently gaining an equitable position in the international market.

Encourage the adoption of a Common Agricultural Policy as a mechanism to secure the development and competitiveness of the agricultural and agribusiness sectors and the rural development of the Andean countries.

D. Border Integration and Development

Consolidate the Border Integration and Development Policy by supporting the establishment of comprehensive development programs for the border regions, particularly the Border Integration Zones, in order to turn these regions into vehicles for reinforcing Andean integration and improving the quality of life of the Subregion's inhabitants. Also to promote the establishment of Border Integration Zones with third countries.

Actively expedite the execution of the "South American Regional Infrastructure Integration Initiative" (IIRSA) with an interrelated vision of the different focal points of integration and development, in order to build a vehicle that will promote further interaction among our nations, more competitiveness and the development of the Andean economies.

E. Sustainable Development

Move ahead with the design and execution of Community programs on strategic fronts, such as the environment, energy development, and disaster prevention and measures that will step up sustainable development in the Subregion.

F. Institutions

Give special attention to the surveillance and enforcement of Community legal provisions and to building up the General Secretariat as the strategist for and executor of the key issues on the multidimensional agenda.

Reaffirm the institutional importance of the Andean Community Court of Justice, whose efforts help to strengthen the Andean Integration System and contribute significantly to juridical stability and certainty in the Subregion.

In order to embark upon a second generation of integration policies that are consonant with the new dimensions of the process and the demands of our peoples, we agree upon the following

Guidelines

Political Dimension of Integration

1. To instruct the Andean Council of Foreign Ministers to propose the elements that would serve as the basis for the possible construction of a governance agenda for the Andean Subregion that would take into consideration the political, economic and social challenges and allow for the promotion of social inclusion and equity, as well as of credibility, in democratic institutions.

2. To instruct the Andean Council of Foreign Ministers to submit to the next Meeting of the Andean Presidential Council draft Andean Common Security Policy guidelines that would develop the parameters of the Lima Commitment and would provide for, among other things, specific plans of action against terrorism and corruption, based on the work that the High-Level Group on Security and Confidence-Building does.

   We deem it essential in this context to expedite the start up of all aspects of the Andean Plan for the Prevention, Combating and Eradication of Small, Light Weapons and its presentation during the Biannual Meeting of States on the Implementation of the United Nations Action Program on the subject.

3. To Instruct the Andean Council of Foreign Ministers to adopt a Program to Disseminate and Implement the Andean Charter for the Promotion and Protection of Human Rights, in order to promote the full effectiveness of that instrument within our Community.

4. To instruct the Andean Council of Foreign Ministers, with the support of the Executive Committee on the Andean Cooperation Plan for the Control of Illegal Drugs and Related Offenses, to move ahead with the application of the Operational Plan, based on the priorities that Committee identifies.

5. To direct the Andean Council of Foreign Ministers to adopt an Andean Plan to Fight Corruption that would encompass both coordinated Subregional efforts and joint participation in international forums.

6. To instruct the Andean Council of Foreign Ministers to lay down the guidelines for a Subregional Food Security Policy that would provide for specific action plans with regard to, among other things, the fight against poverty and marginality, in keeping with the stipulations that the Integrated Social Development Plan establishes.

7. To instruct the Andean Council of Foreign Ministers, in developing the guidelines for the Common Foreign Policy, to continue the negotiations aimed at the signing of a Political Dialogue and Cooperation Agreement with the European Union that should facilitate the launching of

the negotiation of an Association Agreement. The Council should, in addition, hold the First CAN-MERCOSUR and Chile Political Dialogue and Cooperation Meeting and further develop the existing lines of efforts with China, Russia and India, as well as with Japan.

To urge the Andean Council of Foreign Ministers to expedite the creation of a Mechanism for Political Dialogue and Cooperation with the United States and Canada and also to instruct the General Secretariat to study the means for interlinking the Andean Community with the EFTA, the Republic of Korea and the Republic of Cuba, particularly in regard to the Economic Complementary Agreement with the latter country.

Social and Cultural Dimension

8. To request the Andean Council of Foreign Ministers, in its implementation of the approved guidelines, to formulate the Integrated Social Development Plan together with the Ministers responsible for the social area, the General Secretariat and the Andean Development Corporation (CAF).

9. To instruct the Andean Council of Foreign Ministers, in close coordination with the Advisory Council of Labor Ministers, to promote measures to establish regulations for the Decisions on labor migrations, social security and safety and health at work. Also to supplement the socio-labor advances made by adopting the necessary legal provisions to Recognize Professional Licenses, Degrees and Accreditations in the Subregion.

10. To appeal to the Andean Council of Foreign Ministers to organize effective mechanisms to ensure the participation of the social actors and organizations in developing the Andean integration process, with the technical support of the General Secretariat. In this connection, we recommend the immediate establishment of the national chapters that would allow the first meetings of the "Working Committee on Indigenous Peoples' Rights" and the "Andean Working Committee for the Defense of Consumer Rights with the Participation of Civil Society," to be held, respectively, in November 2003 in Ecuador and at the General Secretariat headquarters on a date yet to be defined.

11. To immediately return to the tasks entrusted to the Ministries responsible for our countries' educational, cultural and science and technology policies, under the supervision of the Andean Council of Foreign Ministers and with the technical support of the General Secretariat and the contributions of the Andrés Bello Convention and the Simón Bolívar University, so that at our next regular meeting they can submit guidelines for the adoption of Community policies in each of these program areas aimed at improving the quality, coverage and relevance of education, promoting and respecting the Subregion's

cultural diversity, exercising interculturality and developing technological innovation, among other things, in keeping with the Presidential Guidelines of the Eleventh Andean Presidential Council of
Cartagena de Indias.

12. To instruct the competent national authorities to consolidate the efforts underway in the Subregion to control illegal trafficking in cultural
goods and to promote the application of specific new mechanisms, such
as the red list of endangered cultural goods in Latin America; in this
way, they will help to protect the tangible and intangible, archeologi-
cal, historical, ethnological, paleontological, and artistic heritage of the
Andean Community Member Countries.

13. To instruct the competent national authorities to accede to the International Convention for the Safeguarding of Intangible Cultural
Heritage during the next UNESCO General Conference, inasmuch
as its application will make it possible to reinforce national policies to protect the memory and identity of the Andean peoples and
cultures.

14. To endorse with interest the proposal of the Pan American Health Or-
ganization/ World Health Organization and the Andean Health Body—
the Hipólito Unanue Convention- that creates an "Andean Commission
on Investment in Health" in order to move ahead with a joint strategy
for developing the health sector and to apply to PAHO/WHO for the
necessary funds.

15. To direct the General Secretariat, in coordination with the national authorities of the Member Countries, to promote cooperation among the
Subregional communications media for exchanges of common interest
in the areas of tourism, education, culture, development, etc., in order
to build up their common values and disseminate the wide diversity of
Andean culture.

. . .

Andean Common Market

23. We instructed the Commission, within no more than 30 days and on
the basis of prior deliberations of the Ad Hoc Group, to hold a special
meeting for the sole purpose of adopting decisions that will promote
more development of and a growing and sustained trade in the oil seed
chain.

24. To ensure that the Commission, with the participation of the Ministers
of Agriculture and no later than September 30, 2003, takes a decision
regarding the Common Andean Agriculture Policy, based on the consultations with the corresponding organizations and with the production

sectors, to which end the Andean Agricultural Committee will meet in Caracas in July.

25. To instruct the General Secretariat to draw up a working program, by September 30, 2003, to advance the liberalization of Subregional trade in services.

26. To instruct the pertinent institutions to implement the recommendations of the GRANADUA Project, with the assistance of the General Secretariat, in order to interconnect the Customhouses through the adoption of the Integrated Andean Tariff (ARIAN), the Sole Customs Declaration (DUA), and the harmonization of Special Customs Systems and other mechanisms to avoid distortions, including those caused by differences in the preferences granted to third countries, and expedite the effort to control smuggling and tax evasion in the trade between the Andean countries.

27. To emphasize that the efforts to control smuggling and tax evasion require the interconnection of the Customhouses of the Member Countries, preferably by electronic means.

Border Development and Integration

28. To urge the High-Level Group for Border Integration and Development, based on the accomplishments to date, to establish a Comprehensive Border Integration and Development Plan that will define the necessary juridical, technical and financial instruments; and to ensure the participation of the Member Country planning and cooperation institutions.

29. To request the Inter-American Development Bank (IDB) and the CAF to continue providing technical and financial support to the Border Integration and Development Projects Bank and for all other efforts that the High-Level Group for Border Integration and Development decides upon.

30. To instruct the competent national authorities of the Andean Community countries to ensure that their plans and working programs provide for backing to execute the South American Regional Infrastructure Integration Initiative (IIRSA) and facilitate the coordination of plans, projects and investments in an effort to reconcile and to harmonize both the regulation and the associated policies.

31. To instruct the Advisory Council of Foreign Ministers, in keeping with Andean Community Decision 501, to promote the establishment of Border Integration Zones with third countries adjacent to the Andean Community Member Countries.

. . .

CARIBBEAN COMMUNITY (CARICOM)

Caribbean integration began as a counterintuitive response to European integration. It was meant to be a strategy to tame the inevitable end of British colonial rule over many of the island nations that today are home to 34 million inhabitants. The West Indian Federation, founded so that British influence in the region might persevere, failed in 1962. It was followed by the Caribbean Free Trade Association (CARIFTA) in 1965. A truly postcolonial effort toward regional cooperation and eventual integration was begun in 1973, coinciding with Great Britain's entry into the European Community, which forced the Caribbean island states to reconsider their strategic interests and market patterns. The 1973 Treaty of Chaguaramas established the objectives of the Caribbean Community (CARICOM) and a common market as two separate entities of a broader process eventually heading toward the same goal: greater independence from the global economic centers in both Europe and the US.

The Revised Treaty of Chaguaramas of 2001 came close to a refounding of the Caribbean Community. While the broad objectives essentially remained the same—economic integration, coordination of foreign policies, and functional cooperation—the Caribbean Community has reinforced its efforts to implement its goals. With the incorporation of the Caribbean Community and the CARICOM Single Market and Economy under one legal personality, the revised Treaty of Chaguaramas resembles European efforts, as intended, to overcome structures of parallel institutions and mechanisms of "pillars" distinguishing different degrees of integration and cooperation. Ever since, CARICOM has undergone a period of transition with a limited sense of urgency. The goal was set for a full-fledged Single Market by 2008 with an increased degree of institutionalization that would, however, continue to stop short of introducing elements of supranationality. The EU strongly supports the development of the Caribbean Community. In terms of trade relations, the role of CARICOM is rather marginal to the EU: imports from CARICOM amount to 0.5 percent of total EU imports, exports to CARICOM amount to 0.7 percent of total exports of the EU. The Caribbean Community has shifted much of its economy from sugar and banana to services (tourism, financial services) and remains strongly dependent upon remittances sent by migrant workers from the region who reside in North America and Europe.

Membership in CARICOM includes Antigua and Barbuda, the Bahamas, Barbados, Belize, Dominica, Grenada, Guyana—in whose capital Georgetown the CARICOM Secretariat is located—Haiti, Jamaica, Montserrat, Saint Kitts and Nevis, Saint Lucia, Saint Vincent and the Grenadines, Suriname, and Trinidad and Tobago. Associate members are the British Virgin Islands, Bermuda, Turks and Caicos, Anguilla, and the Cayman Islands. Discussion on membership of the Dominican Republic (and, potentially with the strongest implications, of Cuba) is in a preliminary stage evoking matters of size, contrasting political cultures, and legal traditions. The perspective of a Caribbean Community for the whole Caribbean basin might be a far-fetched vision today, but it is no longer inconceivable. In the Caribbean, the European experience of linking "deepening" and "widening" of the integration process has been carefully studied. The CARICOM dialogue with the European Union might have additional influence.

The original CARICOM suffered from the shortcomings of weak sovereignties and strong ideological rifts among its member states as far as attitudes toward the US and Europe were concerned. The fundamental dilemma of the region has not disappeared as a result of the revision of the Treaty of Chaguaramas: the Caribbean Community must balance national pride among its smaller or smallest countries, but it also needs to pool existing potential in order to make their independence a political and economic reality. Increasing reference to the success of European integration is an indication of the continuous soul-searching in CARICOM. In a certain sense, CARICOM is the most sophisticated regional grouping next to the European Union.

The Caribbean Community has begun to develop a sense of foreign policy identity. CARICOM's support for membership of Suriname and Belize in the continent-wide Organization of American States (OAS) prevented possible escalations of territorial disputes with Venezuela and Guatemala. More important was the positive experience of structured relations with the European Community all the way from the Lomé Agreements (four Lomé Agreements were concluded with the European Community and later the European Union between 1970 and 1995, with preferential trade arrangements for up to 70 developing countries) to the Cotonou Agreement of 2000. CARICOM considered itself instrumental in bringing about these widely praised arrangements between Europe and so many countries in Africa, the Caribbean, and the Pacific. As part of the evolving biregionalism, the EU and most CARICOM member states (i.e., without Montserrat, but including Cuba and the Dominican Republic) were negotiating an Economic Partnership Agreement between 2002 and 2007. It was initialed in December 2007.

The establishment of a Caribbean Commission, an Assembly of Commonwealth Caribbean Parliamentarians, and a Caribbean Supreme Court, along with the replacement of the Community Council of Ministers with the Caribbean Common Market Council as the second highest decision-making body in CARICOM, were the most important institutional additions introduced by the Revised Treaty of Chaguaramas in 2001. The "opting-out clauses" for Denmark on key policy goals of the EU under the Maastricht Treaty found a Caribbean equivalent in the fact that the Bahamas are a member of CARICOM but do not participate in the economic structures and goals of the community. As far as the decision-making mechanism is concerned, the Revised Treaty of Chaguaramas introduced interesting reforms: while the principle of unanimity continues to be applied to decision-making in the Conference of Heads of Government, it has been virtually abolished in the other bodies of the community. Consequently, this facilitates speedy decisions on and reactions to the challenges of neoliberal globalization that require an export-oriented, internationally competitive production of goods and services in CARICOM.

It seems likely that the process of incremental yet steady fusion of economic integration with corresponding political processes will continue in the Caribbean. No matter how mixed the current character of CARICOM may be, the history of the Caribbean will no longer be written with reference to "sugar and slavery" only. Integration has become a new mantra in the region. This coincides with new sensitivity about democratic governance in the Caribbean. Since American pressure in the Caribbean against the revolutionary government in Grenada during the early 1980s, it is also increasingly understood that economic development and democratic governance cannot be separated from a successful and substantial integration strategy. CARICOM's speedy reaction to civil unrest in Haiti in early 2004 was indicative of this realization, following the 2003 Rose Hall Declaration on Regional Governance and Integrated Development.

AGREEMENT ESTABLISHING THE CARIBBEAN FREE TRADE ASSOCIATION (CARIFTA) (15.12.1965)

. . .

Article 2
Objectives

The objectives of the Association shall be:

(a) to promote the expansion and diversification of trade in the area of the Association;

(b) to secure that trade between Member Territories takes place in conditions of fair competition;

(c) to encourage the balanced and progressive development of the economies of the Area in keeping with paragraphs 3 to 10 of the Resolution adopted at the Fourth Conference of the Heads of Government of Commonwealth Caribbean Countries. . .;

(d) to foster the harmonious development of Caribbean trade and its liberalisation by the removal of barriers to it;

(e) to ensure that the benefits of free trade are equitably distributed among the Member Territories.

. . .

Article 4
Import Duties

1. Subject to the provisions of Annex B, Member Territories shall not apply any import duties on goods which are eligible for Area tariff treatment in accordance with Article 5.

2. For the purposes of this Article. . ., the term "import duties" means any tax or surtax of customs and any other charges of equivalent effect—whether fiscal, monetary or exchange—which are levied on imports, except duties notified under Article 7 and other charges which fall within that Article.

3. The provisions of this Article do not apply to fees and similar charges in respect of services rendered and nothing in paragraph 2 of this Article shall be construed to exclude from the application of paragraph 1 of this Article any tax or surtax of customs on any product neither the like of which, nor a competitive substitute for which, is produced in the importing Member Territory, or to extend such application to non-discriminatory internal charges on any such product.

4. For the purposes of paragraph 3 of this Article -

   (a) "non-discriminatory" means non-discriminatory as between goods eligible for Area tariff treatment as aforesaid and goods not so eligible;

   (b) a charge shall not be deemed other than internal by reason only that it is collected at the time and place of importation.

Article 5
Area Origin for Tariff Purposes

1. For the purposes of Articles 4 to 8, goods shall,. . . be accepted as eligible for Area tariff treatment if they are consigned from a Member Territory to a consignee in the importing Member Territory and if they are of Area origin under any one of the following conditions:

   (a) that they have been wholly produced within the Area;

   (b) that they fall within a description of goods listed in a Process list to be established by decision of the Council and have been produced within the Area by the appropriate qualifying process described in that List;

(c) that they have been produced within the Area and that the value of any materials imported from outside the Area or of undetermined origin which have been used at any stage of the production of the goods does not exceed 50 percent of the export price of the goods.

2. For the purposes of sub-paragraphs (a), (b) and (c) of paragraph 1 of this Article, materials listed in the Basic Materials List . . ., which have been used in the state described in that List in a process of production within the Area, shall be deemed to contain no element imported from outside the Area.

3. Nothing in this Agreement shall prevent a Member Territory from accepting as eligible for Area tariff treatment any imports consigned from another Member Territory, provided that the like imports consigned from any Member Territory are accorded the same treatment.

. . .

Article 7
Revenue Duties and Internal Taxation

1. . . . Member Territories shall not -

   (a) apply directly or indirectly to imported goods fiscal charges in excess of those applied directly or indirectly to like domestic goods, nor otherwise apply such charges so as to afford effective protection to like domestic goods; or

   (b) apply fiscal charges to imported goods of a kind which they do not produce, or which they do not produce in substantial quantities, in such a way as to afford effective protection to the domestic production of goods of a different kind which are substitutable for the imported goods, which enter into direct competition with them and which do not bear, directly or indirectly, in the country of importation, fiscal charges of equivalent incidence.

2. A Member Territory shall notify the Council of all fiscal charges applied by it where, although the rates of charge, or the conditions governing the imposition of collection of the charge, are not identical in relation to the imported goods and to the like domestic goods, the Member Territory applying the charge considers that the charge is, or had been made, consistent with sub-paragraph (a) of paragraph 1 of this Article. Each Member Territory shall, at the request of any other Member Territory, supply information about the application of paragraph 1 of this Article.

   . . .

Article 9
Prohibition of export duties

1. Member Territories shall not apply any export duties.

2. The provisions of this Article shall not prevent any Member Territory from taking such measures as are necessary to prevent evasion, by means of re-export, of duties which it applies to exports to territories outside the Area.

3. For the purpose of this Article, "export duties" means any duties or charges with equivalent effect imposed on or in connection with the exportation of goods from any Member Territory to a consignee in any other Member Territory.

4. Nothing in this Article shall preclude a Member Territory from applying to any commodity listed in Annex E, within ten years from the effective date of this Agreement, export duty not exceeding that applicable by the Member Territory to such commodity immediately before the effective date of this Agreement.

5. Any Member Territory which, pursuant to paragraph 4 of this Article, applied or continues to apply export duty to any commodity listed in Annex E shall notify the Council of every commodity on which export duty is applied and the rate of such duty. The Council shall keep under review the question of such export duties and may at any time by majority vote make recommendations designed to moderate any damaging effect of those duties.

Article 10
Cooperation in Customs Administration

Member Territories shall take appropriate measures, including arrangements regarding administrative cooperation, to ensure that the provisions of Articles 4 and 8 and of Annexes B, C and D are effectively and harmoniously applied, taking account of the need to reduce as far as is possible the formalities imposed on trade and of the need to achieve mutually satisfactory solutions of any difficulties arising out of the operation of those provisions.

Article 11
Freedom of Transit

Products imported into, or exported from, a Member Territory shall enjoy freedom of transit within the Area and shall only be subject to the payment of the normal rates for services rendered.

. . .

Article 20
Establishment

1. Each Member Territory recognises that restrictions on the establishment and operation of economic enterprises therein by persons belonging to other Member Territories should not be applied, through accord to such persons of treatment which is less favourable than that accorded in such matters to persons belonging to that Member Territory, in such a way as to frustrate the benefits expected from such removal or absence of duties and quantitative restrictions as is required by this Agreement.

2. Member Territories shall not apply new restrictions in such a way that they conflict with the principle set out in paragraph 1 of this Article.

3. A Member Territory shall notify the Council within such period as the Council may decide of particulars of any restrictions which it applies in such a way that persons belonging to another Member Territory are accorded in the first-mentioned Territory less favourable treatment in respect of the matters set out in paragraph 1 of this Article than is accorded to persons belonging thereto.

4. The Council shall consider before 30th April 1970, and may consider at any time thereafter, whether further or different provisions are necessary to give effect to the principles set out in paragraph 1 of this Article and may decide to make the necessary provisions.

5. Nothing in this Article shall prevent the adoption and enforcement by a Member Territory of measures for the control of entry, residence, activity and departure of persons where such measures are justified by reasons of public order, public health or morality, or national security of that Member Territory.

6. For the purposes of this Article -
   (a) a person shall be regarded as belonging to a Member Territory if such person -
       (i) is a citizen of that Territory;
       (ii) has a connection with that Territory of a kind which entitles him to be regarded as belonging to, or, if it be so expressed, as being a native of, the Territory for the purposes of such laws thereof relating to immigration as are for the time being in force; or
       (iii) is a company or other legal person constituted in the Member Territory in conformity with the law thereof and which that Territory regards as belonging to it, provided that such company or other legal person has been formed for gainful purposes and has its registered office and central administration, and carries on substantial activity, within the Area;

(b) "economic enterprises" means any type of economic enterprises for production of or commerce in goods which are of Area origin, whether conducted by individuals or through agencies, branches or companies or
other legal persons.

. . .

Article 26
General Consultations and Complaints Procedure

1. If any Member Territory considers that any benefit conferred upon it by
this Agreement or any objective of the Association is being or may be
frustrated and if no satisfactory settlement is reached between the Member Territories concerned, any of those Member Territories may refer the
matter to the Council.

. . .

Article 28
The Council

1. It shall be the responsibility of the Council -
   (a) to exercise such powers and functions as are conferred upon it by this
   Agreement;
   (b) to supervise the application of this Agreement and keep its operation under review;
   (c) to consider whether further action should be taken by Member Territories in order to promote the attainment of the objectives of the Association and to facilitate the establishment of closer links with other
   countries, unions of countries and international organisations.
2. Each Member Territory shall be represented in the Council and shall
   have one vote.
3. The Commonwealth Caribbean Regional Secretariat shall be the principal administrative organ of the Association and the Council may entrust it, and may set up other organs, committees and bodies and entrust
   them, with such functions as the Council considers necessary to assist
   it in accomplishing its tasks. Decisions of the Council pursuant to this
   paragraph shall be made by majority vote.
4. In exercising its responsibility under paragraph 1 of this Article, the
   Council may take decisions which shall be binding on all Member Territories and may make recommendations to Member Territories.
5. Decisions and recommendations of the Council shall be made by unanimous vote, except in so far as this Agreement provides otherwise. Decisions or recommendations shall be regarded as unanimous unless any

Member Territory casts a negative vote. A decision or recommendation of the Council pursuant to any such provisions as aforesaid requires the affirmative votes of not less than two-thirds of all Member Territories, and reference in any such provision to a majority shall, in relation to the Council, be construed accordingly.

6. The Council may, by its decision to confer any authority under this Agreement, impose conditions to which such authority shall be subject.

. . .

Article 33
Withdrawal

Any Member Territory may withdraw from participation in this Agreement provided that the Government thereof gives twelve months' notice in writing to the Government of Antigua which shall notify the other Member Territories.

Article 34
Amendment

1. Except where provision for modification is made elsewhere in this Agreement, including the Annexes to it, an amendment to the provisions of this Agreement shall be submitted to the Governments of Member Territories for acceptance if it is approved by decision of the Council, and it shall have effect provided it is accepted by all such Governments. Instruments of acceptance shall be deposited with the Government of Antigua which shall notify the other Member Territories.

. . .

TREATY ESTABLISHING THE
CARIBBEAN COMMUNITY (04.07.1973)

. . .

Chapter I—Principles

Article 1
Establishment of the Caribbean Community

By this Treaty the Contracting Parties establish among themselves a Caribbean Community (hereinafter referred to as "the Community") having the membership, powers and functions hereinafter specified.

Article 2
Membership

    1.   Membership of the Community shall be open to—

        (a)

(i) Antigua	(ii) Bahamas	(iii) Barbados
(iv) Belize	(v) Dominica	(vi) Grenada
(vii)Guyana	(viii)Jamaica	(ix) Montserrat
(x) St. Kitts-Nevis-Anguilla	(xi) St. Lucia	(xii) St. Vincent
(xiii) Trinidad and Tobago.		

      (b) any other State of the Caribbean Region that is in the opinion of the Conference able and willing to exercise the rights and assume the obligations of membership in accordance with Article 29 of this Treaty.

    2.   States listed in paragraph (a) of this Article the Governments of which sign this Treaty in accordance with Article 22 and ratify it in accordance with Article 23 shall become Member States of the Community.

Article 3
Definition of Less Developed Countries and More Developed Countries

For the purposes of this Treaty the States specified in paragraph 1 (iii), (vii), (viii) and (xiii) of Article 2 shall be designated More Developed Countries and the remainder listed in the said Paragraph, other than the Bahamas, shall be designated Less Developed Countries until such time as the Conference otherwise determines by majority decision.

Article 4
Objectives of the Community

The Community shall have as its objectives
      (a) the economic integration of the Member States by the establishment of a common market regime (hereinafter referred to as "the common market") in accordance with the provisions of the Annex to this Treaty with the following aims:
          (i) the strengthening, coordination and regulation of the economic and trade relations among Member States in order to promote their accelerated harmonious and balanced development;
          (ii) the sustained expansion and continuing integration of economic activities, the benefits of which shall be equitably shared taking into account the need to provide special opportunities for the Less Developed Countries;

(iii) the achievement of a greater measure of economic independence and effectiveness of its Member States in dealing with States; groups of states and entities of whatever description;

(b) the coordination of the foreign policies of Member States; and

(c) functional cooperation, including

(i) the efficient operation of certain common services and activities for the benefit of its peoples;

(ii) the promotion of greater understanding among its peoples and the advancement of their social, cultural and technological development;

(iii) activities in the fields specified in the Schedule and referred to in Article 18 of this Treaty.

. . .

Chapter II—Organs of the Community

Article 6
Principal Organs

The principal organs of the Community shall be

(a) the Conference of Heads of Government (hereinafter referred to as "the Conference");

(b) The Common Market Council established under the Annex (hereinafter referred to as "the Council").

Article 7
The Conference—Composition

The Conference shall consist of the Heads of Government of Member States.

Any member of the Conference may, as appropriate, designate an alternate to represent him at any meeting of the Conference.

Article 8
Functions and Powers

1. The primary responsibility of the Conference shall be to determine the policy of the Community.

2. The Conference may establish, and designate as such, institutions of the Community in addition to those specified in paragraphs (a) to (g) of Article 10 of this Treaty, as it deems fit for the achievement of the objectives of the Community.

3. The Conference may issue directions of a general or special character as to the policy to be pursued by the Council and the Institutions of the Community for the achievement of the objectives of the Community, and effect shall be given to any such directions.
4. Subject to the relevant provisions of this Treaty, the Conference shall be the final authority for the conclusion of treaties on behalf of the Community and for entering into relationships between the Community and International Organisations and States.
5. The Conference shall take decisions for the purpose of establishing the financial arrangements necessary for meeting the expenses of the Community and shall be the final authority on questions arising in relation to the financial affairs of the Community.
6. The Conference may regulate its own procedure and may decide to admit at its deliberations observers, representatives of non-Member States or other entities.
7. The Conference may consult with entities and other organisations within the region and for this purpose may establish such machinery as it deems necessary.

Article 9
Voting in the Conference

1. Each member of the Conference shall have one vote.
2. The Conference shall make decisions and recommendations by the affirmative vote of all its members.
3. A decision shall be binding upon each Member State to which it is directed. A recommendation shall have no binding force. Where, however, a Member State fails to observe a recommendation of the Conference, it shall submit a report to the Conference as early as practicable and in any event not later than six months thereafter, giving reasons for its non-compliance.
4. For the purposes of this Article, abstentions shall not be construed as impairing the validity of decisions or recommendation of the Conference provided that not less than three-quarters of its members including at least two of the More Developed Countries vote in favour of any decision or recommendation.

Article 10
Institutions of the Community

Institutions of the Community shall be

(a) the Conference of Ministers responsible for Health
(b) the Standing Committee of Ministers responsible for Education

(c) the Standing Committee of Ministers responsible for Labour

(d) the Standing Committee of Ministers responsible for Foreign Affairs

(e) the Standing Committee of Ministers responsible for Finance

(f) the Standing Committee of Ministers responsible for Agriculture

(g) the Standing Committee of Ministers responsible for Mines

(h) any other institution that may be established and designated as such by the Conference in accordance with Article 18.

Article 11
Composition of the Institutions of the Community

1. Each Institution of the Community as set out in paragraphs (a) to (h) of Article 10 of this Treaty shall consist of representatives of Member States. Each Member State shall designate a Minister of Government as its representative on each such institution.

2. Where the Minister designated under paragraph 1 of this Article is unable to attend a meeting of the institution the Member State may designate any other person as an alternate to attend such meeting in his stead.

3. Where the Conference establishes any other institutions in the exercise of the power conferred on it by paragraph 2 of Article 8 of this Treaty, the composition of such institution shall be determined by the Conference.

Article 12
Functions and Powers

1. Subject to the relevant provisions of Article 8 of this Treaty, the institutions of the Community shall formulate such policies and perform such functions as are necessary for the achievement of the objectives of the Community within their respective spheres of competence.

2. The institutions of the Community may regulate their own procedure and

    (a) may establish such subsidiary committees, agencies and other bodies as they consider necessary for the efficient performance of their functions; and

    (b) may decide to admit at their deliberations observers, representatives of non-Member States or other entities.

Article 13
Voting in Institutions

1. Each Member State represented on an Institution shall have one vote.

2. Unless otherwise provided for, decisions of an Institution shall be made by an affirmative vote of all its members. For the purposes of this

paragraph, abstentions shall not be construed as impairing the validity of decisions of an Institution provided that not less than three-quarters of its members including at least two of the More Developed Countries vote in favour of such decisions.

3. Recommendation shall be made by a two-thirds majority vote of all its members including at least two of the More Developed Countries and shall have no binding force. Where a Member State fails to observe a recommendation of an Institution in whole or in part, it shall submit a report to the Institution making the recommendation as early as practicable and in any event not later than six months after receiving notice of such recommendation giving reasons for its non-compliance.

4. Observers at meetings of Institutions shall not have the right to vote.

Article 14
Associate Institutions

1. The following institutions shall be recognised as Associate Institutions of the Community
    (a) the Caribbean Development Bank;
    (b) the Caribbean Investment Corporation;
    (c) the West Indies Associated States Council of Ministers;
    (d) the East Caribbean Common Market Council of Ministers;
    (e) the Caribbean Examinations Council;
    (f) the Council of Legal Education;
    (g) the University of Guyana;
    (h) the University of the West Indies;
    (I) the Caribbean Meteorological Council;
    (j) the Regional Shipping Council;
    (k) any other institution designated as such by the Conference.

2. The Community shall seek to establish such relationships with its Associate Institutions as will promote the achievement of its objectives.

Article 15
The Community Secretariat

1. The Commonwealth Caribbean Regional Secretariat shall be recognised as the Community Secretariat. The Community Secretariat (hereinafter referred to as "the Secretariat") shall be the principal administrative organ of the Community. The headquarters of the Secretariat shall be located in Georgetown, Guyana.

2. The Secretariat shall comprise a Secretary-General and such staff as the Community may require. The Secretary-General shall be appointed by

the Conference (on the recommendation of the Council) for a term not exceeding 5 years and may be reappointed by the Conference. He shall be the chief administrative officer of the Community.

3. The Secretary-General shall act in that capacity in all meetings of the Conference, the Council and the institutions of the Community. Then Secretary-General shall make an annual report to the Conference on the work of the Community.

4. In the performance of their duties the Secretary-General and his staff shall neither seek nor receive instructions from any government whether of Member States or otherwise or from any other authority. They shall refrain from any action which might reflect on their position as officials of the Community, and shall be responsible only to the Community.

5. Each Member State undertakes to respect the exclusively international character of the responsibilities of the Secretary-General and his staff and shall not seek to influence them in the discharge of their responsibilities.

6. The Conference shall approve the staff Regulations governing the operation of the Secretariat.

7. The Secretary-General shall approve Staff Rules for the operation of the Secretariat.

. . .

Chapter III—Coordination and Functional Cooperation

Article 17
Coordination of Foreign Policies

1. To the end that Member States aim at the fullest possible coordination of their foreign policies within their respective competences and seek to adopt as far as possible common positions in major international issues, there is hereby established a Standing Committee of Ministers responsible for Foreign Affairs.

2. The Committee shall have the power to make recommendations to the Governments of Member States represented on the Committee.

3. Only member States possessing the necessary competence with respect to the matters under consideration from time to time may take part in the deliberations of the Committee.

4. Where after the coming into force of the Treaty a Member State achieves full sovereign status such State shall elect whether it wishes to be bound by the provisions of this Article.

5. The recommendations of the Committee shall be made by an affirmative vote of all the Member States competent and participating in the deliberations.

6. The provisions of Article 13 shall not apply to this Article.

Article 18
Functional Cooperation

Without prejudice to the requirements of any other provision of this Treaty, Member States, in furtherance of the objectives set out in Article 4 of this Treaty, undertake to make every effort to cooperate in the areas set out in the Schedule to this Treaty.

Article 19
Settlement of Disputes

Any dispute concerning the interpretation or application of this Treaty, unless otherwise provided for and particularly in Articles 11 and 12 of the Annex, shall be determined by the Conference.

Chapter IV—General and Final Provisions

Article 20
Legal Capacity

1. The Community shall have full juridical personality.

2. Each Member State shall in its territory accord to the Community the most extensive legal capacity accorded to legal persons under its municipal laws including the capacity to acquire and transfer moveable and immovable property and to sue and be sued in its own name. In any legal proceedings the Community shall be represented by the Secretary-General of the Secretariat.

3. The Community may enter into agreement with Member States, non-Member States and International Organisations.

4. Each Member State hereby agrees to take such action as is necessary to make effective in its territory the provisions of this Article and shall promptly inform the Secretariat of such action.

5. Where necessary, Member States undertake to take steps as expeditiously as possible to give full effect in law to all decisions of the organs and institutions of the Community which are binding on them.

6. Member States shall not participate in decisions with respect to a subject in which they do not possess the necessary competence.

. . .

REVISED TREATY OF CHAGUARAMAS
ESTABLISHING THE CARIBBEAN COMMUNITY
INCLUDING THE CARICOM
SINGLE MARKET AND ECONOMY
(05.07.2001)

. . .

Article 6
Objectives of the Community

The Community shall have the following objectives:
    (a) improved standards of living and work;
    (b) full employment of labour and other factors of production;
    (c) accelerated, coordinated and sustained economic development and convergence;
    (d) expansion of trade and economic relations with third States;
    (e) enhanced levels of international competitiveness;
    (f) organisation for increased production and productivity;
    (g) the achievement of a greater measure of economic leverage and effectiveness of Member States in dealing with third States, groups of States and entities of any description;
    (h) enhanced coordination of Member States' foreign and foreign economic policies;
    (i) enhanced functional cooperation, including -
        (i) more efficient operation of common services and activities for the benefit of its peoples;
        (ii) accelerated promotion of greater understanding among its peoples and the advancement of their social, cultural and technological development;
        (iii) intensified activities in areas such as health, education, transportation, telecommunications.

. . .

Chapter Two—Institutional Arrangements

Article 10
Organs of the Community

1. The principal Organs of the Community are:
   (a) the Conference of Heads of Government; and
   (b) the Community Council of Ministers which shall be the second highest organ.
2. In the performance of their functions, the principal Organs shall be assisted by the following Organs:
   (a) the Council for Finance and Planning (COFAP);
   (b) the Council for Trade and Economic Development (COTED);
   (c) the Council for Foreign and Community Relations (COFCOR); and
   (d) the Council for Human and Social Development.

Article 11
Composition of the Conference

1. The Conference of Heads of Government shall consist of the Heads of Government of the Member States.
2. Any Head of Government may designate a Minister or other person to represent him or her at any Meeting of the Conference.

Article 12
Functions and Powers of the Conference

1. The Conference shall be the supreme Organ of the Community.
   . . .

Article 13
The Community Council of Ministers

1. The Community Council shall consist of Ministers responsible for Community Affairs and any other Minister designated by the Member States in their absolute discretion.
2. The Community Council shall, in accordance with the policy directions established by the Conference, have primary responsibility for the development of Community strategic planning and coordination in the areas of economic integration, functional cooperation and external relations.
   . . .

Article 21
Institutions of the Community

The following entities established by or under the auspices of the Community shall be recognised as Institutions of the Community:

- Caribbean Disaster Emergency Response Agency (CDERA);
- Caribbean Meteorological Institute (CMI);
- Caribbean Meteorological Organisation (CMO);
- Caribbean Environmental Health Institute (CEHI);
- Caribbean Agricultural Research and Development Institute (CARDI);
- Caribbean Regional Centre for the Education and Training of Animal Health and Veterinary Public Health Assistants (REPAHA);
- Assembly of Caribbean Community Parliamentarians (ACCP);
- Caribbean Centre For Developmental Administration (CARICAD);
- Caribbean Food and Nutrition Institute (CFNI), and such other entities as may be designated by the Conference.

Article 22
Associate Institutions of the Community

The following entities with which the Community enjoys important functional relationships which contribute to the achievement of the objectives of the Community shall be recognised as Associate Institutions of the Community:

- Caribbean Development Bank (CDB);

- University of Guyana (UG);

- University of the West Indies (UWI);

- Caribbean Law Institute / Caribbean Law Institute Centre (CLI/CLIC);

- the Secretariat of the Organisation of Eastern Caribbean States; and such other entities as may be designated by the Conference.

Article 23
The Secretariat

1. The Secretariat shall be the principal administrative organ of the Community. The headquarters of the Community shall be located in Georgetown, Guyana.
2. The Secretariat shall comprise a Secretary-General and such other staff as the Community may require. In the recruitment of such staff, consideration shall be given to securing the highest standards of efficiency,

competence and integrity, bearing in mind the principle of equitable geographical distribution.

. . .

Article 26
The Consultative Process

1. In order to enhance the decision-making process in the Community, the Community Council, assisted by the Secretary-General, shall, in collaboration with competent authorities of the Member States, establish and maintain an efficient system of consultations at the national and regional levels.
2. The system of consultations shall be structured to ensure that determinations of Community Organs and the Legal Affairs Committee are adequately informed by relevant information inputs and are reinforced by consultations undertaken at successively lower levels of the decision-making process.

Article 27
Common Voting Procedures in Community Organs and Bodies

1. Subject to paragraph 2 of this Article, each Member State represented on Community Organs and Bodies shall have one vote. A simple majority of Member States shall constitute a quorum.
2. Member States whose contributions to the regular budget of the Community are in arrears for more than two years shall not have the right to vote except on matters relating to the CSME, but may otherwise participate in the deliberations of Community Organs and Bodies. The Conference may, nevertheless, permit such Member States to vote if it is satisfied that the failure to contribute is due to conditions beyond their control.
3. Decisions on procedural issues in Community Organs shall be reached by a simple majority of Member States.
4. Subject to the agreement of the Conference, a Member State may opt out of obligations arising from the decisions of competent Organs provided that the fundamental objectives of the Community, as laid down in the Treaty, are not prejudiced thereby.
5. Prior to taking decisions on any issue falling to be determined by Community Organs, the Secretariat shall bring to the attention of the meeting the financial implications of such decisions and any other matters which may be relevant.

6. Recommendations of Community Organs shall be made by a two-thirds majority of Member States and shall not be legally binding. Member States omitting to comply with recommendations shall inform the Secretariat in writing within six months stating the reasons for their non-compliance.

7. Subject to the relevant provisions of this Treaty, Community Organs and Bodies shall establish their rules of procedure.

Article 28
Voting in the Conference

1. Save as otherwise provided in this Treaty and subject to paragraph 2 of this Article and the relevant provisions of Article 27, the Conference shall take decisions by an affirmative vote of all its members and such decisions shall be binding.

2. For the purpose of this Article abstentions shall not be construed as impairing the validity of decisions of the Conference provided that the Member States constituting three-quarters of the membership of the Community vote in favour of such decisions.

3. Omission by a Member State to participate in the vote shall be deemed an abstention within the meaning of paragraph 2 of this Article.

4. Parties to a dispute or against which sanctions are being considered shall not have the right to vote on the issue falling to be determined.

Article 29
Voting in the Community Council and Ministerial Councils

1. Save as otherwise provided in this Treaty and subject to the provisions of this Article and Article 27, the Ministerial Councils shall take decisions by a qualified majority vote and such decisions shall be binding.

2. For the purposes of paragraph 1 of this Article a qualified majority vote means an affirmative vote of the Member States comprising no less than three-quarters of the membership of the Community.

3. Where issues have been determined to be of critical importance to the national wellbeing of a Member State, in accordance with paragraph 4 of this Article, such decisions shall be reached by an affirmative vote of all Member States.

4. Decisions that an issue is of critical importance to the national wellbeing of a Member State shall be reached by a two-thirds majority of the Member States.

5. For the purposes of paragraph 3 of this Article abstentions shall not be construed as impairing the validity of decisions required to be reached by unanimity provided that Member States constituting not less than three-quarters of the membership of the Community vote in favour of such decisions.

Chapter Three—Establishment, Services, Capital and Movement of Community Nationals

. . .

Article 31
Treatment of Monopolies

1. The Member States may determine that the public interest requires the exclusion or restriction of the right of establishment in any industry or in a particular sector of an industry.
2. Where such a determination has been made:
   (a) if the determination results in the continuation or establishment of a government monopoly, the Member State shall adopt appropriate measures to ensure that the monopoly does not discriminate between nationals of Member States, save as otherwise provided in this Treaty, and is subject to the agreed rules of competition established for Community economic enterprises;
   (b) if the determination results in the continuation or establishment of a private sector monopoly, the Member State shall, subject to the provisions of this Treaty, adopt appropriate measures to ensure that national treatment is accorded to nationals of other Member States in terms of participating in its operations.
   . . .

Article 42
Coordination of Foreign Exchange Policies and Exchange of Information

1. The Member States shall take such measures as are necessary to coordinate their foreign exchange policies in respect of the movement of capital between them and third States.
2. The Member States shall keep the competent authorities in other Member States informed of significant unusual movements of capital within their knowledge to and from third States.
   . . .

Article 45
Movement of Community Nationals

Member States commit themselves to the goal of free movement of their nationals within the Community.

Article 46
Movement of Skilled Community Nationals

1. Without prejudice to the rights recognised and agreed to be accorded by Member States in Articles 32, 33, 37, 38 and 40 among themselves and to Community nationals, Member States have agreed, and undertake as a first step towards achieving the goal set out in Article 45, to accord to the following categories of Community nationals the right to seek employment in their jurisdictions:

   (a) University graduates;
   (b) media workers;
   (c) sportspersons;
   (d) artistes; and
   (e) musicians,

   recognised as such by the competent authorities of the receiving Member States.

2. Member States shall establish appropriate legislative, administrative and procedural arrangements to:

   (a) facilitate the movement of skills within the contemplation of this Article;
   (b) provide for movement of Community nationals into and within their jurisdictions without harassment or the imposition of impediments, including:

      (i) the elimination of the requirement for passports for Community nationals travelling to their jurisdictions;
      (ii) the elimination of the requirement for work permits for Community nationals seeking approved employment in their jurisdictions;
      (iii) establishment of mechanisms for certifying and establishing equivalency of degrees and for accrediting institutions;
      (iv) harmonisation and transferability of social security benefits.

3. Nothing in this Treaty shall be construed as inhibiting Member States from according Community nationals unrestricted access to,

and movement within, their jurisdictions subject to such conditions as the public interest may require.

4. The Conference shall keep the provisions of this Article under review in order to:

    (a) enlarge, as appropriate, the classes of persons entitled to move and work freely in the Community; and

    (b) monitor and secure compliance therewith.

. . .

Article 54
Development of the Services Sector

1. COTED shall, in collaboration with the appropriate Councils, promote the development of the services sector in the Community in order to stimulate economic complementarities among, and accelerate economic development in, the Member States. In particular, COTED shall promote measures to achieve:

    (a) increased investment in services;

    (b) increased volume, value and range of trade in services within the Community and with third States;

    (c) competitiveness in the modes of delivering services; and

    (d) enhanced enterprise and infrastructural development, including that of micro and small service enterprises.

2. In order to achieve the objectives set out in paragraph 1, the Member States shall, through the appropriate Councils, collaborate in:

    (a) designing programmes for the development of human resources to achieve competitiveness in the provision of services;

    (b) establishing a regime of incentives for the development of and trade in services; and

    (c) adopting measures to promote the establishment of an appropriate institutional and administrative framework and, in collaboration with the Legal Affairs Committee, promote the establishment of the appropriate legal framework to support the services sector in the Community.

3. In the establishment of programmes and policies of the Community for the development of the services sector, the relevant Councils shall give priority to:

    (a) the efficient provision of infrastructural services including telecommunications, road, air, maritime and riverine transportation, statistical data generation and financial services;

(b) the development of capacity-enhancing services including education services, research and development services;

(c) the development of services which enhance cross-sector competitiveness;

(d) the facilitation of cross-border provision of services which enhance the competitiveness of the services sector; and

(e) the development of informatics and other knowledge-based services.

Article 55
Sustainable Tourism Development

1. The Community shall, in collaboration with competent international organisations, formulate proposals for sustainable tourism development. These proposals shall recognise the importance of the tourism sub-sector to the economic development of the Region, and the need to conserve its cultural and natural resources and to maintain a balance between a healthy ecology and economic development.

2. The programme for sustainable tourism development shall have the following objectives:

(a) an enhanced image for the Region as a tourist destination;

(b) a diversified tourism product of a consistently high quality;

(c) an expanded market-base;

(d) education programmes designed to ensure that appropriate practices are pursued by service-providers;

(e) linkages with other sectors in the economy;

(f) conservation of the natural and cultural resources of the Region through proper management; and

(g) appropriate infrastructure and other services in support of tourism, considering the natural and social carrying-capacity of the Member States.

. . .

Macro-Economic Policies

1. COFAP shall formulate proposals and adopt appropriate measures to promote a sound macro-economic environment in the Member States, consistent with their obligations under this Treaty and applicable international agreements.

2. COFAP shall, in collaboration with other competent Organs, promote economic development in the Member States through the development and application of convergent macroeconomic policies to ensure fiscal discipline, favourable balance-of-payments, stable currencies and moderate prices without prejudice to securing high levels of employment.

3. COFAP shall collaborate with COFCOR and COTED in coordinating:
   (a) the economic policies of the Member States; and
   (b) the positions and presentations of the Member States in all international economic, financial and trade meetings at which they are represented.

4. In support of the development of macro-economic policies, the Community shall provide for harmonisation of the output of the statistical services of the Member States.

   . . .

Article 80
Coordination of External Trade Policy

1. The Member States shall coordinate their trade policies with third States or groups of third States.
2. The Community shall pursue the negotiation of external trade and economic agreements on a joint basis in accordance with principles and mechanisms established by the Conference.
3. Bilateral agreements to be negotiated by Member States in pursuance of their national strategic interests shall:

   (a) be without prejudice to their obligations under the Treaty; and
   (b) prior to their conclusion, be subject to certification by the CARICOM Secretariat that the agreements do not prejudice or place at a disadvantage the position of other CARICOM States vis-à-vis the Treaty.

4. Where trade agreements involving tariff concessions are being negotiated, the prior approval of COTED shall be required.
5. Nothing in this Treaty shall preclude Belize from concluding arrangements with neighbouring economic groupings provided that treatment not less favourable than that accorded to third States within such groupings shall be accorded to the Member States of the Community, and that the arrangements make adequate provision to guard against the deflection of trade into the rest of CARICOM from the countries of such groupings through Belize.

   . . .

Article 82
Establishment of Common External Tariff

The Member States shall establish and maintain a common external tariff in respect of all goods which do not qualify for Community treatment in accordance with plans and schedules set out in relevant determinations of COTED.

Article 83
Operation of the Common External Tariff

1. Any alteration or suspension of the Common External Tariff on any item shall be decided by COTED.

2. Where:
   (a) a product is not being produced in the Community;
   (b) the quantity of the product being produced in the Community does not satisfy the demand of the Community; or
   (c) the quality of the product being produced in the Community is below the Community standard or a standard the use of which is authorised by COTED,

   COTED may decide to authorise the reduction or suspension of the Common External Tariff in respect of imports of that product subject to such terms and conditions as it may decide, provided that in no case shall the product imported from third States be accorded more favourable treatment than similar products produced in the Member States.

3. The authority referred to in paragraph 2 to suspend the Common External Tariff may be exercised by the Secretary-General on behalf of COTED during any period between meetings of COTED. Any exercise of such authority by the Secretary-General shall be reported to the next meeting of COTED.

4. Each Member State shall, for the purpose of administering the Common External Tariff, appoint a competent authority which shall be notified to COTED.

5. COTED shall continuously review the Common External Tariff, in whole or in part, to assess its impact on production and trade, as well as to secure its uniform implementation throughout the Community, in particular, by reducing the need for discretionary application in the day to day administration of the Tariff.

   . . .

Article 85
Export Promotion

1. COTED shall adopt appropriate measures for the promotion and export of goods and services.

2. In the implementation of measures to promote exports, COTED shall give consideration to:

   (a) the establishment and maintenance of effective trade information systems and services;

(b) the design and implementation of trade facilitation programmes including the conduct of market research and the organisation of trade missions;

(c) the coordination and support of the active participation of the Member States in international trade promotion fora, including trade fairs and exhibitions.

    . . .

Article 87

1. Save as otherwise provided in this Treaty, Member States shall not impose import duties on goods of Community origin.
2. Nothing in paragraph 1 of this Article shall be construed to extend to the imposition of non-discriminatory internal charges on any products or a substitute not produced in the importing Member State.
3. This Article does not apply to fees and similar charges commensurate with the cost of services rendered.
4. Nothing in paragraph 3 of this Article shall be construed to exclude from the application of paragraph 1 of this Article any tax or surtax of customs on any product or a substitute not produced in the importing State.

    . . .

Article 135
Implementation of Community Transport Policy

1. In order to achieve the objectives of the Community Transport Policy, COTED shall, in collaboration with other Organs of the Community as appropriate, promote, inter alia:

    (a) coordination of the national transport policies of the Member States;

    (b) the implementation of uniform regulations and procedures, consistent with standards and recommended practices, for the development of an efficient multi-modal transport system, particularly in respect of operations, safety, licensing and certification;

    (c) the development of required institutional, legal, technical, financial and administrative support for the balanced, sustainable development of the transport sector;

    (d) the establishment of measures:

       (i) to ensure that the development of the transport sector does not impact adversely on the environment of the Member States and, in particular, the Caribbean Sea;

(ii) for the acquisition and transfer of technology in the transport sector; and

(iii) for human resources development in accordance with Article 63;

(e) investment in the transport sector, including ancillary services supportive of the sector through, for example, joint ventures;

(f) the removal of obstacles to the provision of transport services by nationals of the Member States in accordance with the relevant provisions of Chapter Three.

2. COTED shall develop programmes to facilitate the achievement of the objectives set out in Article 134.

3. The Member States shall coordinate their actions in order to secure the best terms and conditions for the provision of transport services by service providers.

. . .

Article 136
Search and Rescue

1. COTED shall promote cooperation in air and maritime search and rescue operations in the Community, bearing in mind such machinery as may exist for the overall coordination of search and rescue services.

2. The Member States shall notify COTED of air and maritime equipment and facilities available for use in search and rescue operations.

3. The Member States shall collaborate with third States and competent international organisations in search and rescue operations.

Article 137
Intra-Community Transport Services

1. The Member States shall adopt uniform standards and recommended practices for the provision of transport services.

2. The Member States shall notify COTED of legislative, regulatory or administrative measures affecting the provision of transport services within their domestic jurisdictions where such measures deviate from uniform standards and recommended practices.

3. The Member States adversely affected by such regulatory or administrative measures may notify COTED of such adverse effects, and shall have recourse to the disputes settlement procedures provided in the Treaty.

. . .

Article 141
Special Status of the Caribbean Sea

The Member States shall cooperate in achieving international recognition for the Caribbean Sea as a Special Area requiring protection from the potentially harmful effects of the transit of nuclear and other hazardous wastes, dumping, pollution by oil or by any other substance carried by sea or wastes generated through the conduct of ship operations.

. . .

Article 147
Promotion of Investment

COFAP shall promote investment in disadvantaged countries by, inter alia, facilitating:

    (a) the establishment of joint ventures among nationals of disadvantaged countries as well as between nationals of disadvantaged countries and nationals of other Member States;

    (b) the establishment of joint ventures between nationals of disadvantaged countries and nationals of third countries;

    (c) investment for economic diversification including diversification of the agricultural sector;

    (d) research, development and the transfer of technology in the development of disadvantaged countries; and

    (e) capital flows from other Member States to disadvantaged countries through the conclusion of double taxation agreements and appropriate policy instruments.

    . . .

Article 158
The Development Fund

    1. There is hereby established a Development Fund for the purpose of providing financial or technical assistance to disadvantaged countries, regions and sectors.

    2. Subject to the provisions of this Article and relevant provisions of this Treaty, the Community Council, in collaboration with COFAP, shall:

        (a) determine the status, composition and functions of the Development Fund;

        (b) determine the contributions of the Member States to the Development Fund.

3. The Development Fund may accept subventions from public or private sector entities of the Member States or from other entities external to the Community. Subventions shall not be accepted nor applied by the Development Fund on conditions which discriminate against Member States, regions or sectors except in accordance with the provisions of this Treaty.

    . . .

Article 170
Implementation of Community Competition Policy

1. In order to achieve the objectives of the Community Competition Policy,
    (a) the Community shall:
        (i)   subject to Articles 164, 177, 178 and 179 of this Treaty, establish appropriate norms and institutional arrangements to prohibit and penalise anti-competitive business conduct; and
        (ii) establish and maintain information systems to enable enterprises and consumers to be kept informed about the operation of markets within the CSME;
    (b) the Member States shall:
        (i)   take the necessary legislative measures to ensure consistency and compliance with the rules of competition and provide penalties for anti-competitive business conduct;
        (ii) provide for the dissemination of relevant information to facilitate consumer choice;
        (iii) establish and maintain institutional arrangements and administrative procedures to enforce competition laws; and
        (iv) take effective measures to ensure access by nationals of other Member States to competent enforcement authorities including the courts on an equitable, transparent and non-discriminatory basis.
2. Every Member State shall establish and maintain a national competition authority for the purpose of facilitating the implementation of the rules of competition.
3. Every Member State shall require its national competition authority to:
    (a) cooperate with the Commission in achieving compliance with the rules of competition;
    (b) investigate any allegations of anti-competitive business conduct referred to the authority by the Commission or another Member State;

(c) cooperate with other national competition authorities in the detection and prevention of anti-competitive business conduct, and the exchange of information relating to such conduct.

4. Nothing in this Article shall be construed as requiring a Member State to disclose confidential information, the disclosure of which would be prejudicial to the public interest or to the legitimate commercial interests of enterprises, public or private. Confidential or proprietary information disclosed in the course of an investigation shall be treated on the same basis as that on which it was provided.

5. Within 24 months of the entry into force of this Treaty, the Member States shall notify COTED of existing legislation, agreements and administrative practices inconsistent with the provisions of this Chapter. Within 36 months of entry into force of this Treaty, COTED shall establish a programme providing for the repeal of such legislation, and termination of agreements and administrative practices.

Article 171
Establishment of the Competition Commission

For the purposes of implementation of the Community Competition Policy, there is hereby established a Competition Commission (hereinafter called "the Commission") having the composition, functions and powers hereinafter set forth.

. . .

Article 181
De Minimis Rule

The Commission may exempt from the provisions of this Part any business conduct referred to it if it considers that the impact of such conduct on competition and trade in the CSME is minimal.

. . .

Accession

1. After the entry into force of this Treaty a State or Territory of the Caribbean may, if Conference so determines, accede to this Treaty.

2. Accession shall be on such terms and conditions as Conference decides and shall take effect one month following the deposit of the instrument of accession with the Secretariat.

. . .

THE ROSE HALL DECLARATION ON "REGIONAL GOVERNANCE AND INTEGRATED DEVELOPMENT" (04.07.2003)

. . .

Mindful of the areas in which we have not yet achieved all the goals agreed for the integration of our economies and the betterment of the lives of the people of our region;

Recognising that the current geopolitical and geostrategic environment is significantly different from that which existed at the time of the establishment of the Community in 1973;

. . .

Recognising that the process of globalisation and economic liberalisation continues to pose significant challenges for the economically fragile and vulnerable member states of the Community as they seek to adjust to a new global trading regime based on reciprocity and open competition;

Determined nevertheless, that we shall go forward with resolution toward realisation of the hopes and expectations of the people of our region and in fulfilment of the aims, purposes, objectives and undertakings of the Revised Treaty of Chaguaramas;

. . .

A. Regional Governance

. . .

1. The reaffirmation that CARICOM is a Community of Sovereign States, and of Territories able and willing to exercise the rights and assume the obligations of membership of the Community, and that the deepening of regional integration will proceed in this political and juridical context.

2. The development of a system of mature regionalism in which critical policy decisions of the Community taken by Heads of Government, or by other Organs of the Community, will have the force of law throughout the Region as a result of the operation of domestic legislation and the Treaty of Chaguaramas appropriately revised, and the authority of the Caribbean Court of Justice in its original jurisdiction—taking into account the constitutional provisions of member states.

3. The establishment of a CARICOM Commission or other executive mechanism, whose purpose will be to facilitate the deepening of regional

integration in the areas of responsibility specified in the next following paragraph. The Commission's function will be to exercise full-time executive responsibility for furthering implementation of Community decisions in such areas as well as to initiate proposals for Community action in any such area.

4. The functions of the Commission will relate to the CARICOM Single Market and Economy and such other areas of the integration process as the Conference of Heads may from time to time determine.

5. In the exercise of its responsibilities the Commission will be accountable to the Conference of Heads of Government and will be responsive to the authority of other Organs of the Community within their areas of competence.

6. The adoption of the principle of automatic resource transfers for the financing of Community institutions, certainly on the establishment of any new tier of governance.

7. The reform of the CARICOM Secretariat to enhance its effectiveness as the administrative and technocratic arm of CARICOM.

8. The recognition that within this framework, it is both legitimate and feasible for a group or groups of CARICOM Member States to forge such closer links among themselves as they collectively consider appropriate.

9. The strengthening of the role of the Assembly of Caribbean Community Parliamentarians in the enhancement of regional integration.

We have also agreed that the Expert Group of Heads of Government, assisted by a technical group, be entrusted with the further task of elaborating these proposals for presentation to a Special Meeting of the Conference later this year, dedicated to taking decisions on them.

We have further agreed to a review of the functioning of the Organs of the Community in order to identify possibilities for rationalisation of their operation including the decentralisation of decision-making.

B. Integrated Development

That, with a view to deepening the integration process in the context of the provisions of the Revised Treaty of Chaguaramas, and the realities of the international economic environment, we have:

1. Agreed to accelerate the establishment of the CARICOM Single Market and Economy, and in that context to promote macro-economic

convergence, the unification of capital and financial markets, and the early unrestricted movement of people within CARICOM.

2. Agreed that in order to stimulate the expansion of output and employment within the framework of the CARICOM Single Market and Economy, a high level expert group be appointed, drawn from the public and private sectors, the labour movement, civil society, the CARICOM and OECS Secretariats, the CDB and the UWI to identify the opportunities and the required institutional and policy measures to promote integrated production in the Community, especially through private sector investment.

3. Reiterated our commitment to collaborate more effectively to exploit the agricultural potential of the Community through, inter alia, the stimulation of increased production, the strengthening of joint research activities, the pursuit within a regional context of additional processing of agricultural raw materials, including sugar in particular, the promotion of increased agricultural trade intra-regionally and extra-regionally and to work towards greater food security within the region.

4. Agreed, in recognition of the critical role played by tourism in the economies of the region, that we will intensify the pursuit of strategies aimed at the sustainable development of the sector. These strategies should include programmes for mobilizing resources and the enhancement of the efficiency of national and regional public and private sector institutions in designing and implementing tourism development policies and programmes.

5. Resolved to pay close attention and take appropriate measures to increase the efficiency of public and private sector investment, so that available investable resources can have maximum impact on poverty alleviation and employment creation.

6. Agreed that in order to effectively protect the Caribbean Sea and promote the sustainable use of its resources Member States will ensure the successful functioning of the recently established Caribbean Regional Fisheries Mechanism and will in due course consider investing it with the authority to administer a comprehensive Common Fisheries Regime.

7. Agreed that a multifaceted programme, including enhanced communication and information flows, be developed and implemented to reinforce and strengthen the sense of common identity and mutual understanding that bind CARICOM people together, and to encourage all feasible initiatives to exploit the economic potential that is inherent in the cultural vitality of our people.

8. Emphasised the importance of CARIFESTA VIII which will be held in Suriname in August 2003 and call upon the people of the region to support the event in order to ensure its success.

9. Agreed further, that the occasion of Cricket World Cup 2007 in the Caribbean be used as a vehicle to showcase Caribbean life and culture.

10. Reaffirmed, in keeping with the Nassau Declaration on Health (2001), our commitment to promote the health and well-being of the people of the Community in recognition of the principle that "the health of the region is the wealth of the region." In this context, special emphasis will be placed on supporting the efforts of the Pan Caribbean Partnership in its fight against HIV/AIDS.

11. Agreed to sustain and seek new ways to improve the dialogue with the private sector, labour and civil society in advancing the objectives of the integration movement.

12. Emphasised the need to intensify efforts to promote human and social development through, inter alia, appropriate education and training in order to improve the overall well being of the people of the Community and to establish the conditions for the creation of a knowledge-based society capable of competing effectively in the new global environment.

13. Agreed that the initiatives we have taken to engage in joint external trade negotiations in relation to the WTO, FTAA and the ACP-EU Cotonou Agreement must be consolidated, and that we shall address attention to building similar joint external negotiating capacity in other aspects of our engagement with the international system.

14. Resolved that Member Governments and the Community Organs work with the public and private sectors and with civil society to strengthen and broaden cultural, social and economic linkages with the West Indian Diaspora, which is an integral part of the Caribbean Community.

15. Agreed that Member States should work towards the strengthening and enlargement of the Caribbean Development Bank, in order to secure the mobilisation of adequate financing to support the economic and social transformation of the region.

16. Agreed that the work of the Regional Task Force on Crime and Security and our recent decisions on the subject be used as a basis for the creation of permanent institutional arrangements for the collective enhancement of security and control of crime within the region.

17. Resolved to create opportunities for the political opposition in Member States to play a more active role in the development of the

Community within a framework of respect for democratic principles and in this context called upon the opposition parties to fully embrace these opportunities.

18. Resolved also that the Charter of Civil Society should be actively applied as an instrument for strengthening democratic governance in the Community.

C. The Community and the International System

That, with a view to establishing a respected place for our countries in the international system, we have:

1. Recognised that, in addition to promoting closer regional integration, the Member States of the Community need to maintain and enhance alliances with other developing countries in advancing their economic interests.
2. Reaffirmed therefore, the need to strengthen relations with other countries in the wider Caribbean, Latin America, Africa, Asia and the Pacific, and in particular to contribute to increased solidarity within the Non-Aligned Movement and the Group of 77.
3. Reiterated the importance of recognising Small Island Developing States (SIDS) as a special and particular grouping in the international system and commit ourselves to the pursuance of appropriate arrangements and measures to facilitate their equitable and beneficial participation in that system.
4. Resolved to work towards a sustained improvement in our relations with developed countries on the basis of mutual respect and mutually beneficial trade and economic arrangements.
5. Reaffirmed our commitment to promote the enhancement of the relevance of the policies and programmes applied by the International Financial Institutions to assist developing countries, including the Member States of our Community
6. Reaffirmed also, our commitment to the provisions of the Charter of the United Nations and to the principles of international law, as well as to the reform of the UN, particularly the Security Council, in order to achieve more equitable representation of the Member States in that Body.
7. Agreed that we will work within the framework of the United Nations to promote multilateralism as the guiding principle of international relations.

. . .

SOUTHERN COMMON MARKET (MERCOSUR)

The Southern Common Market (Mercado Común del Sur, MERCOSUR; MERCOSUL in Portuguese) was founded in 1991 by Argentina, Brazil, Paraguay, and Uruguay upon signing the Treaty of Asuncion. Originally it was meant to create a common market and a customs union between the participating countries. Grown out of the experiences of economic cooperation between Brazil and Argentina since the mid 1980s, MERCOSUR proceeded from their sectoral agreements to wide-ranging liberalization of trade relations. In 1988, Brazil had import tariffs of 51 percent and Argentina of 30 percent. Trade liberalization thus became the first priority in strengthening the partners involved. The Protocol of Ouro Preto of 1994 added much to the institutional structure of MERCOSUR. A transition phase was set into motion with the goal of creating a common market. During the 1990s alone, intra-regional trade jumped from $4.6 billion (US) to $20.4 billion, while foreign investment grew from $22.8 billion to $32.5 billion. Since the mid 1990s, most intra-regional trade has been free of tariffs; in some sensitive areas this was realized by 2001.

In 1996, MERCOSUR signed treaties establishing free trade areas with Chile and Bolivia, which became associate members of MERCOSUR. In 2003 Peru became an associated member of MERCOSUR, as did Ecuador and Colombia in 2004. During the same period, MERCOSUR also established a common mechanism for political consultations. Since 2002, like-minded new presidents in Argentina and Brazil (Kirchner and Lula) have helped to rekindle the idea of institutional advancements in MERCOSUR. Initiatives for a common parliament and the establishment of a Dispute Settlement Court under the Protocol of Olivos went hand in hand with a growing understanding that integration was the only forward-looking strategy to overcome economic and financial constraints to development. The weak institutionalization of MERCOSUR remains the Achilles' heel of the project, although awareness about this deficit is rising in MERCOSUR—not least in light of the weak public legitimacy of national political institutions.

Following the 1999 devaluation in Brazil and the 2002 Argentinian crash, intra-regional trade in MERCOSUR fell by almost 50 percent. Yet since 1999 the European Union has been negotiating an Interregional Association Agreement with MERCOSUR. Though negotiations remain unfinished to date, this planned biregional relationship reflects more than the increasing importance of EU-MERCOSUR trade and investment relations. MERCOSUR, a market with 217 million inhabitants, represents a 2.4 percent share of EU total imports, while the EU export to MERCOSUR is 1.8 percent of total EU exports. EU direct investment in MERCOSUR has increased since the mid 1990s, making the EU the largest investor in MERCOSUR, as it is in all of Latin America, except for Central America. The EU is also the largest donor of developmental aid to the region and to Latin America in general.

Following the US, the EU, and Japan, MERCOSUR is the fourth largest economy in the world and has gained the image of the most advanced regional integration scheme in Latin America, although this is certainly debatable when compared with the structures of CAN. MERCOSUR was as much a response to the American project of NAFTA as it was an echo of the success of regional integration in Europe. The relationship between MERCOSUR and the US-sponsored Free Trade Zone of the Americas remains ambivalent.

MERCOSUR started as an intergovernmental concept and has remained so until now. Nevertheless, it has begun to develop a legal code comparable to the acquis communautaire of the European Union. The original Treaty of Asuncion included the establishment of common external tariffs. The common market was supposed to be finalized in 1995, but it remains incomplete to this day. MERCOSUR has gained the reputation of an unfinished customs union and a free trade zone. In 2005, it took the highly ambivalent step of including Venezuela, under its overly nationalistic and populist President Hugo Chávez, as a new MERCOSUR member state. This may hamper MERCOSUR's ability to deepen solid integration and threatens to limit its global credibility, should MERCOSUR turn into a forum for incessant anti-American rhetoric.

The Common Market Council (Consejo del Mercado Común) is its highest body, consisting of the foreign and economic ministers of MERCOSUR member states. The Council meets once a year in the presence of the heads of state of MERCOSUR member states. The presidency of MERCOSUR rotates and is coordinated by the foreign minister in charge. The Protocol of Ouro Preto specified the competencies of the existing organs and added new ones to MERCOSUR: most notable are the Commerce Commission, the Common Parliamentary Commission, and the Consultative Forum for Economic and Social Affairs. A Secretariat has been established in Montevideo that remains largely technical. A MERCOSUR Court of Justice has been established in Asuncion, for the time being projecting more goodwill than legal power.

Only lately has MERCOSUR been involved in the process of deepening its structures. The most promising step has been the establishment of a MERCOSUR Parliament in December 2005. Its first session was held in December 2006. The MERCOSUR Parliament will have to increase its competencies if it wants to be taken seriously. Plans are being laid for the simultaneous direct election of the MERCOSUR Parliament by all MERCOSUR citizens, which is to take place before 2015. The possibility of a common currency—the "merco-peso"—and the need to improve coordination of macroeconomic policies have been debated in the region. Whether or not the customs union and the incomplete common market will advance, through norm standardization and legislative measures, into a comprehensive Single Market remains to be seen. Much will depend upon the political will generated in the member states of MERCOSUR, notably Brazil and Argentina.

In spite of its shortcomings, MERCOSUR has also begun to "discover" the relevance of foreign and security policy to building regional integration. Joint military maneuvers between Argentina and Brazil and meetings of the chiefs of staff of both countries have taken place, but they are still "light-years" away from the European stage of a Common Foreign and Security Policy. Still, after 150 years of suspicion between Argentina and Brazil, and in the context of the history of Latin America, these efforts constitute a promising step toward understanding the meaning and usefulness of regional cooperation. The end of military dictatorships in both countries, the decrease in power and prestige of the armed forces, and the return to civilian rule in all MERCOSUR member states has been a critical precondition for enhancing the potential of MERCO-SUR integration. The continuous backing of MERCOSUR by the European Union, as well as the EU's resistance to the hasty conclusion of a biregional association agreement, forces MERCOSUR to better implement the original goals of the project and at the same time to enhance its focus on "real," as well as political and supranational, integration. In 2005, intra-regional trade in MERCOSUR again reached the level of 1998. But the new wave of economic dynamism at the end of the first decade of the twenty-first century has not facilitated an immediate recognition of the value added by supranational solutions in MERCOSUR.

Southern Common Market (MERCOSUR) Agreement (Treaty of Asuncion) (26.03.1991)

. . .

Chapter I—Purposes, Principles and Instruments

Article I

The Member States hereby decide to establish a common market, which shall be in place by 31 December 1994 and shall be called the "Common Market of the Southern Cone" (MERCOSUR).

This common market shall involve:

The free movement of goods, services and factors of production between countries through, inter alia, the elimination of customs duties and non-tariff restrictions on the movement of goods, and any other equivalent measures;

The establishment of a common external tariff and the adoption of a common trade policy in relation to third States or groups of States, and the coordination of positions in regional and international economic and commercial forums;

The coordination of macroeconomic and sectoral policies between the Member States in the areas of foreign trade, agriculture, industry, fiscal and monetary matters, foreign exchange and capital, services, customs, transport and communications and any other areas that may be agreed upon, in order to ensure proper competition between the Member States;

The commitment by Member States to harmonize their legislation in the relevant areas in order to strengthen the integration process.

Article 2

The common market shall be based on reciprocity of rights and obligations between the Member States.

. . .

Article 5

During the transition period, the main instruments for putting in place the common market shall be:

(a) A trade liberalization programme, which shall consist of progressive, linear and automatic tariff reductions accompanied by the elimination of non-tariff restrictions or equivalent measures, as well as any other restrictions on trade between the Member States, with a view to arriving at a zero tariff and no non-tariff restrictions for the entire tariff area by 31 December 1994;

(b) The coordination of macroeconomic policies, which shall be carried out gradually and in parallel with the programmes for the reduction of tariffs and the elimination of non-tariff restrictions referred to in the preceding paragraph;

(c) A common external tariff which encourages the foreign competitiveness of the Member States;

(d) The adoption of sectoral agreements in order to optimize the use and mobility of factors of production and to achieve efficient scales of operation.

. . .

Article 7

In the area of taxes, charges and other internal duties, products originating in the territory of one Member State shall enjoy, in the other Member States, the same treatment as domestically produced products.

Article 8

The Member States undertake to abide by commitments made prior to the date of signing of this Treaty, including agreements signed in the framework of the Latin American Integration Association (ALADI), and to coordinate their positions in any external trade negotiations they may undertake during the transitional period. To that end:

(a) They shall avoid affecting the interests of the Member States in any trade negotiations they may conduct among themselves up to 31 December 1994;

(b) They shall avoid affecting the interests of the other Member States or the aims of the common market in any agreements they may conclude with other member coutries of the Latin American Integration Association during the transition period;

(c) They shall consult among themselves whenever negotiating comprehensive tariff reduction schemes for the formation of free trade areas with other member countries of the Latin American Integration Association;

(d) They shall extend automatically to the other Member States any advantage, favour, exemption, immunity or privilege granted to a product originating in or destined for third countries which are not members of the Latin American Integration Association.

Chapter II—Organizational Structure

Article 9

The administration and implementation of this Treaty, and of any specific agreements or decisions adopted during the transition period within the legal framework established thereby, shall be entrusted to the following organs:

(a) The Council of the Common Market

(b) The Common Market Group

Article 10

The Council shall be the highest organ of the common market, with responsibility for its political leadership and for decision-making to ensure compliance with the objectives and time-limits set for the final establishment of the common market.

Article 11

The Council shall consist of the Ministers for Foreign Affairs and the Ministers of the Economy of the Member States.

It shall meet whenever its members deem appropriate, and at least once a year with the participation of the Presidents of the Member States.

Article 12

The presidency of the Council shall rotate among the Member States, in alphabetical order, for periods of six months.

Meetings of the Council shall be coordinated by the Minister for Foreign Affairs, and other ministers or ministerial authorities may be invited to participate in them.

Article 13

The Common Market Group shall be the executive organ of the common market and shall be coordinated by the Ministries of Foreign Affairs.

The Common Market Group shall have powers of initiative. Its duties shall be the following:

- to monitor compliance with the Treaty;
- to take the necessary steps to enforce decisions adopted by the Council;
- to propose specific measures for applying the trade liberalization programme, coordinating macroeconomic policies and negotiating agreements with third parties;
- to draw up programmes of work to ensure progress towards the formation of the common market.

The Common Market Group may set up whatever working groups are needed for it to perform its duties. To start with, it shall have the working groups mentioned in Annex V.

The Common Market Group shall draw up its own rules of procedure within 60 days of its establishment.

Article 14

The Common Market Group shall consist of four members and four alternates for each country, representing the following public bodies:

- Ministry of Foreign Affairs;
- Ministry of Economy or its equivalent (areas of industry, foreign trade and/or economic coordination);
- Central Bank.

In drafting and proposing specific measures as part of its work up to 31 December 1994, the Common Market Group may, whenever it deems appropriate, call on representatives of other government agencies or the private sector.

Article 15

The Common Market Group shall have an administrative secretariat whose main functions shall be to keep the Group's documents and report on its activities. It shall be headquartered in the city of Montevideo.

. . .

Article 18

Prior to the establishment of the common market on 31 December 1994, the Member States shall convene a special meeting to determine the final institutional structure of the administrative organs of the common market, as well as the specific powers of each organ and its decision-making procedures.

. . .

Chapter IV—Accession

Article 20

This Treaty shall be open to accession, through negotiation, by other countries of the Latin American Integration Association; their applications may be considered by the Member States once this Treaty has been in force for five years.

Notwithstanding the above, applications made by countries of the Latin American Integration Association who do not belong to subregional integration schemes or an extraregional association may be considered before the date specified.

Approval of applications shall require the unanimous decision of the Member States.

Chapter V—Denunciation

Article 21

Any Member State wishing to withdraw from this Treaty shall inform the other Member States of its intention expressly and formally and shall submit the document of denunciation within 60 days to the Ministry of Foreign Affairs of the Republic of Paraguay, which shall distribute it to the other Member States.

Article 22

Once the denunciation has been formalized, those rights and obligations of the denouncing State deriving from its status as a Member State shall cease, while those relating to the liberalization programme under this Treaty and any other aspect to which the Member States, together with the denouncing State, may agree within the 60 days following the formalization of the denunciation shall continue. The latter rights and obligations of the denouncing Member State shall remain in force for a period of two years from the date of the above-mentioned formalization.

Chapter VI—General Provisions

Article 23

This Treaty shall be called the "Treaty of Asuncion."

Article 24

In order to facilitate progress towards the formation of the common market, a Joint Parliamentary Commission of MERCOSUR shall be established. The executive branches of the Member States shall keep their respective legislative branches informed of the progress of the common market established by this Treaty.

. . .

SOUTHERN COMMON MARKET—
PROTOCOL OF OURO PRETO (17.12.1994)

. . .

Aware of the importance of the progress made and of the introduction of the customs union as a stage in the establishment of a common market,

. . .

Chapter I—Structure of MERCOSUR

Article 1

The institutional structure of MERCOSUR shall comprise the following organs:

1. The Council of the Common Market (CCM);
2. The Common Market Group (CMG);
3. The MERCOSUR Trade Commission (MTC);
4. The Joint Parliamentary Commission (JPC);
5. The Economic-Social Consultative Forum (ESCF);
6. The MERCOSUR Administrative Secretariat (MAS).

Sole paragraph—Auxiliary organs necessary to attain the objectives of the integration process may be established, under the terms of this Protocol.

Article 2

The following are inter-governmental organs with decision-making powers: the Council of the Common Market, the Common Market Group and the MERCO-SUR Trade Commission.

Section I—Council of the Common Market

Article 3

The Council of the Common Market is the highest organ of MERCOSUR, with responsibility for the political leadership of the integration process and for making the decisions necessary to ensure the achievement of the objectives defined by the Treaty of Asuncion and the final establishment of the common market.

Article 4

The Council of the Common Market shall consist of the Ministers for Foreign Affairs and the Ministers of the Economy of the Member States, or their equivalents.

Article 5

The Presidency of the Council of the Common Market shall be rotated among the Member States, in alphabetical order, for periods of six months.

Article 6

The Council of the Common Market shall meet whenever it deems appropriate, and at least once every six months, with the participation of the Presidents of the Member States.

Article 7

The meetings of the Council of the Common Market shall be coordinated by the Ministers for Foreign Affairs and other ministers or ministerial authorities may be invited to participate.

Article 8

The following are duties and functions of the Council of the Common Market:

1. To supervise the implementation of the Treaty of Asuncion, its protocols, and agreements signed within its context;
2. To formulate policies and promote the measures necessary to build the common market;
3. To assume the legal personality of MERCOSUR;
4. To negotiate and sign agreements, on behalf of MERCOSUR, with third countries, groups of countries and international organisations. These functions may be delegated, by express mandate, to the Common Market Group under the conditions laid down in paragraph VII of Article 14;
5. To rule on proposals submitted to it by the Common Market Group;
6. To arrange meetings of ministers and rule on agreements which those meetings refer to it;
7. To establish the organs it considers appropriate, and to modify or abolish them;

8. To clarify, when it considers necessary, the substance and scope of its decisions;
9. To appoint the Director of the MERCOSUR Administrative Secretariat;
10. To adopt financial and budgetary decisions;
11. To approve the rules of procedure of the Common Market Group.

Article 9

The rulings of the Council of the Common Market shall take the form of Decisions which shall be binding upon the Member States.

Section II — The Common Market Group

Article 10

The Common Market Group is the executive organ of MERCOSUR.

Article 11

The Common Market Group shall consist of four members and four alternates for each country, appointed by their respective governments, who must include representatives of the Ministries of Foreign Affairs, the Ministries of the Economy (or their equivalents) and the Central Banks. The Common Market Group shall be coordinated by the Ministries of Foreign Affairs.

Article 12

When drafting and proposing specific measures in the course of doing its work, the Common Market Group may, whenever it deems appropriate, call on representatives of other organs of government or of the institutional structure of MERCOSUR.

Article 13

The Common Market Group shall hold ordinary or extraordinary meetings, as often as necessary, in accordance with the terms of its rules of procedure.

Article 14

The following are duties and functions of the Common Market Group:

1. To monitor, within the limits of its competence, compliance with the Treaty of Asuncion, its Protocols, and agreements signed within its framework;
2. To propose draft Decisions to the Council of the Common Market;
3. To take the measures necessary to enforce the Decisions adopted by the Council of the Common Market;
4. To draw up programmes of work to ensure progress towards the establishment of the common market;
5. To establish, modify or abolish organs such as working groups and special meetings for the purpose of achieving its objectives;
6. To express its views on any proposals or recommendations submitted to it by other MERCOSUR organs within their sphere of competence;
7. To negotiate, with the participation of representatives of all the Member States, when expressly so delegated by the Council of the Common Market and within the limits laid down in special mandates granted for that purpose, agreements on behalf of MERCOSUR with third countries, groups of countries and international organisations. When so mandated, the Common Market Group shall sign the aforementioned agreements. When so authorised by the Council of the Common Market, the Common Market Group may delegate these powers to the MERCOSUR Trade Commission;
8. To approve the budget and the annual statement of accounts presented by the MERCOSUR Administrative Secretariat;
9. To adopt financial and budgetary Resolutions based on the guidelines laid down by the Council;
10. To submit its rules of procedure to the Council of the Common Market;
11. To organise the meetings of the Council of the Common Market and to prepare the reports and studies requested by the latter;
12. To choose the Director of the MERCOSUR Administrative Secretariat;
13. To supervise the activities of the MERCOSUR Administrative Secretariat;
14. To approve the rules of procedure of the Trade Commission and the Economic-Social Consultative Forum.

Article 15

The decisions of the Common Market Group shall take the form of Resolutions which shall be binding upon the Member States.

. . .

Section IV — The Joint Parliamentary Commission

Article 22

The Joint Parliamentary Commission is the organ representing the parliaments of the Member States within MERCOSUR.

Article 23

The Joint Parliamentary Commission shall consist of equal numbers of members of parliament representing the Member States.

Article 24

The members of the Joint Parliamentary Commission shall be appointed by the respective national parliaments, in accordance with their internal procedures.

Article 25

The Joint Parliamentary Commission shall endeavour to speed up the corresponding internal procedures in the Member States in order to ensure the prompt entry into force of the decisions taken by the MERCOSUR organs provided for in Article 2 of this Protocol. Similarly, it shall assist with the harmonisation of legislations, as required to advance the integration process. When necessary, the Council shall request the Joint Parliamentary Commission to examine priority issues.

Article 26

The Joint Parliamentary Commission shall submit Recommendations to the Council of the Common Market through the Common Market Group.

Article 27

The Joint Parliamentary Commission shall adopt its rules of procedure.

Section V — The Economic-Social Consultative Forum

Article 28

The Economic-Social Consultative Forum is the organ representing the economic and social sectors and shall consist of equal numbers of representatives from each Member State.

Article 29

The Economic-Social Consultative Forum shall have a consultative function and shall express its views in the form of Recommendations to the Common Market Group.

Article 30

The Economic-Social Consultative Forum shall submit its rules of procedure to the Common Market Group, for approval.

Section VI—The MERCOSUR Administrative Secretariat

Article 31

MERCOSUR shall have an Administrative Secretariat to provide operational support. The MERCOSUR Administrative Secretariat shall be responsible for providing services to the other MERCOSUR organs and shall be headquartered in the city of Montevideo.

Article 32

The MERCOSUR Administrative Secretariat shall carry out the following activities:

1. Serve as the official archive for MERCOSUR documentation;
2. Publish and circulate the decisions adopted within the framework of MERCOSUR. In this context, it shall;
   i. Make, in coordination with the Member States, authentic translations in Spanish and Portuguese of all the decisions adopted by the organs of the MERCOSUR institutional structure, in accordance with the provisions of Article 39;
   ii. Publish the MERCOSUR official journal.
3. Organise the logistical aspects of the meetings of the Council of the Common Market, the Common Market Group and the MERCOSUR Trade Commission and, as far as possible, the other MERCOSUR organs, when those meetings are held at its headquarters. In the case of meetings held outside its headquarters, the MERCOSUR Administrative Secretariat shall provide support for the State in which the meeting is held;
4. Regularly inform the Member States about the measures taken by each country to incorporate in its legal system the decisions adopted by the MERCOSUR organs provided for in Article 2 of this Protocol;
5. Compile national lists of arbitrators and experts, and perform other tasks defined in the Brasilia Protocol of 17 December 1991;
6. Perform tasks requested by the Council of the Common Market, the Common Market Group and the MERCOSUR Trade Commission;

7. Draw up its draft budget and, once this has been approved by the Common Market Group, do everything necessary to ensure its proper implementation;
8. Submit its statement of accounts annually to the Common Market Group, together with a report on its activities.

. . .

Chapter II—Legal Personality

Article 34

MERCOSUR shall possess legal personality of international law.

. . .

Chapter III—Decision-Making System

Article 37

The decisions of the MERCOSUR organs shall be taken by consensus and in the presence of all the Member States.

. . .

Chapter V—Legal Sources of MERCOSUR

Article 41

The legal sources of MERCOSUR are:
1. The Treaty of Asuncion, its protocols and the additional or supplementary instruments;
2. The agreements concluded within the framework of the Treaty of Asuncion and its protocols;
3. The Decisions of the Council of the Common Market, the Resolutions of the Common Market Group and the Directives of the MERCOSUR Trade Commission adopted since the entry into force of the Treaty of Asuncion.

Article 42

The decisions adopted by the MERCOSUR organs provided for in Article 2 of this Protocol shall be binding and, when necessary, must be incorporated in the domestic legal systems in accordance with the procedures provided for in each country's legislation.

Chapter VI—Dispute Settlement System

Article 43

Disputes which arise between the Member States concerning the interpretation, application or non-fulfilment of the provisions of the Treaty of Asuncion and the agreements concluded within its framework or of Decisions of the Council of the Common Market, Resolutions of the Common Market Group and Directives of the MERCOSUR Trade Commission shall be subject to the settlement procedures laid down in the Brasilia Protocol of 17 December 1991.

Sole paragraph. The Directives of the MERCOSUR Trade Commission are also incorporated in Articles 19 and 25 of the Brasilia Protocol.

. . .

Chapter VII—Budget

Article 45

The MERCOSUR Administrative Secretariat shall have a budget to cover its operating expenses and the expenses authorised by the Common Market Group. This budget shall be funded by equal contributions from the Member States.

. . .

Chapter IX—Review

Article 47

When they consider it opportune, the Member States shall convene a diplomatic conference for the purpose of reviewing the institutional structure of MERCOSUR established by the present Protocol and the specific functions of each of its organs.

. . .

THE PROTOCOL OF OLIVOS (18.02.2002)

. . .

Chapter I—Disputes Between Member States

Article 1
Scope of application

1. Any disputes between the Member States regarding the interpretation, application or breach of the Treaty of Asuncion, the Protocol of Ouro Preto, the protocols and agreements executed within the framework of the Treaty of Asuncion, the Decisions of the Common Market Council, the Resolutions of the Common Market Group and the Instructions of the MERCOSUR Trade Commission will be subject to the procedures established in this Protocol.

2. Disputes falling within the scope of application of this Protocol that may also be referred to the dispute settlement system of the World Trade Organisation or other preferential trade systems that the MERCOSUR Member States may have entered into, may be referred to one forum or the other, as decided by the requesting party. Provided, however, that the parties to the dispute may jointly agree on a forum.

   Once a dispute settlement procedure pursuant to the preceding paragraph has begun, none of the parties may request the use of the mechanisms established in the other fora, as defined by article 14 of this Protocol.

   Notwithstanding, in connection with the same subject matter, the following in the framework of what has been established in this section, the Common Market Council shall regulate on all aspects related to the choice of forum.

Chapter II—Mechanisms Related To Technical Issues

Article 2
Creating the Mechanisms

1. When deemed necessary, accelerated mechanisms may be established to settle disputes between Member States on technical aspects regulated in common trade policy instruments.

2. The rules of operation, scope of such mechanisms and the nature of the decisions issuing from them shall be defined and approved by a decision of the Common Market Council.

Chapter III—Consultative Opinions

Article 3
Request system

The Common Market Council may establish mechanisms related to the requests for consultative opinions made to the Permanent Review Court and define their scope and procedures.

Chapter IV—Direct Negotiations

Article 4
Negotiations

The States involved in a dispute shall first endeavour to settle it through direct negotiations.

Article 5
Procedure and applicable term

1. Direct negotiations may not exceed, unless otherwise agreed by the parties in the dispute, a fifteen (15) day period as from the date on which one of them communicated to the other the decision to start the dispute settlement proceedings.
2. The States participating in the dispute shall inform the Common Market Group, through the Administrative Secretariat of MERCOSUR, of the steps taken during the negotiations and the results obtained.

Chapter V—Involvement of the Common Market Group

Article 6
Optional procedure before the GMC

1. If no agreement is reached through direct negotiations or if the dispute is settled only in part, any of the States involved in the dispute may directly initiate the arbitration proceedings established in Chapter VI.
2. In addition to the provision contained in the preceding paragraph, the States involved in a dispute may agree to submit it to the Common Market Group for consideration.

    i)   In that case, the Common Market Group will assess the situation, giving the parties to the dispute an opportunity to present their respective positions, requesting, when considered necessary, the advice of experts selected from the list mentioned in article 43 of this Protocol.

    ii)   Any costs incurred in connection with this advice shall be borne equally by the States involved in the dispute or in the proportion determined by the Common Market Group.

3.   The dispute may also be referred to the Common Market Group (GMC) if another State that is not involved in the dispute justifiably requests such procedure at the end of direct negotiations. In that case, the arbitration process initiated by the requesting Member State will not be stopped, unless the States involved in the dispute so agree.

Article 7
Role of the GMC

1.   If the dispute is referred to the Common Market Group by the States involved in it, the Group will make recommendations that, whenever possible, will be specific and detailed with a view to solving the dispute.

2.   If the dispute is referred to the Common Market Group at the request of a State that is not a party to it, the Common Market Group may make comments or recommendations.

Article 8
Time frame for the participation and decision of the GMC

The procedure described in this Chapter may not last more than thirty (30) days as from the date of the meeting during which the dispute was submitted to the Common Market Group.

Chapter VI—Ad Hoc Arbitration Proceedings

Article 9
Beginning of the arbitration period

1.   When it has not been possible to solve a dispute according to the procedure detailed in Chapters IV and V, any of the States involved in the dispute may communicate to the Administrative Secretariat of MERCOSUR its decision to submit to the arbitration proceedings provided for in this Chapter.

2.   The Administrative Secretariat of MERCOSUR will immediately notify such communication to the other State/s involved in the dispute and to the Common Market Group.

3. The Administrative Secretariat of MERCOSUR will undertake the administrative steps required for the proceedings.

Article 10
Composition of the Ad Hoc Arbitration Court

1. The arbitration procedure will be held before an Ad Hoc Court formed by three (3) arbitrators.
2. The arbitrators will be appointed as follows:

   i) Each State involved in the dispute shall appoint one (1) arbitrator from the list provided in Article 11.1 within fifteen (15) days as from the date on which the Administrative Secretariat of MERCOSUR has communicated to the States involved in the dispute the decision taken by one of them to submit the case to arbitration.

   From the same list, one (1) alternate arbitrator will be appointed to replace the head arbitrator in the event of his inability to act or of excusing himself during any of the stages of the arbitration procedure.

   ii) If a State involved in the dispute fails to appoint the arbitrators within the term specified in section 2 i) the arbitrators will be appointed by the Administrative Secretariat of MERCOSUR within two (2) days as from expiration of such term, among the arbitrators from that State included in the list of Article 11.1.

3. The Presiding Arbitrator will be chosen as follows:

   i) The States involved in the dispute will agree on a third arbitrator from the list included in Article 11.2 iii) within fifteen days as from the date on which the Administrative Secretariat of MERCOSUR has communicated to the States involved in the dispute the decision taken by one of them to submit to arbitration. The third arbitrator will preside over the Ad Hoc Arbitration Court.

   The States will simultaneously appoint, from the same list, an alternate arbitrator to replace the head arbitrator in case of his inability to act or of his excluding himself during any stage of the arbitration proceedings.

   The Presiding Arbitrator and his alternate shall not be nationals of the States involved in the dispute.

   ii) If the States involved in the dispute are unable to reach an agreement on the nomination of a third arbitrator within the specified term, the Administrative Secretariat of MERCOSUR, at the request of any of them, will appoint such arbitrator by a draw from the list included in Article 11.2 iii), excluding all nationals of the States involved in the dispute.

iii) The individuals appointed to act as third arbitrators shall answer within three (3) days as from the date of notification of their appointment whether they accept to act in connection with the dispute.

4. The Administrative Secretariat of MERCOSUR shall notify the appointment to the arbitrators.

Article 11
Lists of arbitrators

1. Each Member State shall nominate twelve (12) arbitrators to be included in a list filed with the Administrative Secretariat of the MERCOSUR. The appointment of the arbitrators, together with a detailed curriculum vitae of each one, shall be notified simultaneously to the other Member States and to the Administrative Secretariat of MERCOSUR.

   i) Within thirty (30) days as from notice, each of the Member States may request additional information on the persons appointed by the other Member States to be included in the list mentioned in the previous paragraph.

   ii) The Administrative Secretariat of MERCOSUR shall notify the Member States the consolidated list of arbitrators for MERCOSUR, as well as any subsequent modification thereof.

2. Each Member State shall propose four (4) candidates for the list of third arbitrators. At least one of the arbitrators designated by each Member State for inclusion in the list shall not be a national of any of the Member States of MERCOSUR.

   i) The list shall be notified to the other Member States through the Rotating Presidency, with the curriculum vitae of each of the candidates proposed attached to it.

   ii) Within thirty (30) days as from notification, each of the Member States may ask for additional information on the persons proposed by the other Member States or make well-grounded objections on the designated candidates in accordance with the criteria established in article 35.

   The objections shall be communicated through the Rotating Presidency to the Member State making the proposal. If no solution is found within thirty (30) days as from notification the objection shall prevail.

   iii) The consolidated list of third arbitrators and any subsequent modifications, together with the curriculum vitae of the arbitrators, shall be communicated by the Rotating Presidency to the Administrative Secretariat of MERCOSUR. The Secretariat shall record it and shall notify the Member States.

Article 12
Representatives and advisors

The States involved in the dispute shall appoint their representatives before the Ad Hoc Arbitration Court and may nominate advisors for the defence of their rights.

Article 13
Joint representation

If two or more of the Member States hold the same position in a dispute, they may make a joint presentation before the Ad Hoc Arbitration Court and appoint an arbitration judge jointly, within the time period established in article 10.2.i).

Article 14
Subject matter of the dispute

1. The subject matter of the dispute shall be defined in the written presentations and the answers thereto made before the Ad Hoc Arbitration Court. No additional filings will be allowed thereafter.
2. The matters raised by the parties in the written presentations mentioned in the previous paragraph shall be based on the matters that were considered during the prior stages, considered in this Protocol and in the Annex to the Ouro Preto Protocol.
3. The States involved in the dispute shall inform the Ad Hoc Arbitration Court in the written presentations mentioned in paragraph 1 of this article of the steps taken before the arbitration procedure and shall make a presentations on the facts and the law on which their respective positions are based.

Article 15
Provisional measures

1. The Ad Hoc Arbitration Court may, at the request of the interested party and wherever well grounded suppositions exist that the continuation of a given situation may cause severe and irreparable damage to one of the parties to the dispute, determine that appropriate provisional measures be taken to prevent that damage.
2. The Court may, at any time, discontinue the application of such measures.

3. In the case of a motion for review being filed against the arbitration award, the provisional measures that have not been discontinued prior to the award shall be applicable until they are discussed during the first meeting of the Permanent Review Court that is to decide on their continuation or lifting.

Article 16
Arbitration award

The Ad Hoc Arbitration Court shall issue an award within a period of sixty (60) days, which may be extended by decision of the Court by a maximum thirty (30) additional days as from the date of the communication made by the Administrative Secretariat of MERCOSUR to the parties and the other arbitrators with the information that the Presiding Arbitrator has accepted his nomination.

Chapter VII—Review Procedure

Article 17
Motion from Review

1. Any of the parties to the dispute may file a motion for review with the Permanent Review Court against the award of the Ad Hoc Arbitration Court within fifteen (15) days as from notification thereof.
2. The remedy shall be limited to legal issues dealt with in the dispute and to the legal interpretations set out in the award of the Ad Hoc Arbitration Court.
3. The awards of the Ad Hoc Courts made on the basis of ex aequo et bono principles shall not be subject to review.
4. The Administrative Secretariat of MERCOSUR shall take the administrative steps required for the procedures and shall keep the States involved in the dispute and the Common Market Group informed.

Article 18
Composition of the Permanent Review Court

1. The Permanent Review Court shall include five (5) arbitrators.
2. Each of the MERCOSUR Member States shall appoint one (1) arbitrator and his alternate for a period of two (2) years, renewable for a maximum of two consecutive periods.
3. The fifth arbitrator, to be appointed for a three (3) year non-renewable period unless otherwise agreed by the Member States, shall be chosen

unanimously by the Member States from the list mentioned in this paragraph, at least three (3) months before the end of the fifth arbitrator's term. Such arbitrator shall be a national of one of the Member States of MERCOSUR. All of this in addition to the provisions of item 4 of this article.

If no unanimous decision is made, the appointment will be made by the Administrative Secretariat of MERCOSUR by means of a draw among the names on that list, two (2) days after the expiration of such term.

The list from which the fifth arbitrator will be chosen will include eight (8) members. Each of the Member States shall propose two (2) members that have to be nationals of one of the MERCOSUR countries.

4. The Member States may agree to define other criteria to choose the fifth arbitrator.

5. At least three (3) months before the end of the arbitrators' term, the Member States shall decide on whether to renew their term or propose new candidates.

6. If the term of office of an arbitrator finishes while he is deciding on a dispute, the judge shall remain in office until the end of the dispute.

7. As to the procedures described in this article, the provisions of article 11.2 shall apply.

Article 19
Permanent availability

Once they have accepted their appointment, the members of the Permanent Review Court shall be permanently available to act whenever they are called upon to do so.

Article 20
Operation of the Court

1. Where the dispute involves two Member States, the Court shall be formed by three (3) arbitrators. Two (2) of them shall be nationals of each of the States participating in the dispute and the third one, to be the Presiding Arbitrator, shall be chosen by the Director of the Administrative Secretariat of MERCOSUR by means of a draw among the remaining arbitrators that are not nationals of the States involved in the dispute. The Presiding Arbitrator shall be appointed on the day after the filing of the motion for review, after which date the Court will be considered duly constituted to all intents and purposes.

2. Where the dispute involves more than two of the Member States the Permanent Review Court will be formed by five (5) arbitrators.

3. The Member States may agree to define other criteria for the operation of the Court established by this article.

Article 21
Reply to the motion for review and time limit for the award

1. The other party to the dispute shall have the right to reply to the motion for review filed within fifteen (15) days as from notification of the filing of the motion.
2. The Permanent Review Court shall decide on the motion within thirty (30) days as from the date of the filing of the reply mentioned in the previous paragraph or as from the expiration of the term for such filing, as the case may be. The Court may decide to extend the thirty (30) day term by fifteen (15) days.

Article 22
Scope of the decision

1. The Permanent Review Court may confirm, modify or revoke the juridical basis and the decisions of the Ad Hoc Arbitration Court.
2. The decision of the Permanent Review Court shall be final and shall prevail over the decision of the Ad Hoc Arbitration Court.

Article 23
Direct access to the Permanent Review Court

1. The parties to a dispute, at the end of the procedure described in articles 4 and 5 of this Protocol, may agree expressly to submit directly and in a single instance to the Permanent Review Court. In that case, the Court shall have the same jurisdiction as the Ad Hoc Arbitration Court and the provisions of articles 9, 12, 13, 14, 15 and 16 of this Protocol shall apply.
2. In this case the decisions of the Permanent Review Court shall be binding on the States involved in the dispute as from the date of receipt of the relevant notification, shall not be subject to review appeals and shall have for the parties the effect of res judicata.

Article 24
Exceptional and urgent measures

The Common Market Council may create exceptional procedures to deal with exceptional urgent cases that may cause irreparable damage to the Parties.

. . .

Article 27
The awards have to be enforced

The awards shall be enforced in the way and with the scope determined therein. The adoption of compensatory measures pursuant to the terms of this Protocol shall not release a Member State from its obligations to enforce the award.

. . .

Chapter IX—Compensatory Measures

Article 31
Authorisation to apply compensatory measures

1. If a State involved in a dispute does not comply, totally or partially, with the award of the Arbitration Court, the other party to the dispute shall be authorised, for a one (1) year period starting on the day after the expiration of the term referred to in article 29.1 and without prejudice of the application of the procedures established in article 30, to start the application of temporary compensatory measures, such as the interruption of concessions or other similar obligations, with the aim of complying with the award.
2. The Member State benefited by the award shall, first, try to interrupt the concessions or similar obligations in the same sector or sectors affected. Suspensions within the same sector are considered impracticable or ineffective if they may interrupt concessions or obligations in another sector. The reasons for this decision shall be explained.
3. The compensatory measures to be taken shall be reported formally, by the Member State that will apply them to the Member State that has to comply with the award, at least fifteen (15) days prior to application thereof.

Article 32
Challenging compensatory measures

1. Should the Member State benefiting from the award apply compensatory measures as a result of considering enforcement thereof insufficient and should the Member State bound to comply with the award consider that the measures it has adopted are satisfactory, the latter shall have fifteen (15) days as from the notification provided for in article 31.3 to submit the matter to the Ad Hoc Arbitration Court or to the Permanent Review Court for consideration, as the case may be, which shall have thirty (30) days as from being formed to issue a decision on the matter.

2. Should the Member State bound to enforce the award consider that the applied compensatory measures are excessive, it may request, within fifteen (15) days as from the application of such measures, that the Ad Hoc Court or the Permanent Review Court, as the case may be, issue a decision on the matter, within thirty (30) days as from being formed.

    i) The Court shall decide on the adopted compensatory measures. Depending on the case, it will assess the arguments submitted for application to a sector different from that affected, as well as their proportionality with regard to the consequences arising from failure to comply with the award.

    ii) In analysing proportionality, the Court shall take into account, among other things, the volume and/or value of trade in the sector concerned, as well as any other damage or factor that may have had an influence on the determination of the level or amount of compensatory measures.

3. The Member State that has adopted the compensatory measures shall adapt them to the decision made by the Court within ten (10) days, unless the Court provides for a different term.

. . .

Article 36
Costs

1. Any expenses and fees incurred in connection with the activity of the arbitrators shall be borne by the country appointing them and the expenses of the President of the Ad Hoc Arbitration Court shall be borne equally by the Member States involved in the dispute, unless the Court decides that they are to be distributed in a different proportion.

2. Any expenses and fees incurred in connection with the activity of the arbitrators of the Permanent Review Court shall be borne equally by the State Parties involved in the dispute, unless the Court decides that they are to be distributed in a different proportion.

3. The expenses referred to in the preceding paragraphs may be paid through the Administrative Secretariat of MERCOSUR. Payments may be made through a Special Fund that the State Parties may create by depositing the contributions linked to the budget of the Administrative Secretariat, pursuant to Article 45 of the Protocol of Ouro Preto, or when the procedures provided for in Chapters VI or VII of this Protocol are started. The Fund shall be managed by the Administrative Secretariat of MERCOSUR which shall report to the Member States on the appropriations of the fund.

. . .

Article 38
Venue

The venue of the Permanent Review Court shall be the city of Asuncion. However, when well-grounded reasons exist, the court may exceptionally meet in other cities of MERCOSUR. The Ad Hoc Arbitration Courts may meet in any city of the MERCOSUR Member States.

Chapter XI—Claims by Private Persons

Article 39
Scope of application

The procedure established in this Chapter shall apply to claims filed by private persons (individuals or corporations) in connection with the adoption or application, by any of the Member States, of legal or administrative measures having a restrictive, discriminatory or unfair competition effect in violation of the Treaty of Asunción, the Protocol of Ouro Preto, the protocols and agreements executed within the framework of the Treaty of Asunción, the Decisions of the Common Market Council, the Resolutions of the Common Market Group and the Instructions of the MERCOSUR Trade Committee.

Article 40
Initiation of actions

1. The private persons concerned shall file their claims with the National Chapter of the Common Market Group of the Member State where they have their usual residence or place of business.
2. Such persons shall furnish evidence for the purpose of determining the existence of a violation and the current or imminent damage, in order for the claim to be admitted by the National Chapter and for it to be assessed by the Common Market Group and by the group of experts, if called upon to act.

Article 41
Procedure

1. Unless the claim refers to a matter that has led to a Dispute Settlement procedure in accordance with Chapters IV to VII of this Protocol, the National Chapter of the Common Market Group that has admitted the claim pursuant to Article 40 of this Chapter shall engage in consultations with the National Chapter of the Common Market Group of the Member State charged with the violation, with the aim of finding an immediate solution to the matter raised. Such consultations will be considered automatically

concluded and with no further formal steps if the matter is not settled within fifteen (15) days as from notice of the claim to the Member State charged with the violation, unless the parties agree on a different term.

2. If consultations end without reaching a solution, the National Chapter of the Common Market Group shall forward the claim directly to the Common Market Group.

Article 42
Intervention of the Common Market Group

1. Upon receiving the claim, the Common Market Group shall assess the requirements set forth in Article 40.2 which provided the basis for admission by the National Chapter during the next meeting following receipt thereof. Should it find that the requirements for processing have not been met, it shall reject the claim directly. The decision shall be taken by consensus.

2. Should the Common Market Group not reject the claim, the claim will be deemed accepted. In this case, the Common Market Group shall immediately call upon a group of experts to issue its opinion on admissibility, within thirty (30) days as from their appointment, such term not being subject to extension.

3. Within the said term, the group of experts will give the claiming private person and the States involved in the claim the opportunity to be heard and to submit their arguments at a joint hearing.

Article 43
Group of experts

1. The group of experts referred to in Article 42.2 shall be formed by three (3) members designated by the Common Market Group or, upon failure to reach agreement on one or more experts they shall be appointed by vote by the Member States, choosing from a list of twenty-four (24) experts. The Administrative Secretariat of MERCOSUR shall notify the Common Market Group the name of the expert or experts receiving the largest number of votes. In the latter case, and unless otherwise decided by the Common Market Group, one (1) of the designated experts shall not be a national of the State against which the claim has been filed or a national of the State in which the private person filed his claim, as provided for in Article 40.

2. In order to draw up the list of experts, each of the Member States shall appoint six (6) persons having recognised expertise in the issues that may be the subject matter of the claim. The list will be filed with the Administrative Secretariat of MERCOSUR.

3. Any expenses arising from the involvement of the group of experts shall be borne as determined by the Common Market Group or, if no

agreement is reached, shall be borne equally by the parties directly involved in the claim.

Article 44
Opinion of the group of experts

1. The group of experts shall submit its opinion to the Common Market Group.
    i) If a unanimous opinion were to declare the admissibility of the claim filed against a Member State, any other Member State may request the adoption of corrective measures or annulment by reverse of the challenged measures. If this request is not complied with within fifteen (15) days, the claiming Member State may resort directly to the arbitration procedure, as provided for in Chapter VI of this Protocol.
    ii) Upon receiving the opinion unanimously declaring the inadmissibility of the claim, the Common Market Group shall declare the proceedings ended pursuant to this Chapter.
    iii) Should the group of experts fail to reach unanimity in order to issue its opinion, it shall submit its different conclusions to the Common Market Group, which shall immediately declare the claim proceedings closed pursuant to this Chapter.
2. The closure of the proceedings by the Common Market Group in accordance with paragraphs ii) and iii) of the preceding section shall not prevent the claiming Member State from starting the proceedings provided for in Chapters IV to VI of this Protocol.
    . . .

CONSTITUTIVE PROTOCOL OF THE
MERCOSUR PARLIAMENT (09.12.2005)

. . .

Aware that the installation of a MERCOSUR Parliament, with an appropriate representation of the interests of the citizens of the Participating States, means a contribution to the quality and institutional balance of MERCOSUR, creating a common space which reflects the pluralism and the diversity of the region, and which contributes to the democracy, the participation, the representation, the transparency and the social legitimacy in the development of the integration process and of its norms.

. . .

Article 1
Constitution

. . .

The Parliament replaces the Joint Parliamentary Commission.

The Parliament will be integrated by representatives elected in a universal, direct and secret election, in accordance with the legislation, of each Participating State and the provisions of the present protocol.

The Parliament will be a unicameral organ and its principles, competences and integration are governed as provided by this protocol.

. . .

Article 2
Intentions

Intentions of the Parliament are:

1. To represent the people of MERCOSUR, respecting their ideological and political plurality.
2. To assume the promotion and the permanent defense of democracy, freedom and peace.
3. To impel the sustainable development of the region with social justice and respect for the cultural diversity of its populations.
4. To guarantee the participation of actors of the civil society in the process of integration.
5. To stimulate the formation of a collective conscience of citizens and communitarian values for the integration.
6. To contribute to the consolidation of the Latin-American integration by deepening and expanding MERCOSUR.
7. To promote regional and international solidarity and cooperation.

Article 3
Principles

Principles of the Parliament are:
1. Plurality and tolerance as guarantees of the diversity of the political, social and cultural expressions of the people of the region.
2. Transparency of information and decisions to build trust and to facilitate the participation of the citizens.
3. Cooperation with the other organs of MERCOSUR and regional bodies of citizens' representation.
4. Respect for human rights in all its expressions.

5. Repudiation of all forms of discrimination, especially those referring to gender, color, ethnic group, religion, nationality, age and socio-economic rank.
6. Promotion of the cultural and institutional heritage as well as the heritage of Latin American cooperation in integration processes.
7. Promotion of sustainable development in MERCOSUR and special and differentiated treatment for the countries of lesser economies and the regions with a lower grade of development.
8. Fairness and justice in regional and international matters and the peaceful solution of the controversies.

Article 4
Competences

The Parliament has the following competences:

1. To watch, within its competences, the observation of the norms of MERCOSUR.
2. To watch the preservation of a democratic regime in the Participating States, in conformity with the norms of MERCOSUR and in particular with the Protocol of Ushuaia on the Commitment on Democracy in MERCOSUR, the Republic of Bolivia and the Republic of Chile.
3. To elaborate and publish an annual report on the human rights situation in the Participating States, considering the principles and norms of MERCOSUR.
4. To pass requests for written reports and opinions to the decision-making and consultative organs of MERCOSUR, established in the Protocol of Ouro Preto, on questions concerning the development of the integration process. The requests for reports have to be answered in a maximum period of 180 days.
5. To invite, through the Presidency pro tempore of the CMC, representatives of the organs of MERCOSUR, to report and/or evaluate the development of the integration process, to exchange points of view and to discuss aspects related to activities on the agenda or matters of further consideration.
6. To welcome, at the end of each semester, the Presidency pro Tempore of MERCOSUR, in order of it reporting on the activities done during that period.
7. To welcome, at the beginning of each semester, the Presidency pro Tempore of MERCOSUR, to present the work program agreed upon, with the goals and priorities for the semester.
8. To hold semester meetings with the Socio-Economic Consultative Forum, in order to exchange information and opinions on the development of MERCOSUR.
9. To organize public meetings on matters related to the development of the integration process, with entities of the civil society and the productive sectors.

10. To receive, to examine and if applicable to channel to the decision making organs petitions made by any particular from the Participating States, be it a physical person or a legal entity, related to acts or omissions of the organs of MERCOSUR.

11. To issue declarations, recommendations and reports on issues related to the development of the integration process, at its own initiative or on request of other organs of MERCOSUR.

12. With the goal of accelerating the corresponding internal procedures of putting into effect the norms in the Participating States, the Parliament will elaborate opinions on all the projects of norms of MERCOSUR that require legislative approval in one or several Participating States, within ninety days after carrying out the consultation. These projects shall be sent to the Parliament by the decision-making organ of MERCOSUR, before their approval.

    If the project of a norm of MERCOSUR is approved by the decision-making organ, in conformity with the terms of the opinion of the Parliament, the norm will have to be sent by each of the national Executive Powers to the Parliament of the respective Member State, within forty-five days, with counting starting with this approval.

    In case of the approved norm not being in conformity with the opinion of the Parliament, or if it is not sent in the period mentioned in the first paragraph of the present numeral, the norm will continue the ordinary proceeding of incorporation.

    The national Parliaments, according to the corresponding internal procedures, shall adopt the necessary measures for the instrumentation or creation of a preferential procedure for the consideration of the norms of MERCOSUR which have been adopted in conformity with the terms of the opinion of the Parliament, mentioned in the previous paragraph.

    The maximum term of duration of the procedure foreseen in the preceding Paragraph will be of up to one hundred eighty days, counted from the introduction of the norm into the respective national Parliament.

    If within the term of that preferential procedure the Parliament of the Participating State rejects the norm, it shall be re-sent to the Executive Power to present the norm for reconsideration to the corresponding organ of MERCOSUR.

13. To propose projects of norms of MERCOSUR for their consideration by the Council of the Common Market, which has to report on its treatment each semester.

14. To elaborate studies and drafts of national norms oriented towards the harmonization of the national legislations of the Participating States, which will be communicated to the national parliaments with the effect of their eventual consideration.

15. To develop actions and joint efforts with the national parliaments, with the aim of ensuring the fulfilment of the goals of MERCOSUR, in particular of those related to legislative action.
16. To maintain institutional relationships with the Parliaments of third states and other legislative institutions.
17. To celebrate, within the frame of its attributes, with the advice of the competent organs of MERCOSUR, agreements of cooperation or technical assistance, with public and private organs, of national or international character.
18. To promote the development of instruments of representative and participative democracy in MERCOSUR.
19. To receive within the first semester of each year the report on the execution of the budget of the Secretariat of MERCOSUR for the previous year.
20. To elaborate and approve its budget and inform the Council of the Common Market of its execution within the first semester of the year after the present one.
21. To approve and modify its internal by-laws.
22. To conduct all the tasks corresponding to the exercise of its competences.

Article 5
Integration

1. The Parliament will be integrated in accordance with the criterion of citizens' representation.
2. The members of the Parliament, henceforth Parliamentarians, will have the status of a MERCOSUR Parliamentarian.

Article 6
Election

1. The Parliamentarians will be elected by the citizens of the Participating States through a direct, universal and secret election.
2. The mechanism of election of the Parliamentarians and their substitutes will be governed by the provisions of the legislation of each Participating State, which will adopt measures in order to ensure an adequate representation of gender, ethnic origin and regional provenance according to the realities of each State.
3. The Parliamentarians will be elected together with their substitutes in accordance with the electoral legislation in the respective Participating State, in case of definitive or temporary absence. The substitutes shall

be elected on the same date and in the same procedure as the titular Parliamentarians, as well as for identical periods.

4. On proposal of the Parliament, the Council of the Common Market shall establish the "Day of the MERCOSUR Citizens" for the election of the Parliamentarians, simultaneously in all Participating States, through a direct, universal and secret vote by the citizens.

. . .

Article 20
Budget

1. The Parliament shall elaborate and approve its budget, which will be financed by contributions of the Participating States, as a function of the Gross Domestic Product and the national budget of each of the Participating States.

2. The criteria for the process of the contributions mentioned in the previous paragraph shall be established by a decision of the Council of the Common Market, under consideration of a Parliamentary proposal.

Article 21
Seat of the Parliament

1. The seat of the Parliament shall be the city of Montevideo, capital of the Eastern Republic of Uruguay.

2. MERCOSUR shall sign a Hosting Agreement with the Eastern Republic of Uruguay, which shall define the norms relative to the privileges, the immunity and the exemptions of the Parliament, the Parliamentarians and other civil servants, in accordance with the current norms of International Law.

. . .

3

REGION-BUILDING IN ASIA

ASSOCIATION OF SOUTHEAST ASIAN NATIONS (ASEAN)

The Association of Southeast Asian Nations (ASEAN) is often considered the most favored partner of the European Union. Since its foundation in 1967, ASEAN has indeed put its mark on the world map. The mutually perceived threat of communist expansion in Indochina was the original motive for Indonesia, Malaysia, the Philippines, Singapore, and Thailand to form a system of cooperation. A common response to the threat stemming from escalation of political and military events in Vietnam, Laos, and Cambodia seemed to be a matter of survival. Over time, like the European integration mechanism, ASEAN became a magnetic force for the communist countries in Indochina and generated one of the great economic success stories of twentieth-century Asia. With impressive growth rates, the "Little Tigers" jumped to the forefront of the world economy.

ASEAN has also widened its membership. In 1984, Brunei Darussalam joined. Most notable were the accessions of Vietnam (1995), Laos (1997)—together with Burma/Myanmar—and Cambodia (1999). Of these three war-torn countries, at least Vietnam and Laos formally maintained communist regimes in spite of anti-communist revolutions in Eastern Europe. On the other hand, they began to open their economies to market mechanisms. Cambodian membership also signaled the end of a dramatic and horrible period in the history of this pleasant Southeast Asian country and marked the success of ASEAN as a factor of regional stability. Myanmar's membership remains more controversial than any other because of the continuous military dictatorship in the home country of Nobel Peace Prize winner Aun San Suu Kuyi.

In economic terms, ASEAN pursues cooperation in "common interest areas," as the Bangkok Declaration—the founding document of ASEAN—has phrased the main objective of the group. Over four decades of its existence,

ASEAN has grown into the largest free trade area in the world with its population of 539 million people, yet it remains the smallest one in terms of actual gross domestic product (€659 billion). Although ASEAN has expanded its means of cooperation since its foundation, so far it has fallen short of realizing a Single Market. Intra-regional trade rose to more than 22 percent during the 1990s, underlining the growing complementarity of production in ASEAN. Yet this figure is small compared with the EU's internal trade of more than 50 percent. The other Asian countries, foremost Japan, Korea, and China, that constitute ASEAN's main trading partners account for 50 percent of its export market and provide the region with 60 percent of its imports. ASEAN's share of world trade has grown from 4.2 percent in imports and 4.9 percent in exports (in 1980) to 6.7 percent in imports and 8.3 percent in exports (in 2002). The EU's share of exports from ASEAN was 3.9 percent in 2002, while the EU's import share from ASEAN amounted to 6.3 percent. Intra-regional investment is still limited in ASEAN, although it more than doubled during the 1990s from $12 billion (US) to $26 billion.

ASEAN has reached out beyond the original intention of maximizing economic benefits and has begun to impact regional security and issues of conflict resolution. The Declaration of ASEAN Concord and the Treaty of Amity and Cooperation in Southeast Asia in 1976 and the Declaration of ASEAN Concord II in 2003 frame this period. During the 1980s and 1990s, ASEAN was able to exert pressure on Vietnam in order to resolve the long-standing Cambodian conflict with the rehabilitation of complete national sovereignty and subsequent accession of both Vietnam and Cambodia to ASEAN. The Cambodia policy of ASEAN has to be seen in the larger context of ASEAN's increasing ambition to project itself as a provider of stability and security in the region. In the absence of other regional schemes for security in Asia-Pacific, the ASEAN Regional Forum (ARF) attests to ASEAN's ambition and "pivotal role" in this field. Founded in 1994, the ARF remains to this day the only forum or mechanism devoted to security in Asia.

Since the end of the Cold War, various ASEAN political leaders have challenged the taboo of non-intervention in domestic affairs of member countries. After debates in ASEAN over whether the community should favor "intervention" or "flexible engagement" in the face of new regional crises, ASEAN agreed upon the formula "enhanced interaction." But the conflict in East Timor (1999–2002) did not see any substantial ASEAN involvement. Furthermore, difficulties in dealing with the military dictatorship in Myanmar have demonstrated the limits of ASEAN's negotiation capacities in the absence of supranational mechanisms. ASEAN's strategy remains limited to quiet interventions and soft mediation. ASEAN does not impose sanctions for the poor conduct of any of its member states.

In fact, ASEAN hardly knows any form of institutionalization. It has been suggested that ASEAN member states relate intuitively to a common identity of their region. As much as this is debatable in light of the enormous religious, ethnic, cultural and linguistic diversity of Southeast Asia, the limited degree of institutional structures remains obvious. In 1976 the Treaty of Amity and Cooperation in Southeast Asia introduced elements of arbitration that remain largely on paper. An ASEAN Secretariat was established in Jakarta, thus demonstrating at least the first seeds of supranational potential. The possibility of an ASEAN Parliament has been considered, and some analysts compare the ongoing coordination activity among ASEAN countries to the unwritten constitution of Great Britain.

Eventually, ASEAN began to lay the ground for a genuine ASEAN Constitution with the 2005 Kuala Lumpur Declaration on the Establishment of the ASEAN Charter. On 22 November 2007, forty years after ASEAN's founding, all its member states signed the ASEAN Charter. The ASEAN Charter defines ASEAN as "people oriented." It introduces a Human Rights body as an expression of the region's commitment. New disputes about Myanmar's regime put its strength into doubt even before the ASEAN Charter had been ratified across the region. Yet with the ASEAN Charter, a substantial step to consolidate and institutionalize ASEAN was taken: ASEAN gained legal personality and introduced a vague dispute settlement scheme and a single chairmanship for high-level ASEAN bodies. ASEAN's identity was defined as "one vision, one identity, one community." In December 2008, the ASEAN Charter came into effect after being ratified in all member states.

In the early twenty-first century, more than sixty structures of regional cooperation have been identified in Asia. Formal or informal cooperation is dominant, while continent-wide schemes do not exist. Processes with a continental dimension such as ASEM (Asia-Europe Meeting) and APEC (Asia-Pacific Economic Cooperation) are components of transcontinental free trade areas rather than ambitions toward supranational integration. They are responses to globalization and expressions of multilateralism, but they fall short of generating authentic regional integration schemes. While APEC, which was founded by twelve countries in 1989 on the initiative of Australia, has grown into a membership of twenty-four countries around Asia-Pacific, ASEM is an informal process of dialogue and cooperation between the EU member states and thirteen Asian countries (Brunei, China, Indonesia, Japan, South Korea, Malaysia, the Philippines, Singapore, Thailand, and Vietnam, enlarged in 2006 to India, Pakistan, and Mongolia). The fact that not all ASEAN members participate is as indicative of missing political cohesion as it is of the purely economic approach of ASEM. While APEC was founded with the intention of developing into an OECD-like system for Asia-Pacific (including the Pacific countries of Latin America), ASEM—representing more than three billion people—was largely conceived as a support mechanism for developing global free trade regimes in the context of the WTO.

THE ASEAN-DECLARATION
(BANGKOK DECLARATION) (08.08.1967)

. . .

Mindful of the existence of mutual interests and common problems among countries of South-East Asia and convinced of the need to strengthen further the existing bonds of regional solidarity and cooperation;

Desiring to establish a firm foundation for common action to promote regional cooperation in South-East Asia in the spirit of equality and partnership and thereby contribute towards peace, progress and prosperity in the region;

Conscious that in an increasingly interdependent world, the cherished ideals of peace, freedom, social justice and economic well-being are best attained by fostering good understanding, good neighbourliness and meaningful cooperation among the countries of the region already bound together by ties of history and culture;

Considering that the countries of South East Asia share a primary responsibility for strengthening the economic and social stability of the region and ensuring their peaceful and progressive national development, and that they are determined to ensure their stability and security from external interference in any form or manifestation in order to preserve their national identities in accordance with the ideals and aspirations of their peoples;

. . .

First, the establishment of an Association for Regional Cooperation among the countries of South-East Asia to be known as the Association of South-East Asian Nations (ASEAN).

Second, that the aims and purposes of the Association shall be:

1. To accelerate the economic growth, social progress and cultural development in the region through joint endeavours in the spirit of equality and partnership in order to strengthen the foundation for a prosperous and peaceful community of South-East Asian Nations;

2. To promote regional peace and stability through abiding respect for justice and the rule of law in the relationship among countries of the region and adherence to the principles of the United Nations Charter;

3. To promote active collaboration and mutual assistance on matters of common interest in the economic, social, cultural, technical, scientific and administrative fields;

4. To provide assistance to each other in the form of training and research facilities in the educational, professional, technical and administrative spheres;

5. To collaborate more effectively for the greater utilization of their agriculture and industries, the expansion of their trade, including the study of the problems of international commodity trade, the improvement of their transportation and communications facilities and the raising of the living standards of their peoples;

6. To promote South-East Asian studies;

7. To maintain close and beneficial cooperation with existing international and regional organizations with similar aims and purposes, and explore all avenues for even closer cooperation among themselves.

Third, that to carry out these aims and purposes, the following machinery shall be established:

(a) Annual Meeting of Foreign Ministers, which shall be by rotation and referred to as ASEAN Ministerial Meeting. Special Meetings of Foreign Ministers may be convened as required.

(b) A Standing committee, under the chairmanship of the Foreign Minister of the host country or his representative and having as its members the accredited Ambassadors of the other member countries, to carry on the work of the Association in between Meetings of Foreign Ministers.

(c) Ad-Hoc Committees and Permanent Committees of specialists and officials on specific subjects.

(d) A National Secretariat in each member country to carry out the work of the Association on behalf of that country and to service the Annual or Special Meetings of Foreign Ministers, the Standing Committee and such other committees as may hereafter be established.

Fourth, that the Association is open for participation to all States in the South-East Asian Region subscribing to the aforementioned aims, principles and purposes.

. . .

Declaration of ASEAN Concord (24.02.1976)

. . .

ASEAN cooperation shall take into account, among others, the following objectives and principles in the pursuit of political stability:

1. The stability of each member state and of the ASEAN region is an essential contribution to international peace and security. Each member state resolves to eliminate threats posed by subversion to its stability, thus strengthening national and ASEAN resilience.

2. Member states, individually and collectively, shall take active steps for the early establishment of the Zone of Peace, Freedom and Neutrality.
3. The elimination of poverty, hunger, disease and illiteracy is a primary concern of member states. They shall therefore intensify cooperation in economic and social development, with particular emphasis on the promotion of social justice and on the improvement of the living standards of their peoples.
4. Natural disasters and other major calamities can retard the pace of development of member states. They shall extend, within their capabilities, assistance for relief of member states in distress.
5. Member states shall take cooperative action in their national and regional development programmes, utilizing as far as possible the resources available in the ASEAN region to broaden the complementarity of their respective economies.
6. Member states, in the spirit of ASEAN solidarity, shall rely exclusively on peaceful processes in the settlement of intra-regional differences.
7. Member states shall strive, individually and collectively, to create conditions conducive to the promotion of peaceful cooperation among the nations of Southeast Asia on the basis of mutual respect and mutual benefit.
8. Member states shall vigorously develop an awareness of regional identity and exert all efforts to create a strong ASEAN community, respected by all and respecting all nations on the basis of mutually advantageous relationships, and in accordance with the principles of self-determination, sovereign equality and non-interference in the internal affairs of nations.

    And Do Hereby Adopt

    The following programme of action as a framework for ASEAN cooperation.

A. Political

1. Meeting of the Heads of Government of the member states as and when necessary.
2. Signing of the Treaty of Amity and Cooperation in Southeast Asia.
3. Settlement of intra-regional disputes by peaceful means as soon as possible.
4. Immediate consideration of initial steps towards recognition of and respect for the Zone of Peace, Freedom and Neutrality wherever possible.
5. Improvement of ASEAN machinery to strengthen political cooperation.

6. Study on how to develop judicial cooperation including the possibility of an ASEAN Extradition Treaty.
7. Strengthening of political solidarity by promoting the harmonization of views, coordinating positions and, where possible and desirable, taking common actions.

B. Economic

1. Cooperation on Basic Commodities, particularly Food and Energy
    i)   Member states shall assist each other by according priority to the supply of the individual country's needs in critical circumstances, and priority to the acquisition of exports from member states, in respect of basic commodities, particularly food and energy.
    ii) Member states shall also intensify cooperation in the production of basic commodities, particularly food and energy in the individual member states of the region.
2. Industrial Cooperation
    i)   Member states shall cooperate to establish large-scale ASEAN industrial plants, particularly to meet regional requirements for essential commodities.
    ii) Priority shall be given to projects which utilize the available materials in the member states, contribute to the increase of food production, increase foreign exchange earnings or save foreign exchange and create employment.
3. Cooperation in Trade
    i)   Member states shall cooperate in the fields of trade in order to promote development and growth of new production and trade and to improve the trade structures of individual states and among countries of ASEAN conducive to further development and to safeguard and increase their foreign exchange earnings and reserves.
    ii) Member states shall progress towards the establishment of preferential trading arrangements as a long term objective on a basis deemed to be at any particular time appropriate through rounds of negotiations subject to the unanimous agreement of member states.
    iii) The expansion of trade among member states shall be facilitated through cooperation on basic commodities, particularly in food and energy and through cooperation in ASEAN industrial projects.
    iv) Member states shall accelerate joint efforts to improve access to markets outside ASEAN for their raw material and finished products by seeking the elimination of all trade barriers in those markets, developing new usage for these products and adopting common

approaches and actions in dealing with regional groupings and individual economic powers.

v) Such efforts shall also lead to cooperation in the field of technology and production methods in order to increase the production and to improve the quality of export products, as well as to develop new export products with a view to diversifying exports.

4. Joint Approach to International Commodity Problems and Other World Economic Problems

i) The principle of ASEAN cooperation on trade shall also be reflected on a priority basis in joint approaches to international commodity problems and other world economic problems such as the reform of the international trading system, the reform of the international monetary system and the transfer of real resources, in the United Nations and other relevant multilateral fora, with a view to contributing to the establishment of the New International Economic Order.

ii) Member states shall give priority to the stabilisation and increase of export earnings of those commodities produced and exported by them through commodity agreements including bufferstock schemes and other means.

5. Machinery for Economic Cooperation

Ministerial meetings on economic matters shall be held regularly or as deemed necessary in order to:

i) formulate recommendations for the consideration of Governments of member states for the strengthening of ASEAN economic cooperation;

ii) review the coordination and implementation of agreed ASEAN programmes and projects on economic cooperation;

iii) exchange views and consult on national development plans and policies as a step towards harmonizing regional development; and

iv) perform such other relevant functions as agreed upon by the member Governments.

C. Social

1. Cooperation in the field of social development, with emphasis on the well being of the low-income group and of the rural population, through the expansion of opportunities for productive employment with fair remuneration.

2. Support for the active involvement of all sectors and levels of the ASEAN communities, particularly the women and youth, in development efforts.

3. Intensification and expansion of existing cooperation in meeting the problems of population growth in the ASEAN region, and where possible, formulation of new strategies in collaboration with appropriate international agencies.

4. Intensification of cooperation among member states as well as with the relevant international bodies in the prevention and eradication of the abuse of narcotics and the illegal trafficking of drugs.

D. Cultural and Information

1. Introduction of the study of ASEAN, its member states and their national languages as part of the curricula of schools and other institutions of learning in the member states.

2. Support of ASEAN scholars, writers, artists and mass media representatives to enable them to play an active role in fostering a sense of regional identity and fellowship.

3. Promotion of Southeast Asian studies through closer collaboration among national institutes.

E. Security

Continuation of cooperation on a non-ASEAN basis between the member states in security matters in accordance with their mutual needs and interests.

. . .

TREATY OF AMITY AND COOPERATION IN SOUTHEAST ASIA (24.02.1976)

. . .

Conscious of the existing ties of history, geography and culture, which have bound their peoples together;

. . .

Chapter I—Purpose and Principles

Article 1

The purpose of this Treaty is to promote perpetual peace, everlasting amity and cooperation among their peoples which would contribute to their strength, solidarity and closer relationship.

Article 2

In their relations with one another, the High Contracting Parties shall be guided by the following fundamental principles:

a) Mutual respect for the independence, sovereignty, equality, territorial integrity and national identity of all nations;

b) The right of every State to lead its national existence free from external interference, subversion or coercion;

c) Non-interference in the internal affairs of one another;

d) Settlement of differences or disputes by peaceful means;

e) Renunciation of the threat or use of force;

f) Effective cooperation among themselves.

Chapter II—Amity

Article 3

In pursuance of the purpose of this Treaty the High Contracting Parties shall endeavour to develop and strengthen the traditional, cultural and historical ties of friendship, good neighbourliness and cooperation which bind them together and shall fulfil in good faith the obligations assumed under this Treaty. In order to promote closer understanding among them, the High Contracting Parties shall encourage and facilitate contact and intercourse among their peoples.

Chapter III—Cooperation

Article 4

The High Contracting Parties shall promote active cooperation in the economic, social, technical, scientific and administrative fields as well as in matters of common ideals and aspirations of international peace and stability in the region and all other matters of common interest.

Article 5

Pursuant to Article 4 the High Contracting Parties shall exert their maximum efforts multilaterally as well as bilaterally on the basis of equality, non-discrimination and mutual benefit.

Article 6

The High Contracting Parties shall collaborate for the acceleration of the economic growth in the region in order to strengthen the foundation for a prosperous and peaceful community of nations in Southeast Asia. To this end, they shall promote the greater utilization of their agriculture and industries, the expansion of their trade and the improvement of their economic infrastructure for the mutual benefit of their peoples. In this regard, they shall continue to explore all avenues for close and beneficial cooperation with other States as well as international and regional organisations outside the region.

Article 7

The High Contracting Parties, in order to achieve social justice and to raise the standards of living of the peoples of the region, shall intensify economic cooperation. For this purpose, they shall adopt appropriate regional strategies for economic development and mutual assistance.

Article 8

The High Contracting Parties shall strive to achieve the closest cooperation on the widest scale and shall seek to provide assistance to one another in the form of training and research facilities in the social, cultural, technical, scientific and administrative fields.

Article 9

The High Contracting Parties shall endeavour to foster cooperation in the furtherance of the cause of peace, harmony, and stability in the region. To this end, the High Contracting Parties shall maintain regular contacts and consultations with one another on international and regional matters with a view to coordinating their views, actions and policies.

Article 10

Each High Contracting Party shall not in any manner or form participate in any activity which shall constitute a threat to the political and economic stability, sovereignty, or territorial integrity of another High Contracting Party.

Article 11

The High Contracting Parties shall endeavour to strengthen their respective national resilience in their political, economic, socio-cultural as well as security fields in conformity with their respective ideals and aspirations, free from external interference as well as internal subversive activities in order to preserve their respective national identities.

Article 12

The High Contracting Parties in their efforts to achieve regional prosperity and security, shall endeavour to cooperate in all fields for the promotion of regional resilience, based on the principles of self-confidence, self-reliance, mutual respect, cooperation and solidarity which will constitute the foundation for a strong and viable community of nations in Southeast Asia.

Chapter IV—Pacific Settlement of Disputes

Article 13

The High Contracting Parties shall have the determination and good faith to prevent disputes from arising. In case disputes on matters directly affecting them should arise, especially disputes likely to disturb regional peace and harmony, they shall refrain from the threat or use of force and shall at all times settle such disputes among themselves through friendly negotiations.

Article 14

To settle disputes through regional processes, the High Contracting Parties shall constitute, as a continuing body, a High Council comprising a Representative at ministerial level from each of the High Contracting Parties to take cognizance of the existence of disputes or situations likely to disturb regional peace and harmony.

Article 15

In the event no solution is reached through direct negotiations, the High Council shall take cognizance of the dispute or the situation and shall recommend to the parties in dispute appropriate means of settlement such as good offices, mediation, inquiry or conciliation. The High Council may however offer its good offices, or upon agreement of the parties in dispute, constitute itself into a committee of mediation, inquiry or conciliation. When deemed necessary, the High Council shall recommend appropriate measures for the prevention of a deterioration of the dispute or the situation.

Article 16

The foregoing provision of this Chapter shall not apply to a dispute unless all the parties to the dispute agree to their application to that dispute. However, this shall not preclude the other High Contracting Parties not party to the dispute from offering all possible assistance to settle the said dispute. Parties to the dispute should be well disposed towards such offers of assistance.

. . .

DECLARATION OF ASEAN CONCORD II (07.10.2003)

. . .

Conscious of the need to further consolidate and enhance the achievements of ASEAN as a dynamic, resilient, and cohesive regional association for the well being of its member states and people as well as the need to further strengthen the Association's guidelines in achieving a more coherent and clearer path for cooperation between and among them;

. . .

Reaffirming the fundamental importance of adhering to the principle of non-interference and consensus in ASEAN cooperation;

Reiterating that the Treaty of Amity and Cooperation in Southeast Asia (TAC) is an effective code of conduct for relations among governments and peoples;

Recognizing that sustainable economic development requires a secure political environment based on a strong foundation of mutual interests generated by economic cooperation and political solidarity;

. . .

Do Hereby Declare That:

1. An ASEAN Community shall be established comprising three pillars, namely political and security cooperation, economic cooperation, and socio-cultural cooperation, that are closely intertwined and mutually reinforcing for the purpose of ensuring durable peace, stability and shared prosperity in the region;

2. ASEAN shall continue its efforts to ensure closer and mutually beneficial integration among its member states and among their peoples, and to promote regional peace and stability, security, development and prosperity with a view to realizing an ASEAN Community that is open, dynamic and resilient;

3. ASEAN shall respond to the new dynamics within the respective ASEAN Member Countries and shall urgently and effectively address the challenge of translating ASEAN cultural diversities and different economic levels into equitable development opportunity and prosperity, in an environment of solidarity, regional resilience and harmony;

4. ASEAN shall nurture common values, such as the habit of consultation to discuss political issues and the willingness to share information on

matters of common concern, such as environmental degradation, maritime security cooperation and the enhancement of defense cooperation among ASEAN countries, develop a set of socio-political values and principles, and resolve to settle long-standing disputes through peaceful means;

5. The Treaty of Amity and Cooperation in Southeast Asia (TAC) is the key code of conduct governing relations between states and a diplomatic instrument for the promotion of peace and stability in the region;

6. The ASEAN Regional Forum (ARF) shall remain the primary forum in enhancing political and security cooperation in the Asia Pacific region, as well as the pivot in building peace and stability in the region. ASEAN shall enhance its role in further advancing the stages of cooperation within the ARF to ensure the security of the Asia Pacific region;

7. ASEAN is committed to deepening and broadening its internal economic integration and linkages with the world economy to realize an ASEAN Economic Community through a bold, pragmatic and unified strategy;

8. ASEAN shall further build on the momentum already gained in the ASEAN Plus Three process so as to further draw synergies through broader and deeper cooperation in various areas;

9. ASEAN shall build upon opportunities for mutually beneficial regional integration arising from its existing initiatives and those with partners, through enhanced trade and investment links as well as through IAI process and the RIA;

10. ASEAN shall continue to foster a community of caring societies and promote a common regional identity;

    . . .

A. ASEAN Security Community (ASC)

1. The ASEAN Security Community is envisaged to bring ASEAN's political and security cooperation to a higher plane to ensure that countries in the region live at peace with one another and with the world at large in a just, democratic and harmonious environment. The ASEAN Security Community members shall rely exclusively on peaceful processes in the settlement of intra-regional differences and regard their security as fundamentally linked to one another and bound by geographic location, common vision and objectives.

2. The ASEAN Security Community, recognizing the sovereign right of the member countries to pursue their individual foreign policies and defense arrangements and taking into account the strong interconnections among political, economic and social realities, subscribes to

the principle of comprehensive security as having broad political, economic, social and cultural aspects in consonance with the ASEAN Vision 2020 rather than to a defense pact, military alliance or a joint foreign policy.

3. ASEAN shall continue to promote regional solidarity and cooperation. Member Countries shall exercise their rights to lead their national existence free from outside interference in their internal affairs.

4. The ASEAN Security Community shall abide by the UN Charter and other principles of international law and uphold ASEAN's principles of non-interference, consensus-based decision-making, national and regional resilience, respect for national sovereignty, the renunciation of the threat or the use of force, and peaceful settlement of differences and disputes.

5. Maritime issues and concerns are transboundary in nature, and therefore shall be addressed regionally in a holistic, integrated and comprehensive manner. Maritime cooperation between and among ASEAN member countries shall contribute to the evolution of the ASEAN Security Community.

6. Existing ASEAN political instruments such as the Declaration on ZOPFAN, the TAC, and the SEANWFZ Treaty shall continue to play a pivotal role in the area of confidence building measures, preventive diplomacy and the approaches to conflict resolution.

7. The High Council of the TAC shall be an important component in the ASEAN Security Community since it reflects ASEAN's commitment to resolve all differences, disputes and conflicts peacefully.

8. The ASEAN Security Community shall contribute to further promoting peace and security in the wider Asia Pacific region and reflect ASEAN's determination to move forward at a pace comfortable to all. In this regard, the ARF shall remain the main forum for regional security dialogue, with ASEAN as the primary driving force.

9. The ASEAN Security Community is open and outward looking in respect of actively engaging ASEAN's friends and Dialogue Partners to promote peace and stability in the region, and shall build on the ARF to facilitate consultation and cooperation between ASEAN and its friends and Partners on regional security matters.

10. The ASEAN Security Community shall fully utilize the existing institutions and mechanisms within ASEAN with a view to strengthening national and regional capacities to counter terrorism, drug trafficking, trafficking in persons and other transnational crimes; and shall work to ensure that the Southeast Asian Region remains free of all weapons of mass destruction. It shall enable ASEAN to

demonstrate a greater capacity and responsibility of being the primary driving force of the ARF.

11. The ASEAN Security Community shall explore enhanced cooperation with the United Nations as well as other international and regional bodies for the maintenance of international peace and security.

12. ASEAN shall explore innovative ways to increase its security and establish modalities for the ASEAN Security Community, which include, inter alia, the following elements: norms-setting, conflict prevention, approaches to conflict resolution, and post-conflict peace building.

B. ASEAN Economic Community (AEC)

1. The ASEAN Economic Community is the realisation of the end-goal of economic integration as outlined in the ASEAN Vision 2020, to create a stable, prosperous and highly competitive ASEAN economic region in which there is a free flow of goods, services and investment and a freer flow of capital, equitable economic development and reduced poverty and socio-economic disparities in the year 2020.

2. The ASEAN Economic Community is based on a convergence of interests among ASEAN members to deepen and broaden economic integration efforts through existing and new initiatives with clear timelines.

3. The ASEAN Economic Community shall establish ASEAN as a Single Market and production base, turning the diversity that characterises the region into opportunities for business complementation making the ASEAN a more dynamic and stronger segment of the global supply chain. ASEAN's strategy shall consist of the integration of ASEAN and enhancement of ASEAN's economic competitiveness. In moving towards the ASEAN Economic Community, ASEAN shall, inter alia, institute new mechanisms and measures to strengthen the implementation of its existing economic initiatives including the ASEAN Free Trade Area (AFTA), ASEAN Framework Agreement on Services (AFAS) and ASEAN Investment Area (AIA); accelerate regional integration in the priority sectors; facilitate movement of business persons, skilled labour and talents; and strengthen the institutional mechanisms of ASEAN, including the improvement of the existing ASEAN Dispute Settlement Mechanism to ensure expeditious and legally binding resolution of any economic disputes. As a first step towards the realization of the ASEAN Economic Community, ASEAN shall implement the recommendations of the High Level Task Force on ASEAN Economic Integration.

4. The ASEAN Economic Community shall ensure that deepening and broadening integration of ASEAN shall be accompanied by technical and development cooperation in order to address the development divide and accelerate the economic integration of Cambodia, Lao PDR, Myanmar and Viet Nam through IAI and RIA so that the benefits of ASEAN integration are shared and enable all ASEAN Member Countries to move forward in a unified manner.

5. The realization of a fully integrated economic community requires implementation of both liberalization and cooperation measures. There is a need to enhance cooperation and integration activities in other areas. These will involve, among others, human resources development and capacity building; recognition of educational qualifications; closer consultation on macroeconomic and financial policies; trade financing measures; enhanced infrastructure and communications connectivity; development of electronic transactions through e-ASEAN; integrating industries across the region to promote regional sourcing; and enhancing private sector involvement.

C. ASEAN Socio-Cultural Community (ASCC)

1. The ASEAN Socio-cultural Community, in consonance with the goal set by ASEAN Vision 2020, envisages a Southeast Asia bonded together in partnership as a community of caring societies.

2. In line with the programme of action set by the 1976 Declaration of ASEAN Concord, the Community shall foster cooperation in social development aimed at raising the standard of living of disadvantaged groups and the rural population, and shall seek the active involvement of all sectors of society, in particular women, youth, and local communities.

3. ASEAN shall ensure that its work force shall be prepared for, and benefit from, economic integration by investing more resources for basic and higher education, training, science and technology development, job creation, and social protection. The development and enhancement of human resources is a key strategy for employment generation, alleviating poverty and socio-economic disparities, and ensuring economic growth with equity. ASEAN shall continue existing efforts to promote regional mobility and mutual recognition of professional credentials, talents, and skills development.

4. ASEAN shall further intensify cooperation in the area of public health, including in the prevention and control of infectious diseases, such as HIV/AIDS and SARS, and support joint regional actions to increase

access to affordable medicines. The security of the Community is enhanced when poverty and diseases are held in check and the peoples of ASEAN are assured of adequate health care.

5.   The Community shall nurture talent and promote interaction among ASEAN scholars, writers, artists and media practitioners to help preserve and promote ASEAN's diverse cultural heritage while fostering regional identity as well as cultivating people's awareness of ASEAN.

6.   The Community shall intensify cooperation in addressing problems associated with population growth, unemployment, environmental degradation and transboundary pollution as well as disaster management in the region to enable individual members to fully realize their development potentials and to enhance the mutual ASEAN spirit.

. . .

KUALA LUMPUR DECLARATION ON THE ESTABLISHMENT OF THE ASEAN CHARTER (12.12.2005)

. . .

Acknowledging that the vision, strategy and initiative of ASEAN over the years have made an important contribution to the maintenance of peace, security and stability of the region;

Cognisant that mutual respect for the independence, sovereignty, equality, territorial integrity and national identity of ASEAN Member Countries has fostered a positive environment for the steady development of an ASEAN Community to meet the challenges . . .

. . .

Convinced of the need for an ASEAN Charter to serve as a firm foundation for ASEAN in the years ahead and to facilitate community building towards an ASEAN Community and beyond;

Do hereby declare:

First, we are committed to establish the ASEAN Charter.

Second, the ASEAN Charter will serve as a legal and institutional framework of ASEAN to support the realisation of its goals and objectives.

Third, the ASEAN Charter will codify all ASEAN norms, rules, and values and reaffirm that ASEAN agreements signed and other instruments adopted before the establishment of the ASEAN Charter shall continue to apply and be legally binding where appropriate.

Fourth, the ASEAN Charter will reaffirm principles, goals and ideals contained in ASEAN's milestone agreements, in particular the ASEAN Declaration (1967), the Treaty of Amity and Cooperation in Southeast Asia (1976), the Treaty on Southeast Asia Nuclear Weapon Free Zone (1995), the ASEAN Vision 2020 (1997) and the Declaration of ASEAN Concord II (2003) as well as the principles of inter-state relations in accordance with the UN Charter and established international law that promote and protect ASEAN community interests as well as inter-state relations and the national interests of the individual ASEAN Member Countries. These include among others:

- Promotion of the community interest for the benefit of all ASEAN Member Countries;
- Maintaining the primary driving force of ASEAN;
- Narrowing the development gaps among Member Countries;
- Adherence to a set of common socio-cultural and political community values and shared norms as contained in the various ASEAN documents;
- Continuing to foster a community of caring societies and promote a common regional identity;
- Effective implementation as well as compliance with ASEAN's agreements;
- Promotion of democracy, human rights and obligations, transparency and good governance and strengthening democratic institutions;
- Ensuring that countries in the region live at peace with one another and with the world at large in a just, democratic and harmonious environment;
- Decision making on the basis of equality, mutual respect and consensus;
- Commitment to strengthen ASEAN's competitiveness, to deepen and broaden ASEAN's internal economic integration and linkages with the world economy;
- Promotion of regional solidarity and cooperation;
- Mutual respect for the independence, sovereignty, equality, territorial integrity and national identity of all nations;
- Renunciation of nuclear weapons and other weapons of mass destruction and avoidance of any arms race;
- Renunciation of the use of force and threat of use of force; non-aggression and exclusive reliance on peaceful means for the settlement of differences or disputes;
- Enhancing beneficial relations between ASEAN and its friends and partners;
- Upholding non-discrimination of any ASEAN Member Countries in ASEAN's external relations and cooperative activities;

– Observance of principles of international law concerning friendly relations and cooperation among States; and

– The right of every state to lead its national existence free from external interference, subversion or coercion and non-interference in the internal affairs of one another.

Fifth, the ASEAN Charter will confer a legal personality to ASEAN and determine the functions, developing areas of competence of key ASEAN bodies and their relationship with one another in the overall ASEAN structure.

And do hereby agree:

To establish an Eminent Persons Group (EPG), comprising highly distinguished and well respected citizens from ASEAN Member Countries, with the mandate to examine and provide practical recommendations on the directions and nature of the ASEAN Charter relevant to the ASEAN Community as envisaged in the Bali Concord II and beyond, taking into account, but not limited to, the principles, values and objectives as contained in this Declaration.

To consider their recommendations at our subsequent meetings.

To task our Ministers to establish, as necessary, a High Level Task Force to carry out the drafting of the ASEAN Charter based on the Kuala Lumpur Declaration on the Establishment of the ASEAN Charter and the recommendations of the EPG.

. . .

CHARTER OF THE ASSOCIATION OF SOUTHEAST ASIAN NATIONS (20.11.2007)

. . .

Mindful of the existence of mutual interests and interdependence among the peoples and Member States of ASEAN which are bound by geography, common objectives and shared destiny;

Inspired by and united under One Vision, One Identity and One Caring and Sharing Community;

United by a common desire and collective will to live in a region of lasting peace, security and stability, sustained economic growth, shared prosperity and social progress, and to promote our vital interests, ideals and aspirations;

Respecting the fundamental importance of amity and cooperation, and the principles of sovereignty, equality, territorial integrity, non-interference, consensus and unity in diversity;

Adhering to the principles of democracy, the rule of law and good governance, respect for and protection of human rights and fundamental freedoms;

Resolved to ensure sustainable development for the benefit of present and future generations and to place the well-being, livelihood and welfare of the peoples at the centre

of the ASEAN community building process;

Convinced of the need to strengthen existing bonds of regional solidarity to realise an ASEAN Community that is politically cohesive, economically integrated and socially responsible in order to effectively respond to current and future challenges and opportunities;

Committed to intensifying community building through enhanced regional cooperation and integration, in particular by establishing an ASEAN Community comprising the ASEAN Security Community, the ASEAN Economic Community and the ASEAN Socio-Cultural Community, as provided for in the Bali Declaration of ASEAN Concord II;

Hereby decide to establish, through this Charter, the legal and institutional framework for ASEAN

. . .

Chapter I—Purposes and Principles

Article 1
Purposes

The Purposes of ASEAN are:

1. To maintain and enhance peace, security and stability and further strengthen peace-oriented values in the region;
2. To enhance regional resilience by promoting greater political, security, economic and socio-cultural cooperation;
3. To preserve Southeast Asia as a Nuclear Weapon-Free Zone and free of all other weapons of mass destruction;
4. To ensure that the peoples and Member States of ASEAN live in peace with the world at large in a just, democratic and harmonious environment;
5. To create a Single Market and production base which is stable, prosperous, highly competitive and economically integrated with effective facilitation for trade and investment in which there is free flow of goods, services and investment; facilitated movement of business persons, professionals, talents and labour; and freer flow of capital;

6. To alleviate poverty and narrow the development gap within ASEAN through mutual assistance and cooperation;

7. To strengthen democracy, enhance good governance and the rule of law, and promote and protect human rights and fundamental freedoms, with due regard to the rights and responsibilities of the Member States of ASEAN;

8. To respond effectively, in accordance with the principle of comprehensive security, to all forms of threats, transnational crimes and transboundary challenges;

9. To promote sustainable development so as to ensure the protection of the region's environment, the sustainability of its natural resources, the preservation of its cultural heritage and the high quality of life of its peoples;

10. To develop human resources through closer cooperation in education and life-long learning, and in science and technology, for the empowerment of the peoples of ASEAN and for the strengthening of the ASEAN Community;

11. To enhance the well-being and livelihood of the peoples of ASEAN by providing them with equitable access to opportunities for human development, social welfare and justice;

12. To strengthen cooperation in building a safe, secure and drug-free environment for the peoples of ASEAN;

13. To promote a people-oriented ASEAN in which all sectors of society are encouraged to participate in, and benefit from, the process of ASEAN integration and community building;

14. To promote an ASEAN identity through the fostering of greater awareness of the diverse culture and heritage of the region; and

15. To maintain the centrality and proactive role of ASEAN as the primary driving force in its relations and cooperation with its external partners in a regional architecture that is open, transparent and inclusive.

    . . .

Chapter II—Legal Personality

Article 3
Legal Personality of ASEAN

ASEAN, as an inter-governmental organisation, is hereby conferred legal personality.

    . . .

Chapter IV—Organs

Article 7
ASEAN Summit

1. The ASEAN Summit shall comprise the Heads of State or Government of the Member States.
2. The ASEAN Summit shall:
   (a) be the supreme policy-making body of ASEAN;
   (b) deliberate, provide policy guidance and take decisions on key issues pertaining to the realisation of the objectives of ASEAN, important matters of interest to Member States and all issues referred to it by the ASEAN Coordinating Council, the ASEAN Community Councils and ASEAN Sectoral Ministerial Bodies;
   (c) instruct the relevant Ministers in each of the Councils concerned to hold ad hoc inter-Ministerial meetings, and address important issues concerning ASEAN that cut across the Community Councils. Rules of procedure for such meetings shall be adopted by the ASEAN Coordinating Council;
   (d) address emergency situations affecting ASEAN by taking appropriate actions;
   (e) decide on matters referred to it under Chapters VII and VIII;
   (f) authorise the establishment and the dissolution of Sectoral Ministerial Bodies and other ASEAN institutions; and
   (g) appoint the Secretary-General of ASEAN, with the rank and status of Minister, who will serve with the confidence and at the pleasure of the Heads of State or Government upon the recommendation of the ASEAN Foreign Ministers Meeting.
3. ASEAN Summit Meetings shall be:
   (a) held twice annually, and be hosted by the Member State holding the ASEAN Chairmanship; and
   (b) convened, whenever necessary, as special or ad hoc meetings to be chaired by the Member State holding the ASEAN Chairmanship, at venues to be agreed upon by ASEAN Member States.

Article 8
ASEAN Coordinating Council

1. The ASEAN Coordinating Council shall comprise the ASEAN Foreign Ministers and meet at least twice a year.
2. The ASEAN Coordinating Council shall:

(a) prepare the meetings of the ASEAN Summit;

(b) coordinate the implementation of agreements and decisions of the ASEAN Summit;

(c) coordinate with the ASEAN Community Councils to enhance policy coherence, efficiency and cooperation among them;

(d) coordinate the reports of the ASEAN Community Councils to the ASEAN Summit;

(e) consider the annual report of the Secretary-General on the work of ASEAN;

(f) consider the report of the Secretary-General on the functions and operations of the ASEAN Secretariat and other relevant bodies;

(g) approve the appointment and termination of the Deputy Secretaries-General upon the recommendation of the Secretary-General; and

(h) undertake other tasks provided for in this Charter or such other functions as may be assigned by the ASEAN Summit.

3. The ASEAN Coordinating Council shall be supported by the relevant senior officials.

Article 9
ASEAN Community Councils

1. The ASEAN Community Councils shall comprise the ASEAN Political-Security Community Council, ASEAN Economic Community Council, and ASEAN Socio-Cultural Community Council.

2. Each ASEAN Community Council shall have under its purview the relevant ASEAN Sectoral Ministerial Bodies.

3. Each Member State shall designate its national representation for each ASEAN Community Council meeting.

4. In order to realise the objectives of each of the three pillars of the ASEAN Community, each ASEAN Community Council shall:

(a) ensure the implementation of the relevant decisions of the ASEAN Summit;

(b) coordinate the work of the different sectors under its purview, and on issues which cut across the other Community Councils; and

(c) submit reports and recommendations to the ASEAN Summit on matters under its purview.

5. Each ASEAN Community Council shall meet at least twice a year and shall be chaired by the appropriate Minister from the Member State holding the ASEAN Chairmanship.

6.   Each ASEAN Community Council shall be supported by the relevant senior officials.

Article 10
ASEAN Sectoral Ministerial Bodies

1.   ASEAN Sectoral Ministerial Bodies shall:
     (a) function in accordance with their respective established mandates;
     (b) implement the agreements and decisions of the ASEAN Summit under their respective purview;
     (c) strengthen cooperation in their respective fields in support of ASEAN integration and community building; and
     (d) submit reports and recommendations to their respective Community Councils.

2.   Each ASEAN Sectoral Ministerial Body may have under its purview the relevant senior officials and subsidiary bodies to undertake its functions as contained in Annex 1. The Annex may be updated by the Secretary-General of ASEAN upon the recommendation of the Committee of Permanent Representatives without recourse to the provision on Amendments under this Charter.

Article 11
Secretary-General of ASEAN and ASEAN Secretariat

1.   The Secretary-General of ASEAN shall be appointed by the ASEAN Summit for a non-renewable term of office of five years, selected from among nationals of the ASEAN Member States based on alphabetical rotation, with due consideration to integrity, capability and professional experience, and gender equality.

2.   The Secretary-General shall:
     (a) carry out the duties and responsibilities of this high office in accordance with the provisions of this Charter and relevant ASEAN instruments, protocols and established practices;
     (b) facilitate and monitor progress in the implementation of ASEAN agreements and decisions, and submit an annual report on the work of ASEAN to the ASEAN Summit;
     (c) participate in meetings of the ASEAN Summit, the ASEAN Community Councils, the ASEAN Coordinating Council, and ASEAN Sectoral Ministerial Bodies and other relevant ASEAN meetings;

(d) present the views of ASEAN and participate in meetings with external parties in accordance with the approved policy guidelines and mandate given to the Secretary-General; and

(e) recommend the appointment and termination of the Deputy Secretaries-General to the ASEAN Coordinating Council for approval.

3. The Secretary-General shall also be the Chief Administrative Officer of ASEAN.

4. The Secretary-General shall be assisted by four Deputy Secretaries-General with the rank and status of Deputy Ministers. The Deputy Secretaries-General shall be accountable to the Secretary-General in carrying out their functions.

. . .

Article 12
Committee of Permanent Representatives to ASEAN

1. Each ASEAN Member State shall appoint a Permanent Representative to ASEAN with the rank of Ambassador based in Jakarta.

2. The Permanent Representatives collectively constitute a Committee of Permanent Representatives, which shall:

(a) support the work of the ASEAN Community Councils and ASEAN Sectoral Ministerial Bodies;

(b) coordinate with ASEAN National Secretariats and other ASEAN Sectoral Ministerial Bodies;

(c) liaise with the Secretary-General of ASEAN and the ASEAN Secretariat on all subjects relevant to its work;

(d) facilitate ASEAN cooperation with external partners; and

(e) perform such other functions as may be determined by the ASEAN Coordinating Council.

Article 13
ASEAN National Secretariats

Each ASEAN Member State shall establish an ASEAN National Secretariat which shall:

(a) serve as the national focal point;

(b) be the repository of information on all ASEAN matters at the national level;

(c) coordinate the implementation of ASEAN decisions at the national level;

(d) coordinate and support the national preparations of ASEAN meetings;

(e) promote ASEAN identity and awareness at the national level; and

(f) contribute to ASEAN community building.

Article 14
ASEAN Human Rights Body

1. In conformity with the purposes and principles of the ASEAN Charter relating to the promotion and protection of human rights and fundamental freedoms, ASEAN shall establish an ASEAN human rights body.
2. This ASEAN human rights body shall operate in accordance with the terms of reference to be determined by the ASEAN Foreign Ministers Meeting.

Article 15
ASEAN Foundation

1. The ASEAN Foundation shall support the Secretary-General of ASEAN and collaborate with the relevant ASEAN bodies to support ASEAN community building by promoting greater awareness of the ASEAN identity, people-to-people interaction, and close collaboration among the business sector, civil society, academia and other stakeholders in ASEAN.
2. The ASEAN Foundation shall be accountable to the Secretary-General of ASEAN, who shall submit its report to the ASEAN Summit through the ASEAN Coordinating Council.

   . . .

Chapter VII—Decision-Making

Article 20
Consultation and Consensus

1. As a basic principle, decision-making in ASEAN shall be based on consultation and consensus.
2. Where consensus cannot be achieved, the ASEAN Summit may decide how a specific decision can be made.
3. Nothing in paragraphs 1 and 2 of this Article shall affect the modes of decision-making as contained in the relevant ASEAN legal instruments.
4. In the case of a serious breach of the Charter or noncompliance, the matter shall be referred to the ASEAN Summit for decision.

   . . .

Chapter VIII—Settlement of Disputes

Article 22
General Principles

1. Member States shall endeavour to resolve peacefully all disputes in a timely manner through dialogue, consultation and negotiation.
2. ASEAN shall maintain and establish dispute settlement mechanisms in all fields of ASEAN cooperation.

Article 23
Good Offices, Conciliation and Mediation

1. Member States which are parties to a dispute may at any time agree to resort to good offices, conciliation or mediation in order to resolve the dispute within an agreed time limit.
2. Parties to the dispute may request the Chairman of ASEAN or the Secretary-General of ASEAN, acting in an ex officio capacity, to provide good offices, conciliation or mediation.

Article 24
Dispute Settlement Mechanisms in Specific Instruments

1. Disputes relating to specific ASEAN instruments shall be settled through the mechanisms and procedures provided for in such instruments.
2. Disputes which do not concern the interpretation or application of any ASEAN instrument shall be resolved peacefully in accordance with the Treaty of Amity and Cooperation in Southeast Asia and its rules of procedure.
3. Where not otherwise specifically provided, disputes which concern the interpretation or application of ASEAN economic agreements shall be settled in accordance with the ASEAN Protocol on Enhanced Dispute Settlement Mechanism.

   . . .

Chapter X—Administration and Procedure

Article 31
Chairman of ASEAN

1. The Chairmanship of ASEAN shall rotate annually, based on the alphabetical order of the English names of Member States.

2. ASEAN shall have, in a calendar year, a single Chairmanship by which the Member State assuming the Chairmanship shall chair:
    (a) the ASEAN Summit and related summits;
    (b) the ASEAN Coordinating Council;
    (c) the three ASEAN Community Councils;
    (d) where appropriate, the relevant ASEAN Sectoral Ministerial Bodies and senior officials; and
    (e) the Committee of Permanent Representatives.

Article 32
Role of the Chairman of ASEAN

The Member State holding the Chairmanship of ASEAN shall:
(a) actively promote and enhance the interests and wellbeing of ASEAN, including efforts to build an ASEAN Community through policy initiatives, coordination, consensus and cooperation;
(b) ensure the centrality of ASEAN;
(c) ensure an effective and timely response to urgent issues or crisis situations affecting ASEAN, including providing its good offices and such other arrangements to immediately address these concerns;
(d) represent ASEAN in strengthening and promoting closer relations with external partners; and
(e) carry out such other tasks and functions as may be mandated.
    . . .

Article 34
Working Language of ASEAN

The working language of ASEAN shall be English.

Chapter XI—Identity and Symbols

Article 35
ASEAN Identity

ASEAN shall promote its common ASEAN identity and a sense of belonging among its peoples in order to achieve its shared destiny, goals and values.

Article 36
ASEAN Motto

The ASEAN motto shall be: "One Vision, One Identity, One Community."

Article 37
ASEAN Flag

The ASEAN flag shall be as shown in Annex 3.

Article 38
ASEAN Emblem

The ASEAN emblem shall be as shown in Annex 4.

Article 39
ASEAN Day

The eighth of August shall be observed as ASEAN Day.

Article 40
ASEAN Anthem

ASEAN shall have an anthem.

Chapter XII—External Relations

Article 41
Conduct of External Relations

1. ASEAN shall develop friendly relations and mutually beneficial dialogue, cooperation and partnerships with countries and sub-regional, regional and international organisations and instzitutions.
2. The external relations of ASEAN shall adhere to the purposes and principles set forth in this Charter.
3. ASEAN shall be the primary driving force in regional arrangements that it initiates and maintain its centrality in regional cooperation and community building.
4. In the conduct of external relations of ASEAN, Member States shall, on the basis of unity and solidarity, coordinate and endeavour to develop common positions and pursue joint actions.

5. The strategic policy directions of ASEAN's external relations shall be set by the ASEAN Summit upon the recommendation of the ASEAN Foreign Ministers Meeting.

6. The ASEAN Foreign Ministers Meeting shall ensure consistency and coherence in the conduct of ASEAN's external relations.

7. ASEAN may conclude agreements with countries or subregional, regional and international organisations and institutions. The procedures for concluding such agreements shall be prescribed by the ASEAN Coordinating Council in consultation with the ASEAN Community Councils.

Article 42
Dialogue Coordinator

1. Member States, acting as Country Coordinators, shall take turns to take overall responsibility in coordinating and promoting the interests of ASEAN in its relations with the relevant Dialogue Partners, regional and international organisations and institutions.

2. In relations with the external partners, the Country Coordinators shall, inter alia:

   (a) represent ASEAN and enhance relations on the basis of mutual respect and equality, in conformity with ASEAN's principles;

   (b) co-chair relevant meetings between ASEAN and external partners; and

   (c) be supported by the relevant ASEAN Committees in Third Countries and International Organisations.

Article 43
ASEAN Committees in Third Countries and International Organisations

1. ASEAN Committees in Third Countries may be established in non-ASEAN countries comprising heads of diplomatic missions of ASEAN Member States. Similar Committees may be established relating to international organisations. Such Committees shall promote ASEAN's interests and identity in the host countries and international organisations.

2. The ASEAN Foreign Ministers Meeting shall determine the rules of procedure of such Committees.

   . . .

Gulf Cooperation Council (GCC)

The Gulf Cooperation Council (GCC) was founded by the conservative Gulf monarchies in 1981 as a defensive measure against the threat of a spillover of the Islamic revolution in Iran. Cooperation between Bahrain (with a history of tensions between its Sunni and Shiite populations), Kuwait (which also has a Shiite minority), Oman, Qatar, Saudi Arabia, and the United Arab Emirates has developed considerably. It is poised to transform into regional integration for a population of 28 million, with the implementation of a common currency for the Gulf countries targeted for 2010.

At the time of independence of the smaller Gulf states—Kuwait gained independence from Great Britain in 1961—it seemed possible that all of these new states might replace British suzerainty with a joint system of statehood. After prolonged negotiations, in 1975 only the seven Trucial Sheikhdoms of Abu Dhabi, Dubai, Sharjah, Ajman, Ras al Khaimah, Fujairah and Umm al Quwain agreed to form the United Arab Emirates, while Bahrain and Qatar opted for independent statehood. The Sultanate of Oman gradually opened up during the 1970s. In 1976 Oman hosted a meeting of the Foreign Ministers of Iran, Iraq, Kuwait, Bahrain, Qatar, the United Arab Emirates, Saudi Arabia, and Oman to discuss a coordinated regional security and defense policy. The effort ended without any conclusion all participants were able to agree upon. It took the threat of a possible spread of the Islamic Revolution in Iran in early 1979 to accelerate the thrust for cooperation and integration in the Gulf—as a protective measure against one of the potential participants in any logical cooperation around the Arab/Persian Gulf.

After the Soviet Union invaded Afghanistan in December 1979, the situation looked increasingly dangerous for stability and legitimacy in the Gulf region. Worsening relations between Iran and Iraq, leading into their protracted war between 1980 and 1988, forced the remaining Gulf states to act. At the initiative of Kuwait, they signed the founding Gulf Cooperation Council Charter in May 1981. The charter refers to the "ultimate aim of unity" (Article 4) and an eventual confederal union emanating from the GCC framework.

The highest authority of the Gulf Cooperation Council is the Supreme Council, representing the six heads of state of the member states. When necessary, the Supreme Council can constitute itself as Dispute Settlement Board. In the council, where each country has a single vote, unanimity is required to achieve decisions and approve common policies. The chairmanship in the Supreme Council rotates every year. Below the Supreme Council, the GCC consists of the Ministerial Council, the forum for the foreign ministers of the six member states. This is the working policy group of the GCC, supported by other GCC ministerial and expert committees. The Secretariat in Riyadh administrates the GCC and initiates studies reviewing the potential for integration projects. Within the general framework of the Arab world, the GCC has always been perceived as a force of moderation. It has been involved in mediating the conflicts between the Sultanate of Oman and the then People's Republic of Yemen. After the two Yemenite states were unified in 1990 to form the Arab Republic of Yemen, efforts of gradual approximation of Yemen to the GCC have been pursued on the level of expert and technical cooperation, leading to a cooperation agreement with Yemen in 1998. The issue of Yemenite membership in the Gulf Cooperation Council remains unresolved, not least because of the regime difference between the conservative Arab monarchies and the rather socialist Arab Republic. Nevertheless, the issue of possible Yemenite membership has been discussed as much as the prospect of Iranian and Iraqi membership, which depends on the outcome of the aggravated tensions in both countries and thus within the broader region.

The strategic and defensive rationale behind the creation of the Gulf Cooperation Council led to a speedy spillover into the economic sphere. This was more than logical given the rapid modernization of the Gulf region since the 1970s, based on its oil exports. GCC cooperation soon echoed the need of the oil-producing countries of the Gulf to jointly embark on a strategy of economic diversification in order to strengthen their independence from oil and gas revenues. The member states of the Gulf Cooperation Council hold 45 percent of the world's oil reserves and supply 20 percent of the global production of crude oil. Estimates of the duration of oil and gas reserves indicate that only Kuwait and Qatar might be able to completely rely on oil and gas income for their future. Diversification of the economy has therefore been identified as a crucial challenge for Gulf Cooperation countries in order to make their cooperation sustainable. The structure of their economies makes it difficult to substantially increase intra-regional trade in spite of the ambitions expressed in the Unified Economic Agreement between the Countries of the Gulf Cooperation Council (1981) and its revised version (2001).

The focus shifted from strategic concern about the possible spread of the Islamic Revolution in the 1980s to economic considerations leading to joint efforts in implementing diversification and a customs union with an eventual common currency during the 1990s. A new geostrategic dimension arose in the wake of the terrorist attacks on the United States on 11 September 2001 and the subsequent debate about the stability of Saudi Arabia and the need for the democratic transformation of the Greater Middle East. While some of the smaller Gulf countries embarked on a cautious but steady path toward constitutional monarchy with elements of popular democracy—with local elections in Qatar, elections in Kuwait, new consultative and constitutional elements in Bahrain and Oman—the difference between the smaller Gulf states and the overwhelming size and impact of Saudi Arabia in the region became even more visible.

Integrating the non–raw oil economy has been one of the priorities of the GCC. Common investment in petrochemical, industrial, and livestock projects has taken place. Policies for saving energy, separate passport controls for GCC nationals at the airports in the region, an increase in regional communication and transportation schemes, freedom of capital, and freedom of labor have been realized in the GCC. The necessary steps to advance from a free-trade area without internal customs revenues into a common market and ultimately a monetary union have been supported ever since the establishment of a uniform external tariff system in 1983. All GCC countries remain committed to implementing a common currency by 2010 despite the clouds hanging over the region since the outbreak of Islamic terrorism and the geopolitical tensions in the Greater Middle East since 2001, coinciding with severe generational changes across the region.

THE COOPERATION COUNCIL — CHARTER (25.02.1981)

. . .

Being fully aware of the ties of special relations, common characteristics and similar systems founded on the creed of Islam which bind them; and

Desiring to effect coordination, cooperation and integration between them in all fields;

. . .

Article 1
The Establishment of the Council

A Council shall be established hereby to be named The Cooperation Council for the Arab States of the Gulf hereinafter referred to as the Cooperation Council (GCC).

Article 2

The Cooperation Council shall have its headquarters in Riyadh, Saudi Arabia.

Article 3
Cooperation Council Meetings

The Council shall hold its meetings in the state where it has its headquarters, and may convene in any member state.

Article 4
Objectives

The basic objectives of the Cooperation Council are:

1. To effect coordination, integration and inter-connection between Member States in all fields in order to achieve unity between them.
2. To deepen and strengthen relations, links and areas of cooperation now prevailing between their peoples in various fields.
3. To formulate similar regulations in various fields including the following:
   (a) Economic and financial affairs
   (b) Commerce, customs and communications
   (c) Education and culture
4. To stimulate scientific and technological progress in the fields of industry, mining, agriculture, water and animal resources; to establish scientific research; to establish joint ventures and encourage cooperation by the private sector for the good of their peoples.

Article 5
Council Membership

The Cooperation Council shall be formed of the six states that participated in the Foreign Ministers' meeting held in Riyadh on 4 February 1981.

Article 6
Organization of the Cooperation Council

The Cooperation Council shall have the following main organizations:

1. The Supreme Council to which shall be attached the Commission for Settlement of Disputes.
2. The Ministerial Council.
3. The Secretariat General.

Each of these organizations may establish sub-agencies as may be necessary.

Article 7
Supreme Council

The Cooperation Council shall be formed of the six states that participated in the Foreign Ministers' meeting held in Riyadh on 4 February 1981.

1. The Supreme Council is the highest authority of the Cooperation Council and shall be formed of heads of member states. Its presidency

shall be rotating based on the alphabetical order of the names of the member states.

2. The Supreme Council shall hold one regular session every year. Extraordinary sessions may be convened at the request of any member seconded by another member.

3. The Supreme Council shall hold its sessions in the territories of member states.

4. A Supreme Council's meeting shall be considered valid if attend by two-thirds of the member states.

Article 8
The Functions of the Supreme Council

The Supreme Council shall endeavour to realize the objectives of the Cooperation Council, particularly as concerns the following:

1. Review matters of interest to the member states.
2. Lay down the higher policy for the Cooperation Council and the basic lines it should follow.
3. Review the recommendations, reports, studies and joint ventures submitted by the Ministerial Council for approval.
4. Review reports and studies, which the Secretary-General is charged to prepare.
5. Approve the bases for dealing with other states and international organizations.
6. Approve the rules of procedure of the Commission for the Settlement of Disputes and nominate its members.
7. Appoint the Secretary-General.
8. Amend the Charter of the Cooperation Council.
9. Approve the Council's internal rules of procedure.
10. Approve the budget of the Secretariat General.

Article 9
Voting in the Supreme Council

The Cooperation Council shall be formed of the six states that participated in the Foreign Ministers' meeting held in Riyadh on 4 February 1981.

1. Each member of the Supreme Council shall have one vote.
2. Resolutions of the Supreme Council in substantive matters shall be carried by unanimous approval of the member states participating in the voting, while resolutions on procedural matters shall be carried by majority vote.

Article 10
Commission for the Settlement of Disputes

1. The Cooperation Council shall have a commission called "The Commission for the Settlement of Disputes" which shall be attached to the Supreme Council.
2. The Supreme Council shall establish the composition of the Commission for every case on an ad hoc basis in accordance with the nature of the dispute.
3. If a dispute arises over interpretation or implementation of the Charter and such dispute is not resolved within the Ministerial Council or the Supreme Council, the Supreme Council may refer such dispute to the Commission for the Settlement of Disputes.
4. The Commission shall submit its recommendations or opinion, as applicable, to the Supreme Council for such action as the Supreme Council deems appropriate.

Article 11
Ministerial Council

1. The Ministerial Council shall be formed of the Foreign Ministers of the member states or other delegated ministers. The Council Presidency shall be for the member state which presided over the last ordinary session of the Supreme Council, or if necessary, for the state which is next to preside over the Supreme Council.
2. The Ministerial Council shall convene every three months and may hold extraordinary sessions at the invitation of any member seconded by another member.
3. The Ministerial Council shall determine the venue of its next session.
4. A Council's meeting shall be deemed valid if attended by two-thirds of the member states.

Article 12
Functions of the Ministerial Council

1. Propose policies, prepare recommendations, studies and projects aimed at developing cooperation and coordination between member states in various fields and adopt the resolutions or recommendations required in this regard.
2. Endeavour to encourage, develop and coordinate activities existing between member states in all fields. Resolutions adopted in such matters shall be referred to the Ministerial Council for further submission, with recommendations to the Supreme Council for appropriate action.

3. Submit recommendations to the Ministers concerned to formulate policies whereby the Cooperation Council's resolutions may be put into effect.

4. Encourage means of cooperation and coordination between the various private sector activities, develop existing cooperation between the member states' Chamber of Commerce and Industry, and encourage the movement within the GCC of workers who are citizens of the member states.

5. Refer any of the various aspects of cooperation to one or more technical or specialised committee for study and presentation of appropriate recommendations.

6. Review proposals related to amendments to this Charter and submit appropriate recommendations to the Supreme Council.

7. Approve Rules of Procedure of both the Ministerial Council and the Secretariat General.

8. Appoint the Assistant Secretaries-General, as nominated by the Secretary-General, for a period of three years, renewable.

9. Approve periodic reports as well as internal rules and regulations relating to administrative and financial affairs proposed by the Secretary-General, and submit recommendations to the Supreme Council for approval of the budget of the Secretariat General.

10. Make arrangements for meetings of the Supreme Council and prepare its agenda.

11. Review matters referred to it by the Supreme Council.

Article 13
Voting in the Ministerial Council

1. Every member of the Ministerial Council shall have one vote.

2. Resolutions of the Ministerial Council in substantive matters shall be carried by unanimous vote of the member states present and participating in the vote, and in procedural matters by majority vote.

Article 14
The Secretariat General

1. The Secretariat General shall be composed of a Secretary-General who shall be assisted by assistants and a number of staff as required.

2. The Supreme Council shall appoint the Secretary-General, who shall be a citizen of one of the Cooperation Council states, for a period of three years, which may be renewed once only.

3. The Secretary-General shall nominate the Assistant Secretaries-General.
4. The Secretary-General shall appoint the Secretariat General staff from among the citizens of member states, and may not make exceptions without the approval of the Ministerial Council.
5. The Secretary-General shall be directly responsible for the work of the Secretariat General and the smooth flow of work in its various organizations. He shall represent the Cooperation Council with other parties within the limits of the authority vested in him.

Article 15
Functions of the Secretariat General

The Secretariat General shall:
1. Prepare studies related to cooperation and coordination, and to integrated plans and programmes for member states' action.
2. Prepare periodic reports on the work of the Cooperation Council.
3. Follow up the implementation by the member states of the resolutions and recommendations of the Supreme Council and Ministerial Council.
4. Prepare reports and studies requested by the Supreme Council or Ministerial Council.
5. Prepare the draft of administrative and financial regulations commensurate with the growth of the Cooperation Council and its expanding responsibilities.
6. Prepare the budgets and closing accounts of the Cooperation Council.
7. Make preparations for meetings and prepare agendas and draft resolutions for the Ministerial Council.
8. Recommend to the Chairman of the Ministerial Council the convening of an extraordinary session of the Council when necessary.
9. Any other tasks entrusted to it by the Supreme Council or Ministerial Council.

   . . .

Article 18
Budget of the Secretariat General

The Secretariat General shall have a budget to which the member states shall contribute in equal amounts.

   . . .

Article 20
Amendments to the Charter

1. Any member state may request an amendment of this Charter.

2. Requests for Charter amendments shall be submitted to the Secretary-General who shall refer them to the member states at least four months prior to submission to the Ministerial Council.
3. An amendment shall become effective if unanimously approved by the Supreme Council.

. . .

THE UNIFIED ECONOMIC AGREEMENT BETWEEN THE COUNTRIES OF THE GULF COOPERATION COUNCIL (11.11.1981)

. . .

With the help of God the Almighty; the Governments of the Member States of the Arab Gulf Cooperation Council; in accordance with the Charter thereof, which calls for closer relations and stronger links; and, desiring to develop extend and enhance their economic ties on solid foundations, in the best interest of their peoples and for the sake of working to coordinate and standardize their economic, financial and monetary policies, as well as their commercial and industrial legislation, and Customs regulations have agreed as follows:

Chapter 1—Trade Exchange

Article 1

a) The Member States shall permit the importation and exportation of agricultural, animal, industrial and natural resource products that are of national origin. Also, they shall permit exportation thereof to other Member States.
b) All agricultural, animal, industrial and natural resource products that are from Member States shall receive the same treatment as national products.

Article 2

1. All agricultural, animal, industrial and natural resource products that are of national origin shall be exempted from reciprocal charges.
2. Fees charged for specific services such as demurrage, storage, transportation, freight or unloading, shall not be considered as customs duties when they are levied on domestic products.

Article 3

1. For products of national origin to qualify as national manufactured products, the value added ensuing from their production in Member States shall not be less than 40% of their final value as at the termination of the production phase. In addition Member States citizens' share in the ownership of the producing plant shall not be less than 51%.
2. Every item enjoying exemption hereby shall be accompanied by a certificate of origin duly authenticated by the appropriate government agency concerned

Article 4

1. Member States shall establish a uniform minimum Customs tariff applicable to the products of countries other than G.C.C. Member States.
2. One of the objectives of the uniform Customs tariff shall be the protection of national products from foreign competition
3. The uniform Customs tariff shall be implemented gradually within five years from the date on which this agreement becomes effective. Arrangements for its gradual implementation shall be agreed upon within one year from the said date.

    . . .

Article 7

Member states shall coordinate their commercial policies and relations with other states and regional economic groupings and blocs with a view to creating balanced trade relations and equitable circumstances and terms of trade therewith. To achieve this goal, the Member States shall make the following arrangements:

1. Coordination of import/export policies and regulations.
2. Coordination of policies for building up strategic food stocks.
3. Conclusion of collective economic agreements in cases where joint benefits to Member States would be realized.
4. Taking of action for the creation of collective negotiating power to strengthen their negotiating position vis-à-vis foreign parties in the field of importation of basic needs and exportation of major products.

Chapter 2—The Movement of Capital and Individuals and the Exercise of Economic Activities

Article 8

The Member States shall agree on executive principles to ensure that each Member State shall grant the citizens of all other Member States the same treatment as is granted to its own citizens without any discrimination or differentiation in the following fields:

1. Freedom of movement, work and residence.
2. Right of ownership, inheritance and bequest.
3. Freedom of exercising economic activity.
4. Free movement of capital.

Article 9

The Member States shall encourage their respective private sectors to establish joint ventures in order to link their citizens' economic interests in various spheres of activity.

Chapter 3—Coordination of Development

Article 10

The Member States shall endeavour to achieve the coordination and harmonization of their respective plans with a view to achieving integration in economic affairs.

Article 11

1. The Member States shall endeavour to coordinate their policies with regard to all aspects of the oil industry including extraction, refining, marketing, processing, pricing, the exploitation of natural gas, and development of energy sources.
2. The Member States shall endeavour to formulate united oil policies and adopt common positions vis-à-vis the outside world, and in international and specialized organizations.

Article 12

To achieve the objectives specified in this Agreement, the Member States shall

1. Coordinate industrial activities, formulate policies and mechanisms which will lead to industrial development and the diversification of their products on an integrated basis.
2. Standardize their industrial legislation and regulations and guide their local production units to meet their needs.
3. Allocate industries between Member States according to relative advantages and economic feasibility, and encourage the establishment of basic as well as ancillary industries.

    . . .

Chapter 4—Technical Cooperation

Article 14

The Member States shall collaborate in finding spheres for common technical cooperation aimed at building a genuine local base founded on encouragement and support of research and applied sciences and technology as well as adapting imported technology to meet the needs of the region and to achieve the objectives of progress and development.

Article 15

Member States shall establish procedures, make arrangements and lay down terms for the transfer of technology, selecting the most suitable or introducing such changes thereto as would serve their various needs. Member States shall also, whenever feasible, conclude uniform agreements with foreign governments and scientific or commercial organizations to achieve these objectives.

Article 16

Members States shall formulate policies and implement coordinated programs for technical, vocational and professional training and qualification at all levels and stages. They shall also develop educational curricula at all levels to link education and technology with the development needs of the Member States.

Article 17

Member States shall coordinate their manpower policies and shall formulate uniform and standardized criteria and classifications for the various categories of occupations and crafts in different sectors in order to avoid harmful competition among themselves and to optimize the utilization of available human resources.

Chapter 5—Transport and Communications

Article 18

Member States shall accord passenger and cargo transportation belonging to citizens of the other Member States, when transiting or entering its territory, the same treatment they accord to the means of passenger and cargo transportation belonging to their own citizens, including exemption from all duties and taxes, whatsoever. However, local means of transportation are excluded.

Article 19

1. Member States shall cooperate in the fields of land and sea transportation, and communications. They shall also coordinate and establish infrastructure projects such as seaports, airports, water and power stations and roads, with a view to realizing joint economic development and the linking of their economic activities with each other.
2. The contracting states shall coordinate aviation and air transport policies among them and promote all areas of joint action at various levels.

Article 20

Member States shall allow steamers, ships and boats and their cargoes, belonging to any Member State, freely to use the various port facilities and grant them the same treatment and privileges granted to their own in docking or calling at the ports as concerns fees, pilotage and docking services, freight, loading and unloading, maintenance, repair, storage of goods and other similar services.

Chapter 6—Financial and Monetary Cooperation

Article 21

Member States shall seek to unify investment rules and regulations in order to achieve a joint investment policy aimed at directing their domestic and foreign investments towards serving their interest, and realizing their peoples' aspirations for development and progress.

Article 22

Member States shall seek to coordinate their financial, monetary and banking policies and enhance cooperation between monetary agencies and central banks, including the endeavour to establish a joint currency in order to further their desired economic goals.

Article 23

Member States shall seek to coordinate their external policies in the sphere of international and regional development aid.

. . .

Article 27

In case of conflict with local laws and regulations of Member States, execution of the provisions of this Agreement shall prevail.

. . .

THE ECONOMIC AGREEMENT BETWEEN THE GULF COOPERATION COUNCIL STATES (REVISED) (31.12.2001)

. . .

Seeking to achieve advanced stages of economic Integration that would lead to a common market and an Economic and Monetary Union among Member States according to a specific timetable, while enhancing market mechanisms and fostering the role of the private sector;

. . .

Chapter 1—Trade

Article 1
The Customs Union

Trade between the GCC member States will be conducted within the framework of a customs union that will be implemented no later than the first of January 2003. It shall include, at a minimum, the following:

    i.   A common external customs tariff (CET).
   ii.   Common customs regulations and procedures.
  iii.   Single entry point where customs duties are collected.
  iv.   Elimination of all tariff and non-tariff barriers, while taking into consideration laws of agricultural and veterinarian quarantine, as well as rules regarding prohibited and restricted goods.

v. Goods produced in any Member State shall be accorded the same treatment as national products.

Article 2
International Economic Relations

To secure better terms and more favorable conditions in their international economic relationships, Member States shall draw their policies and conduct economic relations in a collective fashion in dealing with other countries, blocs and regional groupings, as well as other regional and international organizations.

Member States shall take the necessary measures to achieve this objective, including the following:

i. Negotiate collectively in a manner that serves the negotiating position of the Member States.
ii. Collectively conclude economic agreements with trading partners.
iii. Unify import and export rules and procedures.
iv. Unify commercial exchange policies with the outside world.

Chapter 2—GCC Common Market

Article 3

GCC natural and legal citizens shall be accorded, in any Member State, the same treatment accorded to its own citizens, without differentiation or discrimination, in all economic activities, especially the following:

i. Movement and residence
ii. Work in private and government Jobs
iii. Pension and social security
iv. Engagement in all professions and crafts
v. Engagement in all economic, investment and service activities
vi. Real estate ownership
vii. Capital movement
viii. Tax treatment
ix. Stock ownership and formation of corporations
x. Education, health and social Services

Member States shall agree to complete implementation rules sufficient to carry this out and bring into being the Gulf common market.

Chapter 3—Economic and Monetary Union

Article 4
Monetary and Economic Union Requirements

For the purpose of achieving a monetary and economic union between Member States, including currency unification, Member States shall undertake, according to a specified timetable, to achieve the requirements of this union. These include the achievement of a high level of harmonization between Member States in all economic policies, especially fiscal and monetary policies, banking legislation, setting criteria to approximate rates of economic performance related to fiscal and monetary stability, such as rates of budgetary deficit, indebtedness, and price levels.

Article 5
Investment Climate

For the purpose of enhancing local, external, and intra-GCC investment levels, and provide an investment climate characterized by transparency and stability, Member States agree to take the following Steps:

1. Unify all their investment-related laws and regulations.
2. Accord national treatment to all Investments owned by GCC natural and legal citizens.
3. Integrate financial markets in Member States, and unify all related legislation and policies.
4. Adopt unified Standards and specifications for all products, according to the Charter of the GCC Standardization and Metrology Organization.

Article 6
Regional and International Aid

Member States shall coordinate their external policies related to international and regional development aid.

Chapter 4—Development Integration

Article 7
Comprehensive Development

Member States shall adopt the policies necessary to achieve an integrated development process in all fields in all GCC states and deepen coordination between all activities contained in their national development plans. These policies shall include the implementation of the Long-term Comprehensive Development Strategy of the GCC Member States.

Article 8
Industrial Development

    i.   Member States shall adopt the policies necessary to enhance the participation of the industrial sector in the economy, coordination of industrial activity on a GCC-wide integrated basis, including the implementation of the Unified Strategy of Industrial Development for the GCC Member States.

    ii.   Member States shall unify their industrial legislation and regulations, including rules related to industry promotion, anti-dumping, and precautionary safeguards.

Article 9
Oil, Gas, and Natural Resources

For the purpose of achieving Integration between Member States in the fields of petroleum and minerals industries, and other natural resources, and enhancing the competitive position of Member States,

    1.   Member States shall adopt integrated policies in all phases of oil, gas, and minerals industries to achieve optimal exploitation of natural resources, while taking into account environmental considerations and the interests of future generations.

    2.   Member States shall adopt unified policies for oil and gas, and take common positions in this regard towards non-member states and international and specialized organizations.

    3.   Member States and oil and gas companies working within them shall cooperate in supporting and developing research in the fields of oil, gas, and natural resources, and enhance cooperation with universities in these fields.

Article 10
Agricultural Development

Member States shall adopt the policies necessary to achieve agricultural integration between them, and long-tem optimal utilization of available resources, especially water, including the implementation of the Common Agricultural Policy of the GCC Member States and related GCC legislation.

Article 11
Environmental Protection

Member States shall adopt the policies and mechanisms necessary to protect the environment according to all relevant legislation and resolutions adopted within the GCC framework, as representing the minimum level for national rules and legislation.

Article 12
Joint Projects

For the purpose of enhancing ties between Member States in the productive sectors, utilizing economies of scale, achieving economic integration, and improving the distribution of Integration benefits among them, Member States shall undertake the measures necessary to support, finance, and form joint projects, both private and public, including the following:

1. Adopt integrated economic policies between the Member States for infrastructure projects and basic Services such as transport; communications; electricity; information technology; health, education, and tourism projects; and oil and gas industry.
2. Establish joint projects based on comparative advantages of Member States.
3. Provide additional incentives for the private sector to form joint projects that interlink the economic interests of GCC citizens.
4. Eliminate all procedural obstacles encountered by joint projects and accord them, at a minimum, the same treatment given to similar national projects.

Chapter 5—Development of Human Resources

Article 13
Population Strategy

Member States shall implement the "General Framework of Population Strategy of the GCC States," adopt the policies necessary for the development of human resources and their optimal utilization, provision of health care and social services, enhancement of the role of women in development, and the achievement of balance in the demographic structure and labor force to ensure social harmony in Member States, emphasize their Arab and Islamic identity, and maintain their stability and solidarity.

. . .

Article 15
Education

1. Member States shall cooperate to develop programs and curricula of public, higher, and technical education, to ensure high levels of scientific content and compatibility with the development needs of Member States.
2. Member States shall undertake to achieve integration between GCC universities in all fields.
3. Member States shall adopt appropriate policies and mechanisms to ensure compatibility between the Outputs of higher education and scientific and technical research on the one hand, and the needs of the labor market and economic development, on the other.

Article 16
Manpower Nationalization

1. Member States shall undertake the policies necessary to develop and unify their labor rules and legislation, and eliminate all obstacles restricting intra-GCC movement of the national labor force. GCC citizens working in a member State other than their countries of citizenship shall be included within the percentages set for manpower nationalization.

2. Member States shall adopt unified criteria for job description and classification for all professions and trades in all sectors, and undertake to develop and exchange all information related to their labor markets, including unemployment rates, job opportunities and training programs.

Article 17
Increasing Labor Participation Rates and Training of Nationals

1. Member States shall adopt effective policies to increase participation rates of nationals in the labor market, especially in high-skill Jobs, and adopt effective programs to raise the skill levels of the national labor force, develop on-the-job training programs, participate in financing such programs, and provide incentives for Job seekers in the private sector. Aid granted to the private sector shall be linked with the adoption of programs intended for the employment and training of national manpower.

2. Member States shall adopt the policies necessary for rationalizing the employment of foreign workers.

   . . .

Article 27
Settlement of Disputes

1. The Secretariat General shall hear and seek to amicably settle any Claims brought by any GCC citizen or official entity, regarding non-implementation of the provisions of this Agreement or enabled resolutions taken to implement those provisions.

2. If the Secretariat General could not settle a claim amicably, it shall be referred, with the consent of the two parties, to the GCC Commercial Arbitration Center to hear the dispute according to its Charter. Should the two parties not agree to refer the dispute to arbitration, or should the dispute be beyond the competence of the Center, it shall be referred to the judicial body set forth in Paragraph 3 of this Article.

3. A specialized judicial commission shall be formed, when deemed necessary, to adjudicate disputes arising from the implementation of this Agreement or resolutions for its implementation. The Financial and Economic Committee shall propose the Charter of this commission.

   . . .

SOUTH ASIAN ASSOCIATION FOR
REGIONAL COOPERATION (SAARC)

One of the least functional regional integration schemes covers South Asia, with India as its centerpiece. Since its founding in 1985, the South Asian Association for Regional Cooperation (SAARC) has suffered from the dominating power of the largest democracy in the world and from its member states' unwillingness to take up controversial issues. The India-Pakistan controversy has been one of the most dangerous regional conflicts in the world for decades. It comes as a surprise to many that SAARC has not broken down altogether over the contentious issues related to this conflict. Instead, SAARC has continued a quiet path to consolidated institutionalization with the help of a secretariat based in Katmandu. Being itself at the center of violent political controversies since the late 1990s, Nepal has not been able to put discernible weight behind the role that the SAARC Secretariat could possibly play.

SAARC continues to exist with the membership of India, Pakistan, Nepal, Bangladesh, Sri Lanka, Bhutan, and the Maldives, based on the 1985 Charter of the South Asian Association for Regional Cooperation. In 2005, Afghanistan joined SAARC. SAARC is the most impossible combination of countries and political regimes, socioeconomic realities and ethnic composition, and religious and linguistic diversity that the world could possibly offer. Yet the geographical factor has outnumbered all possible reservations against the very idea of a South Asian form of regional cooperation and possibly integration.

South Asia has a total population of almost 1.5 billion people. More than 500 million of them live in extreme poverty, representing 44 percent of the poorest of the poor in the world, who live on less than one dollar per day. South Asia accounts for no more than 2 percent of global GDP, and 2.2 percent of the external trade of the European Union is conducted with the region. India is the most important economic factor of the region, receiving 0.4 percent of foreign direct investment stemming from the EU. SAARC was founded—as stated in its Charter—with the aim of "promoting the well-being of the populations of South Asia and improving their standard of living; this includes speeding up economic growth, social progress and cultural development; reinforcing links between the countries of this area and, lastly, promoting mutual collaboration and assistance in the economic, social, cultural, technical and scientific fields."

The ambitions of SAARC stand in sharp contrast to the real power of the integration scheme. From the beginning, decision-making in SAARC was reduced to unanimity. The consultative nature of the process of cooperation was based on agreement not to deal with controversial issues among the states involved. Given the conflicts in the region—most notably between Pakistan and

India, but also those troubling Sri Lanka and Nepal—this founding principle left SAARC practically impotent from its very beginning. With the improvement of political relations between India and Pakistan in the early years of the twenty-first century, new impulses for strengthened integration were proposed by leaders of both countries.

In light of the conflicting interests on the South Asian subcontinent, it is surprising that SAARC came into being at all. Its founding intention, driven by India's diplomacy, was geared towards broadening the scope for non-aggression and the non-use of force between India and Pakistan. In 1988, during the early days of SAARC, India and Pakistan concluded three agreements prohibiting attacks against nuclear installations and facilities and promoting cultural cooperation and the avoidance of double taxation, thus demonstrating the almost bizarre combination of issues driving the subcontinent's agenda. So far in SAARC, there is enormous resistance to revision of the original Charter and the working mechanisms of its bodies, which include a Standing Committee of Foreign Secretaries, Technical Committees, and Committees of Economic Cooperation. Some observers argue that SAARC has induced a certain dynamic of intensified cooperation among civil society in the region that could eventually also spur a political reassessment of the parameters of regional integration.

To this day, the disputes between India and Pakistan, with their highly explosive dimension of nuclear arms proliferation, have prevented SAARC from developing its potential. In this context it must be considered tremendous progress that all SAARC countries recognized the 1997 Regional Convention on Suppression of Terrorism, defining terrorism as a common threat to them all. Efforts to create an Indian Ocean Rim Economic Growth Area have been curtailed by the disputes. In addition, Sri Lanka's efforts to join ASEAN were refused. Instability of some of the democratic regimes in SAARC, most notably in Bangladesh, the struggle with authoritarianism (the Maldives), the rule of military dictatorship (most notably in Pakistan), and ethnically induced civil war (Sri Lanka) have contributed to a rather negative image of SAARC. Initiatives to generate specific South Asian mechanisms of conflict management have failed so far, leaving South Asia as one of the last regions to "wake up" to the opportunities of regional integration. Conflict resolution in South Asia, such as the India-Bangladesh scheme to regulate the supply of Ganges waters or the search for solutions to the civil war in Sri Lanka, took place outside the SAARC mechanism.

Only in recent years has SAARC begun to emphasize realistic functional progress through economic cooperation and long-term integration. The 1993 Agreement on SAARC Preferential Trading Arrangement (SAPTA) and the 2004 Agreement on South Asia Free Trade Area (SAFTA), followed by the 2005 Agreement for Establishment of SAARC Arbitration Council, demonstrate the growing understanding of what is at stake for the South Asian region if it does not want to be bypassed by the paths of globalization. The most recent economic dynamics nurtured in India were matched by SAARC with a Social Charter (2004) expressing the social sensitivity of the political leadership in South Asia.

In order to make sense and have an impact, regional cooperation and integration in South Asia require more cohesion as regards the nature of the political regimes in the region and a visible increase in the region's economic complementarity. Without democratic structures in all SAARC member states, trust among the participants of the regional grouping will remain limited. Unless these fundamental preconditions are achieved, every effort to promote cooperation and trust on the Indian subcontinent will remain subject to fragile political circumstances. It must, however, be added that SAARC's very existence is a recognition of the potential that might be developed further in the course of the twenty-first century. In fact, it might turn out to be the only path to overcome the socioeconomic pressure in the region that is mounting, notwithstanding the emergence of a middle class. It might be this very middle class that will promote reforms toward both political and economic complementarity in South Asia as a precondition for viable and sustainable regional integration. Still, the path is long and the hope blurred by uncertainties, such as the lingering Islamic radicalism in Pakistan that overshadows the transformation from military dictatorship to democracy. For the time being, this poses a new threat to stable regional integration based on democracy and integrated market economies.

CHARTER OF THE SOUTH ASIAN ASSOCIATION FOR REGIONAL COOPERATION (08.12.1985)

. . .

1. Desirous of promoting peace, stability, amity and progress in the region through strict adherence to the principles of the United Nations Charter and Non-Alignment, particularly respect for the principles of sovereign equality, territorial integrity, national independence, non-use of force and non-interference in the internal affairs of other States and peaceful settlement of all disputes;
2. Conscious that in an increasingly interdependent world, the objectives of peace, freedom, social justice and economic prosperity are best achieved in the South Asian region by fostering mutual understanding, good neighbourly relations and meaningful cooperation among the Member States which are bound by ties of history and culture;
3. Aware of the common problems, interests and aspirations of the peoples of South Asia and the need for joint action and enhanced cooperation within their respective political and economic systems and cultural traditions;

4. Convinced that regional cooperation among the countries of South Asia is mutually beneficial, desirable and necessary for promoting the welfare and improving the quality of life of the peoples of the region;

. . .

Article I
Objectives

The objectives of the Association shall be:

a) to promote the welfare of the peoples of South Asia and to improve their quality of life;

b) to accelerate economic growth, social progress and cultural development in the region and to provide all individuals the opportunity to live in dignity and to realise their full potentials;

c) to promote and strengthen collective self-reliance among the countries of South Asia;

d) to contribute to mutual trust, understanding and appreciation of one another's problems;

e) to promote active collaboration and mutual assistance in the economic, social, cultural, technical and scientific fields;

f) to strengthen cooperation with other developing countries;

g) to strengthen cooperation among themselves in international forums on matters of common interests; and

h) to cooperate with international and regional organisations with similar aims and purposes.

Article II
Principles

1. Cooperation within the framework of the Association shall be based on respect for the principles of sovereign equality, territorial integrity, political independence, non-interference in the internal affairs of other States and mutual benefit.

2. Such cooperation shall not be a substitute for bilateral and multilateral cooperation but shall complement them.

3. Such cooperation shall not be inconsistent with bilateral and multilateral obligations.

Article III
Meeting of the Heads of State or Government

The Heads of State or Government shall meet once a year or more often as and when considered necessary by the Member States.

Article IV
Council of Ministers

1. A Council of Ministers consisting of the Foreign Ministers of the Member States shall be established with the following functions:
   a) formulation of the policies of the Association;
   b) review of the progress of cooperation under the Association;
   c) decision on new areas of cooperation;
   d) establishment of additional mechanisms under the Association as deemed necessary;
   e) decision on other matters of general interest to the Association.
2. The Council of Ministers shall meet twice a year. Extraordinary session of the Council may be held by agreement among the Member States.

Article V
Standing Committee

1. The Standing Committee comprising the Foreign Secretaries shall have the following functions:
   a) overall monitoring and coordination of programmes of cooperation;
   b) approval of projects and programmes, and the modalities of their financing;
   c) determination of inter-sectoral priorities;
   d) mobilisation of regional and external resources;
   e) identification of new areas of cooperation based on appropriate studies.
2. The Standing Committee shall meet as often as deemed necessary.
3. The Standing Committee shall submit periodic reports to the Council of Ministers and make reference to it as and when necessary for decisions on policy matters.

Article VI
Technical Committees

1. Technical Committees comprising representatives of Member States shall be responsible for the implementation, coordination and monitoring of the programmes in their respective areas of cooperation.
2. They shall have the following terms of reference:
   a) determination of the potential and the scope of regional cooperation in agreed areas;
   b) formulation of programmes and preparation of projects;
   c) determination of financial implications of sectoral programmes;

       d)   formulation of recommendations regarding apportionment of costs;
       e)   implementation and coordination of sectoral programmes;
       f)   monitoring of progress in implementation.

3.   The Technical Committees shall submit periodic reports to the Standing Committee.

4.   The Chairmanship of the Technical Committees shall normally rotate among Member States in alphabetical order every two years.

5.   The Technical Committees may, inter-alia, use the following mechanisms and modalities, if and when considered necessary:
       a)   meetings of heads of national technical agencies;
       b)   meetings of experts in specific fields;
       c)   contact amongst recognised centres of excellence in the region.

Article VII
Action Committees

The Standing Committee may set up Action Committees comprising Member States concerned with implementation of projects involving more than two but not all Member States.

Article VIII
Secretariat

There shall be a Secretariat of the Association.

Article IX
Financial Arrangements

1.   The contribution of each Member State towards financing of the activities of the Association shall be voluntary.

2.   Each Technical Committee shall make recommendations for the apportionment of costs of implementing the programmes proposed by it.

3.   In case sufficient financial resources cannot be mobilised within the region for funding activities of the Association, external financing from appropriate sources may be mobilised with the approval of or by the Standing Committee.

Article X
General Provisions

1.   Decisions at all levels shall be taken on the basis of unanimity.

2.   Bilateral and contentious issues shall be excluded from the deliberations.
    . . .

AGREEMENT ON SAARC PREFERENTIAL
TRADING ARRANGEMENT (SAPTA) (11.04.1993)

. . .

Motivated by the commitment to promote regional cooperation for the benefit of their peoples, in a spirit of mutual accommodation, with full respect for the principles of sovereign equality, independence and territorial integrity of all States;

Aware that the expansion of trade could act as a powerful stimulus to the development of their national economies, by expanding investment and production, thus providing greater opportunities of employment and help securing higher living standards for their population;

Convinced of the need to establish and promote regional preferential trading arrangements for strengthening intraregional economic cooperation and the development of national economies;

Bearing in mind the urgent need to promote the intraregional trade which presently constitutes a negligible share in the total volume of the South Asian trade;

. . .

Recognising that a preferential trading arrangement is the first step towards higher levels of trade and economic cooperation in the region;

. . .

Article 2
Establishment and Aims

1. By the present Agreement, the Contracting States establish the SAARC Preferential Trading Arrangement (SAPTA) to promote and sustain mutual trade and the economic cooperation among the Contracting States, through exchanging concessions in accordance with this Agreement.
2. SAPTA will be governed by the provisions of this Agreement and also by the rules, regulations, decisions, understandings and protocols to be agreed upon within its framework by the Contracting States.

Article 3
Principles

SAPTA shall be governed in accordance with the following principles:
   (a) SAPTA shall be based and applied on the principles of overall reciprocity and mutuality of advantages in such a way as to benefit equitably all Contracting States, taking into account their respective levels of economic and industrial development, the pattern of their external trade, trade and tariff policies and systems;

(b) SAPTA shall be negotiated step by step, improved and extended in successive stages with periodic reviews;

(c) The special needs of the Least Developed Contracting States shall be clearly recognised and concrete preferential measures in their favour should be agreed upon;

(d) SAPTA shall include all products, manufactures and commodities in their raw, semi-processed and processed forms.

Article 4
Components

SAPTA may, inter alia, consist of arrangements relating to:

(a) tariffs;

(b) para-tariffs;

(c) non-tariff measures;

(d) direct trade measures.

Article 5
Negotiations

1. The Contracting States may conduct their negotiations for trade liberalisation in accordance with any or a combination of the following approaches and procedures:

   (a) Product by product basis;

   (b) Across the board tariff reductions;

   (c) Sectoral basis;

   (d) Direct trade measures.

2. Contracting States agree to negotiate tariff preferences initially on a product by product basis.

3. The Contracting States shall enter into negotiations from time to time with a view to further expanding SAPTA and the fuller attainment of its aims.

Article 6
Additional Measures

1. Contracting States agree to consider, in addition to the measures set out in Article 4, the adoption of trade facilitation and other measures to support and complement SAPTA to mutual benefit.

2. Special consideration shall be given by Contracting States to requests from Least Developed Contracting States for technical assistance and cooperation arrangements designed to assist them in expanding their trade with other Contracting States and in taking advantage of the potential benefits of SAPTA.

   . . .

Article 7
Schedules of Concessions

The tariff, para-tariff and non-tariff concessions negotiated and exchanged amongst Contracting States shall be incorporated in the National Schedules of Concessions.

. . .

Article 8
Extension of Negotiated Concessions

The concessions agreed to under SAPTA, except those made exclusively to the Least Developed Contracting States in pursuance of Article 10 of this Agreement, shall be extended unconditionally to all Contracting States.

Article 9
Committee of Participants

A Committee of Participants, hereinafter referred to as the Committee, consisting of representatives of Contracting States, is hereby established. The Committee shall meet at least once a year to review the progress made in the implementation of this Agreement and to ensure that benefits of trade expansion emanating from this Agreement accrue to all Contracting States equitably. The Committee shall also accord adequate opportunities for consultation on representations made by any Contracting State with respect to any matter affecting the implementation of the Agreement. The Committee shall adopt appropriate measures for settling such representations. The Committee shall determine its own rules of procedures.

Article 10
Special Treatment for the Least Developed Contracting States

1. In addition to other provisions of this Agreement, all Contracting States shall provide, wherever possible, special and more favourable treatment exclusively to the Least Developed Contracting States as set out in the following subparagraphs:
   (a) Duty-free access, exclusive tariff preferences or deeper tariff preferences for export products,
   (b) The removal of non-tariff barriers,
   (c) The removal, where appropriate, of para-tariff barriers,
   (d) The negotiation of long-term contracts with a view to assisting Least Developed Contracting States to achieve reasonable levels of sustainable exports of their products,

(e) Special consideration of exports from Least Developed Contracting States in the application of safeguard measures,

(f) Greater flexibility in the introduction and continuance of quantitative or other restrictions provisionally and without discrimination in critical circumstances by the Least Developed Contracting States on imports from other Contracting States.

Article 11
Non-Application

Notwithstanding the measures as set out in Articles 4 and 6, the provisions of this Agreement shall not apply in relation to preferences already granted or to be granted by any Contracting State to other Contracting States outside the framework of this Agreement, and to third countries through bilateral, plurilateral and multilateral trade agreements, and similar arrangements. The Contracting States shall also not be obliged to grant preferences in SAPTA which impair the concession extended under those agreements.

Article 12
Communication

Transport and Transit Contracting States agree to undertake appropriate steps and measures for developing and improving communication system, transport infrastructure and transit facilities for accelerating the growth of trade within the region.

Article 13
Balance of Payments Measures

1. Notwithstanding the provisions of this Agreement, any Contracting State facing serious economic problems including balance of payments difficulties may suspend provisionally the concessions as to the quantity and value of merchandise permitted to be imported under the Agreement. When such action has taken place, the Contracting State which initiates such action shall simultaneously notify the other Contracting States and the Committee.

2. Any Contracting State which takes action according to paragraph 1 of this Article shall afford, upon request from any other Contracting State, adequate opportunities for consultations with a view to preserving the stability of the concessions negotiated under SAPTA. If no satisfactory adjustment is effected between the Contracting States concerned within 90 days of such notification, the matter may be referred to the Committee for review.

Article 14
Safeguard Measures

If any product, which is a subject of a concession with respect to a preference under this Agreement, is imported into the territory of a Contracting State in such a manner or in such quantities as to cause or threaten to cause, serious injury in the importing Contracting State, the importing Contracting State concerned may, with prior consultations, except in critical circumstances, suspend provisionally without discrimination, the concession accorded under the Agreement. When such action has taken place the Contracting State which initiates such action shall simultaneously notify the other Contracting State(s) concerned and the Committee shall enter into consultations with the concerned Contracting State and endeavour to reach mutually acceptable agreement to remedy the situation.

In the event of the failure of the Contracting States to resolve the issue within 90 days of the receipt of original notification, the Committee of Participants shall meet within 30 days to review the situation and try to settle the issue amicably. Should the consultations in the Committee of Participants fail to resolve the issue within 60 days, the parties affected by such action shall have the right to withdraw equivalent concession(s) or other obligation(s) which the Committee does not disapprove of.

Article 15
Maintenance of the Value of Concessions

Any of the concessions agreed upon under this Agreement shall not be diminished or nullified by the application of any measures restricting trade by the Contracting States except under the provisions as spelt out in other Articles of this Agreement.

Article 16
Rules of Origin

Products contained in the National Schedules of Concessions annexed to this Agreement shall be eligible for preferential treatment if they satisfy the rules of origin, including special rules of origin, in respect of the Least Developed Contracting States

. . .

Article 19
Consultations

1. Each Contracting State shall accord sympathetic consideration to and shall afford adequate opportunity for consultations regarding such representations as may be made by another Contracting State with respect to any matter affecting the operation of this Agreement.

2. The Committee may, at the request of a Contracting State, consult with any Contracting State in respect of any matter for which it has not been possible to find a satisfactory solution through such consultation under paragraph 1 above.

Article 20
Settlement of Disputes

Any dispute that may arise among the Contracting States regarding the interpretation and application of the provisions of this Agreement or any instrument adopted within its framework shall be amicably settled by agreement between the parties concerned. In the event of failure to settle a dispute, it may be referred to the Committee by a party to the dispute. The Committee shall review the matter and make a recommendation thereon within 120 days from the date on which the dispute was submitted to it. The Committee shall adopt appropriate rules for this purpose.

Article 21
Withdrawal from SAPTA

1. Any Contracting State may withdraw from this Agreement at any time after its entry into force. Such withdrawal shall be effective six months from the day on which written notice thereof is received by the SAARC Secretariat, the depositary of this Agreement. That Contracting State shall simultaneously inform the Committee of the action it has taken.
2. The rights and obligations of a Contracting State which has withdrawn from this Agreement shall cease to apply as of that effective date.
3. Following the withdrawal by any Contracting State, the Committee shall meet within 30 days to consider action subsequent to withdrawal.
   . . .

REGIONAL CONVENTION ON
SUPPRESSION OF TERRORISM (04.11.1997)

. . .

Aware of the danger posed by the spread of terrorism and its harmful effect on peace, cooperation, friendship and good neighbourly relations and which could also jeopardize the sovereignty and territorial integrity of states;

. . .

Article 1

Subject to the overall requirements of the law of extradition, conduct constituting any of the following offences, according to the law of the Contracting State, shall be regarded as terroristic and for the purpose of extradition shall not be regarded as political offence or as an offence connected with a political offence or as an offence inspired by political motives:

a) An offence within the scope of the Convention for the Suppression of Unlawful Seizure of Aircraft, signed at the Hague on December 16, 1970;

b) An offence within the scope of the Convention for the Suppression of Unlawful acts against the safety of Civil Aviation, signed at Montreal on September 23, 1971;

c) An offence within the scope of the Convention on the Prevention and Punishment of Crimes against Internationally Protected Persons, including Diplomatic Agents, signed at New York on December 14, 1973;

d) An offence within the scope of any Convention to which SAARC Member States concerned are parties and which obliges the parties to prosecute or grant extradition;

e) Murder, manslaughter, assault causing bodily harm, kidnapping, hostage-taking and offences relating to firearms, weapons, explosives and dangerous substances when used as a means to perpetrate indiscriminate violence involving death or serious bodily injury to persons or serious damage to property;

f) An attempt or conspiracy to commit an offence described in sub-paragraphs (a) to (e), aiding, abetting or counselling the commission of such an offence or participating as an accomplice in the offences so described.

Article 2

For the purpose of extradition between SAARC Member States, any two or more Contracting States may, by agreement, decide to include any other serious offence involving violence, which shall not be regarded as a political offence or an offence connected with a political offence or an offence inspired by political motives.

Article 3

1. The provisions of all extradition treaties and arrangements applicable between Contracting States are hereby amended as between Contracting States to the extent that they are incompatible with this Convention.

2. For the purpose of this Convention and to the extent that any offence referred to in Article 1 or agreed to in terms of Article 2 is not listed as an extraditable offence in any extradition treaty existing between Contracting States, it shall be deemed to be included as such therein.

3. Contracting States undertake to include these offences as extraditable offences in any future extradition treaty to be concluded between them.

4. If a Contracting State which makes extradition conditional on the existence of a treaty receives a request for extradition from another Contracting State with which it has no extradition treaty, the requested State may, as its option, consider this Convention as the basis for extradition in respect of the offences set forth in Article 1 or agreed to in terms of Article 2. Extradition shall be subject to the law of the requested State.

5. Contracting States which do not make extradition conditional on the existence of a treaty shall recognize the offences set forth in Article 1 or agreed to in terms of Article 2 as extraditable offences between themselves, subject to the law of the requested State.

Article 4

A contracting State in whose territory a person suspected of having committed an offence referred to in Article 1 or agreed to in terms of Article 2 is found and which has received a request for extradition from another Contracting State, shall, if it does not extradite that person, submit the case without exception and without delay, to its competent authorities which shall take their decisions in the same manner as in the case of any offence of a serious nature under the law of the State.

Article 5

For the purpose of Article 4, each Contracting State may take such measures as it deems appropriate, consistent with its national laws, subject to reciprocity, to exercise its jurisdiction in the case of an offence under Article 1 or agreed to in terms of Article 2.

Article 6

A Contracting State in whose territory an alleged offender is found, shall, upon receiving a request for extradition from another Contracting State, take appropriate measures, subject to its national laws, so as to ensure his presence for purposes of extradition or prosecution. Such measures shall immediately be notified to the requesting State.

Article 7

Contracting States shall not be obliged to extradite, if it appears to the requested State that by reason of the trivial nature of the case or by reason of the request for the surrender or return of a fugitive offender not being made in good faith or in the interests of justice or if for any other reason it is unjust or inexpedient to surrender or return the fugitive offender.

Article 8

1. Contracting States shall, subject to their national laws, afford one another the greatest measure of mutual assistance in connection with proceedings brought in respect of the offences referred to in Article 1 or agreed to in terms of Article 2, including the supply of all evidence at their disposal necessary for the proceedings.
2. Contracting States shall cooperate among themselves, to the extent permitted by their national laws, through consultations between appropriate agencies, exchange of information, intelligence and expertise and such other cooperative measures as may be appropriate, with a view to prevention of terroristic activities through precautionary measures.
    . . .

SOCIAL CHARTER (04.01.2004)

Reaffirming that the principal goal of SAARC is to promote the welfare of the people of South Asia, to improve their quality of life, to accelerate economic growth, social progress and cultural development and to provide all individuals the opportunity to live in dignity and to realize their full potential.

Recognising that the countries of South Asia have been linked by age-old cultural, social and historical traditions and that these have enriched the interaction of ideas, values, cultures and philosophies among the people and the States and that these commonalities constitute solid foundations for regional cooperation for addressing more effectively the economic and social needs of people.

Recalling that all Member States attach high importance to the imperative of social development and economic growth and that their national legislative, executive and administrative frameworks provide, in varying degrees, for the progressive realization of social and economic goals, with specific provisions, where appropriate, for the principles of equity, affirmative action and public interest.

Observing that regional cooperation in the social sector has received the focused attention of the Member States and that specific areas such as health, nutrition, food security, safe drinking water and sanitation, population activities, and child development and rights along with gender equality, participation of women in development, welfare of elderly people, youth mobilization and human resources development continue to remain on the agenda of regional cooperation.

Noting that high level meetings convened since the inception of SAARC on the subjects of children, women, human resettlements, sustainable developments, agriculture and food, poverty alleviation etc. have contributed immensely to the enrichment of the social agenda in the region and that several directives of the Heads of State or Government of SAARC Countries at their Summit meetings have imparted dynamism and urgency to adopting regional programmes to fully and effectively realize social goals.

Reiterating that the SAARC Charter and the SAARC Conventions, respectively on Narcotic Drugs and Psychotropic Substances, Preventing and Combating Trafficking in Women and Children for Prostitution, Regional Arrangements for the Promotion of Child Welfare in South Asia and the SAARC Agreement on Food Security Reserve, provide regional frameworks for addressing specific social issues, which require concerted and coordinated actions and strategies for the effective realization of their objectives.

Realizing that the health of the population of the countries of the region is closely interlinked and can be sustained only by putting in place coordinated surveillance mechanisms and prevention and management strategies.

Noting in particular, that Heads of State or Government of SAARC Countries, at their Tenth Summit in Colombo in July 1998, reaffirmed the need to develop, beyond national plans of action, a regional dimension of cooperation in the social sector and that the Eleventh SAARC Summit in Kathmandu in January 2002 directed that a SAARC Social Charter be concluded as early as possible.

Convinced that it was timely to develop a regional instrument which consolidated the multifarious commitments of SAARC Member States in the social sector and provided a practical platform for concerted, coherent and complementary action in determining social priorities, improving the structure and content of social policies and programmes, ensuring greater efficiency in the utilization of national, regional and external resources and in enhancing the equity and sustainability of social programmes and the quality of living conditions of their beneficiaries.

The Member States of the South Asian Association for Regional Cooperation hereby agree to adopt this Charter:

Article 1
General Provisions

1. States Parties shall maintain a social policy and strategy in order to ensure an overall and balanced social development of their peoples. The salient features of individual social policy and programme shall be determined, taking into account the broader national development goals and specific historic and political contexts of each State Party.
2. States Parties agree that the obligations under the Social Charter shall be respected, protected and fulfilled without reservation and that the enforcement thereof at the national level shall be continuously reviewed through agreed regional arrangements and mechanisms.
3. States Parties shall establish a people-centered framework for social development to guide their work and in the future, to build a culture of cooperation and partnership and to respond to the immediate needs of those who are most affected by human distress. States Parties are determined to meet this challenge and promote social development throughout the region.

Article 2
Principles, Goals and Objectives

1. The provisions made herein shall complement the national processes of policymaking, policy-implementation and policy-evaluation, while providing broad parameters and principles for addressing common social issues and developing and implementing result-oriented programmes in specific social areas.
2. In the light of the commitments made in this Charter, States Parties agree to:
   i. Place people at the center of development and direct their economies to meet human needs more effectively;
   ii. Fulfil the responsibility towards present and future generations by ensuring equity among generations, and protecting the integrity and sustainable use of the environment;
   iii. Recognize that, while social development is a national responsibility, its successful achievement requires the collective commitment and cooperation of the international community;
   iv. Integrate economic, cultural and social policies so that they become mutually supportive, and acknowledge the interdependence of public and private spheres of activity;
   v. Recognize that the achievement of sustained social development requires sound, equitable and broad-based economic policies;

vi. Promote participatory governance, human dignity, social justice and solidarity at the national, regional and international levels;

vii. Ensure tolerance, non-violence, pluralism and non-discrimination in respect of diversity within and among societies;

viii. Promote the equitable distribution of income and greater access to resources through equity and equality of opportunity for all;

ix. Recognize the family as the basic unit of society, and acknowledge that it plays a key role in social development and as such should be strengthened, with attention to the rights, capabilities and responsibilities of its members including children, youth and the elderly;

x. Affirm that while State, society, community and family have obligations towards children, these must be viewed in the context of inculcating in children an intrinsic and attendant sense of duty and set of values directed towards preserving and strengthening the family, community, society and nation;

xi. Ensure that disadvantaged, marginalized and vulnerable persons and groups are included in social development, and that society acknowledges and responds to the consequences of disability by securing the legal rights of the individual and by making the physical and social environment accessible;

xii. Promote universal respect for and observance and protection of human rights and fundamental freedoms for all, in particular the right to development; promote the effective exercise of rights and the discharge of responsibilities in a balanced manner at all levels of society; promote gender equity; promote the welfare and interest of children and youth; promote social integration and strengthen civil society;

xiii. Recognize the promotion of health as a regional objective and strive to enhance it by responding to urgent health issues and outbreak of any communicable disease in the region through sharing information with each other, imparting public health and curative skills to professionals in the region, and adopting a coordinated approach to health related issues in international fora;

xiv. Support progress and protect people and communities whereby every member of society is enabled to satisfy basic human needs and to realize his or her personal dignity, safety and creativity;

xv. Recognize and support people with diverse cultures, beliefs and traditions in their pursuit of economic and social development with full respect for their identity, traditions, forms of social organization and cultural values;

xvi. Underline the importance of transparent and accountable conduct of administration in public and private, national and international institutions;

xvii. Recognize that empowering people, particularly women, to strengthen their own capacities is an important objective of development and its principal resource. Empowerment requires the full participation of people in the formulation, implementation and evaluation of decisions and sharing the results equitably;

xviii. Accept the universality of social development, and outline an effective approach to it, with a renewed call for international cooperation and partnership;

xix. Ensure that elderly persons lead meaningful and fulfilling lives while enjoying all rights without discrimination and facilitate the creation of an environment in which they continue to utilize their knowledge, experience and skills;

xx. Recognize that information communication technology can help in fulfilling social development goals and emphasize the need to facilitate easy access to this technology;

xxi. Strengthen policies and programmes that improve, broaden and ensure the participation of women in all spheres of political, economic, social and cultural life, as equal partners, and improve their access to all resources needed for the full enjoyment of their fundamental freedoms and other entitlements.

Article 3
Poverty Alleviation

1. States Parties affirm that highest priority shall be accorded to the alleviation of poverty in all South Asian Countries. Recognizing that South Asia's poor could constitute a huge and potential resource, provided their basis needs are met and they are mobilized to create economic growth, States Parties reaffirm that the poor should be empowered and irreversibly linked to the mainstream of development. They also agree to take appropriate measures to create income-generating activities for the poor.

2. Noting that a large number of the people remain below the poverty line, States Parties re-affirm their commitment to implement an assured nutritional standards approach towards the satisfaction of basic needs of the South Asian poor.

3. Noting the vital importance of biotechnology for the long-term food security of developing countries as well as for medicinal purposes, States Parties resolve that cooperation should be extended to the exchange of expertise in genetic conservation and maintenance of germplasm banks. They stress the importance of the role of training facilities in this area and agree that cooperation in the cataloguing of genetic resources in different SAARC countries would be mutually beneficial.

3. States Parties agree that access to basic education, adequate housing, safe drinking water and sanitation, and primary health care should be guaranteed in legislation, executive and administrative provisions, in addition to ensuring of adequate standard of living, including adequate shelter, food and clothing.
4. States Parties underline the imperative of providing a better habitat to the people of South Asia as part of addressing the problems of the homeless. They agree that each country shall share the experiences gained in their efforts to provide shelter, and exchange expertise for effectively alleviating the problem.

Article 4
Health

1. States Parties re-affirm that they will strive to protect and promote the health of the population in the region. Recognizing that it is not possible to achieve good health in any country without addressing the problems of primary health issues and communicable diseases in the region, the States Parties agree to share information regarding the outbreak of any communicable disease among their populations.
2. Conscious that considerable expertise has been built up within the SAARC countries on disease prevention, management and treatment, States Parties affirm their willingness to share knowledge and expertise with other countries in the region.
3. Noting that the capacity for manufacture of drugs and other chemicals exists in different countries, States Parties agree to share such capacity and products when sought by any other State Party.
4. Realizing that health issues are related to livelihood and trade issues which are influenced by international agreements and conventions, the States Parties agree to hold prior consultation on such issues and to make an effort to arrive at a coordinated stand on issues that relate to the health of their population.
5. States Parties also agree to strive at adopting regional standards on drugs and pharmaceutical products.

Article 5
Education, Human Resource Development and Youth Mobilization

1. Deeply conscious that education is the cutting edge in the struggle against poverty and the promotion of development, States Parties re-affirm the importance of attaining the target of providing free education to all children between the ages of 6–14 years. They agree to share their respective experiences and technical expertise to achieve this goal.

2. States Parties agree that broad-based growth should create productive employment opportunities for all groups of people, including young people.

3. States Parties agree to provide enhanced job opportunities for young people through increased investment in education and vocational training.

4. States Parties agree to provide adequate employment opportunities and leisure time activities for youth to make them economically and socially productive.

5. States Parties shall find ways and means to provide youth with access to education, create awareness on family planning, HIV/AIDS and other sexually-transmitted diseases, and risks of consumption of tobacco, alcohol and drugs.

6. States Parties stress the idealism of youth must be harnessed for regional cooperative programmes. They further stress the imperative of the resurgence of South Asian consciousness in the youth of each country through participation in the development programmes and through greater understanding and appreciation of each other's country. The Organized Volunteers Programme under which volunteers from one country would be able to work in other countries in the social fields shall be revitalized.

7. States Parties recognize that it is essential to promote increased cross-fertilization of ideas through greater interaction among students, scholars and academics in the SAARC countries. They express the resolve that a concerted programme of exchange of scholars among Member States should be strengthened.

Article 6
Promotion of the Status of Women

1. States Parties reaffirm their belief that discrimination against women is incompatible with human rights and dignity and with the welfare of the family and society; that it prevents women realizing their social and economic potential and their participation on equal terms with men, in the political, social, economic and cultural life of the country, and is a serious obstacle to the full development of their personality and in their contribution to the social and economic development of their countries.

2. States Parties agree that all appropriate measures shall be taken to educate public opinion and to direct national aspirations towards the eradication of prejudice and the abolition of customary and all other practices, which are based on discrimination against women. States Parties further declare that all forms of discrimination and violence against women are offences against human rights and dignity and that such offences must be prohibited through legislative, administrative and judicial actions.

3. States Parties shall take all appropriate measures to ensure to women on equal terms with men, an enabling environment for their effective participation in the local, regional and national development processes and for the enjoyment of their fundamental freedoms and legitimate entitlements.

4. States Parties also affirm the need to empower women through literacy and education recognizing the fact that such empowerment paves the way for faster economic and social development. They particularly stress the need to reduce, and eventually eliminate, the gender gap in literacy that currently exists in the SAARC nations, within a time-bound period.

5. States Parties re-affirm their commitment to effectively implement the SAARC Convention on Combating the Trafficking of Women and Children for Prostitution and to combat and suppress all forms of traffic in women and exploitation of women, including through the cooperation of appropriate sections of the civil society.

6. States Parties are of the firm view that at the regional level, mechanisms and institutions to promote the advancement of women as an integral part of mainstream political, economic, social and cultural development shall be established.

Article 7
Promotion of the Rights and Well-being of the Child

1. States Parties are convinced that the child, by reason of his or her physical and mental dependence, needs special safeguards and care, including appropriate legal protection, before as well as after birth.

2. The child, for the full and harmonious development of his or her personality, should grow up in a family environment, in an atmosphere of happiness, love and understanding.

3. States Parties shall protect the child against all forms of abuse and exploitation prejudicial to any aspects of the child's well-being.

4. States Parties shall take necessary actions to implement effectively the SAARC Convention on Regional Arrangements for the Promotion of Child Welfare and to combat and suppress all offences against the person, dignity and the life of the child.

5. States Parties are resolved that the child shall enjoy special protection, and shall be given opportunities and facilities, by law and by other means, to enable him or her to develop its full potential physically, mentally, emotionally, morally, spiritually, socially and culturally in a healthy and normal manner and in conditions of freedom and dignity. The best interests and welfare of the child shall be the paramount consideration and the guiding principle in all matters involving his or her life.

6. States Parties agree to extend to the child all possible support from government, society and the community. The child shall be entitled to grow and develop in health with due protection. To this end, special services shall be provided for the child and its mother, including pre-natal, natal (especially delivery by trained birth attendant) and post-natal care, immunization, early childhood care, timely and appropriate nutrition, education and recreation. States Parties shall undertake specific steps to reduce low birth weight, malnutrition, anemia amongst women and children, infant, child and maternal morbidity and mortality rates through the intergenerational life cycle approach, increase education, literacy, and skill development amongst adolescents and youth, especially girls, and eliminate child/early marriage.
7. States Parties shall take effective measures for the rehabilitation and re-integration of children in conflict with the law.
8. State Parties shall take appropriate measures for the rehabilitation of street children, orphaned, displaced and abandoned children, and children affected by armed conflict.
9. States Parties pledge that a physically, mentally, emotionally or socially disadvantaged child shall be given the special treatment, education and care required by his or her particular condition.
10. States Parties shall ensure that a child of tender years shall not, save in exceptional circumstances, be separated from his or her mother and that society and the public authorities shall be required to extend particular care to children without a family and to those without adequate means of support, including where desirable, provision of State and other assistance towards his or her maintenance.
11. States Parties shall take all appropriate measures, including legislative, administrative, social and educational measures, to protect children from the illicit use of narcotic drugs and psychotropic substances as defined in the relevant international treaties, and to prevent the use of children in the illicit production and trafficking of such substances. In this respect, States Parties shall expedite the implementation of the SAARC Convention on Narcotic Drugs and Psychotropic Substances at the national and regional levels.

Article 8
Population Stabilization

1. States Parties underscore the vital importance of enhanced cooperation in the social development and well-being of the people of South Asia. They agree that national programmes evolved through stakeholder partnership, with enhancement of allocation of requisite resources and

well-coordinated regional programmes, will contribute to a positive atmosphere for the development of a socially content, healthy and sustainable population in the region.

2. States Parties are of the view that population policies should provide for a human centered approach to population and development and aim towards human survival and wellbeing. In this regard, they affirm that national, local or provincial policies and strategies should aim to bring stabilization in the growth of population in each country, through voluntary sustainable family planning and contraceptive methods which do not affect the health of women.

3. States Parties shall endeavour to inculcate a culture of self-contentment and regulation where unsustainable consumption and production patterns would have no place in the society and unsustainable population changes, internal migration resulting in excessive population concentration, homelessness, increasing poverty, unemployment, growing insecurity and violence, environmental degradation and increased vulnerability to disasters would be carefully, diligently and effectively managed.

4. States Parties shall take action to ensure reproductive health, reduction of maternal and infant mortality rates and also provision of adequate facilities to enable an infant to enjoy the warmth of love and support of his/her parents.

5. States Parties also agree to set up a SAARC Network of Focal Institutions on population activities for facilitating the sharing of information, experiences and resources and resources within the region.

. . .

AGREEMENT ON SOUTH ASIAN
FREE TRADE AREA (SAFTA) (06.01.2004)

. . .

Motivated by the commitment to strengthen intra-SAARC economic cooperation to maximise the realization of the region's potential for trade and development for the benefit of their people, in a spirit of mutual accommodation, with full respect for the principles of sovereign equality, independence and territorial integrity of all States;

. . .

Convinced that preferential trading arrangements among SAARC Member States will act as a stimulus to the strengthening of national and SAARC economic resilience, and the development of the national economies of the Contracting States by expanding investment and production opportunities, trade, and foreign exchange earnings as well as the development of economic and technological cooperation;

  . . .

Article 2
Establishment

The Contracting States hereby establish the South Asian Free Trade Area (SAFTA) to promote and enhance mutual trade and economic cooperation among the Contracting States, through exchanging concessions in accordance with this Agreement.

Article 3
Objectives and Principles

1. The Objectives of this Agreement are to promote and enhance mutual trade and economic cooperation among Contracting States by, inter alia:
    (a) eliminating barriers to trade in, and facilitating the cross-border movement of goods between the territories of the Contracting States;
    (b) promoting conditions of fair competition in the free trade area, and ensuring equitable benefits to all Contracting States, taking into account their respective levels and pattern of economic development;
    (c) creating effective mechanisms for the implementation and application of this Agreement, for its joint administration and for the resolution of disputes; and
    (d) establishing a framework for further regional cooperation to expand and enhance the mutual benefits of this Agreement.
2. SAFTA shall be governed in accordance with the following principles:
    (a) SAFTA will be governed by the provisions of this Agreement and also by the rules, regulations, decisions, understandings and protocols to be agreed upon within its framework by the Contracting States;
    (b) The Contracting States affirm their existing rights and obligations with respect to each other under the Marrakesh Agreement Establishing the World Trade Organization and other Treaties/Agreements to which such Contracting States are signatories;
    (c) SAFTA shall be based and applied on the principles of overall reciprocity and mutuality of advantages in such a way as to benefit equitably all Contracting States, taking into account their respective

levels of economic and industrial development, the pattern of their external trade and tariff policies and systems;

(d) SAFTA shall involve the free movement of goods, between countries through, inter alia, the elimination of tariffs, para-tariffs and non-tariff restrictions on the movement of goods, and any other equivalent measures;

(e) SAFTA shall entail adoption of trade facilitation and other measures, and the progressive harmonization of legislations by the Contracting States in the relevant areas; and

(f) The special needs of the Least Developed Contracting States shall be clearly recognized by adopting concrete preferential measures in their favour on a non-reciprocal basis.

Article 4
Instruments

The SAFTA Agreement will be implemented through the following instruments:

1. Trade Liberalisation Programme
2. Rules of Origin
3. Institutional Arrangements
4. Consultations and Dispute Settlement Procedures
5. Safeguard Measures
6. Any other instrument that may be agreed upon.

Article 5
National Treatment

Each Contracting State shall accord national treatment to the products of other Contracting States in accordance with the provisions of Article III of GATT 1994.

Article 6
Components

SAFTA may, inter alia, consist of arrangements relating to:

(a) tariffs;
(b) para-tariffs;
(c) non-tariff measures;
(d) direct trade measures.

Article 7
Trade Liberalisation Programme

1. Contracting States agree to the following schedule of tariff reductions:

(a) The tariff reduction by the Non-Least Developed Contracting States from existing tariff rates to 20% shall be done within a time frame of 2 years from the date of coming into force of the Agreement. Contracting States are encouraged to adopt reductions in equal annual installments. If actual tariff rates after the coming into force of the Agreement are below 20%, there shall be an annual reduction on a Margin of Preference basis of 10% on actual tariff rates for each of the two years.

(b) The tariff reduction by the Least Developed Contracting States from existing tariff rates will be to 30% within the time frame of 2 years from the date of coming into force of the Agreement. If actual tariff rates on the date of coming into force of the Agreement are below 30%, there will be an annual reduction on a Margin of Preference basis of 5 % on actual tariff rates for each of the two years.

(c) The subsequent tariff reduction by Non-Least Developed Contracting States from 20% or below to 0–5% shall be done within a second time frame of 5 years, beginning from the third year from the date of coming into force of the Agreement. However, the period of subsequent tariff reduction by Sri Lanka shall be six years. Contracting States are encouraged to adopt reductions in equal annual installments, but not less than 15% annually.

(d) The subsequent tariff reduction by the Least Developed Contracting States from 30% or below to 0–5% shall be done within a second time frame of 8 years beginning from the third year from the date of coming into force of the Agreement. The Least Developed Contracting States are encouraged to adopt reductions in equal annual installments, not less than 10% annually.

2. The above schedules of tariff reductions will not prevent Contracting States from immediately reducing their tariffs to 0–5% or from following an accelerated schedule of tariff reduction.

3. (a) Contracting States may not apply the Trade Liberalisation Programme as in paragraph 1 above, to the tariff lines included in the Sensitive Lists which shall be negotiated by the Contracting States (for LDCs and Non-LDCs) and incorporated in this Agreement as an integral part. The number of products in the Sensitive Lists shall be subject to a maximum ceiling to be mutually agreed among the Contracting States with flexibility to Least Developed Contracting States to seek derogation in respect of the products of their export interest; and

    (b) The Sensitive List shall be reviewed after every four years or earlier as may be decided by the SAFTA Ministerial Council (SMC), established under Article 10, with a view to reducing the number of items in the Sensitive List.

4. The Contracting States shall notify the SAARC Secretariat all non-tariff and para-tariff measures to their trade on an annual basis. The notified measures shall be reviewed by the Committee of Experts, established under Article 10, in its regular meetings to examine their compatibility with relevant WTO provisions. The Committee of Experts shall recommend the elimination or implementation of the measure in the least trade restrictive manner in order to facilitate intra-SAARC trade.

5. Contracting Parties shall eliminate all quantitative restrictions, except otherwise permitted under GATT 1994, in respect of products included in the Trade Liberalisation Programme.

6. Notwithstanding the provisions contained in paragraph 1 of this Article, the Non- Least Developed Contracting States shall reduce their tariff to 0–5% for the products of Least Developed Contracting States within a timeframe of three years beginning from the date of coming into force of the Agreement.

Article 8
Additional Measures

Contracting States agree to consider, in addition to the measures set out in Article 7, the adoption of trade facilitation and other measures to support and complement SAFTA for mutual benefit. These may include, among others:

(a) harmonization of standards, reciprocal recognition of tests and accreditation of testing laboratories of Contracting States and certification of products;

(b) simplification and harmonization of customs clearance procedure;

(c) harmonization of national customs classification based on HS coding system;

(d) customs cooperation to resolve dispute at customs entry points;

(e) simplification and harmonization of import licensing and registration procedures;

(f) simplification of banking procedures for import financing;

(g) transit facilities for efficient intra-SAARC trade, especially for the land-locked Contracting States;

(h) removal of barriers to intra-SAARC investments;

(i) macroeconomic consultations;

(j) rules for fair competition and the promotion of venture capital;

(k) development of communication systems and transport infrastructure;

(l) making exceptions to their foreign exchange restrictions, if any, relating to payments for products under the SAFTA scheme, as well as repatriation of such payments without prejudice to their rights under Article XVIII of the General Agreement on Tariffs and Trade (GATT) and the relevant provisions of Articles of Treaty of the International Monetary Fund (IMF); and

(m) simplification of procedures for business visas.

Article 9
Extension of Negotiated Concessions

Concessions agreed to, other than those made exclusively to the Least Developed Contracting States, shall be extended unconditionally to all Contracting States.

Article 10
Institutional Arrangements

1. The Contracting States hereby establish the SAFTA Ministerial Council (hereinafter referred to as SMC).
2. The SMC shall be the highest decision-making body of SAFTA and shall be responsible for the administration and implementation of this Agreement and all decisions and arrangements made within its legal framework.
3. The SMC shall consist of the Ministers of Commerce/Trade of the Contracting States.
4. The SMC shall meet at least once every year or more often as and when considered necessary by the Contracting States. Each Contracting State shall chair the SMC for a period of one year on rotational basis in alphabetical order.
5. The SMC shall be supported by a Committee of Experts (hereinafter referred to as COE), with one nominee from each Contracting State at the level of a Senior Economic Official, with expertise in trade matters.
6. The COE shall monitor, review and facilitate implementation of the provisions of this Agreement and undertake any task assigned to it by the SMC. The COE shall submit its report to the SMC every six months.
7. The COE will also act as Dispute Settlement Body under this Agreement.
8. The COE shall meet at least once every six months or more often as and when considered necessary by the Contracting States. Each Contracting State shall chair the COE for a period of one year on rotational basis in alphabetical order.
9. The SAARC Secretariat shall provide secretarial support to the SMC and COE in the discharge of their functions.
10. The SMC and COE will adopt their own rules of procedure.

Article 11
Special and Differential Treatment for the Least Developed Contracting States

In addition to other provisions of this Agreement, all Contracting States shall provide special and more favourable treatment exclusively to the Least Developed Contracting States as set out in the following sub-paragraphs:

(a) The Contracting States shall give special regard to the situation of the Least Developed Contracting States when considering the application of anti-dumping and/or countervailing measures. In this regard, the Contracting States shall provide an opportunity to Least Developed Contracting States for consultations. The Contracting States shall, to the extent practical, favourably consider accepting price undertakings offered by exporters from Least Developed Contracting States. These constructive remedies shall be available until the trade liberalisation programme has been completed by all Contracting States.

(b) Greater flexibility in continuation of quantitative or other restrictions provisionally and without discrimination in critical circumstances by the Least Developed Contracting Sates on imports from other Contracting States.

(c) Contracting States shall also consider, where practical, taking direct trade measures with a view to enhancing sustainable exports from Least Developed Contracting States, such as long and medium-term contracts containing import and supply commitments in respect of specific products, buy-back arrangements, state trading operations, and government and public procurement.

(d) Special consideration shall be given by Contracting States to requests from Least Developed Contracting States for technical assistance and cooperation arrangements designed to assist them in expanding their trade with other Contracting States and in taking advantage of the potential benefits of SAFTA. A list of possible areas for such technical assistance shall be negotiated by the Contracting States and incorporated in this Agreement as an integral part.

(e) The Contracting States recognize that the Least Developed Contracting States may face loss of customs revenue due to the implementation of the Trade Liberalisation Programme under this Agreement. Until alternative domestic arrangements are formulated to address this situation, the Contracting States agree to establish an appropriate mechanism to compensate the Least Developed Contracting States for their loss of customs revenue. This mechanism and its rules and regulations shall be established prior to the commencement of the Trade Liberalisation Programme (TLP).

. . .

Article 14
General Exceptions

(a) Nothing in this Agreement shall be construed to prevent any Contracting State from taking action and adopting measures which it considers necessary for the protection of its national security.

(b) Subject to the requirement that such measures are not applied in a manner which would constitute a means of arbitrary or unjustifiable discrimination between countries where similar conditions prevail, or a disguised restriction on intraregional trade, nothing in this Agreement shall be construed to prevent any Contracting State from taking action and adopting measures which it considers necessary for the protection of:

(i) public morals;

(ii) human, animal or plant life and health; and

(iii) articles of artistic, historic and archaeological value.

Article 15
Balance of Payments Measures

1. Notwithstanding the provisions of this Agreement, any Contracting State facing serious balance of payments difficulties may suspend provisionally the concessions extended under this Agreement.

2. Any such measure taken pursuant to paragraph 1 of this Article shall be immediately notified to the Committee of Experts.

3. The Committee of Experts shall periodically review the measures taken pursuant to paragraph 1 of this Article.

4. Any Contracting State which takes action pursuant to paragraph 1 of this Article shall afford, upon request from any other Contracting State, adequate opportunities for consultations with a view to preserving the stability of concessions under SAFTA.

5. If no satisfactory adjustment is effected between the Contracting States concerned within 30 days of the beginning of such consultations, to be extended by another 30 days through mutual consent, the matter may be referred to the Committee of Experts.

6. Any such measures taken pursuant to paragraph 1 of this Article shall be phased out soon after the Committee of Experts comes to the conclusion that the balance of payments situation of the Contracting State concerned has improved.

. . .

Article 18
Rules of Origin

Rules of Origin shall be negotiated by the Contracting States and incorporated in this Agreement as an integral part.

Article 19
Consultations

1. Each Contracting State shall accord sympathetic consideration to and will afford adequate opportunity for consultations regarding representations made by another Contracting State with respect to any matter affecting the operation of this Agreement.

2. The Committee of Experts may, at the request of a Contracting State, consult with any Contracting State in respect of any matter for which it has not been possible to find a satisfactory solution through consultations under paragraph 1.

Article 20
Dispute Settlement Mechanism

1. Any dispute that may arise among the Contracting States regarding the interpretation and application of the provisions of this Agreement or any instrument adopted within its framework concerning the rights and obligations of the Contracting States will be amicably settled among the parties concerned through a process initiated by a request for bilateral consultations.

2. Any Contracting State may request consultations in accordance with paragraph 1 of this Article with other Contracting States in writing stating the reasons for the request including identification of the measures at issue. All such requests should be notified to the Committee of Experts, through the SAARC Secretariat with an indication of the legal basis for the complaint.

3. If a request for consultations is made pursuant to this Article, the Contracting State to which the request is made shall, unless otherwise mutually agreed, reply to the request within 15 days after the date of its receipt and shall enter into consultations in good faith within a period of no more than 30 days after the date of receipt of the request, with a view to reaching a mutually satisfactory solution.

4. If the Contracting State does not respond within 15 days after the date of receipt of the request, or does not enter into consultations within a period of no more than 30 days, or a period otherwise mutually agreed, after the date of receipt of the request, then the Contracting State that requested the holding of consultations may proceed to request the Committee of Experts to settle the dispute in accordance with working procedures to be drawn up by the Committee.

5. Consultations shall be confidential, and without prejudice to the rights of any Contracting State in any further proceedings.

6. If the consultations fail to settle a dispute within 30 days after the date of receipt of the request for consultations, to be extended by a further period of 30 days through mutual consent, the complaining Contracting State may request the Committee of Experts to settle the dispute. The complaining Contracting State may request the Committee of Experts to settle the dispute during the 60-day period if the consulting Contracting States jointly consider that consultations have failed to settle the dispute.

7. The Committee of Experts shall promptly investigate the matter referred to it and make recommendations on the matter within a period of 60 days from the date of referral.

8. The Committee of Experts may request a specialist from a Contracting State not party to the dispute selected from a panel of specialists to be established by the Committee within one year from the date of entry into force of the Agreement for peer review of the matter referred to it. Such review shall be submitted to the Committee within a period of 30 days from the date of referral of the matter to the specialist.

9. Any Contracting State which is a party to the dispute may appeal the recommendations of the Committee of Experts to the SMC. The SMC shall review the matter within the period of 60 days from date of submission of request for appeal. The SMC may uphold, modify or reverse the recommendations of the Committee of Experts.

10. Where the Committee of Experts or SMC concludes that the measure subject to dispute is inconsistent with any of the provisions of this Agreement, it shall recommend that the Contracting State concerned bring the measure into conformity with this Agreement. In addition to its recommendations, the Committee of Experts or SMC may suggest ways in which the Contracting State concerned could implement the recommendations.

11. The Contracting State to which the Committee's or SMC's recommendations are addressed shall, within 30 days from the date of adoption of the recommendations by the Committee or SMC, inform the Committee of Experts of its intentions regarding implementation of the recommendations. Should the said Contracting State fail to implement the recommendations within 90 days from the date of adoption of the recommendations by the Committee, the Committee of Experts may authorize other interested Contracting States to withdraw concessions having trade effects equivalent to those of the measure in dispute.

. . .

AGREEMENT FOR ESTABLISHMENT OF SAARC ARBITRATION COUNCIL (13.11.2005)

. . .

Desirous of providing a regional forum for settlement of commercial disputes by conciliation and arbitration;

. . .

Article I
Establishment of the SAARC Arbitration Council

1. (1) There is hereby established a body to be known as the SAARC Arbitration Council (hereinafter referred to as the 'Council').
   (2) The Council shall have full legal personality.
   (3) The legal capacity of the Council shall include:
   (a) the capacity to contract;
   (b) to sue and be sued in its name; and
   (c) to acquire, hold and dispose of properties.
2. The location of the Council shall be decided.

Article II
Objectives and Functions of the Council

3. The objectives and functions of the Council are to:
   (a) provide a legal framework within the region for fair and efficient settlement through conciliation and arbitration of commercial, investment and such other disputes as may be referred to the Council by agreement;
   (b) promote the growth and effective functioning of national arbitration institutions within the region;
   (c) provide fair, inexpensive and expeditious arbitration in the region;
   (d) promote international conciliation and arbitration in the region;
   (e) provide facilities for conciliation and arbitration;
   (f) act as a coordinating agency in the SAARC dispute resolution system;
   (g) coordinate the activities of and assist existing institutions concerned with arbitration, particularly those in the region;
   (h) render assistance in the conduct of ad hoc arbitration proceedings;
   (i) assist in the enforcement of arbitral awards;
   (j) maintain registers/panels of:
      i) expert witnesses, and

ii) suitably qualified persons to act as arbitrators as and when required; and

(k) carry out such other activities as are conducive or incidental to its functions.

4. The Council shall have the powers necessary to enable it to carry out its objectives and functions.

Article III
Organisational Set-up of the Council

5. (1) There shall be for the Council a Director-General who shall:
    (a) be a citizen of a SAARC Member State; and
    (b) be appointed, on the principle of alphabetical rotation among SAARC Member States commencing from the Member State hosting the Council, by the Secretary-General of SAARC with the approval of the Council of Ministers.

(2) The Director-General shall hold office for a non-renewable period of three years on such terms and conditions as may be determined by the Council of Ministers. However, the tenure of the first Director-General will be for a period of four years.

(3) The Director-General shall be the chief executive of the Council and be responsible for the day-to-day administration of the Council and will work under the supervision of the Governing Board comprising a Member nominated by each Member State.

(4) The salary and allowances of the Director-General shall be determined by the Council of Ministers.

(5) With regard to matters not covered in this Agreement, including the Service Rules, Provisions relating to Financial and Administrative Matters, Financial Regulations, Financial Rules and Procedures and Rules of Procedures for Governing Boards applicable to the SAARC Regional Centres under the Harmonized Rules will be applicable, mutatis mutandis, to the Council.

6. The Council, its Director-General and staff shall enjoy such immunities and privileges as are essential for the effective functioning of the Council, to be specified in the Headquarters Agreement between the Council and the Host Member State.

Article IV
Rules

7. (1) Subject to the Conciliation Rules to be agreed and annexed to this Agreement, the Governing Board may make any additional rules for

the administration of conciliation proceedings conducted under the auspices of the Council, including the schedule of fees to be charged.

(2) Subject to the Arbitration Rules to be agreed and annexed to this Agreement, the Governing Board may make any additional rules for the administration of arbitrations conducted under the auspices of the Council, including the schedule of fees to be charged.

(3) The Rules made under sub-paras (1) & (2) of this Article shall be made public.

. . .

4

REGION-BUILDING IN AFRICA

AFRICAN UNION (AU)

From the formation of the Organization of African Unity through its 1963 Charter, which aimed to promote African self-government, to the creation in 2001 of the African Union, intended to foster an African Economic Community by 2028, regional efforts in Africa were always considered partial expressions in search of a broader goal, the African Renaissance. The most ambitious effort to integrate Africa is being conducted at the continental level. Ever since the decolonization struggles of the mid twentieth century, African leaders have dreamed of one day bringing about a united continent. The Organization of African Unity (OAU), however, proved incapable of limiting the quest for national sovereignty across the continent, even as it failed to support economic development and good governance. It also failed to prevent the ethnic conflicts and regional crises that have blurred the image of Africa during much of the past three decades.

Africa is by far the poorest continent in the world. Of a total of 770 million inhabitants in sub-Saharan Africa, close to 350 million live below the line of absolute poverty (on less than one US dollar per day). More than 150 million of them are children. During the last decade of the twentieth century, Africa's share in global imports and exports fell to 1.6 percent compared with 4.6 percent in 1980. It was only in light of the recognition of a deep crisis affecting the whole continent—in spite of certain pockets of progress and limited success stories— that leaders from all across Africa made a new beginning. The Treaty Establishing the African Economic Community (Treaty of Abuja), signed at the Summit of the Organization of African Unity in 1991 with the aim of establishing an African Economic Community, and the foundation of the African Union in 2001 after the requisite thirty-six ratifications of the Treaty signed in Lomé in 2000 have begun to generate fresh impulses geared at long-term improvement of the overall prospects for Africa. With fifty-three African states (all except Morocco)

participating, the African Union is the most comprehensive scheme of conti-
nental-wide cooperation and thus is comparable to the Council of Europe rather
than to the European Union. In light of the intricate and mutually reinforcing
relationship between the two during decades of crisis and uncertainty in Europe,
this might not be a bad start for the African Union.

Its Constitutive Act of 2000, ratified by all member states of the African
Union as an instrument of international law, established the African Court of
Justice, the Pan-African Parliament, the African Commission on Human and
Civil Rights, the Monetary Fund, and the Central Bank. Its Secretariat is based
in Addis Ababa. The four institutions of the African Union are: the Assembly, the Executive Council, the Permanent Representatives' Committee, and the
Commission of the Union. Although the terminology echoes the European experience, the principal of supranationality has not been applied to the structures
and competencies of the African Union. It remains an intergovernmental body,
meant to be a proactive organization swiftly responding to the continent's new
challenges. The ambition of Libya's leader Gaddafi, as concerns the creation of
a pan-African defense force and an immediate common market with a common
currency, has not materialized yet.

The African Union is meant to work as a catalyst for bringing various regional
schemes of economic cooperation and integration together under the roof of a
pan-African vision. The structures of the African Union include mechanisms to
deal with human rights protection as well as those intended to contribute to conflict prevention and conflict resolution on the African continent. In the absence
of genuine qualified majority voting as the key to the efficiency and success of
this work, the strength of the indirect effect these reinforced commitments can
have on the member states of the African Union will remain open to long-term
judgment. Self-commitments might produce better results than efforts geared at a
formal limiting of national sovereignty.

Legitimized and refined by the AU's Solemn Declaration on a Common African Defence and Security Policy of 2004, a Peace and Security Council of fifteen
member states of the AU, early warning, and preventive diplomacy, as well as
peacemaking through the use of good offices, mediation, conciliation, and en-
quiry add to the AUu's ambitious plan to change the course of future violent
political crises in the continent. The right to intervene in a member state "pursuant to a decision of the Assembly in respect to grave circumstances, namely: war
crimes, genocide and crimes against humanity" (Article 40h of the Constitutive
Act) stipulates a new direction in African self-rule and self-criticism. It is not
clear whether the Assembly of the AU—comprised of the heads of state and
government—will ever apply the principle of consensus for decisions of this magnitude. The AU's Constitutive Act states that, should the Assembly fail to reach
decisions by consensus, a two-thirds majority is sufficient to proceed with decisions in the framework of the competencies of the Assembly. Alongside issues

of peacekeeping and human rights, this might also include questions relating to the budget of the African Union. The mere wording of the Constitutive Act reflects growing sensitivity toward issues of peace and human rights in Africa. Whether or not this can impact state behavior or that of warring forces remains to be seen. Skepticism also prevails regarding the potential for the Commission of the African Union to truly turn into a supranational executive analogous to the European Commission.

The same uncertainty applies to the African Union's ability to promote economic cooperation and development by advancing the gradual merger of various regional cooperation and integration schemes into an African Economic Community. The AU has identified the following regional schemes of economic cooperation as the engines for creating a pan-African Economic Community: the Economic Community of West Africa (ECOWAS), founded in 1975 and composed of fifteen member states; the Common Market of Eastern and Southern Africa (COMESA) with nineteen member states, founded in 1981 as Preferential Trade Area for Eastern and Southern Africa; the Economic Community of Central African States (ECCAS) with eleven member states, founded in 1983; the Southern African Development Community (SADC), now with fourteen member states, established in 1992 as a successor institution to the Southern African Development Coordination Conference that was founded as an anti-apartheid instrument in 1980, and the five–member state Arab Maghreb Union (AMU), founded in 1989. The New African Initiative and the New Partnership for Africa's Development of 2001 represent ambitious yet reasonable and realistic concepts outlining the path toward an economic renaissance of Africa based on cooperation and integration. No matter how much skepticism is aired in view of African experiences in past decades, the African Union is the promising and ambitious new beginning of a certainly rough and daunting road ahead for the continent.

ORGANIZATION OF AFRICAN UNITY (OAU) CHARTER (25.05.1963)

. . .

Conscious of the fact that freedom, equality, justice and dignity are essential objectives for the achievement of the legitimate aspirations of the African peoples,

Conscious of our responsibility to harness the natural and human resources of our continent for the total advancement of our peoples in all spheres of human endeavour,

Inspired by a common determination to promote understanding among our peoples and cooperation among our states in response to the aspirations of our peoples for brotherhood and solidarity, in a larger unity transcending ethnic and national differences.

. . .

Purposes

Article II

1. The Organization shall have the following purposes:
   (a) To promote the unity and solidarity of the African States
   (b) To coordinate and intensify their cooperation and efforts to achieve a better life for the peoples of Africa
   (c) To defend their sovereignty, their territorial integrity and independence
   (d) To eradicate all forms of colonialism from Africa; and
   (e) To promote international cooperation, having due regard to the Charter of the United Nations and the Universal Declaration of Human Rights.
2. To these ends, the Member States shall coordinate and harmonize their general policies, especially in the following fields:
   (a) Political and diplomatic cooperation
   (b) Economic cooperation, including transport and communications
   (c) Educational and cultural cooperation
   (d) Health, sanitation and nutritional cooperation
   (e) Scientific and technical cooperation; and
   (f) Cooperation for defence and security.

Principles

Article III

The Member States, in pursuit of the purposes stated in Article II, solemnly affirm and declare their adherence to the following principles:

1. The sovereign equality of all Member States
2. Non-interference in the internal affairs of States
3. Respect for the sovereignty and territorial integrity of each State and for its inalienable right to independent existence
4. Peaceful settlement of disputes by negotiation, mediation, conciliation or arbitration

5. Unreserved condemnation, in all its forms, of political assassination as well as of subversive activities on the part of neighbouring States or any other States
6. Absolute dedication to the total emancipation of the African territories which are still dependent
7. Affirmation of a policy of non-alignment with regard to all blocs.

Membership

Article IV

Each independent sovereign African State shall be entitled to become a Member of the Organization.

Rights and Duties of Member States

Article V

All Member States shall enjoy equal rights and have equal duties.

Article VI

The Member States pledge themselves to observe scrupulously the principles enumerated in Article III of the present Charter.

Institutions

Article VII

The Organization shall accomplish its purposes through the following principal institutions:
1. The Assembly of Heads of State and Government
2. The Council of Ministers
3. The General Secretariat
4. The Commission of Mediation, Conciliation and Arbitration.

The Assembly of Heads of State and Government

Article VIII

The Assembly of Heads of State and Government shall be the supreme organ of the Organization. It shall, subject to the provisions of this Charter, discuss matters of common concern to Africa with a view to coordinating and harmonizing the general policy of the Organization. It may in addition review the structure, functions and acts of all the organs and any specialized agencies which may be created in accordance with the present Charter.

Article IX

The Assembly shall be composed of the Heads of State and Government or their duly accredited representatives and it shall meet at least once a year. At the request of any Member State and on approval by a two-thirds majority of the Member States, the Assembly shall meet in extraordinary session.

Article X

1. Each Member State shall have one vote
2. All resolutions shall be determined by a two-thirds majority of the Members of the Organization
3. Questions of procedure shall require a simple majority. Whether or not a question is one of procedure shall be determined by a simple majority of all Member States of the Organization
4. Two-thirds of the total membership of the Organization shall form a quorum at any meeting of the Assembly.

. . .

The Council of Ministers

Article XII

1. The Council of Ministers shall consist of Foreign Ministers or other Ministers as are designated by the Governments of Member States.
2. The Council of Ministers shall meet at least twice a year. When requested by any Member State and approved by two-thirds of all Member States, it shall meet in extraordinary session.

Article XIII

1. The Council of Ministers shall be responsible to the Assembly of Heads of State and Government. It shall be entrusted with the responsibility of preparing conferences of the Assembly.

    . . .

Article XIV

1. Each Member State shall have one vote
2. All resolutions shall be determined by a simple majority of the members of the Council of Ministers
3. Two-thirds of the total membership of the Council of Ministers shall form a quorum for any meeting of the Council.

    . . .

General Secretariat

Article XVI

There shall be a Secretary-General of the Organization, who shall be appointed by the Assembly of Heads of State and Government. The Secretary-General shall direct the affairs of the Secretariat.

. . .

Commission of Mediation, Conciliation and Arbitration

Article XIX

Member States pledge to settle all disputes among themselves by peaceful means and to this end decide to establish a Commission of Mediation, Conciliation and Arbitration, the composition of which and conditions of service shall be defined by a separate Protocol to be approved by the Assembly of Heads of State and Government. Said Protocol shall be regarded as forming an integral part of the present Charter.

. . .

The Budget

Article XXIII

The budget of the Organization prepared by the Secretary-General shall be approved by the Council of Ministers. The budget shall be provided by contributions from Member States in accordance with the scale of assessment of the United Nations; provided, however, that no Member State shall be assessed an amount exceeding twenty percent of the yearly regular budget of the Organization. The Member States agree to pay their respective contributions regularly.

. . .

Interpretation of the Charter

Article XXVII

Any question which may arise concerning the interpretation of this Charter shall be decided by a vote of two-thirds of the Assembly of Heads of State and Government of the Organization.

. . .

Cessation of Membership

Article XXXI

Any State which desires to renounce its membership shall forward a written notification to the Secretary-General. At the end of one year from the date of such notification, if not withdrawn, the Charter shall cease to apply with respect to the renouncing State, which shall thereby cease to belong to the Organization.

. . .

Treaty Establishing the African Economic Community (03.06.1991)

. . .

Chapter II—Establishment, Principles, Objectives, General Undertaking and Modalities

Article 2
Establishment of the Community

The High Contracting Parties hereby establish among themselves an African Economic Community (AEC).

Article 3
Principles

The High Contracting Parties, in pursuit of the objectives stated in Article 4 of this Treaty, solemnly affirm and declare their adherence to the following principles:

(a) Equality and inter-dependence of Member States;

(b) Solidarity and collective self-reliance;

(c) Inter-State cooperation, harmonisation of policies and integration of programmes;

(d) Promotion of harmonious development of economic activities among Member States;

(e) Observance of the legal system of the Community;

(f) Peaceful settlement of disputes among Member States, active cooperation between neighbouring countries and promotion of a peaceful environment as a pre-requisite for economic development;

(g) Recognition, promotion and protection of human and peoples' rights in accordance with the provisions of the African Charter on Human and Peoples' Rights; and

(h) Accountability, economic justice and popular participation in development.

Article 4
Objectives

1. The objectives of the Community shall be:

(a) To promote economic, social and cultural development and the integration of African economies in order to increase economic self-reliance and promote an endogenous and self-sustained development;

(b) To establish, on a continental scale, a framework for the development, mobilisation and utilisation of the human and material resources of Africa in order to achieve a self-reliant development;

(c) To promote cooperation in all fields of human endeavour in order to raise the standard of living of African peoples, and maintain and enhance economic stability, foster close and peaceful relations among Member States and contribute to the progress, development and the economic integration of the Continent; and

(d) To coordinate and harmonize policies among existing and future economic communities in order to foster the gradual establishment of the Community.

2. In order to promote the attainment of the objectives of the Community as set out in paragraph I of this Article, and in accordance with

the relevant provisions of this Treaty, the Community shall, by stages, ensure:

(a) The strengthening of existing regional economic communities and the establishment of other communities where they do not exist;

(b) The conclusion of agreements aimed at harmonising and coordinating policies among existing and future sub-regional and regional economic communities;

(c) The promotion and strengthening of joint investment programmes in the production and trade of major products and inputs within the framework of collective self-reliance;

(d) The liberalisation of trade through the abolition, among Member States, of Customs Duties levied on imports and exports and the abolition, among Member States, of Non-Tariff Barriers in order to establish a free trade area at the level of each regional economic community;

(e) The harmonisation of national policies in order to promote Community activities, particularly in the fields of agriculture, industry, transport and communications, energy, natural resources, trade, money and finance, human resources, education, culture, science and technology;

(f) The adoption of a common trade policy vis-à-vis third States;

(g) The establishment and maintenance of a common external tariff;

(h) The establishment of a common market;

(i) The gradual removal, among Member States, of obstacles to the free movement of persons, goods, services and capital and the right of residence and establishment;

(j) The establishment of a Community Solidarity, Development and Compensation Fund;

(k) The granting of special treatment to Member States classified as least developed countries and the adoption of special measures in favour of land-locked, semi-land-locked and island countries;

(l) The harmonisation and rationalisation of the activities of existing African multinational institutions and the establishment of such institutions, as and when necessary, with a view to their possible transformation into organs of the Community;

(m) The establishment of appropriate organs for trade in agricultural and cultural products, minerals, metals, and manufactured and semi-manufactured goods within the Community;

(n) The establishment of contacts and the promotion of information flow among trading organisations such as State commercial enterprises, export promotion and marketing bodies, chambers of commerce, associations of businessmen, and business and advertising agencies;

(o) The harmonisation and coordination of environmental protection policies; and

(p) Any other activity that Member States may decide to undertake jointly with a view to attaining the objectives of the Community.

. . .

Article 6
Modalities for the Establishment of the Community

1. The Community shall be established gradually in six (6) stages of variable duration over a transitional period not exceeding thirty-four (34) years.

2. At each such stage, specific activities shall be assigned and implemented concurrently as follows:

(a) First Stage:

Strengthening of existing regional economic communities and, within a period not exceeding five (5) years from the date of entry into force of this Treaty, establishing economic communities in regions where they do not exist;

(b) Second Stage:

(i) At the level of each regional economic community and within a period not exceeding eight years, stabilising Tariff Barriers and Non-Tariff Barriers, Customs Duties and internal taxes existing at the date of entry into force of this Treaty; there shall also be prepared and adopted studies to determine the time-table for the gradual removal of Tariff Barriers and Non-Tariff Barriers to regional and intra-Community trade and for the gradual harmonisation of Customs Duties in relation to third States;

(ii) Strengthening of sectoral integration at the regional and continental levels in all areas of activity particularly in the fields of trade, agriculture, money and finance, transport and communications, industry and energy; and

(iii) Coordination and harmonisation of activities among the existing and future economic communities.

(c) Third Stage:

At the level of each regional economic community and within a period not exceeding ten (10) years, establishment of a Free Trade Area through the observance of the time-table for the gradual removal of Tariff Barriers and Non-Tariff Barriers to intra-community trade and the establishment of a customs union by means of adopting a common external tariff.

(d) Fourth Stage:

Within a period not exceeding two (2) years, coordination and harmonisation of tariff and non-tariff systems among the various regional economic communities with a view to establishing a customs union at the continental level by means of adopting a common external tariff.

(e) Fifth Stage:

Within a period not exceeding four (4) years, establishment of an African common market through:

(i) The adoption of a common policy in several areas such as agriculture, transport and communications, industry, energy and scientific research;

(ii) The harmonisation of monetary, financial and fiscal policies;

(iii) The application of the principle of free movement of persons as well as the provisions herein regarding the rights of residence and establishment; and

(iv) Constituting the proper resources of the Community as provided for in paragraph 2 of Article 82 of this Treaty.

(f) Sixth Stage:

Within a period not exceeding five (5) years:

(i) Consolidation and strengthening of the structure of the African common market, through including the free movement of people, goods, capital and services, as well as the provisions herein regarding the rights of residence and establishment;

(ii) Integration of all the sectors namely economic, political, social and cultural; establishment of a single domestic market and a Pan-African Economic and Monetary Union;

(iii) Implementation of the final stage for the setting up of an African Monetary Union, the establishment of a single African Central Bank and the creation of a single African Currency;

(iv) Implementation of the final stage for the setting up of the structure of the Pan-African Parliament and election of its members by continental universal suffrage;

(v) Implementation of the final stage for the harmonisation and coordination process of the activities of regional economic communities;

(vi) Implementation of the final stage for the setting up of the structures of African multi-national enterprises in all sectors; and

(vii) Implementation of the final stage for the setting up of the structures of the executive organs of the Community.

3. All measures envisaged under this Treaty for the promotion of a harmonious and balanced development among Member States, particularly

those relating to the formulation of multi-national projects and programmes, shall be implemented concurrently within the time period
specified for the attainment of the objectives of the various stages outlined in paragraph 2 of this Article.

4. The transition from one stage to another shall be determined when the
    specific objectives, set in this Treaty or pronounced by the Assembly for
    a particular stage, are implemented and all commitments fulfilled. The
    Assembly, on the recommendation of the Council, shall confirm that
    the objectives to a particular stage have been attained and shall approve
    the transition to the next stage.

5. Notwithstanding the provisions of the preceding paragraph, the cumu-
    lative transitional period shall not exceed forty (40) years from the date
    of entry into force of this Treaty.

Chapter III—Organs of the Community

Article 7
Organs

1. The organs of the Community shall be:
    (a) The Assembly of Heads of State and Government;
    (b) The Council of Ministers;
    (c) The Pan-African Parliament;
    (d) The Economic and Social Commission;
    (e) The Court of Justice;
    (f) The General Secretariat; and
    (g) The Specialised Technical Committees.

2. The Organs of the Community shall perform their duties and act within
    the limits of the powers conferred on them by this Treaty.

    . . .

Article 10
Decisions

1. The Assembly shall act by decisions.

2. Without prejudice to the provisions of paragraph (5) Article 18, deci-
    sions shall be binding on Member States and organs of the Community,
    as well as regional economic communities.

3. Decisions shall be automatically enforceable thirty (30) days after the
    date of their signature by the Chairman of the Assembly, and shall be
    published in the official journal of the Community.

4. Unless otherwise provided in this Treaty, decision of the Assembly shall be adopted by consensus, failing that, by a two-thirds majority of Member States.

. . .

Article 13
Regulations

1. The Council shall act by regulations.
2. Without prejudice to the provisions of paragraph (5) of Article 18 of this Treaty, such regulations shall be binding on Member States, subordinate organs of the Community and regional economic communities after their approval by the Assembly. Notwithstanding the foregoing provisions, regulations adopted as aforesaid shall forthwith have a binding effect in the case of delegation of powers by the Assembly pursuant to paragraph 3(j) of Article 8 hereof.
3. Regulations shall be enforceable automatically thirty (30) days after the date of their signature by the Chairman of the Council and shall be published in the official journal of the Community.
4. Unless otherwise provided in this Treaty, regulations shall be adopted by consensus or, failing that, by two-thirds majority of Member States.

Article 14
The Pan-African Parliament

1. In order to ensure that the peoples of Africa are fully involved in the economic development and integration of the Continent, there shall be established a Pan-African Parliament.
2. The composition, functions, powers and organisation of the Pan-African Parliament shall be defined in a Protocol providing thereof.

Article 15
Economic and Social Commission—Composition and Participation

1. The Commission shall be the Economic and Social Commission of the OAU.
2. The Commission shall comprise Ministers responsible for economic development, planning and integration of each Member States. They may be assisted, as and when necessary, by other Ministers.
3. Representatives of regional economic communities shall participate in meetings of the Commission and its subsidiary organs. The modalities

and conditions of their participation shall be prescribed in the protocol concerning relations between the Community and African regional and sub-regional organisations and Third States. Representatives of other organisations may also be invited to participate as observers in the deliberations of the Commission.

. . .

Article 18
Court of Justice Constitution and Functions

1. A Court of Justice of the Community is hereby constituted.
2. The Court of Justice shall ensure the adherence to law in the interpretation and application of this Treaty and shall decide on disputes submitted thereto pursuant to this Treaty
3. To this end, it shall:
   (a) Decide on actions brought by a Member State or the Assembly on grounds of the violation of the provisions of this Treaty, or of a decision or a regulation or on grounds of lack of competence or abuse of powers by an organ, an authority or a Member State; and
   (b) At the request of the Assembly or Council, give advisory opinions.
4. The Assembly may confer on the Court of Justice the power to assume jurisdiction by virtue of this Treaty over any dispute other than those referred to in paragraph 3(a) of this Article.
5. The Court of Justice shall carry out the functions assigned to it independently of the Member States and the other organs of the Community.

Article 19
Decisions of the Court

The Decisions of the Court of Justice shall be binding on Member States and organs of the Community.

. . .

Article 22
Functions of the Secretary-General

1. The Secretary-General shall direct the activities of the Secretariat and shall be its legal representative.
2. The Secretary-General shall:
   (a) Follow up and ensure the implementation of the decisions of the Assembly and the application of the regulations of the Council;

(b) Promote development programmes as well as projects of the Community;

(c) Prepare proposals concerning the programme of activity and budget of the Community and upon their approval by the Assembly ensure the implementation thereof;

(d) Submit a report on the activities of the Community to all meetings of the Assembly, the Council and the Commission;

(e) Prepare and service meetings of the Assembly, the Council, the Commission and the Committees;

(f) Carry out studies with a view to attaining the objectives of the Community and make proposals likely to enhance the functioning and harmonious development of the Community.

To this end, the Secretary-General may request any Member State to furnish him with all necessary information; and

(g) Recruit the staff of the Community and make appointments to all posts except those referred to in paragraph 3(f) of Article 8 of this Treaty.

. . .

Chapter V—Customs Union and Liberalisation of Trade

Article 29
Customs Union

Member States of each regional economic community agree to progressively establish among them, during a transitional period specified in Article 6 of this Treaty, a customs union involving:

(a) The elimination, among Member States of each regional economic community, of customs duties, quota restrictions, other restrictions or prohibitions and administrative trade barriers, as well as all other non-tariff barriers; and

(b) The adoption by Member States of a common external customs tariff.

Article 30
Elimination of Customs Duties among Member States of Regional Economic Communities

1. During the second stage, Member States of each regional economic community shall refrain from establishing among themselves any new customs duties and from increasing those that apply in their mutual trade relations.

2. During the third stage, Member States shall progressively reduce and eliminate finally among themselves, at the level of each regional economic community, customs duties in accordance with such programmes and modalities as shall be determined by each regional economic community.

3. During each stage, the Assembly, on the recommendation of the Council, shall take the necessary measures with a view to coordinating and harmonising the activities of the regional economic communities relating to the elimination of customs duties among Member States.

Article 31
Elimination of Non-Tariff Barriers to Intra-Community Trade

1. At the level of each regional economic community and subject to the provisions of the Treaty, each Member State shall, upon the entry into force of this Treaty, progressively relax and ultimately remove quota restrictions, and all other non-tariff barriers and prohibitions which apply to exports to that State, of goods originating in the other Member States, at the latest by the end of the third stage and in accordance with paragraph (2) of this Article. Except as otherwise provided or permitted by this Treaty, each Member State shall thereafter refrain from imposing any further restrictions or prohibitions on such goods.

2. Subject to the provisions of this Treaty, each regional economic community shall adopt a programme for the progressive relaxation and ultimate elimination, at the latest by the end of the third stage, of all quota restrictions and prohibitions and all other non-tariff barriers that apply in a Member State, to imports originating in the other Member States; it being understood that each regional economic community may subsequently decide that all quota restrictions, other restrictions and prohibitions be relaxed or removed within a shorter period than that prescribed in this paragraph.

3. The arrangements governing restrictions, prohibitions, quota restrictions, dumping subsidies and discriminatory practices shall be the subject of a Protocol concerning Non-Tariff Trade Barriers.

Article 32
Establishment of a Common External Customs Tariff

1. During the third stage, Member States shall, at the level of each regional economic community, agree to the gradual establishment of a common external customs tariff applicable to goods originating from third States and imported into Member States.

2. During the fourth stage, regional economic communities shall, in accordance with a programme drawn up by them, eliminate differences between their respective external customs tariffs.

3. During the fourth stage the Council shall propose to the Assembly the adoption, at Community level, of a common customs and statistical nomenclature for all Member States.

Article 33
System of Intra-Community Trade

1. At the end of the third stage, no Member State shall, at the level of each regional economic community, levy customs duties on goods originating in one Member State and imported into another Member State. The same prohibition shall apply to goods originating from third States which are in free circulation in Member States and are imported from one Member State into another.

2. The definition of the notion of products originating in Member States and the rules governing goods originating in third States and which are in free circulation in Member States shall be governed by a Protocol concerning the Rules of Origin.

3. Goods originating from third States shall be considered to be in free circulation in a Member State if (i) the import formalities relating thereto have been complied with, (ii) customs duties have been paid thereon in that Member State, and (iii) they have not benefited from a partial or total exemption from such customs duties.

4. Member States undertake not to adopt legislation implying direct or indirect discrimination against identical or similar products originating from another Member State.

Article 34
Internal Taxes

1. During the third stage, Member States shall not levy, directly or indirectly on goods originating from a Member State and imported into any Member State, internal taxes in excess of those levied on similar domestic products.

2. Member States, at the level of each regional economic community, shall progressively eliminate any internal taxes levied for the protection of domestic products. Where, by virtue of obligations assumed under a prior agreement signed by a Member State, that Member State is unable to comply with this Article, it shall notify the Council of this fact and shall not extend or renew such agreement when it expires.

. . .

Article 39
Customs Cooperation and Administration

Member States shall, in accordance with the Protocol concerning Customs Cooperation, take all necessary measures for harmonising and standardising their customs regulations and procedures in such a manner as shall be appropriate for ensuring the effective implementation of the provisions of this Chapter and facilitating the movement of goods and services across their frontiers.

. . .

Chapter VI—Free Movement of Persons, Rights of Residence and Establishment

Article 43
General Provisions

1. Member States agree to adopt, individually, at bilateral or regional levels, the necessary measures, in order to achieve progressively the free movement of persons, and to ensure the enjoyment of the right of residence and the right of establishment by their nationals within the Community.
2. For this purpose, Member States agree to conclude a Protocol on the Free Movement of Persons, Right of Residence and Right of Establishment.

Chapter VII—Money, Finance and Payments

Article 44
Monetary, Financial and Payment Policies

1. In accordance with the relevant Protocols, Member States shall, within a time-table to be determined by the Assembly, harmonize their monetary, financial and payments policies, in order to boost intra-community trade in goods and services, to further the attainment of objectives of the Community and to enhance monetary and financial cooperation among Member States.
2. To this end, Member States shall:
    (a) Use their national currencies in the settlement of commercial and financial transactions in order to reduce the use of external currencies in such transactions;
    (b) Establish appropriate mechanisms for setting up multilateral payments systems;

(c) Consult regularly among themselves on monetary and financial matters;

(d) Promote the creation of national, regional and sub-regional money markets, through the coordinated establishment of stock exchanges and harmonising legal texts regulating existing stock exchanges with a view to making them more effective;

(e) Cooperate in an effective manner in the fields of insurance and banking;

(f) Further the liberalisation of payments and the elimination of payment restrictions, if any, among them and promote the integration of all existing payments and clearing mechanisms among the different regions into an African Clearing and Payments House; and

(g) Establish an African Monetary Union through the harmonisation of regional monetary zones.

Article 45
Movement of Capital

1. Member States shall ensure the free movement of capital within the Community through the elimination of restrictions on the transfer of capital funds between Member States in accordance with a timetable to be determined by the Council.

2. The capital referred to in paragraph 1 of this Article is that of Member States or persons of Member States.

3. The Assembly, having regard to the development objectives of national, regional and continental plans, and upon the recommendation of the Commission and after the approval of the Council acting on the recommendation of the Commission, shall prescribe the conditions for the movement within the Community of the capital funds other than those referred to in paragraph (2) of this Article.

4. For the purpose of regulating the movement of capital between Member States and Third States, the Assembly, upon the approval of the Council, acting on the recommendation of the Commission, shall take steps aimed at coordinating progressively the national and regional exchange control policies.

Chapter VIII—Food and Agriculture

Article 46
Agricultural Development and Food Production

1. Member States shall cooperate in the development of agriculture, forestry, livestock and fisheries in order to:

(a) Ensure food security;

(b) Increase production and productivity in agriculture, livestock, fisheries and forestry, and improve conditions of work and generate employment opportunities in rural areas;

(c) Enhance agricultural production through processing locally animal and plant products; and

(d) Protect the prices of export commodities on the international market by means of establishing an African Commodity Exchange.

2. To this end, and in order to promote the integration of production structures, Member States shall cooperate in the following fields:

(a) The production of agricultural inputs, fertilisers, pesticides, selected seeds, agricultural machinery and equipment and veterinary products;

(b) The development of river and lake basins;

(c) The development and protection of marine and fishery resources;

(d) Plant and animal protection;

(e) The harmonisation of agricultural development strategies and policies at regional and Community levels, in particular, in so far as they relate to production, trade and marketing of major agricultural products and inputs; and

(f) The harmonisation of food security policies in order to ensure:

(i) The reduction of losses in food production;

(ii) The strengthening of existing institutions for the management of natural calamities, agricultural diseases and pest control;

(iii) The conclusion of agreements on food security at the regional and continental levels;

(iv) The provision of food aid to Member States in the event of serious food shortage; and

(v) The protection of regional and continental markets primarily for the benefit of African agricultural products.

. . .

Chapter IX—Industry, Science, Technology, Energy, Natural Resources and Environment

Article 48
Industry

1. For the purpose of promoting industrial development of Member States and integrating their economies, Member States shall within the Community harmonize their industrialisation policies.

2. In this connection, Member States shall:

(a) Strengthen the industrial base of the Community, in order to modernize the priority sectors and foster self-sustained and self-reliant development;

(b) Promote joint industrial development projects at regional and Community levels, as well as the creation of African multinational enterprises in priority industrial sub-sectors likely to contribute to the development of agriculture, transport and communications, natural resources and energy.

Article 49
Industrial Development

In order to create a solid basis for industrialisation and promote collective self-reliance, Member States shall:

(a) Ensure the development of the following basic industries essential for collective self-reliance and the modernisation of priority sectors of the economy:
   (i) Food and agro-based industries;
   (ii) Building and construction industries;
   (iii) Metallurgical industries;
   (iv) Mechanical industries;
   (v) Electrical and electronics industries;
   (vi) Chemical and petro-chemical industries;
   (vii) Forestry industries;
   (viii) Energy industries;
   (ix) Textile and leather industries;
   (x) Transport and communications industries; and
   (xi) Biotechnology industries;

(b) Ensure the promotion of small-scale industries with a view to enhancing the generation of employment opportunities in Member States;

(c) Promote intermediate industries that have strong linkages to the economy in order to increase the local component of industrial output within the Community;

(d) Prepare master plans at regional and Community levels for the establishment of African multinational industries, particularly those whose construction cost and volumes of production exceed national financial and absorptive capacities;

(e) Strengthen and establish, where they do not exist, specialised institutions for the financing of African multinational industrial projects;

(f) Facilitate the establishment of African multinational enterprises and encourage and give financial and technical support to African entrepreneurs;

(g) Promote the sale and consumption of strategic industrial products manufactured in Member States;

(h) Promote technical cooperation and the exchange of experience in the field of industrial technology and implement technical training programmes among Member States;

(i) Strengthen the existing multinational institutions, particularly, the African Regional Centre for Technology, the African Regional Centre for Design and Manufacture and the African Industrial Development Fund;

(j) Establish a data and statistical information base to serve industrial development at the regional and continental levels;

(k) Promote South-South and North-South cooperation for the attainment of industrialisation objectives in Africa;

(l) Promote industrial specialisation in order to enhance the complementarity of African economies and expand the intra- Community trade base, due account being taken of national and regional resource endowments; and

(m) Adopt common standards and appropriate quality control systems, which are crucial to industrial cooperation and integration.

. . .

Article 51
Science and Technology

1. Member States shall:
   (a) Strengthen scientific and technological capabilities in order to bring about the socio-economic transformation required to improve the quality of life of their population, particularly that of the rural populations;
   (b) Ensure the proper application of science and technology to the development of agriculture, transport and communications, industry, health and hygiene, energy, education and manpower and the conservation of the environment;
   (c) Reduce their dependence and promote their individual and collective technological self-reliance;
   (d) Cooperate in the development, acquisition and dissemination of appropriate technologies; and
   (e) Strengthen existing scientific research institutions and, where they do not exist, establish new institutions.

2. In the context of cooperation in this field, Member States shall:
   (a) Harmonize, at the Community level, their national policies on scientific and technological research with a view to facilitating their integration into the national economic and social development plans;

(b) Coordinate their programmes in applied research, research for development and scientific and technological services;

(c) Harmonize their national technological development plans by placing special emphasis on local technologies as well as their regulations on industrial property and transfer of technology;

(d) Coordinate their positions on all scientific and technical questions forming the subject of international negotiations;

(e) Carry out a permanent exchange of information and documentation and establish community data networks and data banks;

(f) Develop joint programmes for training scientific and technological cadres, including the training and further training of skilled manpower;

(g) Promote exchanges of researchers and specialists among Member States in order to make full use of the technical skills available within the Community; and

(h) Revise the educational systems in order to better educational, scientific and technical training to the specific developmental needs of the African environment.

. . .

Article 54
Energy and Natural Resources

1. Member States shall coordinate and harmonize their policies and programmes in the field of energy and natural resources.
2. To this end, they shall:
   (a) Ensure the effective development of the continent's energy and natural resources;
   (b) Establish appropriate cooperation mechanisms with a view to ensuring a regular supply of hydrocarbons;
   (c) Promote the development of new and renewable energy in the framework of the policy of diversification of sources of energy;
   (d) Harmonize their national energy development plans;
   (e) Articulate a common energy policy, particularly, in the field of research, exploitation, production and distribution;
   (f) Establish an adequate mechanism of concerted action and coordination for the collective solution of the energy development problems within the Community, particularly, those relating to energy transmission, the shortage of skilled technicians and financial resources for the implementation of energy projects of Member States; and
   (g) Promote the continuous training of skilled manpower.

. . .

Article 64
Broadcasting

1. Member States undertake to:
    (a) Coordinate their efforts and pool their resources in order to promote the exchange of radio and television programmes at bilateral, regional and continental levels;
    (b) Encourage the establishment of programme exchange centres at regional and continental levels. In this connection, Member States shall strengthen the activities and operations of existing programme exchange centres; and
    (c) Use their broadcasting and television systems in order to further close cooperation and better understanding among their peoples and, in particular, to promote the objectives of the Community.
2. Member States further undertake to collect, disseminate and exchange meteorological information at the continental level, particularly with regard to the development of early warning systems for the prevention of natural disasters and for ensuring safety in aerial, coastal and inland navigation.

    . . .

Article 69
Culture

Member states shall:

   (a) Pursue the objectives of the Cultural Charter for Africa;
   (b) Promote and propagate endogenous African cultural values;
   (c) Make every effort to preserve and recover their cultural heritage;
   (d) Ensure that development policies adequately reflect their socio-cultural values in order to consolidate their cultural identity;
   (e) Exchange their cultural programmes and their experiences, particularly in art, literature, entertainment, sports and leisure activities; and
   (f) Promote and develop sports programmes and activities at all levels as factors of integration.

       . . .

Chapter XVI—Solidarity, Development and Compensation Fund

Article 80
Establishment

1. A Solidarity, Development and Compensation Fund of the Community is hereby established.

Article 81
Objectives and Statutes of the Fund

1. The Statutes of the Fund shall be established by the Assembly in a Protocol relating thereto.

2. The Statutes shall determine, inter alia, the objectives, the authorised capital stock, resources of the Fund, contributions of Member States, the currencies in which contributions shall be paid, the functioning, organisation and management of the Fund and any other related matters.

Chapter XVII—Financial Provisions

Article 82
Regular Budget of the Community

1. The annual regular budget of the Community, which constitutes an integral part of the OAU regular budget, shall be prepared by the Secretary-General and approved by the Assembly upon the recommendation of the Council.

2. The budget shall be funded by contributions made by Member States in accordance with the scale of assessment of the OAU. Upon the recommendation of the Council, the Assembly shall determine the conditions under which the financial contributions of Member States may be supplemented or, where necessary, replaced by the proper resources of the Community.

Article 83
Special Budgets

Special budgets shall be made available, where necessary, to meet the extra-budgetary expenditure of the Community. The Assembly shall determine the contributions of Member States to special budgets of the Community.

Article 84
Sanctions Relating to Non-Payment of Contributions

1. Upon the decision of the Assembly, any Member State of the Community having arrears in the payment of its contribution to the budget of the Community, shall not have the right to vote or participate in taking decisions of the Community if the amount of its arrears is equal to, or is in excess of, the contribution payable by such State for the last preceding two financial years. Such Member State shall cease to enjoy other benefits arising by virtue of this Treaty as well as the right to address meetings. In addition, it

shall lose the right to present candidates for vacant posts within the Community and shall not be eligible for office in the deliberative organs of the Community. The Assembly may, where necessary, impose other sanctions on a Member State for non-payment of contributions.

2. Notwithstanding the provisions of paragraph 1 of this Article, the Assembly may suspend the application of the provisions of the said paragraph if it is satisfied, on the basis of a satisfactory explanatory report by the Member State through the Secretary-General, that the non-payment of contributions is due to causes and circumstances beyond the control of the said Member State.

3. The Assembly shall decide on the modalities for the application of this Article.

. . .

Chapter XVIII—Settlement of Disputes

Article 87
Procedure for the Settlement of Disputes

1. Any dispute regarding the interpretation of the application of the provisions of this Treaty shall be amicably settled through direct agreement by the parties to the dispute. If the parties concerned fail to settle such dispute, either party may, within a period of twelve (12) months, refer the matter to the Court of Justice.

2. The decisions of the Court of Justice shall be final and shall not be subject to appeal.

Chapter XIX—Relations between the Community and Regional Economic Communities, Regional Continental Organisations and other Socio-Economic Organisations and Associations

Article 88
Relations between the Community and Regional Economic Communities

1. The Community shall be established mainly through the coordination, harmonisation and progressive integration of the activities of regional economic communities.

2. Member States undertake to promote the coordination and harmonisation of the integration activities of regional economic communities of which they are members with the activities of the Community, it being understood that the establishment of the latter is the final objective

towards which the activities of existing and future regional economic communities shall be geared.

3. To this end, the Community shall be entrusted with the coordination, harmonisation and evaluation of the activities of existing and future regional economic communities.

4. Member States undertake, through their respective regional economic communities, to coordinate and harmonize the activities of their sub-regional organisations, with a view to rationalising the integration process at the level of each region.

Article 89
Relations between the Community and African Continental Organisations

The Community shall closely cooperate with African continental organisations including, in particular, the African Development Bank and African Centre for Monetary Studies in order to ensure the attainment of regional and continental integration objectives. It may conclude cooperation agreements with these Organisations.

Article 90
Relations between the Community and African Non-Governmental Organisations

1. The Community, in the context of mobilising the human and material resources of Africa, shall establish relations of cooperation with African Non-Governmental organisations, with a view to encouraging the involvement of the African peoples in the process of economic integration and mobilising their technical, material and financial support.

2. To this end, the Community shall set up a mechanism for consultation with such Non-Governmental organisations.

. . .

THE CONSTITUTIVE ACT (11.07.2000)

. . .

Inspired by the noble ideals which guided the founding fathers of our Continental Organization and generations of Pan-Africanists in their determination to promote unity, solidarity, cohesion and cooperation among the peoples of Africa and African States;

Considering the principles and objectives stated in the Charter of the Organization of African Unity and the Treaty Establishing the African Economic Community;

Recalling the heroic struggles waged by our peoples and our countries for political independence, human dignity and economic emancipation;

Considering that since its inception, the Organization of African Unity has played a determining and invaluable role in the liberation of the continent, the affirmation of a common identity and the process of attainment of the unity of our continent and has provided a unique framework for our collective action in Africa and in our relations with the rest of the world.

Determined to take up the multifaceted challenges that confront our continent and peoples in the light of the social, economic and political changes taking place in the world;

. . .

Article 2
Establishment

The African Union is hereby established in accordance with the provisions of this Act.

Article 3
Objectives

The objectives of the Union shall be to:

(a) achieve greater unity and solidarity between the African countries and the peoples of Africa;

(b) defend the sovereignty, territorial integrity and independence of its Member States;

(c) accelerate the political and socio-economic integration of the continent;

(d) promote and defend African common positions on issues of interest to the continent and its peoples;

(e) encourage international cooperation, taking due account of the Charter of the United Nations and the Universal Declaration of Human Rights;

(f) promote peace, security, and stability on the continent;

(g) promote democratic principles and institutions, popular participation and good governance;

(h) promote and protect human and peoples' rights in accordance with the African Charter on Human and Peoples' Rights and other relevant human rights instruments;

(i) establish the necessary conditions which enable the continent to play its rightful role in the global economy and in international negotiations;

(j) promote sustainable development at the economic, social and cultural levels as well as the integration of African economies;

(k) promote cooperation in all fields of human activity to raise the living standards of African peoples;

(l) coordinate and harmonize the policies between the existing and future Regional Economic Communities for the gradual attainment of the objectives of the Union;

(m) advance the development of the continent by promoting research in all fields, in particular in science and technology;

(n) work with relevant international partners in the eradication of preventable diseases and the promotion of good health on the continent.

Article 4
Principles

The Union shall function in accordance with the following principles:

(a) sovereign equality and interdependence among Member States of the Union;

(b) respect of borders existing on achievement of independence;

(c) participation of the African peoples in the activities of the Union;

(d) establishment of a common defence policy for the African Continent;

(e) peaceful resolution of conflicts among Member States of the Union through such appropriate means as may be decided upon by the Assembly;

(f) prohibition of the use of force or threat to use force among Member States of the Union;

(g) non-interference by any Member State in the internal affairs of another;

(h) the right of the Union to intervene in a Member State pursuant to a decision of the Assembly in respect of grave circumstances, namely: war crimes, genocide and crimes against humanity;

(i) peaceful co-existence of Member States and their right to live in peace and security;

(j) the right of Member States to request intervention from the Union in order to restore peace and security;

(k) promotion of self-reliance within the framework of the Union;

(l) promotion of gender equality;

(m) respect for democratic principles, human rights, the rule of law and good governance;

(n) promotion of social justice to ensure balanced economic development;

(o) respect for the sanctity of human life, condemnation and rejection of impunity and political assassination, acts of terrorism and subversive activities;

(p) condemnation and rejection of unconstitutional changes of governments.

Article 5
Organs of the Union

1. The organs of the Union shall be:
   (a) The Assembly of the Union;
   (b) The Executive Council;
   (c) The Pan-African Parliament;
   (d) The Court of Justice;
   (e) The Commission;
   (f) The Permanent Representatives Committee;
   (g) The Specialized Technical Committees;
   (h) The Economic, Social and Cultural Council;
   (i) The Financial Institutions;
2. Other organs that the Assembly may decide to establish.

Article 6
The Assembly

1. The Assembly shall be composed of Heads of States and Government or their duly accredited representatives.
2. The Assembly shall be the supreme organ of the Union.
3. The Assembly shall meet at least once a year in ordinary session. At the request of any Member State and on approval by a two-thirds majority of the Member States, the Assembly shall meet in extraordinary session.
4. The Office of the Chairman of the Assembly shall be held for a period of one year by a Head of State or Government elected after consultations among the Member States.

Article 7
Decisions of the Assembly

1. The Assembly shall take its decisions by consensus or, failing which, by a two-thirds majority of the Member States of the Union. However, procedural matters, including the question of whether a matter is one of procedure or not, shall be decided by a simple majority.
2. Two-thirds of the total membership of the Union shall form a quorum at any meeting of the Assembly.

   . . .

Article 10
The Executive Council

1. The Executive Council shall be composed of the Ministers of Foreign Affairs or such other Ministers or Authorities as are designated by the Governments of Member States.

2. The Executive Council shall meet at least twice a year in ordinary session. It shall also meet in an extra-ordinary session at the request of any Member State and upon approval by two-thirds of all Member States.

. . .

Article 17
The Pan-African Parliament

1. In order to ensure the full participation of African peoples in the development and economic integration of the continent, a Pan-African Parliament shall be established.
2. The composition, powers, functions and organization of the Pan-African Parliament shall be defined in a protocol relating thereto.

Article 18
The Court of Justice

1. A Court of Justice of the Union shall be established;
2. The statutes, composition and functions of the Court of Justice shall be defined in a protocol relating thereto.

Article 19
The Financial Institutions

The Union shall have the following financial institutions whose rules and regulations shall be defined in protocols relating thereto:

(a) The African Central Bank;
(b) The African Monetary Fund;
(c) The African Investment Bank.

Article 20
The Commission

1. There shall be established a Commission of the Union, which shall be the Secretariat of the Union.
2. The Commission shall be composed of the Chairman, his or her deputy or deputies and the Commissioners. They shall be assisted by the necessary staff for the smooth functioning of the Commission.
3. The structure, functions and regulations of the Commission shall be determined by the Assembly.

Article 21
The Permanent Representatives Committee

1. There shall be established a Permanent Representatives Committee. It shall be composed of Permanent Representatives to the Union and other Plenipotentiaries of Member States.
2. The Permanent Representatives Committee shall be charged with the responsibility of preparing the work of the Executive Council and acting on the Executive Council's instructions. It may set up such sub-committees or working groups as it may deem necessary.

Article 22
The Economic, Social and Cultural Council

1. The Economic, Social and Cultural Council shall be an advisory organ composed of different social and professional groups of the Member States of the Union.
2. The functions, powers, composition and organization of the Economic, Social and Cultural Council shall be determined by the Assembly.

Article 23
Imposition of Sanctions

1. The Assembly shall determine the appropriate sanctions to be imposed on any Member State that defaults in the payment of its contributions to the budget of the Union in the following manner: denial of the right to speak at meetings, to vote, to present candidates for any position or post within the Union or to benefit from any activity or commitments therefrom;
2. Furthermore, any Member State that fails to comply with the decisions and policies of the Union may be subjected to other sanctions, such as the denial of transport and communications links with other Member States, and other measures of a political and economic nature to be determined by the Assembly.

   . . .

Article 26
Interpretation

The Court shall be seized with matters of interpretation arising from the application or implementation of this Act. Pending its establishment, such matters shall be submitted to the Assembly of the Union, which shall decide by a two-thirds majority.

   . . .

Article 30
Suspension

Governments which shall come to power through unconstitutional means shall not be allowed to participate in the activities of the Union.

. . .

SOLEMN DECLARATION ON A COMMON AFRICAN DEFENCE AND SECURITY POLICY (28.02.2004)

Preamble

. . .

3. Convinced that in order to safeguard and preserve the hard-won liberties of our peoples, the sovereignty and territorial integrity of our countries, our cultures, history and common values, as well as to guarantee peace, security, stability, and socio-economic development of our continent, it is imperative for us to undertake mutually reinforcing actions in the areas of defence and security;

4. Reaffirming our commitments under Article 4(d) of the Constitutive Act, and Article 3(e) of the Protocol Relating to the establishment of the Peace and Security Council of the African Union, which call for the establishment of a common defence policy for the African continent;

. . .

I. Definitions and Scope

4. The adoption of a Common Defence and Security Policy for Africa is premised on a common African perception of what is required to be done collectively by African States to ensure that Africa's common defence and security interests and goals, especially as set out in Articles 3 and 4 of the Constitutive Act of the African Union, are safeguarded in the face of common threats to the continent as a whole.

Defence

5. Ensuring the common defence of Africa involves working on the basis of a definition of defence which encompasses both the traditional, military and state-centric notion of the use of the armed forces of the state

to protect its national sovereignty and territorial integrity, as well as the less traditional, non-military aspects which relate to the protection of the people's political, cultural, social and economic values and ways of life. In terms of the linkage between defence at the national level and that at the regional and continental levels, it is understood, also, that each African country's defence is inextricably linked to that of other African countries, as well as that of other regions and, by the same token, that of the African continent as a whole.

Security

6. Similarly, ensuring the common security of Africa involves working on the basis of a definition which encompasses both the traditional, state-centric, notion of the survival of the state and its protection by military means from external aggression, as well as the non-military notion which is informed by the new international environment and the high incidence of intra-state conflict. The causes of intra-state conflict necessitate a new emphasis on human security, based not only on political values but on social and economic imperatives as well. This newer, multi-dimensional notion of security thus embraces such issues as human rights; the right to participate fully in the process of governance; the right to equal development as well as the right to have access to resources and the basic necessities of life; the right to protection against poverty; the right to conducive education and health conditions; the right to protection against marginalization on the basis of gender; protection against natural disasters, as well as ecological and environmental degradation. At the national level, the aim would be to safeguard the security of individuals, families, communities, and the state/national life, in the economic, political and social dimensions. This applies at the various regional levels also; and at the continental level, the principle would be underscored that the "security of each African country is inseparably linked to that of other African countries and the African continent as a whole."

. . .

II. Principles and Values Underlying the Common African Defence and Security Policy

11. The principles and values informing the Common African Defence and Security Policy include, inter alia, the principles contained in Article 4 of the Constitutive Act of the African Union. These are:

(a) sovereign equality and inter-dependence among Member States of the Union;

(b) respect of borders existing on achievement of independence;

(c) peaceful resolution of conflicts among Member States of the Union, through such appropriate means as may be decided upon by the Assembly;

(d) prohibition of the use of force, or threat of use of force, among Member States of the Union;

(e) non-interference by any Member State in the internal affairs of another;

(f) the right of the Union to intervene in a Member State pursuant to a decision of the Assembly, in respect of grave circumstances, namely: war crimes, genocide and crimes against humanity, as well as a serious threat to legitimate order, in order to restore peace and stability to the Member States of the Union, upon the recommendation of the Peace and Security Council;

(g) peaceful co-existence of Member States and their right to live in peace and security;

(h) the right of Member States to request intervention from the Union in order to restore peace and security;

(i) promotion of self-reliance within the framework of the Union;

(j) respect for democratic principles, human rights, the rule of law and good governance;

(k) promotion of social justice to ensure balanced economic development;

(l) respect for the sanctity of human life, condemnation and rejection of impunity and political assassination, acts of terrorism and subversive activities;

(m) condemnation and rejection of Unconstitutional Changes of Governments;

(n) restraint by any Member State from entering into any treaty or alliance that is incompatible with the principles and objectives of the Union;

(o) prohibition of any Member State from allowing the use of its territory as a base for aggression and subversion against another Member State;

(p) promotion of gender equality.

12. Other principles and values forming the basis of the Common African Defence and Security Policy include the following:

(i) The indivisibility of the security of African States: the security of one African country is inseparably linked to the security of other African countries, and the African continent as a whole. Accordingly, any threat or aggression on one African country is deemed to be a threat or aggression on the others, and the continent as a whole, that needs to be brought to the immediate attention of the Assembly of the Union or the Peace and Security Council for decision and action as appropriate, in conformity with the AU principles and objectives;

(ii) The traditional African principle and value of equal burden-sharing and mutual assistance;

(iii) The fundamental link and symbiotic relationship that exists between security, stability, human security, development and cooperation, in a manner that allows each to reinforce the other;

(iv) African countries shall, subject to the generally accepted norms of free speech, not engage in, or allow non-state entities to engage in, any actions that incite or intend to incite individuals or groups in the territory of other African countries to violence, which actions amount to propaganda for war or advocate hatred based on race, ethnicity, gender or religion;

(v) The plight of African refugees and internally displaced persons shall be given due consideration;

. . .

III. Objectives and Goals of the
Common African Defence and Security Policy

13. Based on the fact that a Common Defence and Security Policy tends to be a common feature of advanced co-operative frameworks, or of regions where integration is highly advanced, and taking into account the common historical, political, economic and international experiences which bind AU Member States together, a Common African Defence Policy is established in pursuit of a number of objectives and goals including among others, the following:

(a) ensure collective responses to both internal and external threats to Africa (as adumbrated above), in conformity with the principles enshrined in the Constitutive Act;

(b) enable the achievement of the objectives of the Constitutive Act, especially those relating to defence and security matters which are contained in Articles 3 and 4 therein;

(c) serve as a tool for the simultaneous enhancement of defence cooperation between and among African States, and the consolidation of national defence;

(d) eliminate suspicions and rivalry among African States, a factor that has traditionally engendered conflicts on the continent and hindered interstate cooperation and integration in Africa;

(e) promote mutual trust and confidence among African States;

(f) provide a framework for AU Member States to cooperate in defence matters, through training of military personnel; exchange of military intelligence and information (subject to restrictions imposed by national security); the development of military doctrine; and the building of collective capacity;

(g) provide for transparency and clarity on national defence and security policies; as well as cost effectiveness;

(h) allow for efficient re-allocation of resources to address the most threatening of the defence and security challenges, such as poverty and the adverse effects of globalization;

(i) advance the cause of integration in Africa and safeguard, not only common values, but also fundamental interests and the independence and integrity of individual states, regions and the continent, as well;

(j) enhance the AU's capacity for, and coordination of, early action for conflict prevention containment, management, resolution and elimination of conflicts, including the deployment and sustenance of peacekeeping missions and thus promote initiatives that will preserve and strengthen peace and development in Africa.

(k) promote a culture of peace and peaceful co-existence among AU Member States and within the regions. This will foster an emphasis on the use of peaceful means of conflict resolution and the non-use of force, such as preventive diplomacy, negotiation, the use of good offices, persuasion, as well as mediation, conciliation and adjudication;

(l) provide best practices and develop strategic capabilities through training and policy recommendations, to strengthen the defence and security sectors in Africa;

(m) develop and enhance the collective defence and strategic capability as well as military preparedness of Member States of the AU and the Continent;

(n) enable the formulation of policies to strengthen the defence and security sectors at the national and continental levels;

(o) facilitate the harmonization of national legislation and executive actions on defence and security matters with the Common Defence and Security Policy;

(p) enhance the capacity of the AU to develop and promote common policies in other areas such as foreign relations and trade, to ensure the security of the continent and the strengthening of its negotiating positions;

(q) provide a framework to establish and operationalize the African Standby Force provided for in the Protocol Establishing the Peace and Security Council;

(r) facilitate the establishment of a threat deterrence and containment capacity within the AU;

(s) integrate and harmonize regional initiatives on defence and security issues;

(t) encourage the conclusion and ratification of non-aggression pacts between and among African States and harmonize such agreements;

(u) create an environment conducive for the implementation of the precepts of the African Charter on Human and People's Rights and promote the acceptance of standards of human rights;

(v) provide a framework for humanitarian action to ensure that international humanitarian law is applied during conflicts between and among African States. It will, further, provide a framework for addressing the problems of refugees and internally displaced persons at the continental, regional and national levels;

(w) provide a framework for the effective participation of women in conflict prevention, management and resolution activities; and provide a framework for delineating the legal parameters for African Civil Society to function with regard to conflict prevention, management and resolution;

(x) provide a framework for post-conflict peace-building and reconstruction;

(y) provide a framework for ensuring that international environmental standards are maintained, including during periods of conflict.

IV. Implementing Organs and Mechanisms of the Common African Defence and Security Policy

. . .

16. The Peace and Security Council is created by the Protocol relating to its establishment, adopted in Durban, South Africa, in July 2002. It is intended, (after the ratification of this Protocol) that it be a "standing decision-making organ for the prevention, management and resolution of conflict." It is also described by the Protocol as "a collective security and early-warning arrangement to facilitate timely and efficient response to conflict and crisis situations in Africa."

17. In addition, the Protocol constitutes an effort to incorporate into a single text, the provisions of certain defence and security instruments already in existence and forming part of the general body of "legislation" and principles on which the African Union, and the Peace and Security Council in particular, will be able to base its actions in the field of defence and security. Similarly, the Council is required to ensure the implementation of the new genre of security instruments such as the OAU Convention on the Prevention and Combating of Terrorism and other relevant international, continental and regional instruments, adopted to combat international terrorism. Further, the Peace and Security Council has the function of promoting and encouraging the implementation of OAU/AU, UN and other relevant international conventions and treaties on arms control and disarmament. These specific provisions of the Protocol could also be usefully incorporated into the proposed Common African Defence and Security Policy.

18. In the Peace and Security Council Protocol, it is provided that there shall also be established a Military Staff Committee to advise and assist the Peace and Security Council on all questions relating to military and security requirements, for the promotion and maintenance of peace and security in Africa. (The Military Staff Committee, composed of the members of the Peace and Security Council, may meet at the level of Chiefs of Defence Staff or at the level of senior military officers.) The African Standby Force should also be an implementing mechanism for the decisions of the Peace and Security Council.

19. The Protocol also addresses the fundamental problem of funding and logistics, a factor which has continued to constrain peace support operations deployed by both the OAU/AU and African regional organizations.

20. The Protocol reaffirms the need to establish a Continental Early Warning System to facilitate the anticipation and prevention of conflicts. It will consist of an observation and monitoring centre to be linked to the observation and monitoring units of the sub-regional mechanisms.

21. There is also provision in the Protocol for the establishment of a Panel of the Wise to advise the Peace and Security Council and the Chairperson of the Commission and to pronounce themselves on issues relating to the promotion and maintenance of peace and security on the continent, particularly in the area of conflict prevention.

22. The Protocol stipulates that the Peace and Security Council shall assist in the restoration of the rule of law, the establishment and development of democratic institutions, and the preparation, organization and supervision of elections in Member States. Further, in areas of relative peace, the Peace and Security Council shall accord priority to the

implementation of policy aimed at reducing degradation of social and economic conditions arising from conflict. In the area of post-conflict peace-building, the Peace and Security Council shall work towards the consolidation of peace agreements that have been negotiated; the establishment of conditions for political, social and economic reconstruction of the society and government institutions; the implementation of disarmament, demobilization and reintegration programmes, including those relating to child soldiers; the settlement and reintegration of refugees and internally displaced persons; and the provision of assistance to vulnerable persons including children, the elderly, women, and other traumatized groups in the society.

23. In an effort to enhance the AU's institutional capacity in the humanitarian field, the Peace and Security Council is required to develop its own capacity to coordinate and efficiently undertake humanitarian action.

24. The Protocol stipulates that the Peace and Security Council shall encourage non-governmental organizations, and community-based and other civil society organizations, particularly women's organizations, to participate actively in the efforts aimed at promoting peace, security and stability in Africa; and that when required, such organizations may be invited to address the Peace and Security Council.

(c) Commission of the African Union

25. The Commission will, among oth5er tasks, deploy efforts and take all initiatives deemed appropriate to prevent, manage and resolve conflicts and support post-conflict and rehabilitation activities.

(d) Regional Economic Groups

26. At the regional level, the implementing organs include the conflict prevention, management and resolution mechanisms existing in the various regional economic organizations. These include those of ECOWAS, ECCAS, IGAD, SADC, the East African Community, CEN-SAD, the Arab Maghreb Union and COMESA.

   . . .

The Building Blocks of a Common African Defence and Security Policy

(A)   Continental Instruments and Mechanisms

1. At the continental level, there are a number of existing intergovernmental defence and security instruments, including treaties, charters,

conventions, agreements, and declarations, which could inform on-going efforts to formulate and implement a Common African Defence and Security Policy. These include:

i. The Constitutive Act of the AU

    The Constitutive Act provides for the establishment of the AU and the relevant policy organs.

ii. AU Peace and Security Council Protocol

    The Protocol provides for the establishment of the Peace and Security Council as the "operational structure for the effective implementation of the decisions taken in the areas of conflict prevention, peacemaking, peace support operations and intervention, as well as peace-building and post-conflict reconstruction."

iii. African Standby Force

    The Protocol of the Peace and Security Council provides for the establishment of an African Standby Force. The African Standby Force shall perform functions in the context of preventive deployment and peace-building, including post-conflict disarmament and demobilization. It shall also provide humanitarian assistance to alleviate the suffering of the civilian population in conflict areas (as well as support efforts to address major natural disasters). The concept of the African Standby Force is based on brigades to be provided by the five African regions. These brigades will be established in two phases, to be completed by the year 2010 with the attendant strengthening of capabilities at both the AU and regional levels. The ASF will have military, police and civilian components and will operate on the basis of various scenarios under African Union mandates, ranging from observer missions to peace-keeping operations and intervention in conformity with the Constitutive Act.

    The ASF will be established to enable the Peace and Security Council perform its responsibilities with respect to the deployment of peace support missions and intervention pursuant to the provisions of the Constitutive Act.

iv. The Convention for the Elimination of Mercenaries in Africa

2. This instrument was adopted at Libreville, Gabon, in July 1977, by the OAU Heads of State in response to the grave threat posed at that time by mercenarism. The Convention criminalizes "mercenarism" by providing for the culpability of States and by specifying the severest penalties, including capital punishment, in connection with the prosecution of offenders.

    . . .

ECONOMIC COMMUNITY OF WEST AFRICAN STATES (ECOWAS)

The eldest among more than a dozen schemes for economic cooperation and integration in Africa is the market-oriented experience in Western Africa with the Economic Community of West African States (ECOWAS). During the critical 1990s, ECOWAS was one of the few regions in Africa that could claim an increase in intra-regional trade. The original Treaty of the Economic Community of West African States, also known as the Treaty of Lagos, signed in 1975, was revised in 1993 in order to make ECOWAS compatible with the planned African Economic Community. In the meantime, Cape Verde, Ivory Coast, Benin, Burkina Faso, Gambia, Ghana, Guinea, Guinea-Bissau, Liberia, Mali, Mauritania, Niger, Nigeria, Senegal, Sierra Leone, and Togo were members of ECOWAS. The total population of 250 million people is experiencing the first effort to overcome the historical and linguistic cleavages between African states. The main objective of ECOWAS, according to its treaty, was the creation of an economic and monetary union by 2004. The plan was outlined in stages, its medium-term goal being the achievement of regional convertibility, before the ten currencies of ECOWAS member states (nine local currencies plus the CFA franc) could create a monetary union at the end of the process. As a practical step in the direction of the overall goal, ECOWAS traveler's checks were introduced to facilitate regional travel and commercial transactions. Eventually, the currency union was due before 2010.

Civil wars in Sierra Leone, Liberia, and Guinea-Bissau slowed down the prospects for speedy economic integration in the region. At the same time, they widened the agenda of ECOWAS and introduced the first elements of security cooperation. The ECOWAS monitoring group ECOMOG (Economic Community of West African States Monitoring Group) became instrumental in ending the seven-year civil war in Liberia and helped manage the bitter conflict in Sierra Leone. During the 1990s, conflict prevention, peacekeeping, and the establishment of a Mediation and Security Council went hand in hand with measures to facilitate the free movement of people and goods and the harmonization of economic policies among ECOWAS countries as the original approach of the economic community was forced to include security challenges inside some of its member states.

Setbacks had already become obvious during the 1980s. Interregional trade decreased by 50 percent during that decade. Labor mobility was blocked through the unilateral measures of Ghana, which closed its borders in 1982, and of Nigeria, where 2 million "illegal immigrants," mostly Ghanaians, were expelled in 1983. Even now, with new impetuses and the pan-continental perspective, there is minimal movement of capital within the region. The ECOWAS Treaty established the Court of Justice, the Parliament, and the Economic and Social

Council. The ECOWAS Commission is based in Abuja. Non-compliance of member states with community decisions has been as notorious as problems with the budget appropriation. But in light of the grave development crisis of Africa in general, it remains the sad truth that ECOWAS must still be considered more of a success than a failed attempt to bring about regional cooperation and integration in one part of Africa.

Of supporting relevance for regional economic integration in Western and Central Africa are the activities of the Central African Customs and Economic Union (Union douanière et économique de l'Afrique centrale, UDEAC) and of the Central African Economic and Monetary Community (Communauté economique et monétaire d'Afrique centrale, CEMAC). UDEAC was founded in 1966 by Cameroon, the Central African Republic, Chad, Congo, and Gabon, replacing the Equatorial African customs union established in 1959 between the four members of the former Federation of French Equatorial Africa (same members as UDEAC minus Cameroon). UDEAC, with 25 million people, aims at achieving a common market, but has not set a deadline for doing so. After decades of failure to deliver its promulgated goals, UDEAC was reinvigorated and in fact transformed into a genuine economic and monetary union, the Central African Economic and Monetary Community, which has been in existence since 1998. Ever since, CEMAC has intended to merge the Economic Union of Central Africa and the Monetary Union of Central Africa. However, its structures—including the Conference of Heads of States, the Council of Ministers, the Executive Secretariat, the Court of Justice, and the Inter-Parliamentary Committee—remain inefficient as long as regional security is not properly established and sustained.

Most relevant in the context of UDEAC and CEMAC is the monetary cooperation arrangement between France and its former west and central African colonies. Existing since the independence of these states in the early 1960s, these countries— fourteen in total—are clustered around the free movement of capital within the zone, pooling of gold and foreign exchange reserves on a common French Treasury account, common rules and regulations for foreign commercial and financial transactions, and free convertibility, at par, of the local CFA franc, first pegged to the French franc and since 2002 to the euro. The French Treasury continues to supply euros to the African Central Banks, which are members of the franc zone.

Another supportive element for the advancement of the overall goals of the African Union is the Economic Community of Central African States (ECCAS). This eleven-nation group, representing 70 million people and consisting of Burundi, Cameroon, the Central African Republic, Chad, Congo, Equatorial Guinea, Gabon, Rwanda, Sao Tome et Principe, Angola, and the Democratic Republic of Congo, aimed at achieving a central African common market and economic community by 1995. Endemic instability and the wars in the Great Lake Region practically ended the activities of ECCAS in the early 1990s.

TREATY OF THE ECONOMIC COMMUNITY OF WEST AFRICAN STATES (ECOWAS) (28.05.1975)

. . .

Recognising that progress towards sub-regional economic integration requires an assessment of the economic potential and interests of each state;

Accepting the need for a fair and equitable distribution of the benefits of co-operation among Member States;

. . .

Affirming as the ultimate objective of their efforts accelerated and sustained economic development of their states and the creation of a homogeneous society, leading to the unity of the countries of West Africa, by the elimination of all types of obstacles to the free movement of goods, capital and persons;

Chapter I—Principles

Article 1
Establishment and Membership of the Community

1. By this Treaty the High Contracting Parties establish among themselves an Economic Community of West African States (ECOWAS) hereinafter referred to as "the Community."
2. The members of the Community, hereinafter referred to as "the Member States," shall be the States that ratify this Treaty and such other West African States as may accede to it.

Article 2
Aims of the Community

1. It shall be the aim of the Community to promote cooperation and development in all fields of economic activity particularly in the fields of industry, transport, telecommunications, energy, agriculture, natural resources, commerce, monetary and financial questions and in social and cultural matters for the purpose of raising the standard of living of its peoples, of increasing and maintaining economic stability, of fostering closer relations among its members and of contributing to the progress and development of the African continent.
2. For the purposes set out in the preceding paragraph and as hereinafter provided for in this Treaty, the Community shall by stages ensure:

    (a) the elimination as between the Member States of customs duties and other charges of equivalent effect in respect of the importation and exportation of goods;

(b) the abolition of quantitative and administrative restrictions on trade among the Member States;

(c) the establishment of a common customs tariff and a common commercial policy towards third countries;

(d) the abolition as between the Member States of the obstacles to the free movement of persons, Services and capital;

(e) the harmonisation of the agricultural policies and the promotion of common projects in the Member States notably in the fields of marketing, research and agro-industrial enterprises;

(f) the implementation of schemes for the joint development of transport, communication, energy and other infrastructural facilities as well as the evolution of a common policy in these fields;

(g) the harmonisation of the economic and industrial policies of the Member States and the elimination of disparities in the level of development of Member States;

(h) the harmonisation, required for the proper functioning of the Community, of the monetary policies of the Member States;

(i) the establishment of a Fund for Cooperation, Compensation and Development; and

(j) such other activities calculated to further the aims of the Community as the Member States may from time to time undertake in common.

Article 3
General Undertaking

The Member States shall make every effort to plan and direct their policies with a view to creating favourable conditions for the achievement of the aims of the Community; in particular, each Member State shall take all Steps to secure the enactment of such legislation as is necessary to give effect to this Treaty.

Chapter II—Institutions of the Community

Article 4
Institutions

1. The institutions of the Community shall be:
   (a) the Authority of Heads of State and Government;
   (b) the Council of Ministers;
   (c) the Executive Secretariat;
   (d) the Tribunal of the Community; and

(e) the following Technical and Specialised Commissions:
  – the Trade, Customs, Immigration, Monetary and Payments Commission;
  – the Industry, Agriculture and Natural Resources Commission;
  – the Transport, Telecommunications and Energy Commission;
  – the Social and Cultural Affairs Commission;

and such other Commissions or bodies as may be established by the Authority of Heads of State and Government or are established or provided for by this Treaty.

2. The institutions of the Community shall perform the functions and act within the limits of the powers conferred upon them by or under this Treaty and by Protocols thereto.

. . .

Article 7
Decisions of the Authority and the Council of Ministers

The Authority shall determine the procedure for the dissemination of its decisions and directions and those of the Council of Ministers and for matters relating to their coming into effect.

. . .

Article 11
Tribunal of the Community

1. There shall be established a Tribunal of the Community which shall ensure the observance of law and justice in the Interpretation of the provisions of this Treaty. Furthermore, it shall be charged with the responsibility of settling such disputes as may be referred to it in accordance with Article 56 of this Treaty.

2. The composition, competence, statutes and other matters relating to the Tribunal shall be prescribed by the Authority.

Chapter III—Customs and Trade Matters

Article 12
Liberalization of Trade

There shall be progressively established in the course of a transitional period of fifteen (15) years from the definitive entry into force of this Treaty, and as prescribed in this Chapter, a customs union among the Member States.

Within this Union, customs duties or other charges with equivalent effect on imports shall be eliminated. Quota, quantitative or like restrictions or prohibitions and administrative obstacles to trade among the Member States shall also be removed. Furthermore, a common customs tariff in respect of all goods imported into the Member States from third countries shall be established and maintained.

Article 13
Customs Duties

1. Member States shall reduce and ultimately eliminate customs duties and any other charges with equivalent effect except duties notified in accordance with Article 17 and other charges which fall within that Article, imposed on or in connection with the importation of goods which are eligible for Community tariff treatment in accordance with Article 15 of this Treaty. Any such duties or other charges are hereinafter referred to as "import duties."

2. Within a period of two (2) years from the definitive entry into force of this Treaty, a Member State may not be required to reduce or eliminate import duties. During this two-year period, Member States shall not impose any new duties and taxes or increase existing ones and shall transmit to the Executive Secretariat all Information on import duties for study by the relevant institutions of the Community.

   . . .

Article 14
Common Customs Tariff

1. The Member States agree to the gradual establishment of a common customs tariff in respect of all goods imported into the Members States from third countries.

2. At the end of the period of eight (8) years referred to in paragraph 3 of Article 13 of this Treaty and during the next succeeding five (5) years, Member States shall gradually, in accordance with a schedule to be recommended by the Trade, Customs, Immigration, Monetary and Payments Commission, abolish existing differences in their external customs tariffs.

3. In the course of the same period, the above-mentioned Commission shall ensure the establishment of a common customs nomenclature and customs statistical nomenclature for all the Member States.

Article 15
Community Tariff Treatment

1. For the purposes of this Treaty, goods shall be accepted as eligible for Community tariff treatment if they have been consigned to the territory of the importing Member State from the territory of another Member State and originate in the Member States.
2. The definition of products originating from Member States shall be the subject of a protocol to be annexed to this Treaty.
3. The Trade, Customs, Immigration, Monetary and Payments Commission shall from time to time examine whether the rules referred to in paragraph 2 of this Article can be amended to make them simpler and more liberal. In Order to ensure their smooth and equitable Operation, the Council of Ministers may from time to time amend them.

   . . .

Article 17
Revenue Duties and Internal Taxation

1. Member States shall not apply directly or indirectly to imported goods from any Member State fiscal charges in excess of those applied to like domestic goods or otherwise impose such charges for the effective protection of domestic goods.
2. Member States shall eliminate all effective internal taxes or other internal charges that are made for the protection of domestic goods not later than one (1) year after the period of two (2) years referred to in paragraph 2 of Article 13 of this Treaty. Where by virtue of obligations under an existing contract entered into by a Member State such a Member State is unable to comply with the provisions of this Article, the Member State shall duly notify the Council of Ministers of this fact and shall not extend or renew such contract at its expiry.
3. Member States shall eliminate progressively all revenue duties designed to protect domestic goods not later than the end of the period of eight (8) years referred to in paragraph 3 of Article 13 of this Treaty.
4. Each Member State shall, not later than the end of the period of two (2) years referred to in paragraph 2 of Article 13 of this Treaty, notify the Council of Ministers of any duty it wishes to apply under the provisions of paragraph 3 of the aforementioned Article.

   . . .

Article 2l
Internal Legislation

Member States shall refrain from enacting legislation which directly or indirectly discriminates against the same or like products of another Member State.

. . .

Chapter IV—Freedom of Movement and Residence

Article 27
Visa and Residence

1. Citizens of Member States shall be regarded as Community citizens and accordingly Member States undertake to abolish all obstacles to their freedom of movement and residence within the Community.
2. Member States shall by agreements with each other exempt Community citizens from holding visitors' visas and residence permits and allow them to work and undertake commercial and industrial activities within their territories.

Chapter V—Industrial Development and Harmonization

Article 28
General Principles

For the purposes of this chapter, Member States shall achieve their industrial development and harmonization in the three stages as set out in Articles 29, 30 and 31.

Article 29
Stage I—Exchange of Information on Major Industrial Projects

Member States undertake to:

(a) furnish one another with major feasibility studies and reports on projects within their territories;

(b) furnish one another, on request, reports on the performance of prospective technical partners who have developed similar projects in their territories;

(c) furnish one another, on request, reports on foreign business groups operating in their territories;

(d) furnish one another, on request, with reports on their experiences on industrial projects and to exchange industrial research information and experts;

(e) commission, where appropriate, joint studies for the identification of viable industrial projects for development within the Community; and

(f) finance, where appropriate, joint research on the transfer of technology and the development of new products through the use of raw materials common in some or all of the Member States and on specific industrial problems.

. . .

Article 31
Stage III—Personnel Exchange, Training and Joint Ventures

Member States shall:

(a) exchange, as may be necessary, skilled, Professional and managerial personnel in the Operation of projects within the Community;

(b) provide places for training in their educational and technical institutions for Community citizens; and

(c) engage, where appropriate, in joint development of projects including those which entail the execution of complementary parts of such projects in different Member States.

. . .

Chapter VI—Cooperation in Agriculture and Natural Resources

Article 33
Cooperation among Member States

Member States shall cooperate as set out in this Chapter in the development of their natural resources particularly agriculture, forestry, animal husbandry and fisheries.

Article 34
Stage I—Harmonisation of Agricultural Policies

1. Member States undertake to work towards the harmonisation of their internal and external agricultural policies in their relations with one another;

2. Member States shall exchange regularly Information on experiments and results of research being carried out in their respective territories and on existing rural development programmes; and

3. Member States shall formulate, as appropriate, joint programmes for both basic and in-service training in existing institutions.

Article 35
Stage II—Evolution of a Common Agricultural Policy

Member States undertake to take all measures necessary for the creation of a common policy especially in the fields of research, training, production, processing and marketing of the products of agriculture, forestry, animal husbandry and fisheries. For this purpose, the Industry, Agriculture and Natural Resources Commission shall, as soon as possible, after its establishment meet to make recommendations to the Council of Ministers for the harmonisation and exploitation of natural resources of the Member States.

Chapter VII—Cooperation in Monetary and Financial Matters

Article 36
Cooperation in Monetary and Fiscal Matters

1. It shall be the responsibility of the Trade, Customs, Immigration, Monetary and Payments Commission, among other things, to:
   (a) as soon as practicable, make recommendations on the harmonisation of the economic and fiscal policies of the Member States;
   (b) give its constant attention to the maintenance of a balance of payments equilibrium in the Member States; and
   (c) examine developments in the economies of the Member States.
2. The recommendations of the Trade, Customs, Immigration, Monetary and Payments Commission under this Article shall be made to the Council of Ministers.

Article 37
Settlement of Payments between Member States

The Trade, Customs, Immigration, Monetary and Payments Commission shall make recommendations to the Council of Ministers on the establishment, in the short term, of bilateral Systems for the settlement of accounts between the Member States and, in the long term, of a multilateral System for the settlement of such accounts.

Article 38
Committee of West African Central Banks

1. For the purpose of overseeing the System of payments within the Community, there is hereby established a Committee of West African Central Banks, which shall consist of the Governors of the Central Banks of the Member States or such other persons as may be designated by Member States. This Committee shall, subject to this Treaty, determine its own procedures.

2. The Committee of West African Central Banks shall make recommendations to the Council of Ministers from time to time on the Operation of the Clearing System of payments and on other monetary issues of the Community.

    . . .

Chapter VIII—Infrastructural Links in the Fields of Transport and Communications

Article 40
Common transport and communications policy

Member States undertake to evolve gradually common transport and Communications policies through the improvement and expansion of their existing transport and Communications links ansd the establishment of new ones as a means of furthering the physical cohesion of the Member States and the promotion of greater movement of persons, goods and Services within the Community.

Article 41
Roads

The Transport, Telecommunications and Energy Commission shall formulate plans for a comprehensive network of all-weather roads within the Community with a view to promoting social and unimpeded commercial intercourse between the Member States through the improvement of existing roads to, and the construction of new ones of international Standards. In the formulation of these plans, the Transport, Telecommunications and Energy Commission shall give priority to a network of roads traversing the territories of the Member States.

Article 42
Railways

The Transport, Telecommunications and Energy Commission shall for the purpose of connecting the railways of the Member States formulate plans for the improvement and reorganisation of such railways.

Article 43
Shipping and international waterways

1. The Transport, Telecommunications and Energy Commission shall formulate plans for the harmonisation and rationalisation of policies on shipping and international waterways of the Member States.

2. Member States undertake to do their utmost to form multinational shipping Companies for both maritime and river navigation.

Article 44
Air transport

Member States shall use their best endeavour to bring about the merger of their national airlines in order to promote efficiency and profitability in the air transportation of passengers and goods within the Community by aircraft owned by the Governments of the Member States and/or their citizens. To this end, they shall coordinate the training of their nationals and policies in air transport and standardize their equipment.

Article 45
Telecommunications

1. Member States shall reorganise and improve, where necessary, their national telecommunications network to meet Standards required for international traffic.
2. Member States undertake to establish a direct, modern, efficient and rational system of telecommunications among themselves.

Article 46
Pan-African Telecommunications Network

The Transport, Telecommunications and Energy Commission shall make urgent recommendations for the rapid realisation in the West African Section of the Pan-African Telecommunications network and, in particular, the establishment of links necessary for the economic and social development of the Community. Member States shall coordinate their efforts in this field and in the mobilisation of national and international financial resources.

Article 47
Postal Services

1. The Transport, Telecommunications and Energy Commission shall study and make recommendations to the Council of Ministers on proposals for speedier, cheaper and more frequent postal Services within the Community.
2. Member States undertake to:

    (a) promote close collaboration among their postal administrations;
    (b) harmonize routes of mails; and

(c) establish among themselves a system of postal remittances and preferential tariffs which are more favourable than those envisaged by the Universal Postal Union.

. . .

Chapter XI—Fund for Cooperation, Compensation and Development

Article 50
Establishment

There is hereby established a Fund to be known as the Fund for Cooperation, Compensation and Development hereinafter referred to as "the Fund."

Article 51
Resources of the Fund

1. The Fund shall derive its resources from:
   (a) contributions of Member States;
   (b) income from Community enterprises;
   (c) receipts from bilateral and multilateral sources as well as other foreign sources; and
   (d) subsidies and contributions of all kinds and from all sources.
2. The contributions of Member States referred to in sub-paragraph (a) of the preceding paragraph shall be determined by the Council of Ministers and shall be of such minimum and maximum amounts as the Council of Ministers may determine.
3. The Method of determining the contribution to be paid by Member States, the regulations governing the payment and the currencies in which they shall be effected, the operation, organisation, management, status of the funds and matters related and incidental thereto shall be the subject of a protocol to be annexed to this Treaty.

Article 52
Uses of the Fund

The Fund shall be used to:

(a) finance projects in Member States;
(b) provide compensation to Member States which have suffered losses as a result of the location of Community enterprises;
(c) provide compensation and other forms of assistance to Member States which have suffered losses arising out of the application of

the provisions of this Treaty on the liberalisation of Trade within the Community;

(d) guarantee foreign Investments made in Member States in respect of enterprises established in pursuance of the provisions of this Treaty on the harmonisation of industrial policies;

(e) provide appropriate means to facilitate the sustained mobilisation of internal and external financial resources for the Member States and the Community; and

(f) promote development projects in the less developed Member States of the Community.

Chapter XII—Financial Provisions

Article 53
Budget of the Community

1. There shall be established a budget of the Community.
2. All expenditures of the Community, other than those in respect of the Fund for Cooperation, Compensation and Development, established under Chapter XI of this Treaty, shall be approved in respect of each financial year by the Council of Ministers and shall be chargeable to the budget.
3. Resources of the budget shall be derived from annual contributions by Member States and such other sources as may be determined by the Council of Ministers.
4. The budget shall be in balance as to revenues and expenditures.
5. A draft budget for each financial year shall be prepared by the Executive Secretary and approved by the Council of Ministers.
6. There shall be special budgets to meet extraordinary expenditures of the Community.

Article 54
Contributions by Member States

1. A protocol to be annexed to this Treaty shall state the mode by which the contribution of Member States shall be determined and the currencies in which the contribution is to be paid.
2. The Member States undertake to pay regularly their annual contributions to the budget of the Community.
3. Where a Member State is in arrears at the end the financial year in the payment of its contributions for reasons other than those caused by public or natural calamity or exceptional circumstances that gravely affect

its economy, such Member States may, by a resolution of the Authority, be suspended from taking part in the activities of the institutions of the Community.

. . .

Chapter XIII—Settlement of Disputes

Article 56
Procedure for the settlement of disputes

Any dispute that may arise among the Member States regarding the interpretation or application of this Treaty shall be amicably settled by direct agreement. In the event of failure to settle such disputes, the matter may be referred to the Tribunal of the Community by a party to such disputes and the decision of the Tribunal shall be final.

. . .

Article 64
Withdrawal

1. Any Member State wishing to withdraw from the Community shall give to the Executive Secretary one year's written notice. At the end of this period of one year, if such notice is not withdrawn, such a State shall cease to be a member of the Community.
2. During the period of one year referred to in the preceding paragraph, such a Member State shall nevertheless observe the provisions of this Treaty and shall remain liable for the discharge of its obligations under this Treaty.

. . .

TREATY OF ECOWAS (REVISED) (24.07.1993)

. . .

Convinced that the integration of the Member States into a viable regional Community may demand the partial and gradual pooling of national sovereignties to the Community within the context of a collective political will;

Accepting the need to establish Community Institutions vested with relevant and adequate powers;

Noting that the present bilateral and multilateral forms of economic cooperation within the region open up perspectives for more extensive cooperation;

Accepting the need to face together the political, economic and socio-cultural challenges of the present and the future, and to pool together the resources of our peoples while respecting our diversities for the most rapid and optimum expansion of the region's productive capacity;

. . .

Chapter II—Establishment, Composition, Aims and Objectives and Fundamental Principles of the Community

Article 2
Establishment and Composition

1. The high contracting parties, by this Treaty, hereby re-affirm the establishment of the Economic Community of West African States (ECOWAS) and decide that it shall ultimately be the sole economic community in the region for the purpose of economic integration and the realization of the objectives of the African Economic Community.

2. The members of the Community, hereinafter referred to as "the Member States," shall be the States that ratify this treaty.

Article 3
Aims and Objectives

1. The aims of the Community are to promote cooperation and integration, leading to the establishment of an economic union in West Africa in order to raise the living standards of its peoples, and to maintain and enhance economic stability, foster relations among Member States and contribute to the progress and development of the African Continent.

2. In order to achieve the aims set out in the paragraph above, and in accordance with the relevant provisions of this Treaty, the Community shall, by stages, ensure;

   (a) the harmonization and coordination of national policies and the promotion of integration programmes, projects and activities, particularly in food, agriculture and natural resources, industry, transport and communications, energy, trade, money and finance, taxation, economic reform policies, human resources, education, information, culture, science, technology, services, health, tourism, legal matters;

   (b) the harmonization and coordination of policies for the protection of the environment;

(c) the promotion of the establishment of joint production enterprises;

(d) the establishment of a common market through:

   (i) the liberalization of trade by the abolition, among Member States, of customs duties levied on imports and exports, and the abolition, among Member States, of non-tariff barriers in order to establish a free trade area at the Community level;

   (ii) the adoption of a common external tariff and a common trade policy vis-à-vis third countries;

   (iii) the removal, between Member States, of obstacles to the free movement of persons, goods, service and capital, and to the right of residence and establishment;

(e) the establishment of an economic union through the adoption of common policies in the economic, financial social and cultural sectors, and the creation of a monetary union.

(f) the promotion of joint ventures by private sector enterprises and other economic operators, in particular through the adoption of a regional agreement on crossborder investments;

(g) the adoption of measures for the integration of the private sectors, particularly the creation of an enabling environment to promote small and medium scale enterprises;

(h) the establishment of an enabling legal environment;

(i) the harmonization of national investment codes leading to the adoption of a single Community investment code;

(j) the harmonization of standards and measures;

(k) the promotion of balanced development of the region, paying attention to the special problems of each Member State particularly those of landlocked and small island Member States;

(l) the encouragement and strengthening of relations and the promotion of the flow of information particularly among rural populations, women's and youth organizations and socio-professional organizations such as associations of the media, business men and women, workers, and trade unions;

(m) the adoption of a Community population policy which takes into account the need for a balance between demographic factors and socioeconomic development;

(n) the establishment of a fund for cooperation, compensation and development; and

(o) any other activity that Member States may decide to undertake jointly with a view to attaining Community objectives.

. . .

Chapter III—Institutions of the Community—
Establishment, Composition and Functions

Article 6
Institutions

1. The Institutions of the Community shall be:
   (a) the Authority of Heads of State and Government;
   (b) the Council of Ministers;
   (c) the Community Parliament;
   (d) the Economic and Social Council;
   (e) the Community Court of Justice;
   (f) the Executive Secretariat;
   (g) the Fund for Cooperation, Compensation and Development;
   (h) Specialized Technical Commissions; and
   (i) any other institutions that may be established by the Authority.
2. The Institutions of the Community shall perform their functions and act within the limits of the powers conferred on them by this Treaty and by the Protocols relating thereto.

Article 7
Authority of Heads of State and Government—
Establishment, Composition and Functions

1. There is hereby established the Authority of Heads of State and Government of Member States which shall be the supreme institution of the Community and shall be composed of Heads of State and/or Government of Member States.
2. The Authority shall be responsible for the general direction and control of the Community and shall take all measures to ensure its progressive development and the realization of its objectives.
3. Pursuant to the provisions of Paragraph 2 of this Article, the Authority shall:
   (a) determine the general policy and major guidelines of the Community, give directives, harmonise and coordinate the economic, scientific, technical, cultural and social policies of Member States;
   (b) oversee the functioning of Community institutions and follow-up implementation of Community objectives;
   (c) prepare and adopt its Rules of Procedure;
   (d) appoint the Executive Secretary in accordance with the provisions of Article 18 of this Treaty;
   (e) appoint, on the recommendation of Council, the External Auditors;

    (f) delegate to the Council, where necessary, the authority to take such decisions as are stipulated in Article 9 of this Treaty;

    (g) refer where it deems necessary any matter to the Community Court of Justice when it confirms that a Member State or institution of the Community has failed to honour any of its obligations or an institution of the Community has acted beyond the limits of its authority or has abused the powers conferred on it by the provisions of this Treaty, by a decision of the Authority or a regulation of the Council;

    (h) request the Community Court of Justice as and when necessary, to give advisory opinion on any legal questions; and

    (i) exercise any other powers conferred on it under this Treaty.

Article 8
Sessions

1. The Authority shall meet at least once a year in ordinary session. An extraordinary session may be convened by the Chairman of the Authority or at the request of a Member State provided that such a request is supported by a simple majority of the Member States.

2. The office of the Chairman shall be held every year by a Member State elected by the Authority.

Article 9
Decisions

1. The Authority shall act by decisions.

2. Unless otherwise provided in this Treaty or in a Protocol decisions of the Authority shall be adopted, depending on the subject matter under consideration by unanimity, consensus or, by a two-thirds majority of the Member States.

3. Matters referred to in paragraph 2 above shall be defined in a Protocol. Until the entry into force of the said Protocol, the Authority shall continue to adopt its decisions by consensus.

4. Decisions of the Authority shall be binding on the Member States and institutions of the Community, without prejudice to the provisions of paragraph (3) of Article 15 of this Treaty.

5. The Executive Secretary shall publish the decisions thirty (30) days after the date of their signature by the Chairman of Authority.

6. Such decisions shall automatically enter into force sixty (60) days after the date of their publication in the Official Journal of the Community.

7. Decisions shall be published in the National Gazette of each Member State within the period stipulated in paragraph 6 of this Article.

Article 10
The Council of Ministers—Establishment, Composition and Functions

1. There is hereby established a Council of Ministers of the Community.
2. The Council shall comprise the Minister in charge of ECOWAS Affairs and any other Minister of each Member State.
3. The Council shall be responsible for the functioning and development of the Community. To this end, unless otherwise provided in this Treaty or a Protocol, the Council shall:
    (a) make recommendations to the Authority on any action aimed at attaining the objectives of the Community;
    (b) appoint all statutory appointees other than the Executive Secretary;
    (c) by the powers delegated to it by the Authority, issue directives on matters concerning coordination and harmonization of economic integration policies;
    (d) make recommendations to the Authority on the appointment of the External Auditors;
    (e) prepare and adopt its rules of procedure;
    (f) adopt the Staff Regulations and approve the organizational structure of the institutions of the Community;
    (g) approve the work programmes and budgets of the Community and its institutions;
    (h) request the Community Court of Justice, where necessary, to give advisory opinions on any legal questions;
    (i) carry out all other functions assigned to it under this Treaty and exercise all powers delegated to it by the Authority.

Article 11
Meetings

1. The Council shall meet at least twice a year in ordinary session. One of such sessions shall immediately precede the ordinary session of the Authority. An extraordinary session may be convened by the Chairman of Council or at the request of a Member State provided that such request is supported by a simple majority of the Member States.
2. The office of Chairman of Council shall be held by the Minister responsible for ECOWAS Affairs of the Member State elected as Chairman of the Authority.

Article 12
Regulations

1. The Council shall act by regulations.
2. Unless otherwise provided in this Treaty regulations of the Council shall be adopted, depending on the subject matter under consideration, by unanimity, consensus or by a two-thirds majority of Member States, in accordance with the Protocol referred to in Article 9 paragraph 3 of this Treaty. Until the entry into force of the said Protocol, the Council shall continue to adopt its regulations by consensus.
3. Regulations of the Council shall be binding on institutions under its authority. They shall be binding on Member States after their approval by the Authority. However, in the case of regulations made pursuant to a delegation of powers by the Authority in accordance with paragraph 3(f) of Article 7 of this Treaty, they shall be binding forthwith.
4. Regulations shall be published and shall enter into force within the same period and under the same conditions stipulated in paragraphs 5, 6 and 7 of Article 9 of this Treaty.

Article 13
The Community Parliament

1. There is hereby established a Parliament of the Community.
2. The method of election of the Members of the Community Parliament, its composition, functions, powers and organization shall be defined in a Protocol relating thereto.

Article 14
The Economic and Social Council

1. There is hereby established an Economic and Social Council which shall have an advisory role and whose composition shall include representatives of the various categories of economic and social activity.
2. The composition, functions and organization of the Economic and Social Council shall be defined in a Protocol relating thereto.

Article 15
The Court of Justice—Establishment and Functions

1. There is hereby established a Court of Justice of the Community.
2. The status, composition, powers, procedure and other issues concerning the Court of Justice shall be as set out in a Protocol relating thereto.

3. The Court of Justice shall carry out the functions assigned to it independently of the Member States and the institutions of the Community.

4. Judgments of the Court of Justice shall be binding on the Member States, the Institutions of the Community and on individuals and corporate bodies.

Article 16
Arbitration Tribunal—Establishment and Functions

1. There is hereby established an Arbitration Tribunal of the Community.

2. The status, composition, powers, procedure and other issues concerning the Arbitration Tribunal shall be as set out in a Protocol relating thereto.

Article 17
The Executive Secretariat—Establishment and Composition

1. There is hereby established an Executive Secretariat of the Community.

2. The Secretariat shall be headed by the Executive Secretary assisted by Deputy Executive Secretaries and such other staff as may be required for the smooth functioning of the Community.

  . . .

Article 20
Relations between the Staff of the Community and Member States

1. In the performance of their duties, the Executive Secretary, the Deputy Executive Secretaries, and other staff of the Community shall owe their loyalty entirely and be accountable only to the Community. In this regard, they shall neither seek nor accept instructions from any government or any national or international authority external to the Community. They shall refrain from any activity or any conduct incompatible with their status as international civil servants.

2. Every Member State undertakes to respect the international character of the office of the Executive Secretary, the Deputy Executive Secretaries, and other staff of the Community and undertakes not to seek to influence them in the performance of their duties.

3. Member States undertake to cooperate with the Executive Secretariat and other institutions of the Community and to assist them in the discharge of the duties assigned to them under this Treaty.

Article 21
Fund for Cooperation, Compensation and Development—Establishment, Status and Functions

1. There is hereby established a Fund for Cooperation, Compensation and Development of the Community.
2. The status, objectives and functions of the fund are defined in the Protocol relating thereto.

Article 22
Technical Commissions—Establishment and Composition

1. There are hereby established the following Technical Commissions:
    (a) Food and Agriculture;
    (b) Industry, Science and Technology and Energy;
    (c) Environment and Natural Resources;
    (d) Transport, Communications and Tourism;
    (e) Trade, Customs, Taxation, Statistics, Money and Payments
    (f) Political, Judicial and Legal Affairs, Regional Security and Immigration;
    (g) Human Resources, Information, Social and Cultural Affairs; and
    (h) Administration and Finance Commission.
2. The Authority may, whenever it deems appropriate, restructure the existing Commissions or establish new Commissions.
3. Each commission shall comprise representatives of each Member State.
4. Each Commission may, as it deems necessary, set up subsidiary commissions to assist it in carrying out its work. It shall determine the composition of any such subsidiary commission.

    . . .

Chapter IV—Cooperation in Food and Agriculture

Article 25
Agricultural Development and Food Security

1. Member States shall cooperate in the development of agriculture, forestry, livestock and fisheries in order to:
    (a) ensure food security;
    (b) increase production and productivity in agriculture, livestock, fisheries and forestry,and improve conditions of work and generate employment opportunities in rural areas;

(c) enhance agricultural production through processing locally, animal and plant products; and

(d) protect the prices of export commodities on the international market.

2. To this end, and in order to promote the integration of production structures, Member States shall cooperate in the following fields:

(a) the production of agricultural inputs, fertilizers, pesticides, selected seeds, Agricultural machinery and equipment and veterinary products;

(b) the development of river and lake basins;

(c) the development and protection of marine and fishery resources;

(d) plant and animal protection;

(e) the harmonization of agricultural development strategies and policies particularly pricing and price support policies on the production, trade and marketing of major agricultural products and inputs; and

(f) the harmonization of food security policies paying particular attention to:

(i) the reduction of losses in food production;

(ii) the strengthening of existing institutions for the management of natural calamities, agricultural diseases and pest control;

(iii) the conclusion of agreements on food security at the regional level; and

(iv) the provision of food aid to Member States in the event of serious food shortage.

(g) the establishment of an early warning system; and

(h) the adoption of a common agricultural policy especially in the fields of research, training, production, preservation, processing and marketing of the products of agriculture, forestry, livestock and fisheries.

Chapter V—Cooperation in Industry, Science and Technology and Energy

Article 26
Industry

1. For the purpose of promoting industrial development of Member States and integrating their economies, Member States shall harmonize their industrialization policies.

2. In this connection, Member States shall:

(a) strengthen the industrial base of the Community, modernize the priority sectors and foster self-sustained and self-reliant development;

(b) promote joint industrial development projects as well as the creation of multinational enterprises in priority industrial sub-sectors likely to contribute to the development of agriculture, transport and communications, natural resources and energy.

. . .

Article 27
Science and Technology

1. Member States shall:
   (a) strengthen their national scientific and technological capabilities in order to bring about the socioeconomic transformation required to improve the quality of life of their population;
   (b) ensure the proper application of science and technology to the development of agriculture, transport and communications, industry, health and hygiene, energy, education and manpower and the conservation of the environment;
   (c) reduce their dependence on foreign technology and promote their individual and collective technological self-reliance;
   (d) cooperate in the development, acquisition and dissemination of appropriate technologies; and
   (e) strengthen existing scientific research institutions and take all necessary measures to prepare and implement joint scientific research and technological development programmes.

   . . .

Article 28
Energy

1. Member States shall coordinate and harmonize their policies and programmes in the field of energy.
2. To this end, they shall:
   (a) ensure the effective development of the energy resources of the region;
   (b) establish appropriate cooperation mechanisms with a view to ensuring a regular supply of hydrocarbons;
   (c) promote the development of new and renewable energy particularly solar energy in the framework of the policy of diversification of sources of energy;
   (d) harmonize their national energy development plans by ensuring particularly the interconnection of electricity distribution networks;

(e) articulate a common energy policy, particularly, in the field of research, exploitation, production and distribution;

(f) establish an adequate mechanism for the collective solution of the energy development problems within the Community, particularly those relating to energy transmission, the shortage of skilled technicians and financial resources for the implementation of energy projects of Member States.

Chapter VI—Cooperation in Environment and Natural Resources

Article 29
Environment

1. Member States undertake to protect, preserve and enhance the natural environment of the region and cooperate in the event of natural disasters.

2. To this end, they shall adopt policies, strategies and programmes at national and regional levels and establish appropriate institutions to protect, preserve and enhance the environment, control erosion, deforestation, desertification, locusts and other pests.

Article 30
Hazardous and Toxic Wastes

1. Member States undertake, individually and collectively, to take every appropriate step to prohibit the importation, transiting, dumping and burying of hazardous and toxic wastes in their respective territories.

2. They further undertake to adopt all necessary measures to establish a regional dump-watch to prevent the importation, transiting, dumping and burying of hazardous and toxic wastes in the region.

Article 31
Natural Resources

1. Member States shall harmonize and coordinate their policies and programmes in the field of natural resources.

2. To this end, they shall:
    (a) seek better knowledge and undertake an assessment of their natural resources potential;
    (b) improve methods of pricing and marketing of raw materials through a concerted policy;

        . . .

Chapter VII—Cooperation in Transport, Communications and Tourism

Article 32
Transport and Communications

    1.   For the purpose of ensuring the harmonious integration of the physical infrastructures of Member States and the promotion and facilitation of the movement of persons, goods and services within the Community, Member States undertake to:

        (a) evolve common transport and communications policies, laws and regulations;

        (b) develop an extensive network of all-weather highways within the Community, priority being given to the inter-State highways;

        (c) formulate plans for the improvement and integration of railway and road networks in the region;

        (d) formulate programmes for the improvement of coastal shipping services and inter-state inland waterways and the harmonization of policies on maritime transport and services;

        (e) coordinate their positions in international negotiations in the area of maritime transport;

        (f) encourage cooperation in flight-scheduling, leasing of aircraft and granting and joint use of fifth freedom rights to airlines of the region;

        (g) promote the development of regional air transportation services and endeavour to bring about the merger of national airlines in order to promote their efficiency and profitability;

        (h) facilitate the development of human resources through the harmonization and coordination of their national training programmes and policies in the area of transportation in general and air transport in particular;

        (i) endeavour to standardize equipment used in transport and communications and establish common facilities for production, maintenance and repair.

    2.   Member States also undertake to encourage the establishment and promotion of joint ventures and Community enterprises and the participation of the private sector in the areas of transport and communications.

Article 33
Posts and Telecommunications

    1.   In the area of postal services, Member States undertake to:

        (a) foster closer cooperation between their postal administrations;

(b) ensure, within the Community, efficient, speedier and. more frequent postal services;

(c) harmonise mail routing;

2. In the area of telecommunications, Member States shall:

(a) develop, modernize, coordinate and standardize their national telecommunications networks in order to provide reliable interconnection among Member States;

(b) complete, with dispatch, the section of the pan-African telecommunications network situated in West Africa;

(c) coordinate their efforts with regard to the operation and maintenance of the West African portion of the pan-African telecommunications network and in the mobilization of national and international financial resources.

3. Member States also undertake to encourage the participation of the private sector in offering postal and telecommunications services, as a means of attaining the objectives set out in this Article.

. . .

Chapter VIII—Cooperation in Trade, Customs, Taxation, Statistics, Money and Payments

. . .

Article 36
Customs Duties

1. Member States shall reduce and ultimately eliminate Customs duties and any other charges with equivalent effect except duties notified in accordance with Article 40 and other charges which fall within that Article, imposed on or in connection with the importation of goods which are eligible for Community tariff treatment in accordance with Article 38 of this Treaty. Any such duties or other charges are herein after referred to as "import duties."

2. Community-originating unprocessed goods and traditional handicraft products shall circulate within the region free of all import duties and quantitative restrictions. There shall be no compensation for loss of revenue resulting from the importation of these products.

3. Member States undertake to eliminate import duties on industrial goods which are eligible for preferential Community tariff treatment in accordance with the decisions of the Authority and Council relating to the liberalization of intra-Community trade in industrial products.

. . .

Article 37
Common External Tariff

1. Member States agree to the gradual establishment of a common external tariff in respect of all goods imported into the Member States from third countries in accordance with a schedule to be recommended by the Trade, Customs, Taxation, Statistics, Money and Payments Commission.

2. Member States shall, in accordance with a schedule to be recommended by the Trade, Customs, Taxation, Statistics, Money and Payments Commission, abolish existing differences in their external Customs tariffs.

3. Member States undertake to apply the common Customs nomenclature and Customs statistical nomenclature adopted by the Council.

Article 38
Community Tariff Treatment

1. For the purposes of this Treaty, goods shall be accepted as eligible for Community tariff treatment if they have been consigned to the territory of the importing Member States from the territory of another Member State and originate from the Community.

2. The rules governing products originating from the Community shall be as contained in the relevant Protocols and Decisions of the Community.

3. The Trade, Customs, Taxation, Statistics, Money and Payments Commission shall from time to time examine whether the rules referred to in paragraph 2 of this Article can be amended to make them simpler and more liberal. In order to ensure their smooth and equitable operation, the Council may from time to time amend them.

   . . .

Article 42
Dumping

1. Member States undertake to prohibit the practice of dumping goods within the Community.

2. For the purposes of this Article, "dumping" means the transfer of goods originating in a Member State to another Member State for sale:

   (a) at a price lower than the comparable price charged for similar goods in the Member States where such goods originate (due allowance being made for the differences in the conditions of sale or in taxation or for any other factors affecting the comparability of prices); and

   (b) under circumstances likely to prejudice the production of similar goods in that Member State.

3. In the event of alleged dumping the importing Member State shall appeal to the Council to resolve the matter.

4. The Council shall consider the issue and take appropriate measures to determine the causes of the dumping.

   . . .

Article 51
Money, Finance and Payments

1. In order to promote monetary and financial integration, and facilitate intra-Community trade in goods and services and the realization of the Community's objective of establishing a monetary union, Member States undertake to:

   (a) study monetary and financial developments in the region;

   (b) harmonize their monetary, financial and payments policies;

   (c) facilitate the liberalization of intra-regional payments transactions and, as an interim measure, ensure limited convertibility of currencies;

   (d) promote the role of commercial banks in intra-community trade financing;

   (e) improve the multilateral system for clearing of payments transactions between Member States, and introduce a credit and guarantee fund mechanism;

   (f) take necessary measures to promote the activities of the West Africa Monetary Agency in order to ensure convertibility of currencies and creation of a single currency zone;

   (g) establish a Community Central Bank and a common currency zone.

Article 52
Committee of West African Central Banks

1. There is hereby established a Committee of West African Central banks comprising the Governors of Central Banks of Member States. This Committee shall, in accordance with the provisions of this Treaty, prepare its own rules of procedure.

2. The Committee shall, from time to time, make recommendations to the Council on the operation of the clearing system of payments and other monetary issues within the Community.

Article 53
Movement of Capital and Capital Issues Committee

1. For the purpose of ensuring the free movement of capital between Member States in accordance with the objectives of this Treaty, there is hereby established a Capital Issues Committee which shall comprise one representative of each of the Member States and which shall, subject to the provisions of this Treaty, prepare its own rules of procedure.
   . . .

Chapter IX—Establishment and Completion of an Economic and Monetary Union

. . .

Article 55
Completion of Economic and Monetary Union

1. Member States undertake to complete within five (5) years following the creation of a Custom Union, the establishment of an economic and monetary union through:
   (i) the adoption of a common policy in all fields of socioeconomic activity particularly agriculture, industry, transport, communications, energy and scientific research;
   (ii) the total elimination of all obstacles to the free movement of people, goods, capital and services and the right of entry, residence and establishment;
   (iii) the harmonization of monetary, financial and fiscal policies, the setting up of West African monetary union, the establishment of a single regional Central Bank and the creation of a single West African currency.
2. The Authority may at any time, on the recommendation of the Council, decide that any stage of the integration process shall be implemented more rapidly than otherwise provided for in this Treaty.

Chapter X—Cooperation in Political, Judicial and Legal Affairs, Regional Security and Immigration

Article 56
Political Affairs

1. In pursuit of the integration objectives of the Community, Member States undertake to cooperate on political matters, and in particular, to

take appropriate measures to ensure effective application of the provisions of this Treaty.

2. The signatory States to the Protocol on Non-Aggression, the Protocol on Mutual Assistance on Defence, the Community Declaration of Political Principles and the African Charter on Human and Peoples' Rights agree to cooperate for the purpose of realizing the objectives of these instruments.

Article 57
Judicial and Legal Matters

1. Member States undertake to cooperate in judicial and legal matters with a view to harmonizing their judicial and legal systems.
2. The modalities for the implementation of this arrangement shall be the subject matter of a Protocol.

Article 58
Regional Security

1. Member States undertake to work to safeguard and consolidate relations conducive to the maintenance of peace, stability and security within the region.
2. In pursuit of these objectives, Member States undertake to cooperate with the Community in establishing and strengthening appropriate mechanisms for the timely prevention and resolution of intra-State and inter-State conflicts, paying particular regard to the need to:
   (a) maintain periodic and regular consultations between national border administration authorities;
   (b) establish local or national joint commissions to examine any problems encountered in relations between neighbouring States;
   (c) encourage exchanges and cooperation between communities, townships and administrative regions;
   (d) organize meetings between relevant ministries on various aspects of inter-State relations;
   (e) employ, where appropriate, good offices, conciliation, meditation and other methods of peaceful settlement of disputes;
   (f) establish a regional peace and security observation system and peace-keeping forces where appropriate;
   (g) provide, where necessary and at the request of Member States, assistance to Member States for the observation of democratic elections.

3. The detailed provisions governing political cooperation, regional peace and stability shall be defined in the relevant Protocols.

Article 59
Immigration

1. Citizens of the community shall have the right of entry, residence and establishment and Member States undertake to recognize these rights of Community citizens in their territories in accordance with the provisions of the Protocols relating thereto.
2. Member States undertake to adopt all appropriate measures to ensure that Community citizens enjoy fully the rights referred to in paragraph 1 of this Article.
3. Member States undertake to adopt, at national level, all measures necessary for the effective implementation of the provisions of this Article.

   . . .

Article 64
Population and Development

1. Member States undertake to adopt, individually and collectively, national population policies and mechanisms and take all necessary measures in order to ensure a balance between demographic factors and socio-economic development.
2. To this end, Member States agree to:
   (a) include population issues as central components in formulating and implementing national policies and programmes for accelerated and balanced socioeconomic development;
   (b) formulate national population policies and establish national population institutions;
   (c) undertake public sensitization on population matters, particularly among the target groups; and
   (d) collect, analyze and exchange information and data on population issues.

Article 65
Information Radio and Television

Member States undertake to:

(a) coordinate their efforts and pool their resources in order to promote the exchange of radio and television programmes at bilateral and regional levels;

(b) encourage the establishment of programme exchange centres at regional level and strengthen existing programme exchange centres;

(c) use their broadcasting and television systems to promote the attainment of the objectives of the Community.

Article 66
The Press

1. In order to involve more closely the citizens of the Community in the regional integration process, Member States agree to cooperate in the area of information.

2. To this end they undertake as follows:

(a) to maintain within their borders, and between one another, freedom of access for professionals of the communication industry and for information sources;

(b) to facilitate exchange of information between their press organs; to promote and foster effective dissemination of information within the Community;

(c) to ensure respect for the rights of journalists;

(d) to take measures to encourage investment capital, both public and private, in the communication industries in Member States;

(e) to modernize the media by introducing training facilities for new information techniques; and

(f) to promote and encourage dissemination of information in indigenous languages, strengthening cooperation between national press agencies and developing linkages between them.

. . .

Chapter XIV—Financial Provisions

Article 69
Budget of the Community

1. There shall be established a budget of the Community and, where appropriate, of any of the Institutions of the Community.

2. All incomes and expenditure of the Community and its institutions shall be approved by the Council or other appropriate bodies for each financial year and shall be charged to the budget of the Community or the institution concerned.

3. A draft budget shall be proposed for each financial year by the Executive Secretary or by the Head of the Institution concerned and approved by the Council or other appropriate body on the recommendation of the Administration and Finance Commission.

4. The Administration and Finance Commission shall consider the draft budget and all financial issues concerning the institutions of the Community and shall examine issues pertaining mainly to administration and personnel management in the institutions of the community.

  . . .

Article 72
Community Levy

1. There is hereby instituted a Community levy for the purpose of generating resources for financing Community activities.

2. The Community levy shall be a percentage of the total value of import duty derivable from goods imported into the Community from third countries.

3. The actual level of the Community levy shall be determined by the Council.

4. The conditions for the application of the Community levy, the modalities for the transfer to the Community of the revenue generated and the utilization of the Community levy shall be defined in the relevant Protocol.

5. Member States undertake to facilitate the application of the provisions of this Article.

Article 73
Contributions by Member States

1. The mode by which the contributions of Member States shall be determined and the currencies in which the contributions are paid shall be as determined by the Council.

2. Member States undertake to promptly transfer their assessed contributions to the Community.

  . . .

Chapter XV—Disputes

Article 76
Settlement of Disputes

1. Any dispute regarding the interpretation or the application of the provisions of this Treaty shall be amicably settled through direct agreement without prejudice to the provisions of this Treaty and relevant Protocols.
2. Failing this, either party or any other Member States or the Authority may refer the matter to the Court of the Community whose decision shall be final and shall not be subject to appeal.

Chapter XVI—Sanctions

Article 77
Sanctions Applicable for Non-Fulfilment of Obligations

1. Where a Member State fails to fulfil its obligations to the Community, the Authority may decide to impose sanctions on that Member State.
2. These sanctions may include:
   (i) suspension of new Community loans or assistance,
   (ii) suspension of disbursement to on-going Community projects or assistance programmes;
   (iii) exclusion from presenting candidates for statutory and professional posts;
   (iv) suspension of voting rights; and
   (v) suspension from participating in the activities of the Community.
3. Notwithstanding the provisions of paragraph 1 of this Article, the Authority may suspend the application of the provisions of the said Article if it is satisfied on the basis of a well supported and detailed report prepared by an independent body and submitted through the Executive Secretary, that the non-fulfillment of its obligations is due to causes and circumstances beyond the control of the said Member State;
4. The Authority shall decide on the modalities for the application of this Article.
   . . .

Article 85
International Negotiations

1. Member States undertake to formulate and adopt common positions within the Community on issues relating to international negotiations with third parties in order to promote and safeguard the interests of the region.
2. To this end, the Community shall prepare studies and reports designed to help Member States to harmonize better their positions on the said issues.

    . . .

Article 90
Amendments and Revisions

1. Any Member State may submit proposals for the amendment or revision of this Treaty.
2. Any such proposals shall he submitted to the Executive Secretary who shall notify other Member States thereof not later thirty (30) days after the receipt of such proposals. Amendments or revisions shall not be considered by the Authority unless Member States shall have been given at least three months' notice thereof.
3. Amendments or revisions shall be adopted by the Authority in accordance with the provisions of Article 9 of this Treaty and shall be submitted for ratification by all Member Sates in accordance with their respective constitutional procedures. They shall enter into force in accordance with Article 89 of this Treaty.

Article 91
Withdrawal

1. Any Member State wishing to withdraw from the Community shall give to the Executive Secretary one year's notice in writing who shall inform Member States thereof. At the expiration of this period, if such notice is not withdrawn, such a State shall cease to be a member of the Community.
2. During the period of one year referred to in the preceding paragraph, such a Member State shall continue to comply with the provisions of this. Treaty and shall remain bound to discharge its obligations under this Treaty.

    . . .

SOUTHERN AFRICAN DEVELOPMENT COMMUNITY (SADC)

Southern and Eastern Africa have been struggling with concepts of regional cooperation and integration in the shadow of decolonization and on the long road to overcoming apartheid regimes in Southern Africa. The effort to create an East African Community failed in 1977 after ten years of promising activity because of fundamental ideological differences between socialist Tanzania and pro-Western, market-oriented Kenya. However, this was not the end of integration efforts in Eastern and South Eastern Africa. The struggle against apartheid brought the front-line states of Southern and Eastern Africa together under the roof of the Southern African Development Coordination Conference (SADCC) in 1980. Angola, Botswana, Lesotho, Malawi, Mozambique, Swaziland, Tanzania, Zambia, and Zimbabwe were united in their search to reduce economic dependency on South Africa. After the peaceful end of apartheid in 1992, SADCC was transformed into the Southern African Development Community (SADC). Namibia had already joined after its independence in 1990. South Africa did the same after the end of apartheid (in 1994), followed by Mauritius (in 1995), the Seychelles, and the Democratic Republic of Congo (in 1997). Ever since, SADC has been considered the most viable engine for economic cooperation and potentially for regional integration in Southern Africa. South Africa has turned from being the unifying enemy of SADCC into the center of power and engine of SADC. SADC countries are home to 240 million people with a combined gross domestic product of $379 billion (US).

The founding treaty of SADC of 1992—officially labeled the Consolidated Text of the Treaty of the Southern African Development Community—makes reference to the noble goals of preserving human rights, peace, and security, the rule of law, the peaceful settlement of disputes, the development of common political values, systems, and institutions, and the harmonization of policies, including foreign policy. One of the main organs of SADC is the Inter-State Defense and Security Committee. A regional satellite communications network, actions (no matter how vague) against coup attempts, peacekeeping training in a Regional Peacekeeping Training Institute, and standardized operating procedures for peacekeeping operations have been among the activities of SADC. In the economic field, SADC aims for a free trade area by 2008, paving the way for customs union and subsequently for a common market. Intra-regional trade has increased and stands now at 22 percent, the highest intra-regional trade level in all of sub-Saharan Africa. Progress on the realization of the free trade area—by substantially reducing tariff and non-tariff barriers—has been accompanied by improvement of transport corridors that are supposed to bring development into the most depressed areas of the regions. Since 1995, the region has had an integrated power grid.

SADC's institutional arrangements include the SADC Parliamentary Forum, the SADC Tribunal, the SADC Electoral Commission Forum, the SADC Lawyers Association, and various other civil society forums. SADC's Secretariat is based in Gaborone, the capital of Botswana. SADC was confronted with difficult adaptation challenges after South Africa joined. Economically this could not have come as a surprise since South Africa accounts for almost 70 percent of SADC's GDP, but the hegemonic potential of South Africa's economy affects political cooperation in SADC. A South Africa–Zimbabwe political conflict over control of SADC organs "stretched it almost to the breaking point." European disputes with Zimbabwe over growing authoritarianism in that country did not affect SADC's stance toward its member state Zimbabwe. In light of this background, SADC's 2004 Principles and Guidelines Governing Democratic Elections will be of long-term importance. The military intervention of SADC in Lesotho in 1998 caused further disputes among members of the integration scheme. Nevertheless, the potential of SADC remains strong compared to past or parallel efforts in sub-Saharan Africa. The 2001 Protocol on Politics, Defence and Security Cooperation indicates potential and direction.

SADC, as the engine of regional integration in Southern Africa, is supported by the activities of the Common Market for Eastern and Southern Africa (COMESA). COMESA was established by a treaty signed in Kampala, Uganda, in 1993 by the member states of the former Preferential Trade Area for Eastern and Southern Africa (PTA), namely Burundi, Comoros, Djibouti, Ethiopia, Kenya, Lesotho, Malawi, Mauritius, Mozambique, Rwanda, Somalia, Swaziland, Tanzania, Uganda, Zambia, and Zimbabwe. While Tanzania, Namibia, Lesotho, Mozambique, and Somalia left COMESA, Angola, the Democratic Republic of Congo, Egypt, Eritrea, Madagascar, Namibia, the Seychelles, and Sudan joined COMESA after its creation. COMESA's main goal remains the fulfillment of a common market. The target dates for realizing a free trade area by 2000 and a common external tariff by 2004 could not be achieved. Yet COMESA claims considerable achievement as far as facilitating trade and institution-building in the region is concerned. Headquartered in Lusaka, Zambia, the accounts of COMESA are denominated in the organization's unit of account, the COMESA dollar, which is equal to one US dollar.

The main organ of COMESA is the Authority of Heads of State and Government. The Council of Ministers, the Court of Justice, the Committee of Governors of Central Banks and other institutional mechanisms resemble European experiences. Yet the practical performance of COMESA has not been very impressive. Overlapping membership in COMESA, SADC, and ECCAS has been identified as only one of the factors hindering progress toward the implementation of COMESA's goals. The weak development level of most African economies is as much an impediment to early integration as the political obstacles that weaken Africa's political structures. Weak economic and political sovereignty do not make fertile breeding ground for a rapid and substantial shift toward regional integration and shared sovereignty as a strategy for both stronger economic and political systems on the national level and a changing perception of the overall potential of Africa on the continental level. Nevertheless, Africa has begun to focus on the need for and potential of regional and even continental integration more than at any time since the beginning of modern independent statehood on the continent. Since 2000, the East African Community has been revived, aiming at an East African Federation by 2010.

CONSOLIDATED TEXT OF THE TREATY OF THE SOUTHERN AFRICAN DEVELOPMENT COMMUNITY (17.08.1992)

. . .

Conscious of our duty to promote the interdependence and integration of our national economies for the harmonious, balanced and equitable development of the Region;

Convinced of the need to mobilise our own and international resources to promote the implementation of national, interstate and regional policies, programmes and projects within the framework for economic integration;

Dedicated to secure, by concerted action, international understanding, support and cooperation;

Mindful of the need to involve the people of the Region centrally in the process of development and integration, particularly through the guarantee of democratic rights, observance of human rights and the rule of law;

. . .

Chapter 2—Establishment and Legal Status

Article 2
Establishment

1. By this Treaty, the High Contracting Parties establish the Southern African Development Community (hereinafter referred to as SADC).
2. The Headquarters of SADC shall be at Gaborone, Republic of Botswana.

Article 3
Legal Status

1. SADC shall be an international organisation, and shall have legal personality with capacity and power to enter into contract, acquire, own or dispose of movable or immovable property and to sue and be sued.

2. In the territory of each Member State, SADC shall, pursuant to paragraph 1 of this Article, have such legal capacity as is necessary for the proper exercise of its functions.

Chapter 3—Principles, Objectives, SADC Common Agenda and General Undertakings

Article 4
Principles

SADC and its Member States shall act in accordance with the following principles:
   (a) sovereign equality of all Member States;
   (b) solidarity, peace and security;
   (c) human rights, democracy and the rule of law;
   (d) equity, balance and mutual benefit; and
   (e) peaceful settlement of disputes.

Article 5
Objectives

1. The objectives of SADC shall be to:
   (a) promote sustainable and equitable economic growth and socio-economic development that will ensure poverty alleviation with the ultimate objective of its eradication, enhance the standard and quality of life of the people of Southern Africa and support the socially disadvantaged through regional integration;
   (b) promote common political values, systems and other shared values which are transmitted through institutions which are democratic, legitimate and effective;
   (c) consolidate, defend and maintain democracy, peace, security and stability;
   (d) promote self-sustaining development on the basis of collective self-reliance, and the interdependence of Member States;
   (e) achieve complementarity between national and regional strategies and programmes;
   (f) promote and maximise productive employment and utilisation of resources of the Region;
   (g) achieve sustainable utilisation of natural resources and effective protection of the environment;
   (h) strengthen and consolidate the long standing historical, social and cultural affinities and links among the people of the Region;
   (i) combat HIV/AIDS and other deadly and communicable diseases;

(j) ensure that poverty eradication is addressed in all SADC activities and programmes; and

(k) mainstream gender in the process of community building.

2. In order to achieve the objectives set out in paragraph 1 of this Article, SADC shall:

(a) harmonise political and socio-economic policies and plans of Member States;

(b) encourage the people of the Region and their institutions to take initiatives to develop economic, social and cultural ties across the Region, and to participate fully in the implementation of the programmes and projects of SADC;

(c) create appropriate institutions and mechanisms for the mobilisation of requisite resources for the implementation of programmes and operations of SADC and its institutions;

(d) develop policies aimed at the progressive elimination of obstacles to the free movement of capital and labour, goods and services, and of the people of the Region generally, among Member States;

(e) promote the development of human resources;

(f) promote the development, transfer and mastery of technology;

(g) improve economic management and performance through regional cooperation;

(h) promote the coordination and harmonisation of the international relations of Member States;

(i) secure international understanding, cooperation and support, and mobilise the inflow of public and private resources into the Region; and

(j) develop such other activities as Member States may decide in furtherance of the objectives of this Treaty.

Article 5A
SADC Common Agenda

1. The SADC Common Agenda shall be as reflected in Article 5 of this Treaty.

2. Without prejudice to paragraph 1 of this Article, the Council shall develop and implement the SADC Common Agenda.

Article 6
General Undertakings

1. Member States undertake to adopt adequate measures to promote the achievement of the objectives of SADC, and shall refrain from taking any measure likely to jeopardise the sustenance of its principles, the

achievement of its objectives and the implementation of the provisions of this Treaty.

2. SADC and Member States shall not discriminate against any person on grounds of gender, religion, political views, race, ethnic origin, culture, ill health, disability, or such other ground as may be determined by the Summit.

3. SADC shall not discriminate against any Member State.

4. Member States shall take all steps necessary to ensure the uniform application of this Treaty.

5. Member States shall take all necessary steps to accord this Treaty the force of national law.

6. Member States shall cooperate with and assist institutions of SADC in the performance of their duties.

    . . .

Chapter 5—Institutions

Article 9
Establishment of Institutions

1. The following institutions are hereby established:
    (a) the Summit of Heads of State or Government;
    (b) the Organ on Politics, Defence and Security Cooperation;
    (c) the Council of Ministers;
    (d) the Integrated Committee of Ministers;
    (e) the Standing Committee of Officials;
    (f) the Secretariat;
    (g) the Tribunal; and
    (h) SADC National Committees.

2. Other institutions may be established as necessary.

Article 9A
Troika

1. The Troika shall apply with respect to the following institutions:
    (a) the Summit;
    (b) the Organ;
    (c) the Council;
    (d) the Integrated Committee of Ministers; and
    (e) the Standing Committee of Officials.

2. The Troika of the Summit shall consist of:
    (a) the Chairperson of SADC;

(b) the Incoming Chairperson of SADC who shall be the Deputy Chairperson of SADC; and

(c) the Outgoing Chairperson of SADC.

3. The respective offices of the Troika of the Summit shall be held for a period of one year.

4. The membership and term of office of the Troika of the Council, the Integrated Committee of Ministers and the Standing Committee of Officials shall correspond to the membership and term of office of the Troika of the Summit.

5. The Troika of the Organ shall consist of:

(a) the Chairperson of the Organ;

(b) the Incoming Chairperson of the Organ who shall be the Deputy Chairperson of the Organ; and

(c) the Outgoing Chairperson of the Organ.

6. The Troika of each institution shall function as a steering committee of the institution and shall, in between the meetings of the institution, be responsible for:

(a) decision-making;

(b) facilitating the implementation of decisions; and

(c) providing policy directions.

7. The Troika of each institution shall have power to create committees on an ad hoc basis.

8. The Troika of each institution shall determine its own rules of procedure.

9. The Troika of each institution may co-opt other members as and when required.

Article 10
The Summit

1. The Summit shall consist of the Heads of State or Government of all Member States, and shall be the supreme policy-making Institution of SADC.

2. The Summit shall be responsible for the overall policy direction and control of the functions of SADC.

3. Subject to Article 22 of this Treaty, the Summit shall adopt legal instruments for the implementation of the provisions of this Treaty; provided that the Summit may delegate this authority to the Council or any other institution of SADC as the Summit may deem appropriate.

4. The Summit shall elect a Chairperson and a Deputy Chairperson of SADC from among its members for one year on the basis of rotation.

5. The Summit shall meet at least twice a year.

6. The Summit may create committees, other institutions and organs as it may consider necessary.

7. The Summit shall appoint the Executive Secretary and the Deputy Executive Secretary, on the recommendation of the Council.
8. Subject to Article 8 of this Treaty, the Summit shall decide on the admission of new members to SADC.
9. Unless otherwise provided in this Treaty, the decisions of the Summit shall be taken by consensus and shall be binding.

Article 10A
Organ on Politics, Defence and Security Cooperation

1. The Summit shall select a Chairperson and a Deputy Chairperson of the Organ on the basis of rotation from among the members of the Summit except that the Chairperson of the Summit shall not simultaneously be the chairperson of the Organ.
2. The term of office of the Chairperson, Incoming Chairperson and the Outgoing Chairperson of the Organ shall be one year respectively.
3. The Chairperson of the Organ shall consult with the Troika of the Summit and report to the Summit.
4. There shall be a Ministerial Committee of the Organ, consisting of the Ministers responsible for:
   (a) foreign affairs;
   (b) defence;
   (c) public security; or
   (e) state security,

   from each of the Member States, which shall be responsible for the co-ordination of the work of the Organ and its structures.
5. The structure, functions, powers and procedures of the Organ and other related matters shall be prescribed in a Protocol.
6. The Secretariat shall provide Secretariat services to the Organ.
7. Decisions of the Organ shall be taken by consensus.

Article 11
The Council

1. The Council shall consist of one Minister from each Member State, preferably a Minister responsible for Foreign or External Affairs.
2. It shall be the responsibility of the Council to:
   (a) oversee the functioning and development of SADC;
   (b) oversee the implementation of the policies of SADC and the proper execution of its programmes;
   (c) advise the Summit on matters of overall policy and efficient and harmonious functioning and development of SADC;

(d) approve policies, strategies and work programmes of SADC;

(e) direct, coordinate and supervise the operations of the institutions of SADC subordinate to it;

(f) recommend, for approval to the Summit, the establishment of directorates, committees, other institutions and organs;

(g) create its own committees as necessary;

(h) recommend to the Summit persons for appointment to the posts of Executive Secretary and Deputy Executive Secretary;

(i) determine the Terms and Conditions of Service of the staff of the institutions of SADC;

(j) develop and implement the SADC Common Agenda and strategic priorities;

(k) convene conferences and other meetings as appropriate, for purposes of promoting the objectives and programmes of SADC; and

(l) perform such other duties as may be assigned to it by the Summit or this Treaty.

3. The Chairperson and Deputy Chairperson of the Council shall be appointed by the Member States holding the Chairpersonship and Deputy Chairpersonship of SADC respectively.

4. The Council shall meet at least four times a year.

5. The Council shall report and be responsible to the Summit.

6. Decisions of the Council shall be taken by consensus.

7. The Council shall consider and recommend to the Summit any application for membership to SADC.

Article 12
Integrated Committee of Ministers

1. The Integrated Committee of Ministers shall consist of at least two ministers from each Member State.

2. It shall be the responsibility of the Integrated Committee of Ministers to:

(a) oversee the activities of the core areas of integration which include:

(i) trade, industry, finance and investment;

(ii) infrastructure and services;

(iii) food, agriculture and natural resources; and

(iv) social and human development and special programmes;

(b) monitor and control the implementation of the Regional Indicative Strategic Development Plan in its area of competence;

(c) provide policy guidance to the Secretariat;

(d) make decisions on matters pertaining to the directorates;

(e) monitor and evaluate the work of the directorates; and

(f) create such permanent or ad hoc subcommittees as may be necessary to cater for cross-cutting sectors.

3. The Integrated Committee of Ministers shall, with respect to its responsibilities under paragraph 2 of this Article, have decision making powers to ensure rapid implementation of programmes that would otherwise wait for a formal meeting of the Council.

4. The Chairperson and Deputy Chairperson of the Integrated Committee of Ministers shall be appointed from the Member States holding the Chairpersonship and Deputy Chairpersonship, respectively, of the Council.

5. The Integrated Committee of Ministers shall meet at least once a year.

6. The Integrated Committee of Ministers shall report and be responsible to the Council.

7. Decisions of the Integrated Committee of Ministers shall be taken by consensus.

Article 13
The Standing Committee of Officials

1. The Standing Committee shall consist of one permanent secretary or an official of equivalent rank from each Member State, from the Ministry that is the SADC National Contact Point.

2. The Standing Committee shall be a technical advisory committee to the Council. The Standing Committee shall process documentation from the Integrated Committee of Ministers to the Council.

3. The Standing Committee shall report and be responsible to the Council.

4. The Chairperson and Deputy Chairperson of the Standing Committee shall be appointed from the Member States holding the Chairpersonship and the Deputy Chairpersonship, respectively, of the Council.

5. The Standing Committee shall meet at least four times a year.

6. Decisions of the Standing Committee shall be taken by consensus.

Article 14
The Secretariat

1. The Secretariat shall be the principal executive institution of SADC, and shall be responsible for:
   (a) strategic planning and management of the programmes of SADC;
   (b) implementation of decisions of the Summit, Troika of the Summit, Organ on Politics, Defence and Security Cooperation, Troika of the Organ on Politics, Defence and Security Cooperation, Council, Troika of the Council, Integrated Committee of Ministers and Troika of the Integrated Committee of Ministers;

(c) organisation and management of SADC meetings;

(d) financial and general administration;

(e) representation and promotion of SADC;

(f) coordination and harmonisation of the policies and strategies of Member States;

(g) gender mainstreaming in all SADC programmes and activities;

(h) submission of harmonized policies and programmes to the Council for consideration and approval;

(i) monitoring and evaluating the implementation of regional policies and programmes;

(j) collation and dissemination of information on the Community and maintenance of a reliable database;

(k) development of capacity, infrastructure and maintenance of intra-regional information communications technology;

(l) mobilization of resources, coordination and harmonization of programmes and projects with cooperating partners;

(m) devising appropriate strategies for self financing and income generating activities and investment;

(n) management of special programmes and projects;

(o) undertaking research on Community building and the integration process; and

(p) preparation and submission to the Council, for approval, administrative regulations, standing orders and rules for management of the affairs of SADC.

2. The Secretariat shall be headed by the Executive Secretary.

3. The Deputy Executive Secretary shall have delegated powers and assist the Executive Secretary in the execution of his or her functions.

4. The Secretariat shall have such other staff as may be determined by the Council from time to time.

5. Except as otherwise provided in this Treaty, the structures of the Secretariat and specifications, descriptions and grading of jobs of the staff of the Secretariat shall be as determined from time to time by the Council.

. . .

Article 16
The Tribunal

1. The Tribunal shall be constituted to ensure adherence to and the proper interpretation of the provisions of this Treaty and subsidiary instruments and to adjudicate upon such disputes as may be referred to it.

2. The composition, powers, functions, procedures and other related matters governing the Tribunal shall be prescribed in a Protocol, which

shall, notwithstanding the provisions of Article 22 of this Treaty, form an integral part of this Treaty, adopted by the Summit.

3. Members of the Tribunal shall be appointed for a specified period.
4. The Tribunal shall give advisory opinions on such matters as the Summit or the Council may refer to it.
5. The decisions of the Tribunal shall be final and binding.

Article 16A
SADC National Committees

1. Each Member State shall create a SADC National Committee.
2. Each SADC National Committee shall consist of key stakeholders.
3. Each SADC National Committee shall, in its composition, reflect the core areas of integration and coordination referred to in paragraph 2 of Article 12 of this Treaty.
4. It shall be the responsibility of each SADC National Committee to:

    (a) provide input at the national level in the formulation of SADC policies, strategies and programmes of action;
    (b) coordinate and oversee, at the national level, implementation of SADC programmes of action;
    (c) initiate projects and issue papers as input to the preparation of the Regional Indicative Strategic Development Plan, in accordance with the priority areas set out in the SADC Common Agenda; and
    (d) create a national steering committee, sub-committees and technical committees.

5. Each national steering committee shall consist of the chairperson of the SADC National Committee and the chairpersons of sub-committees.
6. Sub-committees and technical committees of the SADC National Committee shall operate at ministerial and official levels.
7. A national steering committee shall be responsible for ensuring rapid implementation of programmes that would otherwise wait for a formal meeting of the SADC National Committee.
8. Sub-committees and technical committees shall endeavour to involve key stakeholders in their operations.
9. Each Member State shall create a national secretariat to facilitate the operation of the SADC National Committee.
10. Each national secretariat of a SADC National Committee shall produce and submit reports to the Secretariat at specified intervals.
11. Each Member State shall provide funds for the operation of its national secretariat which shall be structured according to the core areas of integration referred to in paragraph 2 of Article 12 of this Treaty.
12. Each SADC National Committee shall meet at least four times a year.

13. For purposes of this Article, key stakeholders include:

    (a) government;
    (b) private sector;
    (c) civil society;
    (d) non-governmental organizations; and
    workers and employers organizations.

    . . .

Article 19
Decisions

Except as otherwise provided in this Treaty, decisions of the institutions of SADC shall be taken by consensus.

. . .

Article 23
Stakeholders

1. In pursuance of the objectives of this Treaty, SADC shall seek to involve fully, the people of the Region and key stakeholders in the process of regional integration.
2. SADC shall cooperate with, and support the initiatives of the peoples of the Region and key stakeholders, contributing to the objectives of this Treaty in the areas of cooperation in order to foster closer relations among the communities, associations and people of the Region.
3. For the purposes of this article, key stakeholders include:

    (a) private sector;
    (b) civil society;
    (c) non-governmental organisations; and
    (d) workers and employers organisations.

    . . .

Chapter 9—Resources, Funds and Assets

Article 25
Resources

1. SADC shall be responsible for the mobilisation of its own and other resources required for the implementation of its programmes and projects.
2. SADC shall create such institutions as may be necessary for the effective mobilisation and efficient application of resources for regional development.

3. Resources acquired by SADC by way of contributions, loans, grants or gifts, shall be the property of SADC.

4. The resources of SADC may be made available to Member States in pursuance of the objectives of this Treaty, on terms and conditions mutually agreed between SADC and the Member States involved.

5. Resources of SADC shall be utilised in the most efficient and equitable manner.

Article 26
Funds

The funds of SADC shall consist of contributions of Member States, income from SADC enterprises and receipts from regional and non-regional sources.

Article 26A
Regional Development Fund

1. There is hereby established a special fund of SADC to be known as the Regional Development Fund in which shall be accounted receipts and expenditure of SADC relating to the development of SADC.

2. The Regional Development Fund shall, subject to this Treaty, consist of contributions of Member States and receipts from regional and non-regional sources, including the private sector, civil society, non-governmental organisations and workers and employers organisations.

3. The Council shall determine the modalities for the institutionalization, operation and management of the Regional Development Fund.

4. The Regional Development Fund shall be governed in terms of financial regulations made in accordance with Article 30 of this Treaty.

Article 27
Assets

1. Property, both movable and immovable, acquired by or on behalf of SADC shall constitute the assets of SADC, irrespective of their location.

2. Property acquired by Member States, under the auspices of SADC, shall belong to the Member States concerned, subject to provisions of paragraph 3 of this Article, and Articles 25 and 34 of this Treaty.

3. Assets acquired by Member States under the auspices of SADC shall be accessible to all Member States on an equitable basis.

Chapter 10—Financial Provisions

Article 28
The Budget

1. The budget of SADC shall be funded by financial contributions made by Member States, and such other sources as may be determined by the Council.
2. Member States shall contribute to the budget of SADC based upon a formula agreed upon by the Summit.
3. The Executive Secretary shall cause to be prepared, estimates of revenue and expenditure for the Secretariat, and submit them to the Council, not less than three months before the beginning of the financial year.
4. The Council shall approve the estimates of revenue and expenditure before the beginning of the financial year.
5. The financial year of SADC shall be determined by the Council.

Article 29
External Audit

1. The Council shall appoint external auditors and shall fix their fees and remuneration at the beginning of each financial year.
2. The Executive Secretary shall cause to be prepared and audited annual statements of accounts for the Secretariat and submit them to the Council for approval.

Article 30
Financial Regulations

The Executive Secretary shall prepare and submit to the Council for approval financial regulations, standing orders and rules for the management of the affairs of SADC.

Chapter 11—Immunities and Privileges

Article 31

1. SADC, its institutions and staff shall, in the territory of each Member State, have such immunities and privileges as are necessary for the proper performance of their functions under this Treaty, and which shall be similar to those accorded to comparable international organisations.

2. The immunities and privileges conferred by this Article shall be prescribed in a Protocol.

Chapter 12—Settlement of Disputes

Article 32

Any dispute arising from the interpretation or application of this Treaty, the interpretation, application or validity of Protocols or other subsidiary instruments made under this Treaty, which cannot be settled amicably, shall be referred to the Tribunal.

Chapter 13—Sanctions, Withdrawal and Dissolution

Article 33
Sanctions

1. Sanctions may be imposed against any Member State that:
   (a) persistently fails, without good reason, to fulfil obligations assumed under this Treaty;
   (b) implements policies which undermine the principles and objectives of SADC; or
   (c) is in arrears in the payment of contributions to SADC, for reasons other than those caused by natural calamity or exceptional circumstances that gravely affect its economy, and has not secured the dispensation of the Summit.
2. The Summit shall determine on a case-by-case basis sanctions to be imposed under subparagraphs a) and b) of paragraph 1 of this Article.
3. Subject to subparagraph c) of paragraph 1 of this Article, sanctions against a Member State which is in arrears shall be imposed as follows:
   (a) when in arrears for one year, suspension of the Member State's right to speak and receive documentation at meetings of SADC;
   (b) when in arrears for two years, suspension:
      (i) of the Member State's right to speak and receive documentation at meetings of SADC; and
      (ii) by SADC of recruitment, and renewal of contracts of employment, of personnel from the Member State;
   (c) when in arrears for three years, suspension:
      (i) of the Member State's right to speak and receive documentation at meetings of SADC;

      (ii) by SADC of recruitment, and renewal of contracts of employ-ment, of personnel from the Member State; and

      (iii) of provision by SADC of funds for new projects in the Member State; and

(d) when in arrears for four or more years, suspension:

      (i)   of the Member State's right to speak and receive documenta-tion at meetings of SADC;

      (ii) by SADC of recruitment, and renewal of contracts of employ-ment, of personnel from the Member State; and

      (iii) of provision by SADC of funds for new projects in the Member State; and of cooperation, between SADC and the Member State, in the areas of cooperation spelt out in Article 21 of this Treaty.

4.   The sanctions referred to in paragraph 3 of this Article shall be applied by the Secretariat without reference to the Summit or Council except that the application of the sanctions shall be subject to the Secretariat notifying:

(a) prior to any meeting of SADC, Member States in default; and

(b) Member States at the beginning of any meeting of SADC.

Article 34
Withdrawal

1.   A Member State wishing to withdraw from SADC shall serve notice of its intention in writing, a year in advance, to the Chairperson of SADC, who shall inform other Member States accordingly.

2.   At the expiration of the period of notice, the Member State shall, unless the notice is withdrawn, cease to be a member of SADC.

3.   During the one year period of notice referred to in paragraph 1 of this Article, the Member State wishing to withdraw from SADC shall com-ply with the provisions of this Treaty, and shall continue to be bound by its obligations under this Treaty up to the date of its withdrawal.

4.   A Member State which has withdrawn shall not be entitled to claim any property or rights until the dissolution of SADC.

5.   Assets of SADC situated in the territory of a Member State which has withdrawn, shall continue to be the property of SADC and be available for its use.

Article 35
Dissolution

1.   The Summit may decide by a resolution supported by three-quarters of all members to dissolve SADC or any of its institutions, and determine the terms and conditions of dealing with its liabilities and disposal of its assets.

2. A proposal for the dissolution of SADC may be made to the Council by any Member State, for preliminary consideration, provided, however, that such a proposal shall not be submitted for the decision of the Summit until all Member Sates have been duly notified of it and a period of twelve months has elapsed after the submission to the Council.

Chapter 14—Amendment of the Treaty

Article 36

1. An amendment of this Treaty shall be adopted by a decision of three-quarters of all the Members of the Summit.
2. A proposal for the amendment of this Treaty may be made to the Executive Secretary by any Member State for preliminary consideration by the Council, provided, however, that the proposed amendment shall not be submitted to the Council for preliminary consideration until all Member States have been duly notified of it, and a period of three months has elapsed after such notification.

PROTOCOL ON POLITICS, DEFENCE AND SECURITY COOPERATION(14.08.2001)

. . .

Convinced that peace, security and strong political relations are critical factors in creating a conducive environment for regional cooperation and integration;

Convinced further that the Organ constitutes an appropriate institutional framework by which Member States could coordinate policies and activities in the area of politics, defence and security;

. . .

Article 2
Objectives

1. The general objective of the Organ shall be to promote peace and security in the Region.
2. The specific objectives of the Organ shall be to:
   (a) protect the people and safeguard the development of the Region against instability arising from the breakdown of law and order, intra-state conflict, inter-state conflict and aggression;

(b) promote political cooperation among State Parties and the evolution of common political values and institutions;

(c) develop common foreign policy approaches on issues of mutual concern and advance such policies collectively in international fora;

(d) promote regional coordination and cooperation on matters related to security and defence and establish appropriate mechanisms to this end;

(e) prevent, contain and resolve inter-and intra-state conflict by peaceful means;

(f) consider enforcement action in accordance with international law and as a matter of last resort where peaceful means have failed;

(g) promote the development of democratic institutions and practices within the territories of State Parties and encourage the observance of universal human rights as provided for in the Charters and Conventions of the Organisation of African Unity and United Nations respectively;

h) consider the development of a collective security capacity and conclude a Mutual Defence Pact to respond to external military threats;

    (i) develop close cooperation between the police and state security services of State Parties in order to:

    (i) address cross border crime; and

    (ii) promote a community based approach to domestic security;

(j) observe, and encourage State Parties to implement United Nations, African Union and other international conventions and treaties on arms control, disarmament and peaceful relations between states;

(k) develop peacekeeping capacity of national defence forces and co-ordinate the participation of State Parties in international and regional peacekeeping operations; and

(l) enhance regional capacity in respect of disaster management and coordination of international humanitarian assistance.

Article 3
Structures

1. The Organ shall be an institution of SADC and shall report to the Summit.

2. The Organ shall have the following structures:

    (a) the Chairperson of the Organ;

    (b) the Troika;

    (c) a Ministerial Committee;

    (d) an Inter-State Politics and Diplomacy Committee (ISPDC);

    (e) an Inter-State Defence and Security Committee (ISDSC); and

(f) such other sub-structures as may be established by any of the ministerial committees.

3. The Troika shall consist of:

(a) the Chairperson of the Organ;

(b) the Incoming Chairperson who shall be the Deputy Chairperson of the Organ; and

(c) the Outgoing Chairperson.

Article 4
Chairperson of the organ

1. The Summit shall elect a Chairperson and a Deputy Chairperson of the Organ on the basis of rotation from among the members of the Summit except that the Chairperson and the Deputy Chairperson of the Summit shall not simultaneously be the Chairperson of the Organ.

2. The term of office of the Chairperson and Deputy Chairperson of the Organ shall be one year respectively.

3. The Chairperson of the Organ shall consult with the Troika of SADC and report to the Summit.

4. The Chairperson, in consultation with the Troika of SADC, shall be responsible for the overall policy direction and the achievement of the objectives of the Organ.

5. The Chairperson may request reports from any ministerial committee of the Organ on any matter which is within the competence of the committee.

6. The Chairperson may request any ministerial committee of the Organ to consider any matter which is within the competence of the committee.

7. The Chairperson may request the Chairperson of SADC to table for discussion of any matter that requires consideration by the Summit.

Article 5
Ministerial Committee

1. The Ministerial Committee shall comprise the ministers responsible for foreign affairs, defence, public security and state security from each of the State Parties.

2. The Committee shall be responsible for the coordination of the work of the Organ and its structures.

3. The Committee shall report to the Chairperson.

4. The Committee shall be chaired by a Minister from the same country as the Chairperson for a period of one year on a rotation basis.

5. The Chairperson of the Committee shall convene at least one meeting on an annual basis.

6. The Chairperson of the Committee may when necessary convene other meetings of the Ministerial Committee at a request of either ISPDC or ISDSC.

7. The Committee may refer any relevant matter to, and may request reports from, ISPDC and ISDSC.

Article 6
Inter-State Politics and Diplomacy Committee

1. ISPDC shall comprise the ministers responsible for foreign affairs from each of the State Parties.

2. ISPDC shall perform such functions as may be necessary to achieve the objectives of the Organ relating to politics and diplomacy.

3. ISPDC shall report to the Ministerial Committee without prejudice to its obligation to report regularly to the Chairperson.

4. ISPDC shall be chaired by a Minister from the same country as the Chairperson for a period of one year and on a rotation basis.

5. The Chairperson of ISPDC shall convene at least one meeting on an annual basis.

6. The Chairperson of ISPDC may convene such other meetings as he or she deems necessary or as requested by another Minister serving on ISPDC.

7. ISPDC may establish such sub-structures as it deems necessary to perform its functions.

Article 7
Inter-State Defence and Security Committee

1. ISDSC shall comprise the ministers responsible for defence, ministers responsible for public security and ministers responsible for state security from each of the State Parties.

2. ISDSC shall perform such functions as may be necessary to achieve the objectives of the Organ relating to defence and security, and shall assume the objectives and functions of the existing Inter-State Defence and Security Committee.

3. ISDSC shall report to the Ministerial Committee without prejudice to its obligation to report regularly to the Chairperson.

4. ISDSC shall be chaired by a Minister from the same country as the Chairperson for a period of one year and on a rotating basis.

5. The Chairperson of ISDSC shall convene at least one meeting on an annual basis.

6. The Chairperson of ISDSC may convene such other meetings as he or she deems necessary or as requested by another minister serving on ISDSC.

7. ISDSC shall retain the Defence, State Security and Public Security Sub-Committees and other subordinate structures of the existing Inter-State Defence and Security Committee.

8. ISDSC may establish such other structures as it deems necessary to perform its functions.

. . .

Article 11
Conflict Prevention, Management and Resolution

1. Obligation of the Organ under International Law
   (a) In accordance with the Charter of the United Nations, State Parties shall refrain from the threat or use of force against the territorial integrity or political independence of any state, other than for the legitimate purpose of individual or collective self-defence against an armed attack.
   (b) State Parties shall manage and seek to resolve any dispute between two or more of them by peaceful means.
   (c) The Organ shall seek to manage and resolve inter- and intra-state conflict by peaceful means.
   (d) The Organ shall seek to ensure that the State Parties adhere to and enforce all sanctions and arms embargoes imposed on any party by the United Nations Security Council.

2. Jurisdiction of the Organ
   (a) The Organ may seek to resolve any significant inter-state conflict between State Parties or between a State Party and non-State Party and a "significant inter-state conflict" shall include:
       (i) a conflict over territorial boundaries or natural resources;
       (ii) a conflict in which an act of aggression or other form of military force has occurred or been threatened; and
       (iii) a conflict which threatens peace and security in the Region or in the territory of a State Party which is not a party to the conflict.
   (b) The Organ may seek to resolve any significant intra-state conflict within the territory of a State Party and a "significant intra-state conflict" shall include:
       (i) large-scale violence between sections of the population or between the state and sections of the population, including genocide, ethnic cleansing and gross violation of human rights;
       (ii) a military coup or other threat to the legitimate authority of a State;
       (iii) a condition of civil war or insurgency; and
       (iv) a conflict which threatens peace and security in the Region or in the territory of another State Party.

(c) In consultation with the United Nations Security Council and the Central Organ of the Organisation of African Unity Mechanism for Conflict Prevention, Management and Resolution, the Organ may offer to mediate in a significant inter-or intra-state conflict that occurs outside the Region.

3. Methods

(a) The methods employed by the Organ to prevent, manage and resolve conflict by peaceful means shall include preventive diplomacy, negotiations, conciliation, mediation, good offices, arbitration and adjudication by an international tribunal.

(b) The Organ shall establish an early warning system in order to facilitate timely action to prevent the outbreak and escalation of conflict.

(c) Where peaceful means of resolving a conflict are unsuccessful, the Chairperson acting on the advice of the Ministerial Committee may recommend to the Summit that enforcement action be taken against one or more of the disputant parties.

(d) The Summit shall resort to enforcement action only as a matter of last resort and, in accordance with Article 53 of the United Nations Charter, only with the authorization of the United Nations Security Council.

(e) External military threats to the Region shall be addressed through collective security arrangements to be agreed upon in a Mutual Defence Pact among the State Parties.

4. Procedures

(a) In respect of both inter- and intra-state conflict, the Organ shall seek to obtain the consent of the disputant parties to its peace-making efforts.

(b) The Chairperson, in consultation with the other members of the Troika, may table any significant conflict for discussion in the Organ.

(c) Any State Party may request the Chairperson to table any significant conflict for discussion in the Organ and in consultation with the other members of the Troika of the Organ, the Chairperson shall meet such requests expeditiously.

(d) The Organ shall respond to a request by a State Party to mediate in a conflict within the territory of that State and the Organ shall endeavour by diplomatic means to obtain such request where it is not forthcoming.

(e) The exercise of the right of individual or collective self-defence shall be immediately reported to the United Nations Security Council and to the Central Organ of the Organisation of African Unity Mechanism for Conflict Prevention, Management and Resolution.

. . .

PRINCIPLES AND GUIDELINES GOVERNING
DEMOCRATIC ELECTIONS (19.08.2004)

. . .

2. Principles for Conducting Democratic Elections

2.1   In the event a Member State decides to extend an invitation to SADC
        to observe its elections, this shall be based on the provisions of the
        Protocol on Politics, Defence and Security Cooperation.

2.2   SADC Member States shall adhere to the following principles in the
        conduct of democratic elections:

2.1.1   Full participation of the citizens in the political process;

2.1.2   Freedom of association;

2.1.3   Political tolerance;

2.1.4   Regular intervals for elections as provided for by the respective Na-
        tional Constitutions;

2.1.5   Equal opportunity for all political parties to access the state
        media;

2.1.6   Equal opportunity to exercise the right to vote and be voted for;

2.1.7   Independence of the Judiciary and impartiality of the electoral institu-
        tions; and

2.1.8   Voter education.

2.1.9   Acceptance and respect of the election results by political parties pro-
        claimed to have been free and fair by the competent National Elec-
        toral Authorities in accordance with the law of the land.

2.1.10 Challenge of the election results as provided for in the law of the
        land.

3. Mandate and Constitution of the SADC Observers Mission

3.1   In the event a Member State deems it necessary to invite SADC
        to observe is elections, the SADC Electoral Observation Missions
        (SEOM) have an Observation role. The mandate of the Mission
        shall be based on the Treaty and the Protocol on Politics, Defence
        and Security Cooperation.

3.2   The Chairperson of the Organ shall officially constitute the Mission
        upon receipt of an official invitation from the Electoral Authority of a
        Member State holding the elections.

3.3 The Chairperson of the Organ shall mandate the Executive Secretary to issue a Letter of Credential to each Member of the SEOM prior to their deployment into the Member State holding elections.

3.4 The constitution of the Mission should comply with the SADC policies relating to gender balance. While recognising that the Members of the Mission may come from different political parties in the home countries, they should behave as a team.

4. Guidelines for the Observation of Elections

4.1 SADC Member States shall be guided by the following guidelines to determine the nature and scope of election observation:

4.1.1 Constitutional and legal guarantees of freedom and rights of the citizens;

4.1.2 Conducive environment for free, fair and peaceful elections;

4.1.3 Non-discrimination in the voters' registration;

4.1.4 Existence of updated and accessible voters roll;

4.1.5 Timely announcement of the election date;

4.1.6 Where applicable, funding of political parties must be transparent and based on agreed threshold in accordance with the laws of the land;

4.1.7 Polling Stations should be in neutral places;

4.1.8 Counting of the votes at polling stations;

4.1.9 Establishment of the mechanism for assisting the planning and deployment of electoral observation missions; and

4.1.10 SADC Election Observation Missions should be deployed at least two weeks before the voting day.

5. Code of Conduct for Election Observers

5.1 The code of conduct for the elections observers of SADC are consistent with those of the OAU/AU Declaration on the Principles Governing Democratic Elections in Africa—AHG/DECL. 1 (XXXVIII). In this regard, the SADC Election Observation Missions shall adhere to the following code of conduct:

5.1.1 Must comply with all national laws and regulations;

5.1.2 Shall maintain strict impartiality in the conduct of their duties, and shall at no time express any bias or preference in relation to national authorities, parties and candidates in contention in the Election process. Furthermore they will not display or wear any partisan symbols, colours or banners;

5.1.3   Shall neither accept nor attempt to procure any gifts, favours or inducements from a candidate, their agent, the parties or any other organisation or person involved in the electoral process;

5.1.4   Shall immediately disclose to the relevant SADC structures any relationship that could lead to a conflict of interest with their duties or with the process of the observation and assessment of the elections;

5.1.5   Will base all reports and conclusions on well documented, factual, and verifiable evidence from a multiple number of credible sources as well as their own eye witness accounts;

5.1.6   Shall seek a response from the person or organisation concerned before treating any unsubstantiated allegation as valid;

5.1.7   Shall identify in their reports the exact information and the sources of the information they have gathered and used as a basis for their assessment of the electoral process or environment;

5.1.8   Shall report all information gathered or witnessed by them honestly and accurately;

5.1.9   Shall, when meeting election officials, relevant state authorities and public officials, parties, candidates and their agents, inform them of the aims and objectives of the SEOM;

5.1.10   May wish to bring irregularities to the attention of the local election officials, but must never give instructions or countermand decisions of the election officials;

5.1.11   Will carry any prescribed identification issued at all times, and will identify themselves to any interested authority upon request;

5.1.12   Will undertake their duties in an unobtrusive manner, and will not interfere with the election process, polling day procedures, or the vote count;

5.1.13   Will refrain from making personal or premature comments or judgements about their observations to the media or any other interested persons, and will limit any remarks to general information about the nature of their activity as observers;

5.1.14   Must participate in the briefings/training provided by the SEOM;

5.1.15   Must provide their reports on time to their supervisors and attend any debriefings as required; and

5.1.16   Should work harmoniously with each other and with observers from other organisations in their area of deployment.

6. Rights and Responsibilities of SADC Election Observers

6.1   The rights and responsibilities of the SOEM are based on the SADC experience and the AU Guidelines for Electoral Observation and Monitoring Missions. Accordingly the following shall be the rights and responsibilities of the SADC Elections Observers:

6.1.1   Freedom of movement within the host country;

6.1.2.   Accreditation as election observers on a non-discriminatory basis:

6.1.3.   Unhindered access to and free communication with the media;

6.1.4   Free access to all legislation and regulations governing the electoral process and environment;

6.1.5   Free access to electoral registers or voters' roll;

6.1.6   Unimpeded and unrestricted access to all polling stations and counting centres;

6.1.7   Free communication with all competing political parties, candidates, other political associations and organisations, and civil society organisations;

6.1.8   Communicate freely with voters without prejudice to the electoral law proscribing such communication in order to protect the secrecy of the vote;

6.1.9   Communicate with and have unimpeded and unrestricted access to the National Election Commission or appropriate electoral authority and all other election administrators;

6.1.10   The SEOM shall be headed by an appropriate official from the Office of the Chairperson of the Organ who shall also be the spokesperson of the Mission;

6.1.11   Send regular reports on the electoral observation process to the Representative of the Organ on issues that may require urgent consideration;

6.1.12   Issue a statement on the conduct and outcome of the elections immediately after the announcement of the result; and

6.1.13   Prepare a Final Report within 30 (thirty) days after the announcement of the results.

7. Responsibilities of the Member State Holding Elections

7.1   Take necessary measures to ensure the scrupulous implementation of the above principles, in accordance with the constitutional processes of the country;

7.2   Establish, where none exist, appropriate institutions where issues such as codes of conduct, citizenship, residency, age requirements for eligible voters and compilation of voters' registers, would be addressed;

7.3   Establish impartial, all-inclusive, competent and accountable national electoral bodies staffed by qualified personnel, as well as competent legal entities including effective constitutional courts to arbitrate in the event of disputes arising from the conduct of elections;

7.4   Safeguard the human and civil liberties of all citizens including the freedom of movement, assembly, association, expression, and campaigning as well as access to the media on the part of all stake-holders, during electoral processes as provided for under 2.1.5 above;

7.5 Take all necessary measures and precautions to prevent the perpetration of fraud, rigging or any other illegal practices throughout the whole electoral process, in order to maintain peace and security;

7.6 Ensure the availability of adequate logistics and resources for carrying out democratic elections;

7.7 Ensure that adequate security is provided to all parties participating in elections;

7.8 Ensure the transparency and integrity of the entire electoral process by facilitating the deployment of representatives of political parties and individual candidates at polling and counting stations and by accrediting national and/other observers/monitors;

7.9 Encourage the participation of women, disabled and youth in all aspects of the electoral process in accordance with the national laws;

7.10 Issue invitation by the relevant Electoral Institutions of the country in election to SADC 90 (ninety) days before the voting day in order to allow an adequate preparation for the deployment of the Electoral Observation Mission;

7.11 Ensure freedom of movement of the members of the SEOM within the host country;

7.12 Accredit the members of the SEOM as election observers on a non-discriminatory basis;

7.13 Allow the members of the SEOM to communicate freely with all competing political parties, candidates, other political associations and organisations, and civil society organizations;

7.14 Allow the members of the SEOM to communicate freely with voters except when the electoral law reasonably proscribes such communication in order to protect the secrecy of the vote;

7.15 Allow the members of the SEOM unhindered access to and free communication with the media;

7.16 Allow the members of the SEOM to communicate with and have unimpeded access to the National Election Commission or appropriate electoral authority and all other election administrators;

7.17 Allow the members of the SEOM free access to all legislation and regulations governing the electoral process and environment;

7.18 Allow the members of the SEOM free access to all electoral registers or voters' list;

7.19 Ensure that the members of the SEOM have unimpeded and unrestricted access to all polling stations and counting centres.

. . .

5

REGION-BUILDING IN EURASIA

COMMONWEALTH OF INDEPENDENT STATES (CIS)

The Commonwealth of Independent States (CIS) was created on 21 December 1991. Its official founding document, the Alma-Ata Declaration, signed by Russia, Ukraine, and Belarus, stated that the Soviet Union had disappeared as subject of international law and geopolitical reality. The CIS was thereupon enlarged, with not only Turkmenistan, Uzbekistan, Tajikistan, Kazakhstan, and Kyrgyzstan, but also Moldova, Armenia, and Azerbaijan joining. The CIS committed itself to compliance with responsibilities stemming from international treaties signed by the Soviet Union and the common control of nuclear weapons. It stated its support for human rights, the protection of national minorities, and respect for the territorial integrity of its member states. Georgia joined the CIS in 1993.

The Commonwealth of Independent States (CIS) does not carry any supranational competencies. Accordingly, it is fundamentally different from the European Union. On the other hand, it is rooted in the long common history of former Soviet republics with their specific form of state-controlled industrialization and an integrated market. This market has broken down as a consequence of the demise of the Soviet Union and its economic imperatives. Yet traditional mentality prevails in a post-Soviet transformation that began in 1991 and had not ended by the time the CIS celebrated its tenth anniversary in Moscow in November 2001.

The founding Charter of the Commonwealth of Independent States of 22 January 1993 declared sovereign equality among its member states and recognized each of them as a sovereign member of the international state system. With the signing of the CIS Treaty on the Formation of an Economic Union in September 1993, the CIS embarked on the path of stronger integration, as if by then the European Union was perceived as a distant model. The Treaty on the Formation of an Economic Union is based on the goal of transforming the interaction of economic relations among CIS member states. It states the principles of free movement of goods, capital, services, and workers, thus recalling the original goals of a single market under the provisions of the European Economic Community. It elaborates concerted money and credit policies as well as tax, customs, and foreign economic policies. It outlines mechanisms that favor direct production links among CIS countries and a harmonization of the methods of management of economic affairs. The CIS has addressed issues as diverse as transport corridors in its vast territory and common health protection methods. The proliferation of drugs originating in Afghanistan, for example, has been a concern for the CIS.

In 2003, a single budget of the CIS was adopted for the first time. The goal of a free trade zone was promulgated but never implemented. More than anything else, the CIS has remained an instrument of managing the post-Soviet decline. Even official documents stated that some member states were falling behind in the early implementation of measures agreed upon by all CIS member states. The 2003 Agreement on the Creation of a Common Economic Space, aimed at enforcing the Treaty on the Formation of an Economic Union, was signed only by Belarus, Russia, Kazakhstan, and Ukraine. In 2005, Turkmenistan reduced its status to that of an associate member of the CIS. In 2006, Georgia left the CIS Council of Defense Ministers.

The main interest of Russia was the potential of the Commonwealth of Independent States as a foreign policy instrument. The CIS Treaty on Collective Security of May 1992 laid the ground for the projection of Russia's ambition as the dominant leader in the grouping. The Agreement on Collective Peacekeeping Forces and Joint Measures on their Material and Technical Supply of September 1993 reinforced Russia's intention but also provoked counterreactions among other CIS member states. Notwithstanding the role of Russia, the need for more efficient foreign policy measures became a perennial issue for the CIS. The conduct of joint anti-terrorist actions in all CIS countries echoed not only the change in the global arena since the terrorist attacks of 11 September 2001 in the US, but also the ongoing bitter conflicts in the Northern Caucasus region. The existence of a CIS Commission on Human Rights has not helped change the direction these conflicts have taken so far. CIS peacekeeping was developed early on, and CIS peacekeeping missions had their first experiences in Tajikistan and Abkhazia.

CIS structures remain intergovernmental well into the second decade of their existence. The Council of Heads of State, the Council of Heads of Government, including various ministerial councils, the Inter-Parliamentary Assembly, a Council of Joint Border Troop Commanders, and the Secretariat of the CIS are the most important bodies. The Secretariat of the Commonwealth of Independent States is based in Minsk, the capital of Belarus. Although its functions were widened over time, like all CIS organs it lacks cohesive orders of competencies. Most important, however, is the uncertainty about the very concept on which CIS is based. While some countries still consider the CIS a mild "divorce" from Russia and a means to protect their fragile sovereignty, Russia considers the CIS an instrument to project its ambitions of power throughout the post-Soviet sphere. The three Baltic republics Estonia, Latvia, and Lithuania—the only former Soviet republics with a definitely new geopolitical orientation—joined both the European Union and NATO in 2004. The future of the other twelve former Soviet republics remains as unsettled as the CIS itself.

The CIS has tried to encourage the development of a common economic sphere in Eurasia, but it has not contributed to the stabilization of processes heading toward rule of law and democratic governance in the post-Soviet environment. Democracy remains a promise more than a reality. Foremost, the CIS member states have not concluded the ultimate goal of their endeavor. This shortcoming is related to the ongoing search for a new identity in post-Soviet Eurasia. While concepts of "Eurasianism" have rekindled since the end of the Soviet Union, several of the new states—most notably Ukraine, Russia, Georgia, and to a lesser degree Belarus, Moldova, and Armenia—have favored a closer relationship with Europe, including the possibility of EU membership. All in all, for the first one and half decades of its existence, the CIS has remained weak and rather lacking in authority. Unable to transform itself into the nucleus of a new and positive frame for regional integration, it remains an organism for managing disintegration. The peaceful disintegration of the former Soviet Union represents its biggest success so far as a scheme to move from enforced integration to sovereign statehood across Eurasia. Some hopeful optimists saw this as the beginning of a new and voluntary integration, but for the time being this remains illusionary. While interstate borders among CIS member states did not become impermeable, new visa regimes were established between CIS member states, making freedom of movement more difficult than it was during the time of the Soviet Union.

The Alma-Ata Declaration (21.12.1991)

. . .

The Declaration

Cooperation between members of the Commonwealth will be carried out in accordance with the principle of equality through coordinating institutions formed on the basis of parity and operating in the way established by the agreements between members of the Commonwealth, which is neither a state nor a supra-state structure.

In order to ensure international strategic stability and security, allied command of the military-strategic forces and unified control over nuclear weapons will be preserved, and the sides will respect one another's desire to attain the Status of a non-nuclear and (or) neutral state.

The Commonwealth of Independent States is open, with the agreement of all its participants, to states-members of the former USSR, as well as other states that share the goals and principles of the Commonwealth.

The allegiance to cooperation in the formation and development of the common economic space, and all-European and Eurasian markets, is being confirmed.

With the formation of the Commonwealth of Independent States the USSR ceases to exist. Member states of the Commonwealth guarantee, in accordance with their constitutional procedures, the fulfilment of international obligations, stemming from the treaties and agreements of the former USSR.

Member states of the Commonwealth pledge to observe strictly the principles of this declaration.

Decision of the Heads of State of the Commonwealth of Independent States

The member states of the Commonwealth, citing Article 12 of the agreement on the Creation of a Commonwealth of Independent States,

Proceeding from the intention of each state to fulfil the obligations set down by the UN Charter and to participate in that organization's work as full-fledged members,

In view of the fact that the Republic of Belarus, the USSR and Ukraine were original members of the United Nations,

Expressing satisfaction with the fact that the Republic of Belarus and Ukraine are continuing to participate in the United Nations as sovereign independent states,

Firmly resolved to promote the strengthening of international peace and security on the basis of the UN Charter and in the interests of their peoples and the entire international community,

Have declared that:

1. The states of the Commonwealth support Russia in its continuation of the USSR's membership in the United Nations, including the USSR's membership in the Security Council and other international organizations.
2. The Republic of Belarus, the Russian FSR and Ukraine will support the other states of the Commonwealth in resolving the question of their full-fledged membership in the United Nations and other international organizations.

   . . .

CIS Treaty on Collective Security (15.05.1992)

. . .

Article 1

The participating states confirm their commitment to refrain from the use or threat of force in Interstate relations. They pledge to resolve all disagreements among themselves and with other states by peaceful means.

The participating states will not enter into military alliances or participate in any groupings of states, nor in actions directed against another participating state.

In the event of the creation of a System of collective security in Europe and Asia and the conclusion of treaties on collective security to the end, for which the contracting parties will strive unswervingly, the participating states will enter into immediate consultations with each other for the purpose of incorporating the necessary intentions in the present treaty.

Article 2

The participating states will consult with each other on all important questions of international security affecting their interests and will coordinate their positions on these questions.

In the event of a threat to the security, territorial integrity, and sovereignty of one or several participating states or of a threat to international peace and security, the participating states will immediately activate the mechanism of joint consultations for the purpose of coordinating their positions and taking measures to eliminate the threat that has emerged.

Article 3

The participating states will form a Collective Security Council consisting of the heads of participating states and the commander-in-chief of the CIS Joint Armed Forces.

Article 4

If one of the participating states is subjected to aggression by any state or groups of states, this will be perceived as aggression against all participating states to this treaty.

In the event of an act of aggression being committed against any of the participating states they will give it the necessary assistance, including military assistance, and will also give support with the means at their disposal by way of exercising the right to collective defense in accordance with Article 51 of the UN Charter.

The participating states will immediately inform the UN Security Council of any measures taken on the basis of this article. When implementing these measures, the participating states will abide by the corresponding provisions of the UN Charter.

Article 5

The Collective Security Council of the participating states and the organs to be created by it undertake the coordination and ensuring of joint activities by the participating states in accordance with this treaty. Until the aforementioned organs have been created, the activities of the armed forces of the participating states will be coordinated by the High Command of the Commonwealth Joint Armed Forces.

Article 6

Any decision to use armed forces for the purpose of repulsing aggression in accordance with Article 3 of the present treaty is adopted by the heads of the participating states.

The use of armed forces outside the territory of the participating states can be effected exclusively in the interests of international security in strict compliance with the UN Charter and the legislation of participating states in the present treaty.

Article 7

The location and functioning of installations in the collective security system on the territory of participating states is regulated by special agreements.

Article 8

The present treaty does not affect any rights and commitments under other bilateral and multilateral treaties and agreements currently in force concluded by the participating states with other states, and it is not directed against third countries.

The present treaty does not affect the participating states' right to individual and collective defense against aggression in accordance with the UN Charter.

The participating states pledge not to conclude international agreements that are incompatible with the present treaty. |

Article 9

Any questions arising between the participating states in connection with the Interpretation or application of any provision of the present treaty will be resolved jointly in the spirit of friendship, mutual respect, and mutual understanding.

Amendments to the present treaty may be incorporated on the initiative of one or several of the participating states and adopted on the basis of mutual agreement.

Article 10

The present treaty is open to all interested states which share its aims and principles.

Article 11

The present treaty is concluded after five years with a subsequent renewal.

Any of the participating states has the right to withdraw from the present treaty if it notifies the other parties of its intention at least six months in advance and fulfills all the commitments resulting from withdrawal from the present treaty.

. . .

CHARTER OF THE COMMONWEALTH OF INDEPENDENT STATES (22.01.1993)

. . .

The states which have voluntarily united within the Commonwealth of Independent States (hereinafter the Commonwealth), basing themselves on the historic community of their peoples and the ties established between them, acting in accordance with the generally recognized principles and norms of international law, the provisions of the UN Charter and the Helsinki Final Act, and other documents of the CSCE,

- seeking to ensure by joint efforts the economic and social progress of their peoples, fully resolved to implement the provisions of the Agreement on the Creation of the Commonwealth of Independent States, the protocol to that Agreement, and the provisions of the Alma-Ata Declaration,

- developing cooperation among themselves to ensure international peace and security and equally for the purpose of maintaining civil peace and interethnic accord,
- desiring to create conditions for the preservation and development of the cultures of all the peoples of the member states,

. . .

Section I—Aims and Principles

Article l

The Commonwealth is founded on the principles of the sovereign equality of all its members. The member states are autonomous and equal subjects of international law.

The Commonwealth promotes the further development and strengthening of the relations of friendship, good neighborliness, interethnic accord, trust, mutual understanding, and mutually advantageous cooperation among the member states.

The Commonwealth is not a state and does not possess supranational powers.

Article 2

The aims of the Commonwealth are:

- cooperation in the political, economic, ecological, humanitarian, cultural, and other spheres;
- the all-around and balanced economic and social development of member states within the framework of the common economic space, and interstate cooperation and Integration;
- the guaranteeing of human rights and basic freedoms in accordance with the generally recognized principles and norms of international law and documents of the CSCE;
- cooperation among member states to ensure international peace and security, the implementation of effective measures to reduce arms and military expenditure, the elimination of nuclear and other types of weapons of mass destruction, and the achievement of general and complete disarmament;
- assistance to citizens of member states in free association, contacts, and movement within the Commonwealth;
- reciprocal legal assistance and cooperation in other spheres of legal relations;
- peaceful solution of disputes and conflicts between Commonwealth states.

Article 3

In order to achieve the Commonwealth's aims member states, proceeding on the basis of the generally recognized norms of international law and the Helsinki Final Act, build their relations in accordance with the following interconnected principles of equal value:

- respect for the sovereignty of member states, for the inalienable right of peoples to self-determination, and for the right to determine their future without external interference;

- inviolability of state borders, recognition of existing borders, and rejection of unlawful territorial acquisitions;
- territorial integrity of states and rejection of any actions aimed at dismembering another state's territory;
- non-use of force or the threat of force against the political independence of a member state;
- resolution of disputes by peaceful means in such a way as to avoid jeopardizing international peace, security, and justice;
- supremacy of international law in interstate relations;
- non-interference in one another's internal and external affairs;
- the guaranteeing of human rights and basic freedoms for all regardless of race, ethnic origin, language, religion, and political or other convictions;
- conscientious discharge of commitments assumed under Commonwealth documents, including this charter;
- consideration of one another's interests and of the interests of the Commonwealth as a whole, provision of assistance in all spheres of their mutual relations on the basis of mutual assent;
- the pooling of efforts and provision of support to one another for the purpose of creating peaceful conditions of life for the peoples of Commonwealth member states, and the ensuring of their political, economic, and social progress;
- development of mutually advantageous economic, scientific, and technical cooperation, and expansion of the processes of integration;
- spiritual unity of their peoples, based upon respect for their identity, and close cooperation in the preservation of cultural values and cultural exchange.

Article 4

The following belong to the spheres of joint activity of member states and are carried out on an equitable basis via common coordinating institutions in accordance with the commitments assumed by member states within the framework of the Commonwealth:

- guaranteeing human rights and basic freedoms;
- coordinating foreign policy activity;
- cooperating in forming and developing a common economic space, the pan-European and Eurasian markets, and customs policy;
- cooperating in developing systems of transport and communications;
- protecting health and the environment;
- questions of social and migration policy;
- struggle against organized crime;
- cooperating in the sphere of defense policy and the protection of external borders;

This list may be extended by the mutual assent of member states.

Article 5

Multilateral and bilateral agreements in various spheres of member states' mutual relations form the fundamental legal basis of interstate relations within the framework of the Commonwealth.

Agreements concluded within the framework of the Commonwealth should correspond to the aims and principles of the Commonwealth and the commitments of member states under this Charter.

Article 6

Member states promote the cooperation and development of ties among state organs, public associations, and economic structures.

Section II—Membership

. . .

Article 9

A member state has the right to secede from the Commonwealth. A member state shall inform the depositary of the Charter of such intention in writing twelve months prior to secession.

The commitments which arise during the period of participation in this Charter are binding upon the relevant states until they are discharged in full.

. . .

Section III—Collective Security and Military-Political Cooperation

Article 11

Member states shall pursue a coordinated policy in the sphere of international security, disarmament, arms control, and the organizational development of the armed forces and shall maintain security in the Commonwealth by, inter alia, groups of military observers and collective peacekeeping forces.

Article 12

In the event of a threat to the sovereignty, security, and territorial integrity of one or several member states or to international peace and security, member states shall immediately activate the mechanism of mutual consultations with the aim of coordinating positions and adopting measures to eliminate the threat, including peacemaking operations and the use, where need be, of Armed Forces in exercise of the right to individual or collective self-defense in accordance with Article 51 of the UN Charter.

The decision on the joint use of the armed forces shall be made by the Council of Heads of State of the Commonwealth or the interested member states of the Commonwealth in line with their national legislation.

Article 13

Each member state shall take appropriate measures to ensure a stable situation along the Commonwealth member states' external borders. On the basis of mutual assent member states shall coordinate the activity of border troops and other competent services which exercise control and bear responsibility for ensuring observance of the prescribed procedure governing the crossing of member states' external borders.

Article 14

The Council of Heads of State is the Commonwealth's supreme organ on questions concerning the defense and protection of member states' external borders. Coordination of the Commonwealth's military-economic activity shall be exercised by the Council of Heads of Government.

Collaboration by member states in the implementation of international agreements and the resolution of other questions in the sphere of security and disarmament shall be organized by joint consultations.

Article 15

Specific questions of member states' military-political cooperation shall be regulated by special agreements.

Section IV—Preventing Conflicts and Resolving Disputes

Article 16

Member states shall take all possible measures to prevent conflicts, primarily along interethnic and interreligious lines, which could entail violation of human rights.

They shall, on the basis of mutual agreement, render assistance to one another in settling such conflicts, including within the framework of international organizations.

Article 17

Commonwealth member states shall refrain from actions which could be detrimental to other member states and result in the exacerbation of potential disputes.

Member states shall conscientiously and in a spirit of cooperation make efforts toward a fair and peaceful resolution of their disputes through talks of the achievement of accord in an appropriate alternative procedure for settling the dispute.

If member states do not resolve the dispute via the means indicated in the second part of this article, they may refer it to the Council of Heads of State.

Article 18

The Council of Heads of State is empowered, at any stage of a dispute whose continuation could threaten the maintenance of peace or security in the Commonwealth, to recommend to the parties an appropriate procedure or method for settling the dispute.

Section V—Cooperation in the Economic, Social, and Legal Spheres

Article 19

Member states shall cooperate in the economic and social spheres along the following avenues:

- forming a common economic space on the basis of market relations and the free movement of goods, Services, capital, and labor;
- coordinating social policy, elaborating joint social programs and measures to ease social tension in connection with the implementation of economic reforms;
- developing systems of transport and communications and energy systems;
- coordinating credit and financial policy;
- promoting the development of member states' trade and economic ties;
- encouraging and mutually protecting investments;
- promoting the standardization and certification of industrial goods and commodities;
- legally protecting intellectual property;
- promoting the development of a common information space;
- implementing joint environmental protection measures, providing mutual assistance in eliminating the consequences of environmental disasters and other emergency situations;

– implementing joint projects and programs in the spheres of science and technology, education, health care, culture, and sports.

Article 20

Member states shall cooperate in the sphere of the law, in particular by concluding multilateral and bilateral treaties on affording legal assistance, and shall promote the alignment of national legislation.

In the event of conflicts between the norms of member states' national legislation regulating relations in spheres of joint activity, member states shall hold consultations and talks for the purpose of elaborating proposals to remove those conflicts.

Section VI—Organs of the Commonwealth

The Council of Heads of State and the Council of Heads of Government

Article 21

The Council of Heads of State is the supreme organ of the Commonwealth.

The Council of Heads of State, in which all member states are represented at top level, shall discuss and resolve fundamental questions connected with member states' activity in the sphere of their common interests.

The Council of Heads of State shall assemble for sessions twice a year. Extraordinary sessions of the council may be convened on the initiative of any one of the member states.

Article 22

The Council of Heads of Government shall coordinate the cooperation of member states' organs of executive power in the economic, social, and other spheres of common interest.

The Council of Heads of Government shall assemble for sessions four times a year. Extraordinary sessions of the council may be convened on the initiative of any one of the member states' governments.

Article 23

Decisions of Council of Heads of State and the Council of Heads of Government shall be made by common assent-consensus. Any state may declare it has no interest in a particular question, which should not be regarded as an obstacle to the adoption of a decision.

The Council of Heads of State and the Council of Heads of Government may hold joint sessions.

The working procedure of the Council of Heads of State and the Council of Heads of Government shall be regulated by the Rules of Procedure,

Article 24

The heads of states and heads of governments shall take the chair at sessions of the Council of Heads of State and Council of Heads of Government by rotation in the Russian alphabetical order of the names of the Commonwealth member states.

Sessions of the Council of Heads of State and Council of Heads of Government shall be held as a rule in the city of Minsk.

Article 25

The Council of Heads of State and the Council of Heads of Government shall create working and auxiliary organs on both a Standing basis and a temporary basis.

These organs shall be formed from representatives of the member states vested with the corresponding powers.

Experts and consultants may be invited to participate in their sessions.

Article 26

Conferences of leaders of the corresponding state organs shall be convened to resolve questions of cooperation in individual spheres and to elaborate recommendations for the Council of Heads of State and the Council of Heads of Government.

The Foreign Ministers Council

Article 27

The Foreign Ministers Council, on the basis of decisions of the Council of Heads of State and the Council of Heads of Government, shall coordinate the foreign policy activity of the member states, including their activity in international organizations, and shall organize consultations on questions of world policy of mutual interest.

The Foreign Ministers Council shall perform its activity in accordance with the Statute approved by the Council of Heads of State.

. . .

The Defense Ministers Council; The Joint Armed Forces High Command

Article 30

The Defense Ministers Council is an organ of the Council of Heads of State on questions of military policy and the military organizational development of the member states.

The Joint Armed Forces High Command exercises leadership of the Joint Armed Forces, as well as of groups of military observers and collective forces maintaining peace in the Commonwealth.

The Defense Ministers Council and the Joint Armed Forces High Command perform their activity on the basis of the relevant Statutes ratified by the Council of Heads of State.

The Council of Commanders of Border Troops

Article 31

The Council of Commanders of Border Troops is an organ of the Council of Heads of State on questions of the protection of the external borders of member states and the provision of a stable situation along them.

The Council of Commanders of Border Troops performs its activity on the basis of the relevant Statute ratified by the Council of Heads of State.

The Economic Court

Article 32

The Economic Court operates for the purpose of ensuring the fulfilment of economic commitments within the framework of the Commonwealth.

The jurisdiction of the Economic Court includes the settlement of disputes arising in the fulfilment of economic commitments. The court may also settle other disputes referred to its jurisdiction by agreements of member states.

The Economic Court is empowered to interpret the provisions of agreements and other Commonwealth acts on economic issues.

The Economic Court performs its activity in accordance with the Agreement on the Status of the Economic Court and the Statute on it ratified by the Council of Heads of State.

The seat of the Economic Court is in the city of Minsk.

Commission on Human Rights

Article 33

The Commission on Human Rights is a consultative organ of the Commonwealth and monitors the fulfilment of commitments on human rights which the member states have assumed within the framework of the Commonwealth.

The commission comprises representatives of Commonwealth member states and operates on the basis of the Statute ratified by the Council of Heads of State.

The seat of the Commission on Human Rights is in the city of Minsk.

Organs of Sectoral Cooperation

Article 34

On the basis of agreements between the member states on cooperation in the economic, social, and other spheres, organs of sectoral cooperation may be established to carry out the elaboration of agreed principles and rules of such cooperation to promote their practical implementation.

The organs of sectoral cooperation (councils, committees) perform the functions envisaged in the present charter and in the provisions on them, ensuring the examination and settlement on a multilateral basis of questions of cooperation in the relevant spheres.

Leaders of the corresponding organs of executive power of the member states are members of the organs of sectoral cooperation.

The organs of sectoral cooperation adopt recommendations within the limits of their competence and, whenever necessary, also submit proposals for consideration by the Council of Heads of Government.

The Working Language of the Commonwealth

Article 35

The working language of the Commonwealth is Russian.

Section VII—Interparliamentary Cooperation

Article 36

The Interparliamentary Assembly holds interparliamentary consultations, discusses questions of cooperation within the framework of the Commonwealth, and elaborates joint proposals in the sphere of the activity of national parliaments.

Article 37

The Interparliamentary Assembly comprises parliamentary delegations.

The organization of the activity of the Interparliamentary Assembly is carried out by the Council of the Assembly, which comprises leaders of the parliamentary delegations.

Procedural questions of the activity of the Interparliamentary Assembly are regulated by its standing orders.

The seat of the Interparliamentary Assembly is the city of St. Petersburg.

Section VIII—Finances

Article 38

Expenditure on financing the activity of the Commonwealth organs is apportioned on the basis of proportional participation by the member states and is set in accordance with special agreements on the budgets of the Commonwealth organs.

The budgets of the Commonwealth organs are ratified by the Council of Heads of State on the basis of proposals by the Council of Heads of Government.

Article 39

Questions of the financial and economic activity of the Commonwealth organs are examined according to the procedure established by the Council of Heads of Government.

Article 40

Member states are autonomously responsible for the expenditure associated with the participation of their representatives, experts, and consultants in the work of Commonwealth Conferences and organs.

. . .

CIS Treaty on the Formation of an Economic Union (24.09.1993)

. . .

- Based on the historic closeness of their peoples and realizing the importance of expansion and intensification of versatile and mutually advantageous economic relations;
- Respecting the sovereignty of every nation and confirming their commitment to the goals and principles expressed in the constituent documents on the formation of the Commonwealth of Independent States;
- In order to create favorable conditions for the dynamic and harmonious development of the economies and for the implementation of economic reforms aimed at the improvement of the living Standards of their peoples;
- - Realizing the objective necessity of forming and developing a single economic space, based on the free movement of goods, Services, labor, and

capital, as well as the necessity to strengthen the direct ties between the economic subjects of the agreeing parties;
– Realizing also the importance of technological interconnections of highly integrated scientific and technical, as well as industrial potentials of the states;
– In order to create favorable conditions for organic integration of their economies into the world economy.

Chapter 1—Goals and Principles of Economic Union

Article 1

The Economic Union shall be established on the basis of voluntary participation, respect for sovereignty and territorial integrity, equal rights and mutual responsibilities among the agreeing parties for the implementation of the principles of this Treaty.

In their activities within the borders of the Economic Union the agreeing parties shall adhere to international legal principles, including:

– non-interference in the internal affairs of others, respect for human rights and liberties;
– peaceful solution of conflicts and non-use of any kind of economic pressure in interstate relations;
– responsibility for assumed commitments;
– elimination of race or of any other kind of discrimination in relation to any legal entities or individuals of the agreeing parties;
– mutual consultations with the purpose of coordinating positions and in order to take appropriate measures in the event of economic encroachment against any of the agreeing parties, on the part of any state or group of states, which are not the participants of this treaty.

Article 2

The goals of the Economic Union are as follows:

– creation of conditions for stable development of the economies of the agreeing parties with the purpose of improving the living Standards of their populations;
– gradual formation of the single economic space on the basis of market relations;
– provision of equal possibilities and guarantees for all economic subjects;
– joint implementation of economic projects, which are of interest to all agreeing parties;

– joint efforts to resolve ecological problems and liquidation of consequences of natural disasters and catastrophes.

Article 3

The Economic Union envisages:

– free movement of goods and Services, capital and labor;
– coordination of monetary, credit, budgetary, taxation, foreign economic, customs, currency, and price policies;
– harmonization of the economic legislation of the agreeing parties;
– availability of a common statistical base.

Article 4

The agreeing parties agree that the Economic Union shall be formed through gradual deepening of Integration and coordination of actions in the process of implementation of economic reforms, through:

– an international (multilateral) free trade association;
– a Single Market of goods and Services, capital and labor;
– a currency (monetary) union.
– Each form of Integration shall be realized through a complex of special interconnected measures, which shall be adopted and implemented in accordance with other agreements and this one.

Chapter 2—Trade and Economic Relations

Article 5

In accordance with Article 4 of this treaty, in order to create an international free trade association, the agreeing parties concurred on the following principles:

– a gradual decrease in and final abolition of customs duties, taxes and collections, quantitative and other restrictions and limitations;
– harmonization of customs legislation and mechanisms of tariff and non-tariff regulations;
– simplification of customs procedures;
– unification of statistical customs forms and documentation;
– gradual equalization of tariffs for cargo and passenger transportation, as well as transit tariffs, preserving the principle of free transit;
– prohibition of non-legitimate re-export to third countries.

Article 6

In the process of establishing a customs union, the agreeing parties agreed to abolish tariff and non-tariff regulation of the movement of goods, services, and labor, as well as to:

- establish common tariffs with states which are not participants in this treaty;
- coordinate foreign trade policies with states which are not participants in this treaty.

Article 7

In the process of making the transition to a Single Market the agreeing parties shall:

- create the necessary legal, economic, and organizational conditions for free movement of capital and labor;
- create conditions for fair competition, including the elaboration of anti-monopoly regulations;
- conduct coordinated policy in the fields of transport and communications, aimed at realizing effective cargo and passenger transportation;
- ensure equal economic conditions for capital investment in the development of the economies, and elaborate effective mechanisms for protection of rights and interests of investors.

Article 8

Trade relations will be based on free market prices, which will be set through the Integration of internal markets of the agreeing parties. The agreeing parties pledge not to use discriminatory price policies toward their economic subjects, regardless of nationality.

Article 9

Agreeing parties shall not conduct without coordination any unilateral activities of a non-economic character with the aim of limiting access to their markets.

Chapter 3—Entrepreneurship and Investments

Article 10

Agreeing parties shall ensure legal national regulation of economic activity by residents on the territories of member states of this Treaty.

Article 11

Agreeing parties shall promote the development of direct economic relations between economic subjects, creating favorable conditions for strengthening productive cooperation.

Article 12

Agreeing parties shall promote the creation of joint ventures, transnational corporations, networks of commercial and financial credit institutions and organizations.

Article 13

Agreeing parties shall coordinate their investment policies, including the attraction of foreign investment and credits in branches of mutual interest, and shall conduct joint capital Investments, including those made on a barter basis.

Chapter 4—Relations in the Sphere of Money, Credits, Finance, and Currencies

Article 14

Agreeing parties shall coordinate their policy in the sphere of money, credits, currency, and financial regulations.

Article 15

In the functioning of interstate free trade, the agreeing parties shall use in their financial relations:

- a multicurrency system, which shall include national currencies functioning in separate states;
- a system based on the Russian Federation ruble.

The transition to a single currency system for mutual payments will be ensured whenever a currency union has been created. This system should be based on a common (reserve) currency, which shall be the most utilized and stable currency.

Article 16

The creation of a monetary and currency system based on national currencies shall be implemented in stages through the creation of a Payments Union based on the following principles:

- mutual recognition of national currencies and recognition of their quoted values;
- the realization of payments in national currencies with the use of multilateral Clearing mechanisms through the Interstate Bank and other payment centers;
- the introduction of a mechanism for coordinating deficits in balance of payments;
- establishing a standard conversion rate for national currencies in current operations;

As the Integration process deepens, the Payments Union shall be transformed into a unified currency System which shall stipulate:

- the use of floating exchange rates and the coordination of limits on their standard fluctuations;
- the introduction of a banking mechanism for controlling exchange fluctuation rates;
- the achievement of full currency conversion between national currencies.

Article 17

The agreeing parties will join a unified ruble zone based on the use as legal tender of the Russian ruble in accordance with the undermentioned:

- until the activity of the Interstate Bank commences as the emissions institute of the states using the ruble as a national currency, the authorities of the central (national) banks which make credit and monetary emissions shall be delegated to the Central Bank of the Russian Federation. Central (national) banks of these states commit themselves to coordinate their credit emission with the Russian Federation Central Bank;
- relations between central (national) banks shall be established through a special interbank treaty;
- limitations on the use of rubles in the interstate payments of states which use the Russian ruble shall be removed;

    . . .

Article 18

The states of the common ruble zone commit themselves to common principles in the implementation of monetary and credits policies:

- on deposits of jointly owned money on their territories in keeping with anticipated price indices;
- on standards governing obligatory reserve demands on commercial banks acting on the territories of the agreeing parties;

- on the maximum volume of credits to be issued to government and local power organs by the commercial banks of the agreeing parties;
- on the level of the discount rate on loans granted by central (national) banks to commercial banks;
- on the rules of payment between economic subjects, and also between commercial banks, including rules of opening an account by a bank and by a non-resident economic subject from a third country;
- on regulation of commercial banking activities;
- on a regular basis provide each other with the balances of central (national) banks and of the banking system as a whole, as well as with other required information.

These states will apply a coordinated ruble exchange rate to hard currency and to the currency of third countries including participants in the Economic Union who use their own currencies.

Article 19

Agreeing parties which enter into the ruble zone will carry out a coordinated budget policy, which stipulates:

- coordinated limitations on the consolidated budget deficit, as compared with the gross national product;
- methods of financing states' budget deficits;
- conditions, kinds, and magnitude of non-budget fund formation;
- limits on increases in the amount of internal debt on the emission base.

The agreeing parties commit themselves to the implementation of coordinated measures aimed at the consecutive decrease of consolidated budget deficits and non-budget funds.

Agreeing parties which exceed the coordinated deficit of their consolidated budgets, should, during a stipulated term, take measures for their normalization.

Article 20

The agreeing parties shall implement a harmonization of their taxation systems. They shall unify basic types of taxes, and the legal regulations which govern the procedures of taxation and taxation rates.

The harmonization of the agreeing parties' taxation systems will be implemented through a special treaty on taxation policy within the framework of the Economic Union, and through a unified methodology of cost accounting.

. . .

AGREEMENT ON COLLECTIVE PEACEMAKING
FORCES AND JOINT MEASURES ON THEIR MATERIAL
AND TECHNICAL SUPPLY (24.09.1993)

. . .

Article 1

For the purposes of the present agreement the term "Collective Peacemaking Forces" (CPF) shall signify:

The military units of the Republic of Kazakhstan, the Kyrgyz Republic, the Russian Federation, the Republic of Tajikistan, the Republic of Uzbekistan, and other member-states of the Commonwealth of Independent States with their armaments, munitions, military technology and property, which have been allocated by member-states to carry out missions geared at stabilizing the situation and maintaining peace and being under United Command (CPFUC).

. . .

Article 2

The member-states allocate to the CPF a coordinated number of forces and means.

Article 3

The member-states bear responsibility for the formation, studies, training, financing, and material and technical supply of the forces and means allocated to the CPF.

Any dearth of material means shall be acquired by the member-states from each other on the basis of treaties and mutual settlements on common price formation principles.

Article 4

Expenses related to the activity and maintenance of the personnel of the United Command of the Collective Peacemaking Forces shall be borne through proportional contributions of the member-states, allocated in keeping with Appendix 2.

Article 5

A member-state, which is the Recipient, shall ensure the reception and deployment of troops (forces) integrated in the CPF and grant the requisite infrastructure to accomplish the missions set to the CPF.

Article 6

Every member-state shall ensure the timely and uninterrupted transportation through its territory of military cargoes delivered by air and surface transport for the material and technical supply of the CPF without import and export licenses, customs duties, taxes, and other fees on the basis of military passes issued by the defense ministries of the member-states.

Article 7

The member-states shall take measures to ensure the security of transit transportation of CPF military cargoes through their territory.

Every member-state shall ensure transit transportation by land or air through its territory of CPF servicemen and also members of their families.

Article 8

To guarantee the activity of the CPF, the member-states shall grant their air space and airdromes, ensure the parking and maintenance of airplanes (helicopters) and attendance of personnel on a gratis basis and refuelling for pay, and refrain from actions disturbing or complicating their normal operation.

Article 9

Issues linked with the organization and conduct of military intelligence in the CPF interests are defined by special agreements between the Russian Federation and other member-states.

Article 10

Member-states shall take the requisite measures to provide material and technical supply of their troops integrated in the CPF with the help of the stocks of armaments, military technology, munitions, and other materiel created and kept at military bases located on the territory of member-states.

Article 11

Member-states shall repair military technology and armaments and replenish the losses of their military units with their own forces on the territory of a member-state, which is a Recipient, and, if necessary, on their territory.

The Recipient shall not prevent the withdrawal of military technology and armaments for repair.

Article 12

Member-states shall resolve all disputes arising during the implementation of this Agreement via mutual consultations and additional agreements.

Article 13

This Agreement is open to any member-state of the Commonwealth of Independent States and also to other states sharing the goals of the given Agreement.

Article 14

The present Agreement shall enter into force for each of the member-states, in accordance with its legislative procedures.

Article 15

The present Agreement shall be effective until adoption of a new resolution on the given issue.

. . .

AGREEMENT ON THE CREATION OF A COMMON ECONOMIC SPACE (CES) (19.09.2003)

. . .

Recognizing the Parties' right to define their participation in the process of the creation of the CES taking into account their readiness for further deepening of integration processes;

. . .

Article 1

For the purpose of creating conditions for a stable and effective development of the Parties' economies and increasing the living standards of their peoples, the Parties start the process of creating the CES.

Under Common Economic Space the Parties understand an economic zone uniting the customs areas of the Parties with functioning mechanisms of economic regulation based on common principles providing free movement of goods, services, capital and labour and with the implementation of a common external trade policy and taxation, fiscal and monetary policy sufficiently coordinated to provide equal competition and to maintain macroeconomic stability.

The Parties intend to promote: the development of trade and investments between the Parties, which will provide sustainable development of their economies based on the generally recognized principles and norms of international law and rules of the WTO; the strengthening of the unity and the development of economic potential and the increased competitiveness of the Parties' economies in external markets.

Article 2

The gradual fulfilment of the tasks of deepening of integration depends on the fulfilment of the Parties' obligations and the actual implementation of the following tasks: creation of the free trade area without exemptions and restrictions, which implies refraining in mutual trade from dumping, compensational and special protectionist measures as the basis of common policy of tariff and non-tariff regulation; common rules on competition, subsidies and other forms of State support; unification of principles of creation and application of technical regulations and standards, sanitary and phytosanitary norms; harmonization of macroeconomic policy; creation of conditions for free movement of goods, services, capital and labour; harmonization of the Parties' legislation to an extent sufficient for the functioning of the CES, including trade and competition policy; formation of common principles of regulation of the activities of natural monopolies (in the sphere of railway transport, main telecommunications, electricity, oil and gas transportation and other spheres), common competition policy and the promotion of non-discriminatory access and equal tariffs for the services of natural monopolies.

Article 3

In accordance with goals and tasks mentioned in Articles 1 and 2 of the Agreement, the Parties take measures envisaged in the Conception of the Creation of the Common Economic Space attached to this Agreement and constituting its inalienable part.

For implementation of this Agreement the Parties will elaborate a Complex of Fundamental Measures on the Creation of Common Economic Space.

Article 4

The coordination of the processes of the creation and functioning of the CES is conducted by the appropriate bodies, the structure of which is determined by the level of integration.

The bodies of the CES are formed on the basis of a combination of intergovernmental elements and the partial transfer of the Parties' powers to a common regulatory body with a gradual increase of the importance of the latter.

Coordination and control of the creation and the functioning of CES on the intergovernmental level is conducted by the Council of Heads of States (CHS).

The votes within the Council are distributed according to the principle 'one country—one vote'. Decisions are made on the basis of consensus.

The Parties establish an integrated regulatory body and on the basis of international agreements delegate their power to it. Decisions of the latter are obligatory for all the Parties.

All decisions of the integrated regulatory body are made by voting. The number of votes each party possesses is determined with regard to its economic potential. Distribution of votes is conducted on the basis of the Parties' agreement.

Each Party can submit a proposal to the Council to change a decision of the integrated regulatory body.

Special agreements will provide for compensation in cases where a decision made causes economic damage to one or more Parties.

Article 5

The CES is being formed gradually, with regard to a possibility of integration at different speeds and levels.

Transit to a subsequent stage is conducted by those Parties who to a full extent fulfil tasks envisaged in the previous stage of the Complex of Fundamental Measures on the Creation of the Common Economic Space.

The Parties accede to international treaties on the creation and the functioning of the CES according to their readiness. In doing so every Party should follow an agreed sequence of acceding to such international treaties. No Party can prevent other Parties from a faster achievement of a higher degree of integration.

Integration at different speeds and levels implies that each Party is free to decide in which aspects of integration or special integration events it would like to engage and to what extent.

Article 6

The legal basis for the creation and the functioning of the CES is constituted by international agreements and decisions by the CES bodies made with regard to the Parties' legislation and in accordance with generally recognized norms and principles of international law.

Article 7

The parties' disagreements over the interpretation or/and implementation of the Provisions of this Agreement will be resolved by means of negotiations and consultations.

Article 8

This Agreement is open to the accession of other countries sharing its goals and principles and on the conditions negotiated by all the Parties of this Agreement.

The Agreement comes into force for an acceding Party from the date of the depositary's obtainment of the final notification from the Parties of their agreement on such an accession.

Article 9

On mutual consent the Parties can introduce changes and modifications into this Agreement in the form of separate protocols, constituting inalienable parts of this Agreement and coming into power according to the order stipulated by Article 10 of this Agreement.

Article 10

This Agreement enters into force from the date of the depositary's obtainment of the final written notification of the fulfilment by the Parties of the domestic procedures needed for this Agreement to enter into force.

Article 11

This Agreement is concluded without delay.

Each Party can withdraw from the Agreement by submitting a written notification to the depositary not later than 12 months before such withdrawal.

. . .

6

REGION-BUILDING IN THE PACIFIC OCEAN

PACIFIC ISLANDS FORUM (PIF)

The Pacific Islands Forum (PIF) was established relatively recently, in 2000. But from 1971 to 1999, a precursor was in effect: the South Pacific Forum. Founded in Wellington on 5–7 August 1971, it remained a structure largely dominated by New Zealand, much as the South Pacific Commission was defined by the strong role of Australia. The South Pacific Forum was by and large a confidence-building measure. It was never institutionalized and had neither legal personality nor a formal voting structure. Decision-making among its members was done by consensus. No issue was taboo, while all matters of common concern were discussed in a semiformal manner. The Cook Islands, Nauru, Fiji, Tonga, and Samoa were founding countries along with Australia and New Zealand, although the latter two were initially only observers, becoming full members in 1972. Australia and New Zealand remained the main sources of funding for the South Pacific Forum, each of them with over a third of the budget, while the islands collectively contributed to less than one third of the budget. The South Pacific Forum never had a founding treaty. Over time, the seven founding members were joined by nine new members, eventually including almost all future members of the Pacific Islands Forum.

The 30th Forum Summit, held in Koror on Palau from 3–5 October 1999, was the occasion for refounding the basis for regional cooperation and eventual integration in the Pacific. The forum was renamed Pacific Islands Forum (PIF). The Agreement Establishing the Pacific Islands Forum Secretariat was signed on 30 October 2000 in Tarawa. It was replaced by a completely new constitutive treaty at the 36th Forum Summit on 27 October 2005 in Papua New Guinea. The Agreement Establishing the Pacific Islands Forum indicates the future objectives: "The purpose of the Forum is to strengthen regional cooperation and integration, including through the pooling of regional resources of governance and the alignment of policies, in order to further Forum members' shared goals of economic growth, sustainable development, good governance and security" (Article II). The ultimate vision is a region "where people can all lead free and worthwhile lives." The Pacific Islands Forum considers itself "an international organization in its own right." It distinguishes between membership, associate membership, and observer status. The PIF consists of the following members: Australia, the Cook Islands, the Federated States of Micronesia, Fiji, Kiribati, the Marshall Islands, Nauru, New Zealand, Niue, Palau, Papua New Guinea, Samoa, the Solomon Islands, Tonga, Tuvalu, Vanuatu.

Alongside the Pacific Islands Forum Secretariat and the annual leaders' Summit, a Forum Officials' Committee was introduced as an Executive Committee. By and large, the Pacific Islands Forum remains a deliberative body that excludes controversial issues and is short of legally binding mechanisms that would help to implement decisions. This is problematic for development goals as well as for security matters. More rooted in the Pacific than ever, New Zealand and Australia play an increasing role in Pacific affairs. An Australian became the PIF's Secretary General in 2004. Australia and New Zealand each continue to provide a third of the budget of the Pacific Islands Forum. In the meantime, the involvement of New Zealand and Australia in the Pacific Islands Forum is undoubtedly constructive. They have become recognized as Pacific countries, while their own attitude toward the Pacific islands region has also changed. The fact that the number of Pacific migrants to New Zealand has increased from 3,600 in 1951 to more than a quarter million today has contributed to this change in outlook in New Zealand. As for Australia, the dilemma of being often perceived as big brother while trying to play the constructive role of a simple partner country prevails.

The Pacific Islands Forum has begun to transform the structures of the former South Pacific Forum into more viable institutions of regional cooperation. When the South Pacific Forum created the South Pacific Organization Coordinating Committee in 1988, it was charged with the task of improving harmonization and collaboration among the economic areas in the region. In 1999, the Pacific Islands Forum changed the clumsy name of the committee to the Council of Regional Organizations in the Pacific (CROP). CROP was identified as the umbrella organization for a wide array of functional institutions of regional cooperation.

The European Union has a genuine interest in the promotion of regional cooperation and integration in the Pacific region. The EU is pursuing this interest with a considerable normative approach, coupled with a broad set of instruments that are not, however, always fully coherent. The European Union might not necessarily serve as a model for the Pacific Islands Forum, yet it must be considered its strongest external advocate and strongest engine. Following four Lomé Conventions with its partners in Africa, the Caribbean, and the Pacific (ACP countries), the European Union concluded the Cotonou Agreement with them in 2000. Between 2002 and 2008, the European Union conducted several region-based negotiations with its Cotonou partner regions in order to conclude Regional Economic Partnership Agreements. The Lomé mechanism of preferential trade agreements was to be replaced by biregional economic partnerships, largely a code word for mutually recognized free trade. The Pacific Island Countries Trade Agreement (PICTA) and the Pacific Agreement on Closer Economic Relations (PACER), both of 2001, were the Pacific countries' preliminary steps in that direction. As for the EU strategy of promoting regional economic partnership with the Pacific island countries, the negotiation approach was incoherent: membership in the Pacific Islands Forum is not identical to membership in the Pacific sub-grouping of the ACP countries (with which the EU was negotiating the specific Pacific Economic Partnership Agreement). In spite of this incoherence in its approach to the region, the EU claims to support close cohesion, deeper cooperation, and eventual integration also in Oceania. The Pacific Islands Forum, meanwhile, will continue to follow its own pace and agenda toward these very goals. The Pacific Plan presented by the Pacific Islands Forum in 2005 echoes this perspective.

AGREEMENT ESTABLISHING THE PACIFIC ISLANDS FORUM SECRETARIAT (30.10.2000)

. . .

Desiring also that consideration should be given to the possibility of establishing a free trade area for the Pacific region,

Noting that the collection and dissemination of information and the preparation of reports and studies will be essential to facilitate these ends,

Concerned to ensure coordination of studies relating to transport services within the region,

. . .

Article I
The Pacific Islands Forum

1. For the purposes of this Agreement, the Pacific Islands Forum (hereinafter called "the Forum") comprises the Heads of Government of Australia, the Cook Islands, Fiji, Nauru, New Zealand, Samoa and Tonga being founding members of the Forum together with the Heads of Government of the Federated States of Micronesia, Kiribati, Niue, Palau, Papua New Guinea, the Republic of the Marshall Islands, Solomon Islands, Tuvalu and Vanuatu and such other Heads of Government as

may be admitted to the Forum membership with the approval of the Forum.

2. It is duly noted that the name of the Forum is hereby changed from that at its inception as the South Pacific Forum and is henceforth called the Pacific Islands Forum.

Article II
Establishment of the Pacific Islands Forum Secretariat

1. There is hereby established the Pacific Islands Forum Secretariat (hereinafter called "the Secretariat").

2. The Secretariat shall be located in Suva and shall operate in accordance with the provisions of this Agreement.

Article III
Purpose

The purpose of the Secretariat is to facilitate, develop and maintain cooperation and consultation between member governments on economic development, trade, transport, tourism, energy, telecommunications, legal, political, security and such other matters as the Forum may direct.

. . .

Article V
Pacific Islands Forum Officials Committee

1. The Secretariat shall have an Executive Committee to be known as the Pacific Islands Forum Officials Committee (hereinafter called 'the Committee').

2. The Committee shall be composed of one representative of each of the members of the Secretariat.

3. The powers and functions of the Committee shall be to give general policy directions to the Secretary General and to make reports and recommendations to the Forum. In particular the Committee shall:

   (a) approve, reject or amend the annual budget estimates and any interim budget submitted by the Secretary General;

   (b) receive, examine and comment on the Annual Report of the Secretary General on the operation of the Secretariat; and

   (c) lay down staff establishment, salary policy and scales.

4. The Committee shall appoint a Chairman at its first and subsequent annual meetings who shall remain in office until the next annual meeting.

5. The Chairmanship shall rotate annually as decided by the Committee.
6. The Committee shall hold a meeting at least once in each calendar year and shall meet prior to meetings of the Forum.
7. The Secretary General, in consultation with and at the request of the Chairman, shall convene meetings of the Committee.
8. All matters shall be decided wherever possible by consensus or if necessary by a majority of the representatives present and voting. Each representative on the Committee shall have one vote.
9. The Committee shall establish its own rules of procedure.

   . . .

Article VIII

1. The Secretary General shall act as Secretary to the Forum. He shall also act as Secretary to the Committee and such other councils, committees or working groups that may be established by the Forum or the Committee.
2. The Secretary General shall also perform such other functions and duties directed to him by the Forum, the Committee or such other bodies referred to in paragraph 1 of this Article.
3. The Secretary General shall be responsible for the management of the Secretariat.

Article IX
Functions of the Secretariat Staff

1. The functions of the Secretariat shall be carried out by the Staff.
2. Subject to the direction of the Committee, the Staff may:

   (a) prepare studies in order to identify and promote opportunities for a modification of present trade patterns in the Pacific region, and between the region and other countries, having in mind the objectives of regional trade expansion;

   (b) prepare studies as required on political, security and legal issues affecting the Forum or member governments;

   (c) carry out necessary investigations in connection with development of free trade among the Forum Island Countries (hereinafter called "FICs");

   (d) prepare studies of the development plans and policies of member governments in an effort to promote cooperation in the region; and investigate the scope for regional development planning aimed among other things at a rationalisation of manufacturing and processing industries and the achievement of economies of scale in certain regional enterprises;

(e) establish an advisory service on sources of technical assistance, aid and investment finance, both official and private, that is available to member governments;

(f) undertake studies of regional transport, as necessary, and help coordinate action, both government and private, in this sector;

(g) advise and assist member governments with the operation of regional trade and tourist promotion services;

(h) provide a means of regular and rapid consultation among FICs on the region's import requirements to enable the bulk ordering of essential imports by official agencies;

(i) act as a clearing house for information on trade, production and economic development in the region and in areas outside the region which are of interest to member governments;

(j) carry out research and statistical studies on production and trade on a continuing basis as requested by the Committee;

(k) prepare reports, studies and working papers;

(l) establish means for the collection, dissemination and exchange of information and statistics;

(m) cooperate with member governments in research projects and the obtaining and collating of statistics and other information;

(n) cooperate and coordinate its work with that of other international and regional organisations; and

(o) undertake such other activities as the Committee may from time to time consider necessary for the attainment of the Secretariat's purpose.

3. The Staff shall provide secretarial support services to the Forum, the Committee and other councils, committees or working groups established by the Forum or the Committee.

Article X
Budget

1. The annual budget of the Secretariat shall be prepared by the Secretary General for the approval or otherwise by the Committee.

2. The costs of operating the Secretariat shall be borne by the member governments in the shares set out in the Annex to this Agreement, subject to review from time to time by the Forum.

3. In advance of the Committee's approval of the budget, the Secretary General shall be entitled to incur expenditure up to a limit not exceeding two-thirds of the previous year's approved budgetary expenditure.

. . .

PACIFIC ISLAND COUNTRIES
TRADE AGREEMENT (PICTA) (18.08.2001)

. . .

Mindful of the close historical, political, economic, geographic and cultural links that bind them;

Desiring to foster and strengthen trade in the Pacific region;

. . .

Article 2

Objectives

The objectives of the Parties in concluding this Agreement are to:

(a) strengthen, expand and diversify trade between the Parties;
(b) promote and facilitate this expansion and diversification through the elimination of tariff and non-tariff barriers to trade between the Parties in a gradual and progressive manner, under an agreed timetable, and with a minimum of disruption;
(c) develop trade between the Parties under conditions of fair competition;
(d) promote and facilitate commercial, industrial, agricultural and technical cooperation between the Parties;
(e) further the development and use of the resources of the Pacific region with a view to the eventual creation of a single regional market among the Pacific Island economies in accordance with the respective social and economic objectives of the Parties, including the advancement of indigenous peoples; and
(f) contribute to the harmonious development and expansion of world trade in goods and Services and to the progressive removal of barriers to it.

Part II—Trade in Goods

Article 3
Free Trade Area

1. The Parties shall gradually establish a free trade area in accordance with the provisions of this Agreement, with the understanding that Least Developed Countries and Small Island States may be integrated in accordance with different structures and by different time frames than other Parties. The Area shall consist of the territories of the Parties to this Agreement.

2. The Parties may agree to extend the Area to include any other State, Territory or Self-Governing Entity, subject to terms consistent with this Agreement which shall be negotiated between the Parties and the other State, Territory or Self-Governing Entity.

. . .

Article 5
Rules of Origin

1. Goods shall be treated as originating in a Party if they comply with the Rules of Origin set out in Annex I of this Agreement, hereinafter "the Rules."
2. Each Party shall establish a mechanism to provide on request a binding ruling on the originating Status of goods to be imported, available at least six months in advance of shipment of such goods, and valid for a period of at least six months after the arrival of the first shipment.
3. The Parties shall establish a Rules of Origin Committee which shall consist of representatives, whether from the public or private sector, from five Parties, including at least one representative from a Least Developed Country or Small Island State. The Committee members:

   (a) shall initially be the representatives appointed by each of the first five Parties to ratify this Agreement that are willing to provide such a representative, and shall meet within 60 days of the entry into force of this Agreement;
   (b) shall thereafter be the representatives of the five Parties which have been decided by the consensus agreement of the Parties bi-annually; and
   (c) may serve more than one term.

4. The Committee may act with a quorum of three, and where appropriate employ the Services of expert advisers.
5. The Forum Secretariat shall provide secretariat Services to the Committee.
6. The functions of the Rules of Origin Committee shall be to:

   (a) regularly review the implementation of the Rules to ensure that they are applied effectively, uniformly and in accordance with this Agreement, and report its findings and make appropriate recommendations to the Parties;
   (b) regularly review the Rules to ensure that:

      (i) they are fully supportive of the objectives of this Agreement; and
      (ii) if appropriate, they conform to the guidelines produced by bodies such as the World Customs Organisation and the World Trade Organisation; and report its findings and recommend any desirable amendments to the Parties;

(c) in consultation with the Parties, make recommendations on the adoption of standardised operating and documentation procedures;

(d) provide technical and investigative assistance to the Parties in respect of the interpretation, implementation and Operation of the Rules;

(e) receive from the parties requests for derogation, and approve as appropriate those requests in accordance with Paragraph 7;

(f) provide, as appropriate, training to Parties on the application and Operation of the Rules;

(g) provide, if requested by the Parties, assistance, consultation or mediation to assist in the resolution of disputes arising from, or related to the Rules;

(h) provide binding rulings on disputes related to the Rules or derogation from them, if requested by the relevant Parties;

(i) notify the Parties of any disputes between the Parties and the results of any consultation, mediation or rulings, pursuant to subparagraphs (g) and (h);

(j) develop guidelines and procedures, consistent with international best practices, to be used in determining 'substantial transformation' for the purposes of Paragraph 7 (c) (i), and notify these guidelines and procedures and any subsequent changes to the Parties, which may make amendments as appropriate;

(k) ensure that the Committee's Operation is functional, transparent and within the resources of the Parties;

(l) establish operating procedures for carrying out its functions, including by means of remote Communications where desirable, and notify these procedures and any subsequent changes to the Parties, which may make amendments as appropriate; and

(m) when making recommendations for future cooperation, have regard to the resource and capacity constraints of the Parties, in particular the Small Island States and Least Developed Countries.

7. Where origin cannot be achieved under the normal criteria, the Rules of Origin Committee may permit the Rules to be derogated from where their Operation in specific cases is considered unduly restrictive of trade. Derogation from the Rules shall be permitted where it has been established on the basis of objective evidence that the derogation sought:

(a) will not have significant adverse effects, including arbitrary or unjustifiable discrimination on any Parties; and

(b) relates to goods which are not ordinarily produced or obtained in any Party affected by the derogation; and

(c) relates to goods which,

    (i) have undergone substantial transformation in the territory of the exporting Party; or

    (ii) are temporarily unable to qualify as originating goods due to exceptional circumstances.

     . . .

Article 7
Tariffs

1. Each Party shall notify the other Parties of that Party's most-favoured nation tariff rate on all goods in effect on the date of entry into force of this Agreement. The notified tariffs shall be the base tariffs.

2. Originating goods which were free of tariffs on the date of entry into force of this Agreement, or which subsequently become free of tariffs pursuant to the obligations imposed by this Agreement on each Party, shall remain free of tariffs.

3. Tariffs on originating goods shall not be increased above the levels permitted by this Agreement.

     . . .

Article 9
Trade Distorting Measures

1. All import or export prohibitions or restrictions on trade in originating goods, other than tariffs, customs duties and taxes, whether effected through quotas, import or export licences or other similar measures, shall be eliminated upon the entry into force of this Agreement. No new such measures shall be introduced.

2. No Party shall seek, take or maintain any voluntary export restraints, orderly marketing arrangements or any other similar measures on any trade in originating goods.

3. Originating goods imported into the territory of any Party shall not be subject, either directly or indirectly, to internal taxes or other internal charges of any kind in excess of those applied, directly or indirectly, to like domestic products.

4. Originating goods imported into the territory of any Party shall be accorded treatment no less favourable than that accorded to like domestic products in respect of all laws, regulations and requirements affecting their internal sale, offering for sale, purchase, transportation, distribution or use.

5. Notwithstanding Paragraphs 1 and 2, where any measures prohibited by Paragraphs 1 and 2 restricting Imports into any Party are identified,

that Party may within six months from the day on which this Agreement comes into force convert such measures into the equivalent tariffs. Where any Party converts import restrictions into tariffs pursuant to this Paragraph that Party shall immediately notify the other Parties of the import restriction, the equivalent tariff, and the method by which the equivalent tariff was calculated. Such tariffs shall be reduced and eliminated in accordance with the timetables set out in Annex II to this Agreement. The time periods within which such tariffs shall be reduced and eliminated shall be calculated on the basis of the dates provided in Annex II to this Agreement.

6.   If any Party considers that another Party has failed to carry out its obligations under Paragraphs 1 to 5 and that failure has nullified or impaired any benefit accruing directly or indirectly to the first Party that Party may initiate consultations under Article 21.

7.   The provisions of this Article shall not prevent the payment of subsidies not prohibited . . . under Article 12.

8.   The provisions of this Article shall not apply to measures pertaining to government procurement, which shall be subject exclusively to the provisions of Article 15.

9.   The Parties shall periodically review the implementation of this Article in accordance with Article 23, with a view to ensuring that all trade distorting measures in the Area have been eliminated.

. . .

Article 12
Dumped or Subsidised Imports

1.   Where a Party has conducted an investigation under Article 10 and has determined that goods being imported into it from another Party, or other Parties, are being dumped, as defined in Article VI of the General Agreement on Tariffs and Trade and the World Trade Organization Agreement on Implementation of Article VI, so as to cause or threaten to cause serious injury to a domestic industry producing like or directly competitive goods or to materially retard the establishment of a domestic industry to produce like or directly competitive goods, it shall enter into consultations with the other Party or Parties, in accordance with Article 21, with a view to agreeing on measures to reduce or prevent injury or retardation which are consistent with the objectives of this Agreement.

2.   Where a Party has conducted an investigation under Article 10 and has determined that goods being imported into it from another Party, or other Parties, are subsidised by the Party or Parties so as to cause or

threaten to cause serious injury to a domestic industry producing like or directly competitive goods or to materially retard the establishment of a domestic industry to produce like or directly competitive goods, it shall enter into consultations with the other Party or Parties, in accordance with Article 21, with a view to agreeing on measures to reduce or prevent injury or retardation which are consistent with the objectives of this Agreement.

3.   Where a mutually acceptable solution to the problem is not achieved within 60 days of the commencement of consultations under Paragraph 1 or 2, the first Party shall give notice to the other Party, or Parties, of its intention to levy anti-dumping or countervailing duties on the goods.

4.   No agreed solution shall be inconsistent with the provisions of Paragraph 2 of Article 9.

5.   If further consultations between the Parties fail to resolve the issue, the first Party may, pursuant to Paragraph 10 of Article 10, no earlier than 60 days after notice was given to the other Party or Parties, levy anti-dumping or countervailing duties on the dumped or subsidised products. Such duties shall not exceed the rate of dumping or subsidisation.

6.   Duties levied pursuant to Paragraph 5 shall be reviewed by the Party imposing the duties, after one year, and annually thereafter, to determine whether the conditions necessary for the imposition of anti-dumping or countervailing duties under this Article, still apply. If the review determines that dumping or subsidisation has ceased, the duties shall be immediately eliminated. If the review determines otherwise the duties may continue to be applied, but shall not exceed the rate of dumping or subsidisation found to exist at the time of the review.

7.   The Parties agree to eliminate any subsidies that cause or threaten to cause serious injury to a domestic industry producing like or directly competitive goods, or to materially retard the establishment of a domestic industry to produce like or directly competitive goods, in another Party. Such Parties shall enter into consultations, in accordance with Article 21, with a view to agreeing on measures to reduce or prevent injury or retardation which are consistent with the objectives of this Agreement.

Article 13
Balance of Payments

1.   Where a Party has conducted an investigation under Article 10 and has determined that:

   (a) there is a serious decline or an imminent threat of serious decline in its monetary reserves; or

      (b) in the case of a Party with very low monetary reserves, its monetary reserves have failed to achieve a reasonable rate of increase; that Party may impose or increase tariffs for the minimum period necessary and to the minimum extent necessary to arrest or prevent the serious decline in reserves or to enable reserves to increase at a reasonable rate.

2.   Parties applying restrictions under this Article may determine the incidence of the restrictions on imports of different products or classes of products in such a way as to give priority to the importation of those products which are more essential.

3.   In applying restrictions under this Article, Parties shall:
      (a) avoid unnecessary damage to the commercial or economic interests of any other Party;
      (b) not prevent unreasonably the importing of any goods in minimum commercial quantities, the exclusion of which would impair regular channels of trade; and
      (c) not prevent the importing of commercial samples or prevent compliance with patent, trade mark, Copyright, or similar procedures.

4.   If there is a persistent and widespread application of restrictions under this Article, indicating the existence of a general disequilibrium which is restricting international trade, the Parties shall review the Agreement to consider whether other measures might be taken to remove the underlying causes of the disequilibrium.

Article 14
Protection of Developing Industries

1.   Notwithstanding Article 7, where a Party has determined that a product is being imported into its territory from another Party in such quantities and under such conditions as to materially retard the establishment of a domestic industry in like or directly competitive products in the first Party, the first Party may raise tariffs where permitted by Paragraph 2. Before raising tariffs, that Party shall notify the other Parties of its Intention to do so, in accordance with Article 20.

2.   No Party shall raise tariffs under this Article unless it can demonstrate, on the basis of objective evidence, the existence of the causal link between imports of the good concerned and the material retardation of the establishment of the domestic industry. Tariffs shall not be raised further than necessary to prevent the material retardation caused by the imports.

3.   Subject to Paragraph 4, the initial period of action taken under this Article shall not exceed five years, or ten years in the case of measures

taken by Small Island States or Least Developed Countries. This period shall not be extended unless the domestic industry has been established and there is evidence that the action continues to be necessary in order for it to adjust to competition. The total period of action taken under this Article shall not exceed ten years, or fifteen years in the case of measures taken by Small Island States or Least Developed Countries.

4. Where the expected duration of action taken under this Article is over one year, the Party taking the action shall review the necessity of such action every two years and promptly notify all Parties of the results of this review.

5. No tariffs shall be raised under this Article before the developing domestic industry has commenced production.

6. The Parties shall, in accordance with Article 23, periodically review the Operation of this Article and the time limits provided therein, with a view to preventing unjustifiable restrictions on trade between the Parties and ensuring that the objectives of this Agreement on fair competition in trade between the Parties are being achieved.

Part III—Government Procurement

Article 15
Principles Governing Government Procurement

1. The Parties are committed to the objective of liberalising government procurement within the Area as soon as possible.

2. In order to achieve this objective, the Parties agree:

    (a) to identify existing measures and practices which prohibit or restrict the achievement of the objective set out in Paragraph 1;

    (b) to adopt transparent measures and practices in respect of contract valuations, technical specifications, qualification and performance requirements, tendering procedures, and invitation, selection and challenge processes;

    (c) that each Party shall, as soon as possible, take appropriate measures needed to minimise and remove the measures and practices identified in Paragraph 2(a);

    (d) within two years of the entry into force of this Agreement, to conclude arrangements for detailed rules on government procurement. Those rules shall be included as a protocol to this Agreement;

    (e) in accordance with Article 23, to periodically review progress made in liberalising government procurement and shall endeavour to resolve any problems arising in respect of the implementation of this Article.

Part IV—General Provisions

Article 16
Exceptions

1. Provided that such measures are not used as a means of arbitrary or unjustifiable discrimination between the Parties, or as a disguised restriction on trade between the Parties, nothing in this Agreement shall prevent the adoption or enforcement by a Party of measures:

   (a) necessary to protect public morals;
   (b) necessary to protect human, animal or plant life or health;
   (c) relating to trade in gold or silver;
   (d) necessary to secure compliance with laws and regulations which are not inconsistent with the provisions of this Agreement;
   (e) necessary to secure compliance with laws and regulations which are not inconsistent with the provisions of this Agreement relating to the protection of patents, trade marks and Copyrights, and the prevention of deceptive practices;
   (f) necessary for the prevention of disorder or crime;
   (g) relating to products of prison labour;
   (h) imposed for the protection of national treasures of artistic, historical, anthropological, palaeontological, archaeological or other cultural or scientific value;
   (i) necessary to reserve for approved purposes the use of Royal Arms or national, state, provincial and territorial arms, flags, crests and seals;
   (j) necessary to protect its indigenous flora and fauna;
   (k) undertaken in pursuance of its rights and obligations under a multilateral international commodity agreement or arrangement;
   (l) necessary to prevent or relieve shortages of foodstuffs or other essential goods; or
   (m) relating to the conservation of exhaustible natural resources if such measures are made effective in conjunction with restrictions on domestic production or consumption.

2. Nothing in this Agreement shall prevent the adoption and enforcement by a Party of measures:

   (a) necessary to protect its essential security interests or implement its international obligations or national policies:

       (i) relating to the non-proliferation of biological and chemical weapons, nuclear weapons or other nuclear explosive devices;
       (ii) relating to the traffic in arms, ammunition and implements of war, and to such traffic in other goods, materials and Services

       as is carried on directly or indirectly for the purpose of supply-
       ing a military establishment; or

     (iii) in time of war or other serious international tension.

  (b) to prevent any Party from taking any action in pursuance of its ob-
      ligations under the United Nations Charter for the maintenance of
      peace and security.

Article 17
Transparency

1. Each Party shall publish promptly and, except in emergency situations, at the latest by the time of their entry into force, all measures, including judicial decisions and administrative rulings, of general application which pertain to or affect the Operation of this Agreement.

2. Each Party shall endeavour to provide as much opportunity as possible for interested parties and persons to comment on proposed measures that may affect trade or government procurement.

3. Nothing in Paragraphs 1 and 2 shall be interpreted as requiring a Party to disclose confidential information contrary to its national security or the public interest, or to prejudice legitimate commercial interests.

4. Each Party shall administer in a uniform, impartial and reasonable manner all measures of general application pertaining to trade and government procurement.

Article 18
Measures to Facilitate Trade

1. The Parties shall endeavour to implement measures which will facilitate trade within the Area and, where appropriate, shall encourage government bodies and other organisations and institutions to work towards the implementation of such measures.

2. The Parties shall examine the scope for taking action to facilitate trade within the Area by harmonising their laws, regulations and administrative practices.

3. Where possible, trade facilitation initiatives shall be coordinated with wider regional and international initiatives.

4. Where a Party believes harmonisation of measures, or their implementation, will facilitate trade or reduce or eliminate distortions of trade, it may notify any other Party of its wish to enter into consultations. The Party so requested shall enter into consultations in good faith, and as soon as possible, with a view to seeking a mutually satisfactory solution.

Article 19
Evolving Relationship

1. Where a Party considers it is desirable to extend the matters covered by this Agreement, or extend the territorial scope of this Agreement, or otherwise develop or deepen the relationship established by this Agreement, it may notify the other Parties of its wish to enter into consultations with a view to negotiating the terms and conditions of the extension.

2. The Parties undertake to periodically review the Status of the relationship established by this Agreement, in accordance with Article 23.

Article 20
Notification

1. Each Party shall give the other Parties notice of any proposed or actual measure which might materially affect trade or government procurement in the Area.

2. The notice referred to in Paragraph 1 shall be given as soon as possible, but in any event not later than 15 days after implementing the measure or taking the action.

3. Each Party shall, on another Party's request, promptly provide information and respond to questions pertaining to any actual or proposed measure or action which might materially affect trade or government procurement in the Area.

4. The provisions of Paragraphs 1, 2 and 3 are to be interpreted as widely as possible consistent with not requiring a Party to disclose confidential information contrary to its national security or the public interest, or to prejudice legitimate commercial interests.

5. Any notice given in terms of this Agreement shall be in writing and shall be effective from the date on which it is received.

6. Where this Agreement requires a Party to notify the other Parties it shall be sufficient for that Party to notify the Forum Secretariat. The Forum Secretariat shall immediately disseminate the notice to all other Parties. Notifications which are made directly to other Parties shall also be made to the Forum Secretariat.

Article 21
Consultations

1. If a Party considers that:

   (a) an Obligation under this Agreement has not been, or is not being, fulfilled;

(b) any benefit conferred upon it by this Agreement is being, or may be, denied;

(c) the achievement of any objective of this Agreement is being, or may be, frustrated;

(d) a case of difficulty has arisen or may arise; or

(e) a change in circumstances necessitates, or might necessitate, an amendment of this Agreement; it may notify any other Party of its wish to enter into consultations. The Party so requested shall enter into consultations in good faith and as soon as possible, with a view to seeking a mutually satisfactory solution.

2. For the purposes of this Agreement, consultations between the Parties shall be considered to have commenced on the day on which notice requesting the consultations is received.

Article 22
Dispute Resolution

1. The Parties shall endeavour, as far as is possible, to settle any differences concerning the interpretation, implementation or Operation of this Agreement through amicable consultations in accordance with Article 21. Such consultations shall be undertaken with appropriate regard to relevant cultural values and customary procedures for resolving differences in the Pacific region.

2. Where the consultations referred to in Paragraph 1 have failed within 60 days to resolve the dispute between the Parties, any Party to the dispute may notify the Secretary General and the other Parties to the dispute of its wish to resolve the dispute by mediation. The Parties may agree on a mediator or request the Secretary General to appoint a mediator. Any costs relating to such mediation shall be borne by the Parties to the dispute in equal shares.

3. Where the mediation process referred to in Paragraph 2 has failed within 60 days, or such time period as agreed to by the Parties to the dispute, to resolve the dispute between the Parties, any Party to the dispute may notify the Secretary General and the other Parties to the dispute of its decision to submit the dispute to arbitration, pursuant to the provisions of Annex V.

4. The Secretary General in consultation with the Parties, shall develop, maintain and, from time to time, amend a list of individuals who may be designated as Arbitrators for the purpose of this Article and Annex V. The Parties, in consultation with Secretary General, shall establish the criteria for individuals to be included in the list of potential arbitrators.

5. The list described in the preceding Paragraph shall identify each individual, including that individual's nationality, and briefly describe the

individual's experience with respect to both international trade and international arbitration, the individual's training or qualifications for Services as an arbitrator, and any areas of special expertise which the individual possesses.

6. Where a Party fails to comply with the arbitrator's award, any Party affected by this failure may enter into consultations with the other Parties with a view to persuading the defaulting Party to comply. Where such consultations are unsuccessful within 60 days, any affected Party may suspend the application to the defaulting Party of concessions or the performance of any other obligations under this Agreement, until such time as the defaulting Party complies with the arbitrator's award. The level of the Suspension of concessions or performance of other obligations by the affected Party shall be equivalent to the level of nullification or impairment of benefits under this Agreement to that Party caused by the defaulting Party.

7. Once the defaulting Party complies with the decision of the Arbitrator, all action taken under the preceding Paragraph shall be terminated.

Article 23
Review

1. The Parties shall meet at the time of the Forum Trade Ministers' Meeting or otherwise as appropriate to review relevant aspects of the implementation and Operation of this Agreement.

2. The Parties undertake to conduct a general review of the Operation of this Agreement no later than five years after it enters into force, and thereafter at no later than five-year intervals. Under the general review, the Parties shall:

   (a) monitor progress made in implementing this Agreement, and in particular, progress made in:
      (i) ensuring the effectiveness and appropriateness of the Rules (Article 5);
      (ii) implementing timetables for reduction and elimination of tariffs (Article 7);
      (iii) removing goods from the lists of excepted imports (Article 8);
      (iv) eliminating measures distorting trade in goods (Article 9);
      (v) liberalising developing industries (Article 14);
      (vi) liberalising government procurement (Article 15);
      (vii) implementing measures to facilitate trade and harmonise business laws and other measures (Article 18); and
      (viii) broadening and deepening the relationship established by this Agreement (Article19);

(b) assess whether the Agreement is operating effectively;

(c) evaluate the need for additional measures or modifications to increase its effectiveness;

(d) endeavour, in the spirit of this Agreement, to identify ways to accelerate the time frames for liberalisation, including the removal of items from their lists of exempted imports; and

(e) consider any other matter relating to the implementation of this Agreement or trade within the Area or in the Pacific region.

. . .

Pacific Agreement on Closer Economic Relations (PACER) (18.08.2001)

. . .

Desiring to encourage trade liberalisation and economic integration in the Pacific region, with a view to the eventual full and complete integration of all sectors of their economies;

Convinced of the benefits of an outward-looking approach to trade and economic integration, and a clearly established and secure framework of rules for trade and economic integration;

Desiring to promote the gradual integration of all of the Parties into the world economy, with due regard for their national circumstances and their right to regulate in accordance with national, social and economic policy objectives;

Mindful of the differing levels of economic development and special vulnerability of some Parties to this Agreement, and recognising that any economic integration among the Forum members should be gradual;

Concerned to minimise any disruptive effects and adjustment costs to the economies of the Forum Island Countries resulting from trade liberalisation and economic integration;

. . .

Article 2
Objectives

1. The Parties wish to establish a framework for the gradual trade and economic Integration of the economies of the Forum members in a way that is fully supportive of sustainable development of the Forum Island Countries and to contribute to their gradual and progressive integration into the international economy.

2. The objectives of this Agreement include the following:

(a) to provide a framework for cooperation leading over time to the development of a single regional market;

(b) to foster increased economic opportunities and competitiveness through more effective regional trade arrangements;

(c) to minimise any disruptive effects and adjustment costs to the economies of the Forum Island Countries, including through the provision of assistance and support for the Forum Island Countries to undertake the necessary structural and economic adjustments for integration into the international economy;

(d) to provide economic and technical assistance to the Forum Island Countries in order to assist them in implementing trade liberalisation and economic integration and in securing the benefits from liberalisation and integration; and

(e) to be consistent with the obligations of any of the Parties under the Marrakesh Agreement Establishing the World Trade Organization.

Part 2—Pacific Economic Integration Initiatives

Article 3
Guiding Principles

1. The objectives of sustainable development of the Forum Island Countries and gradual and progressive integration of the Forum Island Countries into the international economy shall guide all aspects of all stages of the development of the trade and economic partnership established under this Agreement.

2. The trade arrangements established in accordance with Part 2 of this Agreement are intended to provide "stepping stones" to allow the Forum Island Countries to gradually become part of a single regional market and integrate into the international economy.

3. The Parties recognise that the purpose of free trade areas should be to facilitate trade between the constituent parties and not to raise barriers to the trade of other Parties to this Agreement, and shall endeavour to act consistently with that purpose.

4. Nothing in this Agreement shall be construed as restricting the right of the Parties to undertake an arrangement between two or more of them to regulate trade and economic relations between them as they may agree, except when necessary to achieve the objectives of this Agreement.

5. The Parties shall use their best endeavours to follow international best practice in formulating the rules governing the trade relations between them, taking into account the development Status, capacity and resource constraints of Forum Island Countries.

6. Consistent with the objectives set out in Paragraph 1, Least Developed Countries and Small Island States may be integrated in accordance with different structures and by different time frames than other Parties.

7. This Agreement is not intended to be:

    (a) a customs union, an Interim agreement leading to the formation of a customs union, a free trade area, or an interim agreement leading to the formation of a free trade area notifiable under Article XXIV of the General Agreement on Tariffs and Trade;

    (b) an agreement notifiable under Article V of the General Agreement on Trade in Services; or

    (c) in derogation of any pre-existing arrangements, obligations or treaties.

Article 4
Arrangements among Forum Island Countries

1. The Parties agree that it is desirable for the Forum Island Countries to commence trade liberalisation and economic Integration among themselves first.

2. The Forum Island Countries may liberalise trade among themselves and integrate their economies at a different pace and with different priorities than those with which they liberalise trade, and integrate their economies with the economies of Australia and New Zealand.

3. Any arrangements established in accordance with this Article shall:

    (a) be consistent with the objectives and guiding principles of this Agreement; and

    (b) confer no rights or obligations on any Party not party to that arrangement.

Article 5
Future Negotiation of Forum-wide Trade Arrangements

1. In accordance with the objectives of this Agreement, and notwithstanding the process for further Integration established in the following Paragraph, eight years after the PICTA has entered into force, unless earlier agreed as part of the general review of this Agreement under Paragraph 2 of Article 16 or otherwise triggered by the provisions of Article 6, the Parties will enter into negotiations with a view to establishing reciprocal free trade arrangements between the Forum Island Countries and Australia and New Zealand.

2. Where a Party considers it desirable to establish new trading and economic integration arrangements between all the Forum Island

Countries and Australia and New Zealand, or to extend the matters covered by or to deepen the relationship established by such arrangements, it may notify the Forum Secretariat, which will notify the other Parties to this Agreement, of its wish to enter into consultations with a view to negotiating the terms and conditions of the new arrangement or extension.

3. With respect to any Forum Island Country, Australia and New Zealand shall maintain all existing arrangements relating to market access in effect at the time this Agreement enters into force, until such time as that particular Forum Island Country has concluded new and/ or improved trade arrangements providing equal or better access to their markets.

. . .

Article 7
Terms of Trade Arrangements between Forum Island Countries and Australia and New Zealand

The terms of any new trade arrangements between Forum Island Countries and Australia and New Zealand established pursuant to Articles 5 or 6 shall:

(a) be consistent with the objectives and guiding principles of this Agreement;

(b) provide Forum Island Countries with no less favourable treatment than exists under the arrangements referred to in Paragraph 3 of Article 5;

(c) recognise the differences in development Status of the Parties by the inclusion of appropriate measures providing for special and differential treatment of developing countries;

(d) not discriminate between any Forum Island Country which is a Party to this Agreement, unless the discrimination is to provide special and differential treatment for Least Developed Countries or Small Island States; and

(e) not discriminate between Australia and New Zealand.

Article 8
Voluntary Tariff Liberalisation

1. The Parties acknowledge the importance of gradual reduction of their tariffs as part of their overall trade strategy, and welcome all such tariff reductions by any Forum member.

2. Each Party shall periodically review its tariff schedule with a view to making voluntary unilateral reductions to its tariffs.

Part 3—Trade Facilitation and Economic and Technical Assistance

Article 9
Trade Facilitation

1. The Parties believe that the development of an appropriate, efficient and transparent framework of trade facilitation measures in the Pacific region will enhance the effectiveness and benefits of trade liberalisation among Forum members.
2. The Parties shall establish detailed programmes for the development, establishment and implementation of trade facilitation measures in accordance with Annex I.
3. To assist the Integration of Forum Island Countries into the international economy, trade facilitation programmes shall, to the extent practicable, be consistent with other regional and international trade facilitation agreements and initiatives.
4. The design of trade facilitation programmes, including the level of financial commitment and other resources required for the implementation of the Programme, shall take into account the special needs and resource and capacity constraints of Least Developed Countries and Small Island States.

   . . .

Article 11
Financial and Technical Assistance

1. The Parties recognise the need for significant additional resources for the development of a programme of work to support the objectives of this Agreement.
2. The Parties, and other Pacific island Countries or Territories as agreed, in conjunction with the Forum Secretariat, shall develop a programme of work for financial and technical assistance in areas such as trade facilitation and promotion, capacity building, and structural adjustment, which may include fiscal reform measures.
3. This programme of work, administered by a Unit within the Forum Secretariat, should be incorporated into the Forum Secretariat's "Budget Summary and Work Programme" without diverting resources from other Forum Secretariat programmes.
4. This programme of work shall be supported by an adequate level of funding from Australia and New Zealand and other interested donors to promote the timely implementation of the objectives of this Agreement,

including trade facilitation programmes to be established in accordance with Annex I.

Article 12
Mutual Assistance in International Fora

1. The Parties shall provide mutual assistance in international trade and economic fora, in particular in the World Trade Organization, in all matters related to the terms and objectives of this Agreement, and in other matters where the Parties have common interests in international economic and trade cooperation.
2. The Parties agree on the importance of effective implementation of special and differential provisions designed to take account of Parties' differing levels of development and vulnerability in international trade and economic agreements and arrangements.
3. Australia and New Zealand shall continue to assist the Forum Island Countries in their efforts to become active members of international trade and economic organisations by developing the necessary capacity to negotiate, participate effectively in, monitor and implement these agreements.

Part 4—General Provisions

. . .

Article 15
Consultations

If a Party considers that:

(a) an Obligation under this Agreement has not been, or is not being, fulfilled;
(b) any benefit conferred upon it by this Agreement is being, or may be, denied;
(c) the achievement of any objective of this Agreement is being, or may be, frustrated;
(d) a change in circumstances necessitates, or might necessitate, an amendment of this Agreement;

it may notify any other Party, through the Forum Secretariat, of its wish to enter into consultations. The Party so requested shall enter into consultations in good faith and as soon as possible, with a view to seeking a mutually satisfactory solution.

Article 16
Decision-Making and Review

1. The Parties shall meet at least once per year, at the time of the Forum Trade Ministers' Meeting or otherwise as appropriate, to review the implementation and operation of this Agreement and all aspects of trade and economic cooperation between the Parties.

2. The Parties undertake to conduct a general review of the Operation of this Agreement no later than 3 years after it enters into force, and thereafter at 3-year intervals, or as otherwise agreed to by the Parties.

3. The purpose of the reviews shall be to:

   (a) make decisions, as required, on the opening and timetabling of negotiations for agreements or arrangements to provide for the broadening and deepening of the economic integration of the Parties, and to monitor the progress of those negotiations;

   (b) reach agreement on actions necessary to harmonise and coordinate the trade and economic integration arrangements of the Parties;

   (c) reach agreement, as required, to establish or modify trade facilitation programmes, review the implementation and success of established programmes, and make any decisions necessary for the development, establishment and implementation of trade facilitation programmes and specific trade facilitation measures;

   (d) examine the implementation of the programme of work under Paragraph 2 of Article 11 and identify any issues which should be taken into account in subsequent development of the programme of work; and

   (e) consider any other issue agreed to by the Parties.

Article 17
Functions of the Pacific Islands Forum Secretariat

1. The Parties agree that the Forum Secretariat shall provide secretariat Services for this Agreement and other international agreements established pursuant to Part 2 of this Agreement.

2. Subject to the direction of the Parties, the functions of the Forum Secretariat in respect of this Agreement shall include:

   (a) the preparation and transmission of documentation, including an annual report, required under this Agreement, including the transmission of Communications between the Parties;

   (b) the provision of administrative support for meetings convened to review this Agreement or conduct negotiations or consultations under this Agreement;

(c) the provision of administrative support for the Operation of financial and technical assistance under Article 11;

(d) liasing, as appropriate, between the Parties or with any other Organisation;

(e) the provision of technical support to the Parties in the gathering and dissemination of information relevant to this Agreement;

(f) the provision of technical support to the Parties in the implementation of their obligations under this Agreement;

(g) the provision of other administrative or technical support, as determined by the Parties, in respect of matters that relate to trade facilitation covered by this Agreement, including as required under Annex I; and

(h) ensuring the smooth and orderly functioning of the Unit referred to in Article 11.

. . .

AGREEMENT ESTABLISHING THE
PACIFIC ISLANDS FORUM (08.11.2005)

. . .

Treasuring the diversity of the Pacific and seeking a future in which its cultures, traditions and religious beliefs are valued, honoured and developed;

Seeking a Pacific region that is respected for the quality of its governance, the sustainable management of its resources, the full observance of democratic values, and for its defence and promotion of human rights;

Determined to work in partnership with each other and with others beyond our region to achieve our shared goals of economic growth, sustainable development, good governance and security;

. . .

Article I
The Pacific Islands Forum

1. The Pacific Islands Forum (hereinafter called "the Forum") is hereby established as an international Organisation.

2. The Forum comprises Australia, the Cook Islands, Fiji, Nauru, New Zealand, Samoa and Tonga, being founding members of the Forum, together with the Federated States of Micronesia, Kiribati, Niue, Palau, Papua New Guinea, the Republic of the Marshall Islands, Solomon Islands, Tuvalu and Vanuatu; and such other states as may be admitted

to Forum membership with the approval of the Forum Leaders and in accordance with Article XI.

3. Territories in the Pacific Islands region may be admitted to associate membership of the Forum, if a request for associate membership is approved by the Forum Leaders. The criteria for associate membership, and the nature and extent of the rights and obligations of such members, shall be determined by the Forum Leaders from time to time.

4. The Forum Leaders may as they see fit invite other territories, and intergovernmental organisations whose membership includes a significant number of Forum members, to be Forum observers. The entitlements of observers shall be determined by the Forum Leaders from time to time.

Article II
Purpose

The purpose of the Forum is to strengthen regional cooperation and Integration, including through the pooling of regional resources of governance and the alignment of policies, in order to further Forum members' shared goals of economic growth, sustainable development, good governance, and security.

Article III
The Forum Leaders' Meeting

1. The preeminent decision-making body of the Forum shall be the Forum Leaders' Meeting.

2. The Forum Leaders Meeting shall be held annually. The Forum Leaders shall appoint one of their number to be Chair at each annual Meeting (hereinafter called "the Forum Chair") who shall hold the position of Forum Chair until the next annual Meeting. The venue, agenda and procedures for the Forum Leaders' Meeting shall be as determined by the Forum Leaders from time to time.

3. In addition to the annual Forum Leaders' Meeting, the Forum Leaders may convene special meetings at any time as they see fit.

Article IV
Establishment of the Pacific Islands Forum Secretariat

1. The Forum shall have a secretariat to be known as the Pacific Islands Forum Secretariat (hereinafter called "the Secretariat").

2. The headquarters of the Secretariat shall be located in Suva.

Article V
Pacific Islands Forum Officials' Committee

1. The Forum shall have an executive committee to be known as the Pacific Islands Forum Officials' Committee (hereinafter called "the Committee").

2. The Committee shall comprise one representative of each member of the Forum.

3. The powers and functions of the Committee shall be to give general policy directions to the Secretariat and to make reports and recommendations to the Forum Leaders. In particular the Committee shall:

   (a) approve, reject or amend the annual work programme and budget of the Secretariat and any interim budget submitted by the Secretariat;

   (b) receive, examine and comment on the Annual Report of the Secretary General on the Operation of the Secretariat; and

   (c) determine the staff establishment and the remuneration policy of the Secretariat, and approve its Staff Regulations.

4. The Committee shall meet each year prior to the Forum Leaders' Meeting, and at such other times as may be required.

5. The Committee Chair shall rotate annually in alphabetical order of members or as otherwise decided by the Committee.

6. The Secretary General, in consultation with and at the request of the Committee Chair, shall convene meetings of the Committee.

7. All decisions of the Committee shall be taken by consensus, wherever possible, or if necessary by a majority of the representatives present and voting, except as provided for in Article IX (2) of this Agreement.

8. The Committee shall establish its own rules of procedure.

Article VI
Appointment of Secretariat Staff

1. The Secretariat staff (hereinafter called "the Staff") shall consist of a Secretary General and such other staff as may be appointed by the Secretary General in accordance with this Article.

2. The Secretary General shall be appointed by the Forum Leaders under such conditions as the Forum Leaders may determine. If for any reason the post of Secretary General is vacant, a Deputy Secretary General shall be directed by the Forum Chair to carry out the functions of the Secretary General on an interim basis until the position is filled.

3. The Secretary General shall appoint all other staff in accordance with the Staff Regulations, the staff establishment and the remuneration policy determined by the Committee.

4. The Secretary General shall be appointed for a term of three years and shall be eligible for reappointment. The Secretary General's appointment shall not, however, exceed two consecutive terms.

Article VII
Functions of the Secretary General

1. The Secretary General shall act as secretary to the Forum Leaders' Meeting. The Secretary General shall also act as secretary to Ministerial meetings, the Committee and such other councils, committees or working groups as may be established by the Forum.
2. The Secretary General shall be responsible, in close consultation with the Forum Chair and within the limits set by the Forum Leaders from time to time, for setting Forum Leaders' Meeting agendas and coordinating responses by members to regional events, particularly crises. The Secretary General shall also perform other functions and duties as directed by the Forum Leaders. Where appropriate the Secretary General shall act on the advice of and in consultation with the Committee and other bodies referred to in paragraph 1 of this Article.
3. The Secretary General shall be responsible for the management of the Secretariat.

Article VIII
Functions of the Secretariat

1. The functions of the Secretariat shall be carried out by the Staff.
2. The primary roles of the Secretariat are to provide policy advice, coordination and assistance in implementing the decisions of the Forum Leaders.
3. Subject to the direction of the Forum Leaders and the Committee, the Secretariat shall also:

    (a) build upon the important basis for regional cooperation established by the Forum by working to further strengthen and deepen links between the countries of the region in accordance with the purpose of the Forum, including through the ongoing development and implementation of the Pacific Plan;
    (b) promote the identity and activities of the Forum;
    (c) work to advance partnerships between the Forum and its stakeholders within and beyond the Pacific region; and
    (d) undertake such other activities as are necessary for the attainment of the Forum's purpose.
4. The Secretariat shall work in cooperation and coordination with other intergovernmental organisations in the Pacific region, with the aim of ensuring that the most effective use is made of regional resources.

5. In the performance of its functions the Secretariat shall have regard to the particular needs of the most vulnerable Forum members, communities and peoples, including the smaller Island states, and shall embrace the cultural diversity of the region with tolerance and respect.
6. The Secretariat shall provide Support Services to Forum Leaders' Meetings, Ministerial meetings, and meetings of the Committee and such other councils, committees or working groups as may be established by the Forum.
7. The Secretariat shall communicate with members through their Ministries of Foreign Affairs, or such other contact points as may be nominated by the respective members.

Article IX
Budget

1. The annual budget of the Forum shall be prepared by the Secretary General for consideration and approval by the Committee.
2. The costs of operating the Forum shall be borne by the members in the shares determined by the Committee by consensus from time to time, subject to review by the Forum Leaders at their discretion.
3. In advance of the Committee's approval of the budget, the Secretary General shall be entitled to authorise expenditure up to a limit not exceeding one third of the previous year's actual expenditure.

BIBLIOGRAPHY

---◆---

1. REGION-BUILDING IN EUROPE

European Union (EU)
www.europa.eu

Documents

Treaty Establishing the European Economic Community (The Treaties of Rome) (25.03.1957). Online at: eur-lex.europa.eu/en/treaties/dat/12002E/htm/C_2002325EN.003301.html.

Single European Act (01.07.1987). Online at: www.europa.eu.int/eur-lex/lex/en/treaties/treaties_other.htm.

The Treaty on European Union (07.02.1992). Online at: www.eur-lex.europa.eu/en/treaties/dat/11992M/htm/11992M.html.

Treaty of Lisbon Amending the Treaty on European Union and the Treaty Establishing the European Community (13.12.2007). Online at: www.eur-lex.europa.eu/JOHtml.do?uri=OJ:C:2007:306:SOM:EN:HTML.

af Malmborg, Mikael, and Bo Strath (eds.). The Meaning of Europe: Variety and Contention Within and Among Nations. Oxford and New York: Berg, 2002.

Banchoff, Thomas, and Mitchell P. Smith (eds.). Legitimacy and the European Union: The Contested Polity. London and New York: Routledge, 1999.

Bischof, Günter, Michael Gehler, Ludger Kühnhardt, and Rolf Steininger (eds.). Towards a European Constitution: A Historical and Political Comparison with the United States. Vienna: Böhlau, 2005.

Bulmer, Simon, and Christian Lequesne. The Member States of the European Union. Oxford: Oxford University Press, 2005.

Caporaso, James A., et al. Transforming Europe: Europeanization and Domestic Change. Ithaca, NY: Cornell University Press, 2001.

Checkel, Jeffrey T. "Social Construction and European Integration." In Thomas Christiansen et al. (eds.), The Social Construction of Europe. London: Sage Publications, 2001: 50–64.

Dedman, Martin. The Origins and Development of the European Union 1945–1995. London: Routledge, 1996.

Dinan, Desmond. Europe Recast: A History of European Union. Boulder, CO: Lynn Rieffer, 2004.

Dunkerley, David et al. (eds.). Changing Europe: Identities, Nations and Citizens. London and New York: Routledge, 2002.

Dyson, Kenneth (ed.). European States and the EURO: Europeanization, Variation, and Convergence. New York: Oxford University Press, 2002.

Featherstone, Kevin, and Claudio M. Raedelli (eds.). *The Politics of Europeanization.* Oxford: Oxford University Press, 2003.

Fratianni, Michele, and Jürgen von Hagen (eds.). *The European Monetary System and European Monetary Union.* Boulder, CO: Westview Press, 1992.

Gillingham, John. *European Integration 1950–2003: Superstate or New Market Economy?* Cambridge: Cambridge University Press, 2003.

Hug, Simon. *Voices of Europe: Citizens, Referendums and European Integration.* Lanham, MD: Rowman and Littlefield, 2002.

Jachtenfuchs, Marcus. "The Governance Approach to European Integration." *Journal of Common Market Studies* 39, no. 2 (2001): 245–264.

Kühnhardt, Ludger. *Implications of Globalization on the Raison d`Etre of European Integration.* Oslo: ARENA, 2002.

Kühnhardt, Ludger. *Constituting Europe: Identity, Institution-Building and the Search for a Global Role.* Baden-Baden: Nomos, 2003.

Kühnhardt, Ludger. *European Union—The Second Founding: The Changing Rationale of European Integration.* Baden-Baden: Nomos, 2008.

Kühnhardt, Ludger (ed.). *Crises in European Integration: Challenge and Response 1945–2005.* Oxford and New York: Berghahn Books, 2008.

Lipgens, Walter (ed.). *Documents on the History of European Integration Vol.1: Continental Plans for European Union, 1939–1945.* Berlin and New York: de Gruyter, 1985.

Lipgens, Walter (ed.), *Documents on the History of European Integration Vol. 2: Plans for European Union in Great Britain and in Exile, 1939–1945.* Berlin and New York: de Gruyter, 1986.

Lipgens, Walter (ed.). *45 Jahre Ringen um eine europäische Verfassung.* Bonn: Europa Union Verlag, 1986.

Lipgens, Walter, and Wilfried Loth (eds.). *Documents on the History of European Integration, Vol. 3: The Struggle for European Union by Political Parties and Pressure Groups in Western European Countries 1945–1950.* Berlin and New York: de Gruyter, 1988.

Murray, Philomena. "Towards a Research Agenda on the European Union as a Model of Regional Integration." *Asia-Pacific Journal of EU Studies* 2, no. 1 (2004): 33–51.

Nelsen, Brent F., and Alexander Stubb (eds.). *The European Union: Readings on the Theory and Practice of European Integration.* Houndmills: Palgrave, 2003.

Nicolaidis, Kalypso, and Robert Howse (eds.). *The Federal Vision: Legitimacy and Levels of Governance in the United States and the European Union.* New York: Oxford University Press, 2001.

Pernice, Ingolf. "Multi-Level Constitutionalism in the European Union." *European Law Review* 27, nos. 1–6 (2002): 511–529.

Weiler, Joseph H.H., and Marlene Wind (eds.). *European Constitutionalism Beyond the State.* Cambridge: Cambridge University Press, 2003.

Zielonka, Jan. *Europe as Empire: The Nature of the Enlarged European Union.* Oxford: Oxford University Press, 2006.

Zielonka, Jan (ed.). *Paradoxes of European Foreign Policy.* The Hague: Kluwer, 1998.

2. REGION-BUILDING IN SOUTH AMERICA

Central American Integration System
(Sistema de la Integración Centroamericana, SICA)

www.sica.int/sgsica/

Documents

General Treaty on Central American Economic Integration (13.12.1960). Online at: www.sice.oas.org/trade/camertoc.asp.

Tegucigalpa Protocol to the Charter of the Organization of Central American States (13.12.1991). In United Nations General Assembly—Security Council, A/46/829 S/23310. New York: United Nations, 1991: 15–29.

Convention on the Statute of the Central American Court of Justice (10.12.1992). In United Nations Treaty Series, Vol.1821, No. I-31191. New York: United Nations, 1994: 292–303.

Framework Treaty on Democratic Security in Central America (15.12.1995). Online at: www.state. gov/t/ac/csbm/rd/4368.htm.

Axline, Andrew W. "Free Trade in the Americas and Sub-Regional Integration in Central America and the Caribbean." *Canadian Journal of Development Studies* 21, no. 1 (2000): 31–53.

Bulmer-Thomas, Victor. *Central America 2002: Towards a New Regional Development Model*. Hamburg: Institut für Iberoamerika-Kunde, 2000.

Devlin, Robert, and Ricardo French-Davis. *Towards an Evaluation of Regional Integration in Latin America in the 1990s*. INTAL/ITD-Working Paper-2. Buenos Aires: Institute for the Integration of Latin America and the Caribbean, 1998. Online at: http://idbdocs.iadb.org/wsdocs/getdocument. aspx?docnum=417959.

Gallep, Bernd. "Der zentralamerikanische Integrationsprozess: Probleme und Scheinprobleme." *KAS-Auslandsinformationen* 10 (2005): 30–81.

Herrera Cáceres, Hector Roberto. *El Sistema de la Integración Centroamericana : Memoria y Prospectiva : Hacia la Convergencia Funcional Dinámica para el Desarrollo Integral Sostenible de Centroamérica*. San Salvador: Secretaría General del SICA, 1996.

Kose, M. Ayhan, and Alessandro Rebucci. "How Might CAFTA Change Macroeconomic Fluctuations in Central America? Lessons from NAFTA." *Journal of Asian Economics* 16, no. 1 (2005): 77–104.

Minkner-Bünjer, Mechthild. "Zentralamerikas 'China(alb)träume': Herausforderungen und Zukunftsaussichten." *Brennpunkt Lateinamerika* 17 (2005): 197–208.

Nicholls, Shelton et al. "Open Regionalism and Institutional Developments among the Smaller Integration Schemes of CARICOM, the Andean Community and the Central America Common Market." In Victor Bulmer-Thomas (ed.), *Regional Integration in Latin America and the Caribbean: The Political Economy of Open Regionalism*. London: University of London/Institute of Latin American Studies, 2001: 141–164.

O'Keefe, Thomas Andrew. "Central American Integration System (S.I.C.A.) at the Dawn of a New Century: Will the Central American Isthmus Finally Be Able to Achieve Economic and Political Unity?" *Florida Journal of International Law* 3 (2001): 243–261.

Papageorgiou, Giannis F. "The Regional Integration Process of Central America." In *The Federalist Debate: Papers for Federalists in Europe and the World*, No. 3. Torino: The Einstein Center for International Studies, 2001: 26–28.

Rodlauer, Markus, and Alfred Schipke. *Central America: Global Integration and Regional Cooperation*. Occasional Paper No. 243. Washington D.C.: International Monetary Fund, 2005.

Sánchez, Rafael. "Rebuilding the Central American Bloc in the 1990s: An Intergovernmentalist Approach to Integration." In Finn Laursen (ed.), *Comparative Regional Integration: Theoretical Perspectives*. Aldershot: Ashgate, 2003: 31–52.

Taccone, Juan José, and Uziel Nogueira (eds.). *Central American Report No.2*. Buenos Aires: Institute for the Integration of Latin America and the Caribbean, 2004. Online at: www.iadb.org/intal/ aplicaciones/uploads/publicaciones/i-Central_American_Report_2.pdf.

Zimmek, Martin. *Integrationsprozesse in Lateinamerika: Aktuelle Herausforderungen in Mittelamerika und der Andenregion*. Bonn: Center for European Integration Studies, 2005.

Andean Community of Nations (Comunidad Andina de Naciones, CAN)
www.comunidadandina.org

Documents

Andean Subregional Integration Agreement—Cartagena Agreement (26.05.1969). Online at: www.comunidadandina.org/ingles/normativa/ande_trie1.htm.

Trujillo Act (10.03.1996). online at: www.un.org/documents/ga/docs/51/plenary/a51–87.htm.

Treaty Creating the Court of Justice of the Cartagena Agreement (10.03.1996). Online at: www.comunidadandina.org/ingles/normativa/ande_trie2.htm.

Sucre Protocol (25.06.1997. Online at: www.comunidadandina.org/ingles/normativa/ande_trie4.htm.

Additional Protocol on the Treaty Establishing the Andean Parliament (23.04.1997). Online at: www.comunidadandina.org/ingles/treaties/trea/ande_trie5.htm.

Additional Protocol to the Cartagena Agreement—Andean Community Commitment to Democracy (27.10.1998). Online at: www.comunidadandina.org/ingles/normativa/democracy.htm.

Quirama Declaration (28.06.2003). Online at: www.comunidadandina.org/ingles/documentos/documents/Quirama.htm.

Campaña, Víctor Alejandro. *Desarrollo, Conocimiento y Participación en la Comunidad Andina*. Riobamba: Federación de Organizaciones Indígenas de las Faldas del Chimborazo, 2001.

Cárdenas, Miguel E., and Christian Arnold. *La Experiencia de la Unión Europea y sus Anécdotas para la Comunidad Andina de Naciones (CAN)*. Bonn: Center for European Integration Studies, 2005.

Carrión, Fernando (ed.). *Procesos de Decentralisación en la Comunidad Andina*. Quito: FLACSO, 2003.

Creamer, Germán. "Open Regionalism in the Andean Community: A Trade Flow Analysis." *World Trade Review* 2, no. 1 (2003): 101–118.

Devlin, Robert, and Antoni Estevadeordal. *What's New in the New Regionalism in the Americas?* INTAL/ITD Working Paper No. 2. Buenos Aires: Institute for the Integration of Latin America and the Caribbean, 2001. Online at: http://idbdocs.iadb.org/wsdocs/getdocument.aspx?docnum=776254.

Fairlie Reinoso, Alan. *Las Relaciones Comunidad Andina-Unión Europea y la Zona de Libre Comercio del Sur*. Lima: Pontificia Universidad Católica del Perú, 2000.

Garrón Bozo, Rodrigo Javier. *Derecho Comunitario: Principes, Fuentes y Sistema Jurisdiccional de la Comunidad Andina de Naciones y la Union Europea*. La Paz: Edicion Cima, 2004.

Lauer, Rene. *Las Políticas Sociales en la Integración Regional: Estudio Comparativa de la Union Europea y la Comunidad Andina de Naciones*. Quito: Universidad Andina Simón Bolívar, 2001.

Luis Socas, Jaime. *Areas Monetarias y Convergencia Macroeconómica: Comunidad Andina*. Caracas: Universidad Católica Andrés Bello, 2002.

Mandani, Dorsati. *South-South Regional Integration and Industrial Growth: The Case of the Andean Pact*. Washington D.C.: World Bank, 2001.

Moncayo Jiménez, Edgar. *Geografía Económica de la Comunidad Andina : Regiones Nuevos Actores de la Integración*. Lima: Comunidad Andina, Secretaría General, 2003.

Mutschler, Claudia. "Comparative International Experiences: Latin America." In Christopher Clapham et al. (eds.), *Regional Integration in Southern Africa: Comparative International Perspectives*. Johannesburg: The South African Institute of International Affairs, 2001: 137–165.

Nicholls, Shelton, et al. "Open Regionalism and Institutional Developments among the Smaller Integration Schemes of CARICOM, the Andean Community and the Central America Common Market." In Victor Bulmer-Thomas (ed.). *Regional Integration in Latin America and the Caribbean: The Political Economy of Open Regionalism*. London: University of London/Institute of Latin American Studies, 2001: 141–164.

Turck, Mary. *South American Community of Nations*. Minneapolis: Resource Center of the Americas, 2005.

Caribbean Community (CARICOM)

www.caricom.org

Documents

Agreement establishing the Caribbean Free Trade Association (CARIFTA) (15.12.1965). Online at: www.caricom.org/jsp/secretariat/legal_instruments/agreement_carifta.pdf.

Treaty Establishing the Caribbean Community (04.07.1973). Online at: www.caricom.org/jsp/community/original_treaty-text.pdf.

The Revised Treaty of Chaguaramas Establishing the Caribbean Community including the CARICOM Single Market and Economy (05.07.2001). Online at: www.caricom.org/jsp/community/revised_treaty-text.pdf.

The Rose Hall Declaration on Regional Governance and Integrated Development (04.07.2003). Online at: www.caricomlaw.org/docs/rosehalldeclaration.htm.

Caribbean Community Secretariat (ed.). *Regional Cultural Policy of the Caribbean Community*. Georgetown: Caribbean Community Secretariat, 1997.

Clegg, Peter. "From Insiders to Outsiders: Caribbean Banana Interests in the New International Trading Framework." In Stephen J. H. Dearden (ed.), *The European Union and the Caribbean*. Aldershot: Ashgate, 2002: 79–113.

Economic Commission for Latin America and the Caribbean (ed.). *Latin America and the Caribbean in the World Economy*. Santiago de Chile: United Nations Publications, 2004.

Grugel, Jean, and Anthony J. Payne. "Regionalist Responses in the Caribbean Basin." In Björn Hettne et al. (eds.), *National Perspectives on the New Regionalism in the South*. London: Macmillan, 2000: 198–220.

Hall, Kenneth O. *Re-inventing CARICOM: The Road to a New Integration: A Documentary Record*. Kingston: Ian Randle, 2003.

Hall, Kenneth O. (ed.). *The Caribbean Community: Beyond Survival*. Kingston: Ian Randle, 2001.

Harding, Alan, and Jan Hoffman. *Trade between Caribbean Community (CARICOM) and Central American Common Market (CAM) Countries: The Role to Play for Ports and Shipping Services*. Santiago de Chile: CEPAL, 2003.

Ishmael, Len. *The OECS Model of Integration in the Context of Caribbean Regionalism*. Castries: Organization of Eastern Caribbean States, 2006.

Itam, Samuel, et al. *Developments and Challenges in the Caribbean Region*. Washington, D.C.: International Monetary Fund, 2000.

Jessen, Anneke, and Ennio Rodríguez. *The Caribbean Community: Facing the Challenges of Regional and Global Integration*. Buenos Aires: Institute for the Integration of Latin America and the Caribbean, 1999.

Jessen, Anneke, and Christopher Vignoles. *CARICOM Report No. 2*. Buenos Aires: Institute for the Integration of Latin America and the Caribbean, 2005.

Laurent, Edwin. *Understanding International Trade: The Trading System from the Perspective of the Eastern Caribbean*. Castries: Organization of Eastern Caribbean States, 2006.

Levitt, Kari. *Reclaiming Development: Independent Thought and Caribbean Community*. Kingston: Randle, 2005.

Payne, Anthony, and Paul Sutton. *Charting Caribbean Developments*. Gainsville, FL: University Press of Florida, 2001.

Pollard, Duke (ed.). *The CARICOM System: Basic Instruments*. Kingston: The Caribbean Law Publishing Company, 2003.

Southern Common Market (Mercado Común del Sur, MERCOSUR)

www.mercosur.int/msweb/

Documents

Southern Common Market (MERCOSUR) Agreement (Treaty of Asuncion) (26.03.1991). Online at: www.itcilo.it/english/actrav/telearn/global/ilo/blokit/mercoa.htm.

Southern Common Market—Protocol of Ouro Preto (17.12.1994). Online at: www.itcilo.it/english/actrav/telearn/global/ilo/blokit/mercopro.htm.

The Protocol of Olivos (18.02.2002). Online at: www.mercosul.gov.br/textos/default.asp?Key=232.

Constitutive Protocol of the MERCOSUR Parliament (09.12.2005). ZEI translation.

Arestis, Philip, and Luiz Fernando de Paula (eds.). *Monetary Union in South America: Lessons from EMU*. Cheltenham and Northampton: Edward Elgar, 2003.

Crawley, Andrew. *MERCOSUR in Search of a New Agenda: Rapporteur's Report*. Buenos Aires: Institute for the Integration of Latin America and the Caribbean, 2004. Online at: http://idbdocs.iadb.org/wsdocs/getdocument.aspx?docnum=548062.

Da Motta Veiga, Pedro. *Mercosur: In Search of a New Agenda: Mercosur's Institutionalization Agenda, The Challenges of a Project in Crisis*. Buenos Aires: Institute for the Integration of Latin America and the Caribbean, 2004. Online at: http://idbdocs.iadb.org/wsdocs/getdocument.aspx?docnum=548061.

De Lombaerde, Philippe. *El Nuevo Regionalismo en América Latina*. UNU-CRIS Occasional Papers, 0–2005/3. Bruges: United Nations University-CRIS, 2005. Online at: www.cris.unu.edu/fileadmin/workingpapers/20050225143924.OP%202005%203%20PDL-RegionalismoAm%E9ricas-2005.pdf.

De Lombaerde, Philippe, and Liliana Lizarazo. *La Problématique de l'Intégration Monétaire en Amérique Latine et dans les Caraibes*. UNU-CRIS Occasional Papers, 0–2004/13. Bruges: United Nations University-CRIS, 2004. Online at: www.cris.unu.edu/fileadmin/workingpapers/OP%20De%20Lombaerde%20LizarazoProbl%E9matiqueIntMonAL2003.pdf.

Devlin, Robert, and Ziga Vodusek. *Trade Related Capacity Building: An Overview in the Context of Latin American Trace Policy and the Mercosur-EU Association Agreement*. Buenos Aires: Institute for the Integration of Latin America and the Caribbean, 2005. Online at: http://idbdocs.iadb.org/wsdocs/getdocument.aspx?docnum=548075.

Diaz Labrano, Roberto Ruiz. *Mercosur, Integracion y Derecho*. Buenos Aires: Ciudadargentina, 1998.

García Pelufo, Juan Ignacio. *Mercosur: In Search of a New Agenda: Mercosur's Insertion into a Globalized World*. Buenos Aires: Institute for the Integration of Latin America and the Caribbean, 2004. Online at: www.iadb.org/intal/aplicaciones/uploads/publicaciones/i_ieci_wp_06b_garciapelufo.pdf.

Giordano, Paolo. *The External Dimension of the Mercosur: Prospects for North-South Integration with the European Union*. London: Royal Institute for International Affairs, 2002. Online at: www.iadb.org/intal/aplicaciones/uploads/publicaciones/i_INTALITDSTA_OP_19_2003_Giordano.pdf.

Gomes Saraiva, Miriam. *The European Union as an International Actor and the Mercosur Countries*. Rio de Janeiro: Universidade do Estado do Rio de Janeiro, 2004. Online at: www.iscte.pt.

Guira, Jorge. *MERCOSUR: Trade and Investment Amid Financial Crisis*. London and New York: Kluwer Law International, 2003.

Hallberg, Anna. *Regional Integration in Latin America: The MERCOSUR Experience*. Stockholm: Latinamerika-Institutet, 2000.

Jaguaribe, Helio, and Alvaro Vasconcelos (eds.). *The European Union, Mercosul and the New World Order*. London: Frank Cass, 2003.

Magone, José. *Challenging the Monroe Doctrine? The Relations between the European Union and Mercosur*. Hull: University of Hull, 2002. Online at: www.psa.ac.uk/journals/pdf/5/2002/magone.pdf.

Malamud, Andrés. "Presidentialism and Mercosur: A Hidden Cause for a Successful Experience." In Finn Laursen (ed.), *Comparative Regional Integration: Theoretical Perspectives*. Aldershot: Ashgate, 2003: 53–73.

Pena, Celina, and Ricardo Rozemberg. "Mercosur: A Different Approach to Institutional Development." *FOCAL Policy Paper* 6 (2005). Online at: www.focal.ca/pdf/mercosur.pdf.

Peña, Felix. *Civil Society, Transparency and Legitimacy in Integration Processes and Trade Negotiations: Mercosur's Experience and Lessons for the Negotiations with the European Union*. Chaire Mercosur de Sciences Po, Working Group on EU-Mercosur Negotiations Annual Seminar. Paris: Chaire Mercosur de Sciences Po, 2003. Online at: www.felixpena.com.ar/index.php?contenido=wpapers&wpagno=documentos/2003–09-eng.

Peña, Felix, and Ramón Torrent (eds.). *Hacia Una Nueva Etapa en las Relaciones Unión Europea-América Latina: Un Diagnóstico Inicial.* Barcelona: Universidad de Barcelona (Observatorio de Relaciones Unión Europea-América Latina), 2005.

Sanguinetti, Pablo, et al. *Economic Integration and Location of Manufacturing Activities: Evidence from Mercosur.* Bonn: Center for European Integration Studies, 2004.

Smith, Hazel. "Actually Existing Foreign Policy—Or Not? The EU in Latin and Central America." In John Petersen and Helene Sjursen (eds.), *A Common Foreign Policy for Europe? Competing Visions of the CFSP.* London and New York: Routledge, 1998: 152–168.

3. Region-Building in Asia

Association of Southeast Asian Nations (ASEAN)
www.aseansec.org

Documents

The ASEAN-Declaration (Bangkok Declaration) (08.08.1967). Online at: www.aseansec.org/1629.htm.

Declaration of ASEAN Concord (24.02.1976). Online at: www.aseansec.org/1649.htm.

Treaty of Amity and Cooperation in Southeast Asia (24.02.1976). Online at:www.aseansec.org/1654.htm.

Declaration of ASEAN Concord II (07.10.2003). Online at: www.aseansec.org/15160.htm.

Kuala Lumpur Declaration on the Establishment of the ASEAN Charter (12.12.2005). Online at: www.aseansec.org/18031.htm.

Charter of the Association of Southeast Asian Nations (20.11.2007). Online at: www.aseansec.org/21069.pdf.

Acharya, Amitav. *The Quest for Identity: International Relations of South East Asia.* Oxford: Oxford University Press, 2000.

Apotheker, Thierry, et al. (eds.). *New Business Opportunities for EU Companies in the ASEAN Area: How to Benefit from the ASEAN Integration: An Investor's Guidebook.* Luxembourg: Office for Official Publications of the European Communities, 2005.

Bayoumi, Tamin, et al. *On Regional Monetary Arrangements for ASEAN.* London: Centre for Economic Policy Research 2000.

David, Harald. *Die ASEAN zwischen Konflikt, Kooperation und Integration.* Hamburg: Institut für Asienkunde, 2003.

Davidson, Paul J. *ASEAN: The Evolving Legal Framework for Economic Cooperation, Legal Studies.* Singapore: Times Academic Press, 2002.

Dent, Christopher. "The Asia-Europe Meeting (ASEM) Process: Beyond the Triadic Political Economy?" In Heiner Hänggi et al. (eds.), *Interregionalism and International Relations.* Abingdon and New York: Routledge, 2006: 113–127.

Erling, Alvestad. *The ASEAN Regional Forum: A Catalyst for Change?* Oslo: University of Oslo, 2001.

Fisher, C.A. "Southeast Asia: The Balkans of the Orient? A Study in Continuity and Change." *Geography* 47 (1962): 347–367.

Gates, Carolyn L., and Mya Than (eds.). *ASEAN Enlargement: Impacts and Implications.* Singapore: Institute of Southeast Asian Studies, 2001.

Hoa, Tran Van, and Charles Harvie (eds.). *New Asian Regionalism: Responses to Globalisation and Crises.* Basingstoke: Macmillan, 2003.

Kuroda, Haruhiko. "ASEAN Economic Outlook and Policy Issues." 2008. Online at: http://www.adb.org/Documents/Speeches/2008/ms2008018.asp.

Low, Linda. *ASEAN Economic Cooperation and Challenges*. Singapore: Institute of Southeast Asian Studies, 2004.

McDougall, Derek. "Humanitarian Intervention and Peacekeeping as Issues for Asia-Pacific Security." In James J. Hentz and Marten Boas (eds.), *New and Critical Security and Regionalism: Beyond the Nation-State*. Aldershot: Ashgate, 2003: 33–54.

Nathan, K.S. (ed.). *The European Union, United States and Asean: Challenges and Prospects for Cooperative Engagement in the 21st Century*. London: ASEAN Academic Press, 2002.

Öjendal, Joakim. "Regional Hydropolitics in Mainland Southeast Asia: A New Deal in a New Era?" In Björn Hettne et al. (eds.), *The New Regionalism and the Future of Security and Development*. London: Macmillan, 2000: 176–209.

Öjendal, Joakim. "South East Asia at a Constant Crossroads: An Ambiguous 'New Region.'" In Michael Schulz et al. (eds.), *Regionalization in a Globalizing World: A Comparative Perspective on Forms, Actors and Processes*. London: Zed Books, 2001: 147–172.

Pennetta, Piero. *Il Regionalismo Multipolare Asiatico: Contributo al Diritto Della Cooperazione Istituzionalizzata fra Stati*. Torino: G. Giappichelli, 2003.

Plummer, Michael G. "The EU and ASEAN: Real Integration and Lessons in Financial Cooperation." In P.K.M. Tharakan (ed.), *The World Economy, European Union and Preferential Arrangements*. Oxford and Boston: Blackwell Publishers, 2002: 1469–1500.

Robles, Alfredo C., Jr. "The Association of Southeast Asian Nations (ASEAN) and the European Union: Limited Interregionalism." In Heiner Hänggi et al. (eds.), *Interregionalism and International Relations*. Abingdon and New York: Routledge, 2006: 97–112.

Rüland, Jürgen. *ASEAN and the European Union: A Bumpy International Relationship*. Bonn: Center for European Integration Studies, 2001.

Schmidt, Axel. "Die ASEAN-Charter: Die Quadratur des Kreises oder der Scheideweg der Region?" *FES-Kurzberichte aus der internationalen Entwicklungszusammenarbeit* 11 (2005): 1–4.

Solidum, Estrella D. *The Politics of ASEAN: An Instrument on Southeast Asian Regionalism*. Singapore: Eastern University Press, 2003.

Solingen, Etel. "ASEAN: Quo Vadis?: Domestic Coalitions and Regional Cooperation." *Contemporary South East Asia* 21, no. 1 (1999): 30–53.

Strange, Roger, et al. (eds.). *The European Union and ASEAN: Trade and Investment Issues*. New York: St. Martin's Press, 2000.

Tan, Gerald. *ASEAN Economic Development and Cooperation*. Singapore: Eastern University Press, 2003.

Wolters, O.W. *History, Culture and Religion in Southeast Asian Perspectives*. Ithaca, NY: Cornell University Press, 2000.

Gulf Cooperation Council (GCC)

www.gcc-sg.org/eng/index.php

Documents

The Cooperation Council–Charter (25.05.1981).
Online at: www.gcc-sg.org/eng/index.php?action=Sec-Show&ID=1.

The Unified Economic Agreement between the Countries of the Gulf Cooperation Council (11.11.1981).
Online at: www.worldtradelaw.net/fta/agreements/gccfta.pdf.

The Economic Agreement between the Countries of the Gulf Cooperation Council (Revised) (31.12.2001). Riyadh: Secretariat General of the Cooperation Council for the Arab States of the Gulf, 2003: 7–28.

Aftab Kamal Pasha. *India, Iran and the GCC States: Political Strategy and Foreign Policy*. New Delhi: Manas Publications, 2000.

al-Alkim, Hassan. *The GCC States in an Unstable World: Foreign Policy Dilemmas of Small States*. London: Saqi Books, 1994.

Chami, Sade, et al. *What are the Potential Economic Benefits of Enlarging the Gulf Cooperation Council?* Washington D.C.: International Monetary Fund, 2004.

Christie, John. "History and Development of the Gulf Cooperation Council: A Brief Overview." In John A. Sandwick (ed.), *The Gulf Cooperation Council: Moderation and Stability in an Interdependent World.* Boulder, CO: Westview Press, 1987: 7–20.

Cooper, Scott, and Brock Taylor. "Power and Regionalism: Explaining Regional Cooperation in the Persian Gulf." In Finn Laursen (ed.), *Comparative Regional Integration: Theoretical Perspectives.* Aldershot: Ashgate, 2003: 105–124.

Fassano, Ugo, and Rina Bhattacharya (eds.). *Monetary Union Among the Member Countries of the Gulf Cooperation Council.* Washington, D.C.: International Monetary Fund, 2003.

Hanna, Daniel. *A New Fiscal Framework for GCC Countries Ahead of Monetary Union.* International Economic Programme Briefing Paper 06/02. London: Chatham House, 2006.

Koppers, Simon. *Economic Evaluation of the Gulf Cooperation Council (GCC).* 2nd ed. Frankfurt: Lang, 2004.

Nakleh, Emile A. *The Gulf Cooperation Council: Policies, Problems and Prospects.* New York, Westport, CT, and London: Praeger, 1986.

Peterson, Erik R. *The Gulf Cooperation Council: Search for Unity in a Dynamic Region.* Boulder, CO: Westview Press, 1988.

Peterson, John E. "Succession in the States of the Gulf Cooperation Council." *The Washington Quarterly* 24, no. 4 (2001): 173–186.

Rabi, Uzi. "The Dynamics of Gulf Cooperation Council (GCC): The Ceaseless Quest for Regional Security in a Changing Region." *Orient* 45, no. 2 (2004): 281–295.

Sturm, Michael, and Siegfried Nikolaus. *Regional Monetary Integration in the Member States of the Gulf Cooperation Council.* Frankfurt: European Central Bank, 2003.

Tripp, Charles. "Regional Organization in the Arab Middle East." In Louise Fawcett and Andrew Hurrell (eds.), *Regionalism in World Politics: Regional Organization and International Order.* Oxford: Oxford University Press, 1995: 283–309.

South Asian Association for Regional Cooperation (SAARC)
www.saarc-sec.org/main.php

Documents

Charter of the South Asian Association for Regional Cooperation (08.12.1985). Online at: www.saarc-sec.org/main.php?id=10&t=4.

Agreement on SAARC Preferential Trading Arrangement (SAPTA) (11.04.1993). Online at: www.saarc-sec.org/main.php?id=44&t=2.1.

Regional Convention on Suppression of Terrorism (04.11.1997). Online at: www.untreaty.un.org/English/Terrorism/Conv18.pdf.

Social Charter (04.01.2004). Online at: www.saarc-sec.org/main.php?id=13.

Agreement on South Asian Free Trade Area (SAFTA) (06.01.2004). Online at: www.saarc-sec.org/data/agenda/economic/safta/SAFTA%20AGREEMENT.pdf.

Agreement for Establishment of SAARC Arbitration Council (13.11.2005). Online at: www.209.85.129.104/search?q=cache:AFGrgsTUtysJ:www.mofa.gov.bd/13saarcsummit/Agreement%2520on%2520%2520SAARC%2520Arbitration%2520Council%2520final.pdf+agreement+for+establishment+of+SAARC+arbitration+council&hl=de&ct=clnk&cd=1&gl=de.

Bhargava, Kant K. *EU-SAARC: Comparisons and Prospects for Cooperation.* Bonn: Center for European Integration Studies, 1998.

Fernando, P.D. *Has the South Asian Association for Regional Cooperation (SAARC) Achieved a Substantial Progress?* Colombo: Konrad-Adenauer-Foundation, 2001.

Gonsalves, Eric, and Nancy Jetly (eds.). *The Dynamics of South Asia: Regional Cooperation and SAARC*. New Delhi: Sage Publications, 1999.

Hettne, Björn. "Security Regionalism in Europe and South Asia." In James J. Hentz and Morten Boas (eds.), *New and Critical Security and Regionalism:Beyond the Nation-State*. Aldershot: Ashgate, 2003: 149–166.

Hossain, Masud. *Regional Conflict Transformation: A Reinterpretation of South Asian Association for Regional Cooperation (SAARC)*. Helsinki: Institute of Development Studies, 2002.

Jayatilleke, Bandara S., and Wusheng Yu. "How Desirable is the South Asian Free Trade Area? A Quantitative Economic Assessment." *World Economy* 26, no. 9 (2003): 1293–1323.

Jorgensen, Bent D. "South Asia: An Anxious Journey towards Regionalization?" In Michael Schulz et al. (eds.), *Regionalization in a Globalizing World: A Comparative Perspective on Forms, Actors and Processes*. London: Zed Books, 2001: 125–146.

Kalam, Abdul. *Subregionalism in Asia: ASEAN and SAARC Experiences*. New Delhi: UBS Publishers, 2001.

Muni, S.D. "India in SAARC: A Reluctant Policy-Maker." In Björn Hettne et al. (eds.), *National Perspectives on the New Regionalism in the South*. London: Macmillan Press, 2000: 108–131.

Pola, Kumaran. *South Asian Association for Regional Cooperation (SAARC): Retrospects and Prospects*. Mumbai: MVIRDC World Trade Center, 2001.

Rahman, S.M. *SAARC in The New Millennium*. Rawalpindi: Friends, 2001.

Reddy, K.C., and T. Nirmala Devi. *Regional Cooperation in South Asia: New Dimensions*. New Delhi: Kanishka Publishers, 2002.

Sabur, A.K.M. Abdus, and Mohammad Humayun Kabir. *Conflict Management and Sub-Regional Cooperation in ASEAN: Relevance for SAARC*. Dhaka: Academic Press and Publishers, 2000.

Sobhan, Rehman. *Promoting Cooperation in South Asia: An Agenda for the 13th SAARC Summit*. Dhaka: University Press Limited, 2004.

Sudhakar, E. *SAARC, Origin, Growth, and Future*. New Delhi: Gyan Publishing House, 1994.

Syed, M.H. *SAARC Challenges Ahead*. New Delhi: Kilaso Books, 2003.

Upreti, B.C., (ed.). *Dynamics of Regional Cooperation in South Asia*. 2 vols. New Delhi: Kalinga Publications, 2000.

4. REGION-BUILDING IN AFRICA

African Union (AU)

www.africa-union.org

Documents

Organization of African Unity (OAU) Charter (25.05.1963). Online at: www.africa-union.org/root/au/Documents/Treaties/text/ OAU_Charter_1963.pdf.

Treaty Establishing the African Economic Community (03.06.1991). Online at: www.africa-union.org/root/au/Documents/Treaties/Text/AEC_Treaty_1991.pdf.

The Constitutive Act (11.07.2000). Online at: www.africa-union.org/About_AU/AbConstitutive_Act.htm.

Solemn Declaration on a Common African Defence and Security Policy (28.02.2004). Online at: www.africa-union.org/News_Events/2ND%20EX%20ASSEMBLY/Declaration%20on%20a%20Comm.Af%20Def%20Sec.pdf.

Agubuzu, Lawrence O.C. *From the OAU to AU: The Challenges of African Unity and Development in the Twenty-First Century*. Lagos: Nigerian Institute of International Affairs, 2004.

Babarinde, Olufemi, and Gerrit Faber. "From Lomé to Cotonou: Business as Usual?" *European Foreign Affairs Review* 9, no. 1 (2004): 27–47.

Bach, Daniel. "The Global Politics of Regionalism: Africa." In Mary Farrell, et al. (eds.), *Global Politics of Regionalism: Theory and Practice*. London: Pluto Press, 2005: 171–186.

Chabal, Patrick. "The Quest for Good Governance in Africa: Is NEPAD the Answer?" *International Affairs* 74, no. 2 (2002): 289–303.

Cheru, Fantu. *African Renaissance: Roadmaps to the Challenge of Globalization*. London and New York: Zed Books, 2002.

Dennis, Peter M., and M. Leann Brown. "The ECOWAS: From Regional Economic Organization to Regional Peacekeeping." In Finn Laursen (ed.), *Comparative Regional Integration: Theoretical Perspectives*. Aldershot: Ashgate, 2003: 229–249.

De Waal, Alex. "What's New in the 'New Partnership for Africa's Development'?" *International Affairs* 78, no. 3 (2002): 463–475.

Dinka, Tesfaye, and Walter Kennes. "Africa's Regional Integration Arrangements: History and Challenges." ECDPM Discussion Paper No. 74. Maastricht: European Centre for Development Policy, 2007.

Economic Commission for Africa (ed.). *Assessing Regional Integration in Africa*. Addis Ababa: Economic Commission for Africa, 2004.

Francis, David J. *The Politics of Economic Regionalism*. Ashgate: Aldershot, 2001.

Francis, David J. *Uniting Africa: Building Regional Peace and Security Systems*. Ashgate: Aldershot, 2006.

Genge, Manelisi, et al. *African Union and a Pan-African Parliament*. Pretoria: Africa Institute of South Africa, 2000.

Gottschalk, Keith, and Siegmar Schmidt. "The African Union and the New Partnership for Africa's Development—Strong Institutions for Weak States?" *International Politics and Society* 4 (2004): 138–158.

Grant, Andrew J., and Fredrik Söderbaum (eds.). *The New Regionalism in Africa*. Aldershot: Ashgate, 2003.

Hofmeier, Rolf. "Regionale Kooperation und Integration." In Mir A. Ferdowsi (ed.), *Afrika—Ein verlorener Kontinent?* Munich: Wilhelm Fink, 2004: 189–224.

Hurt, Stephen R. "Cooperation and Coercion? The Cotonou Agreement between the European Union and ACP States and the End of the Lomé Convention." *Third World Quarterly* 24, no. 1 (2003): 161–176.

Krause, Alexandra. "The European Union's Africa Policy: The Commission as Policy Entrepreneur in the CFSP." *European Foreign Affairs Review* 8, no. 1 (2003): 221–237.

Kühnhardt, Ludger. *Stufen der Souveränität: Staatsverständnis und Selbstbestimmung in der "Dritten Welt."* Bonn: Bouvier, 1992.

Mair, Stefan. "Die regionale Integration und Kooperation in Afrika südlich der Sahara." *Aus Politik und Zeitgeschichte* 52, nos. 13–14 (2002): 15–23. Online at: www.bpb.de/popup/popup_druckversion.html?guid=6CR2Z3.

Masson, Paul, and Catherine Pattillo. "A Single Currency for Africa?" *Finance & Development* 12 (2004): 8–15.

Masson, Paul, and Catherine Pattillo. *The Monetary Geography of Africa*. Washington, D.C.: Brookings Institution Press, 2005.

Mbeki, Thabo. *African Renaissance, South Africa and the World*. Speech at the United Nations University, 9 April 1998. Online at: www.unu.edu/unupress/mbeki.html.

Melber, Henning. *The New African Initiative and the African Union: A Preliminary Assessment and Documentation*. Uppsala: Nordiska Afrikainstitutet, 2001.

Moreau, Françoise. "The Cotonou Agreement—New Orientations." *The Courier* 9 (2000): 6–10.

Pennetta, Piero. *Le Organizzazioni Internazionali dei Paesi in Via di Svipullo: Le Organizzazioni Economiche Regionali Africane*. Bari: Cacucci Editore, 1998.

Rye Olsen, Gorm. "The Africa-Europe (Cairo Summit) Process: An Expression of 'Symbolic Politics.'" In Heiner Hänggi et al. (eds.), *Interregionalism and International Relations*. Abingdon and New York: Routledge, 2006: 199–214.

Schmidt, Siegmar. "Aktuelle Aspekte der EU-Entwicklungspolitik: Aufbruch zu neuen Ufern?" *Aus Politik und Zeitgeschichte* 19–20 (2002): 29–38.

Shaw, Timothy M. "Africa in the Global Political Economy: Globalization, Regionalization, or Marginalization?" In Björn Hettne et al. (eds.), *The New Regionalism and the Future of Security and Development*. London: Macmillan, 2000: 97–120.

United Nations Economic Commission for Africa (ed.). *Assessing Regional Integration in Africa*. Addis Ababa: Economic Commission for Africa, 2004.

Van Ginkel, Hans, et al. (eds.). *Integrating Africa: Perspectives on Regional Integration and Development*. Tokyo: United Nations University, 2003.

Williams, Paul D. "From Non-Intervention to Non-Indifference: The Origins and Development of the African Union's Security Culture." *African Affairs* 106 (2007): 253–279.

Economic Community of West African States (ECOWAS)

www.ecowas.int.

Documents

Treaty of the Economic Community of West African States (ECOWAS) (28.05.1975). United Nations Treaty Series, Vol. 1010, No. I-14843. New York, United Nations, 1976: 17–41.

Treaty of ECOWAS (Revised) (24.07.1993). Online at: www.iss.co.za/AF/RegOrg/unity_to_union/pdfs/ecowas/3ECOWASTreaty.pdf.

Agbohou, Nicolas. *Le Franc CFA et l'Euro Contre Afrique: Pour Une Monnaie Africaine et la Coopération Sud-Sud*. Paris: Editions Solidarité Mondiale, 1999.

Baudouhat, Virginie. *The Impact of the Euro in the CFA Franc Zone*. Oslo: Høgskolen i Oslo, 2002.

Chambas, Mohammed Ibn. *The ECOWAS Agenda: Promoting Good Governance, Peace, Stability and Sustainable Development*. Lagos: Nigerian Institute of International Affairs, 2005.

Dembélé, Demba Moussa. "Mauvais Comptes du Franc CFA: l'Afrique de l'Ouest Toujours Sous le Coup de Dévaluation." *Le Monde Diplomatique* 51 (2004): 19.

Francis, David J. *The Politics of Economic Regionalism: Sierra Leone in ECOWAS*. Aldershot: Ashgate, 2001.

Gambari, Ibrahim A. *Political and Comparative Dimensions of Regional Integration: The Case of ECOWAS*. New Jersey and London: Humanities Press International, 1991.

Gehle, Silke. *Die Franc-Zone als inhomogener Währungsraum: Zur Optimalität der Währungskooperation der Franc-Zone für ihre afrikanischen Mitgliedsländer*. Baden-Baden: Nomos, 1998.

Gibert, Marie V. *Monitoring a Region in Crisis: The European Union in West Africa*. Chaillot Paper No. 96. Paris: European Union Institute for Security Studies, 2007.

Hadjimichael, Michael J., and Michel Galy. *The CFA Franc Zone and the EMU*. Washington, D.C.: International Monetary Fund, 1997.

Hefeker, Carsten. *Fiscal Reform and Monetary Union in West Africa*. Hamburg: Hamburger Weltwirtschafts-Archiv, 2003. Online at: www.hwwa.de/Forschung/Publikationen/Discussion_Paper/2003/224.pdf.

Hettmann, Jens-U., and Fatima Kyari Mohammed. *Opportunities and Challenges of Parliamentary Oversight of the Security Sector in West Africa: The Regional Level*. Bonn: Friedrich-Ebert-Stiftung, 2005. Online at: www.fes.de/in_afrika/documents/SB_ECOWAS_Parl_1_1105_001.pdf.

Irving, Jacueline. "Varied Impact on Africa Expected from New European Currency." *Africa Recovery* 12, no. 4 (1999): 24–29. Online at: www.un.org/ecosocdev/geninfo/afrec/vol12no4/euro.htm.

Jouve, Edmond. "Les Relations Eurafrique dans le Cadre de la Régionalisation." *Revue Juridique et Politique* 58, no. 3 (2004): 361–476.

Laakso, Liisa (ed.). *Regional Integration for Conflict Prevention and Peace Building in Africa*. Helsinki: University of Helsinki, 2002.

Lavergne, Réal (ed.). *Regional Integration in West Africa: A Multidimensional Perspective.* Trenton, NJ and Asmara: Africa World Press, 1997.

Nivet, Bastien. *Security By Proxy? The EU and (Sub-)Regional Organisations: The Case of ECOWAS.* Paris: European Union Institute for Security Studies, 2006.

Ouédraogo, Ousmane. *Une Monnaie Unique Pour Toute l'Afrique de l'Ouest? Le Dossier Économique.* Paris: Karthala, 2003.

Qualmann, Regine. "Währungsanbindung als Chance oder Hindernis für die afrikanische Franc-Zone? Erfahrungen mit dem Festkurssystem und Entwicklungsperspektiven nach der Euro-Anbindung des CFA-Franc." *Nord-Süd Aktuell* 13 (1999): 3.

Söderbaum, Fredrik. "The Role of the Regional Factor in West Africa." In Björn Hettne et al. (eds.), *The New Regionalism and the Future of Security and Development.* London: Macmillan, 2000: 121–143.

Söderbaum, Fredrik. "Turbulent Regionalization in West Africa." In Michael Schulz et al. (eds.), *Regionalization in a Globalizing World: A Comparative Perspective on Forms, Actors and Processes.* London: Zed Books, 2001: 61–81.

Stasavage, David. *The Political Economy of a Common Currency: The CFA Franc Zone Since 1945.* Aldershot: Ashgate, 2003.

Van den Boogaerde Pierre, and Charalambros Tsangarides. *Ten Years After the CFA Franc Devaluation: Progress Toward Regional Integration in the WAEMU.* Washington, D.C.: International Monetary Fund, 2005.

Walthier, Claude. "Grand Manoeuvre Françafricaine." *Le Monde Diplomatique* 50 (2003): 12–13.

Zafar, Ali. *The Impact of the Strong Euro on the Real Effective Exchange Rates of the Two Francophone African CFA Zones.* Washington, D.C.: World Bank, 2005.

Zafar, Ali, and Keiko Kubota. *The CEMAC: Regional Integration in Central Africa: Key Issues.* The World Bank Working Papers- Africa Region Working Papers 52, 2003. Online at: http://www.worldbank.org/afr/wps/wp52.pdf.

Southern African Development Community (SADC)
www.sadcreview.com

Documents

Consolidated Text of the Treaty of the Southern African Development Community (17.08.1992). Online at: www.sadc.int/english/documents/legal/treaties/amended_declaration_and_treaty_of_sadc.php.

Protocol on Politics, Defence and Security Cooperation (14.08.2001). Online at: www.sadc.int/english/documents/legal/protocols/politics.php.

Principles and Guidelines Governing Democratic Elections (19.08.2004). Online at: www.sadc.int/english/documents/political_affairs/index.php.

Adelmann, Martin. *Regionale Kooperation im südlichen Afrika.* Freiburg: Arnold-Bergstraesser-Institut, 2003.

Clapham, Christopher, et al. (eds.). *Regional Integration in Southern Africa: Comparative International Perspectives.* Johannesburg: South African Institute of International Affairs, 2001.

Economic Commission for Africa (ed.). *Assessing Regional Integration in Africa.* Addis Ababa: Economic Commission for Africa, 2004.

Fisher, L.M., and Naison Ngoma. *The SADC Organ: Challenges in the New Millennium.* Institute for Security Studies Occasional Paper 114, 2005. Online at: http://www.iss.co.za/index.php?link_id=3&slink_id=388&link_type=12&slink_type=12&tmpl_id=3.

Harvey, Charles, et al. *The Prerequisites for Progress Towards a Single Currency in COMESA.* Lusaka: COMESA Regional Integration Research Network, 2001.

Jenkins, Carolyn, and Lynne Thomas. "African Regionalism and the SADC." In Mario Telò (ed.), *European Union and New Regionalism: Regional Actors and Global Governance in a Post-Hegemonic Era.* Aldershot: Ashgate, 2001: 153–174.

Kagira, B.M. *The Effects of Regional Integration on the Performance of Intra-Industry Trade in Eastern and Southern Africa*. Lusaka: COMESA Regional Integration Research Network, 2001.

Kalabi, Hope, and Susan Mpande. *An Assessment of the European Union Bilateral Agreement and Lessons to Be Learnt for the Economic Partnership Agreement Negotiations*. Lusaka: COMESA Secretariat, 2004.

Kasonga, Raphael Abel. *The Process of Monetary Integration in Eastern and Southern Africa*. Lusaka: COMESA Regional Integration Research Network, 2001.

Khandelwal, Padamja. *COMESA and SADC: Prospects and Challenges for Regional Trade Integration*. Washington, D.C.: International Monetary Fund, 2004.

Koesler, Ariane. *The Southern African Development Community and its Relations to the European Union: Deepening Integration in Southern Africa?* Bonn: Center for European Integration Studies, 2007.

Laakso, Liisa (ed.). *Regional Integration for Conflict Prevention and Peace Building in Africa*. Helsinki: University of Helsinki, 2002.

Mwase, Ngila R.L. *Co-ordination and Rationalisation of Sub-Regional Integration Institutions in Eastern and Southern Africa*. Lusaka: COMESA Regional Integration Research Network, 2001.

Nieuwkerk, Antoni van. "Regionalism into Globalism? War into Peace? SADC and ECOWAS Compared." *African Security Review*, Vol. 10, no. 2 (2001): 7–18. Online at: http://www.iss.co.za/pubs/ASR/10No2/Vannieuwkerk.html.

Odén, Bertil. "The Southern Africa Region and the Regional Hegemon." In Björn Hettne et al. (eds.), *National Perspectives on the New Regionalism in the South*. London: Macmillan, 2000: 242–264.

Odén, Bertil. "Regionalization in West Africa." In Michael Schulz et al. (eds.), *Regionalization in a Globalizing World: A Comparative Perspective on Forms, Actors and Processes*. London: Zed Books, 2001: 82–99.

Söderbaum, Fredrik. *The Political Economy of Regionalism: The Case of Southern Africa*. Basingstoke: Palgrave, 2004.

Söderbaum, Fredrik, and Ian Taylor (eds.). *Regionalism and Uneven Development in Southern Africa*. Aldershot: Ashgate, 2003.

Swatuk, Larry A. "Power and Water: The Coming Order of Southern Africa." In Björn Hettne, et al. (eds.), *The New Regionalism and the Future of Security and Development*. London: Macmillan, 2000: 210–247.

Trivedi, Sonu. "Common Market for Eastern and Southern Africa (COMESA)." *African Quarterly/Indian Journal of African Affairs* 44, no. 2 (2004): 89–111.

Weiland, Heribert. "The European Union and Southern Africa: Interregionalism between Vision and Reality." In Heiner Hänggi et al. (eds.), *Interregionalism and International Relations*. Abingdon and New York: Routledge, 2006: 185–198.

5. REGION-BUILDING IN EURASIA

The Commonwealth of Independent States (CIS)
www.cisstat.com/eng/cis.htm.

Documents

The Alma-Ata Declaration (21.12.1991). In Zbigniew Brzezinski and Paine Sullivan (eds.), *Russia and the Commonwealth of Independent States: Documents, Data, and Analysis*. Armonk, NY: M.E. Sharpe, 1997: 47–48.

CIS Treaty on Collective Security (15.05.1992). In Zbigniew Brzezinski and Paine Sullivan (eds.), *Russia and the Commonwealth of Independent States: Documents, Data, and Analysis*. Armonk, NY: M.E. Sharpe, 1997: 539–540.

Charter of the Commonwealth of Independent States (22.1.1993). In Zbigniew Brzezinski and Paine Sullivan (eds.), *Russia and the Commonwealth of Independent States: Documents, Data, and Analysis*. Armonk, NY: M.E. Sharpe, 1997: 506–511.

CIS Treaty on the Formation of an Economic Union (24.9.1993). In Zbigniew Brzezinski and Paine Sullivan (eds.), *Russia and the Commonwealth of Independent States: Documents, Data, and Analysis*. Armonk, NY: M.E. Sharpe, 1997: 518–522.

Agreement on Collective Peacekeeping Forces and Joint Measures on their Material and Technical Supply (24.09.1993). *Military News Bulletin* 10 (1993): 1–2.

Agreement on the Creation of a Common Economic Space (CES) (19.09.2003). ZEI translation.

Ahrens, Geert-Hinrich. *Die Präsidentschaftswahlen in der Ukraine: Der schwierige Weg der OSCE/ODIHR-Wahlbeobachter*. Bonn: Center for European Integration Studies, 2005.

Butler, William Elliott. *The Law of Treaties in Russia and the Commonwealth of Independent States: Text and Commentary*. Cambridge: Cambridge University Press, 2002.

Freinkman, Lev, et al. *Trade Performance and Regional Integration of the CIS Countries*. Washington, D.C.: The World Bank, 2004.

Jonson, Lena, and Clive Archer (eds.). *Peacekeeping and the Role of Russia in Eurasia*. Boulder, CO, and Oxford: Westview Press, 1996.

Marchetti, Andreas. *The European Neighbourhood Policy: Foreign Policy at the EU's Periphery*. Bonn: Center for European Studies, 2006.

McCormack, Mark H., and William E. Butler (eds.). *The Laws of Treaties in Russia and the Commonwealth of Independent States: Texts and Comments*. Cambridge: Cambridge University Press, 2002.

Mickiewicz, Tomasz. *Economic Transition in Central Europe and in the Commonwealth of Independent States*. Basingstoke: Palgrave, 2005.

Molchanov, Mikhail. "Regionalism and Globalization in the Post-Soviet Sphere." *Studies in Post-Communism* 9 (2005): 1–28. Online at: www.stfx.ca/pinstitutes/cpcs/studies-in-post-communism/Molchanov2005.pdf.

Olcott, Martha Brill, et al. *Getting It Wrong: Regional Cooperation and the Commonwealth of Independent States*. Washington, D.C.: Carnegie Endowment for International Peace, 1999.

Shenfield, Stephen D. (ed.). *Transborder and Interregional Cooperation Between Russia and the Commonwealth of Independent States*. Armonk, NY: M.E. Sharpe, 2005.

Slay, Benjamin. *The Commonwealth of Independent States and the Global Commons*. New York: Sharpe, 2003.

Stadelbauer, Jörg. "Die GUS zwischen Integration und Fragmentierung: Zehn Jahre GUS—eine Zwangsgemeinschaft von Erben." *Praxis Geographie* 32, no. 1 (2002): 4–9.

Strezhneva, Marina. *Social Culture and Regional Governance: Comparison of the European Union and Post-Soviet Experiences*. Commack: Nova Science Publishers, 1999.

6. Region-Building in the Pacific Ocean

Pacific Islands Forum (PIC)
www.forumsec.org.

Documents

Agreement Establishing the Pacific Islands Forum Secretariat (30.10.2000). Online at: www.austlii.edu.au/au/other/dfat/treaties/notinforce/2000/14.html.

Pacific Island Countries Trade Agreement (PICTA) (18.08.2001). Online at: www.ftib.org.fj/uploaded_documents/Picta.pdf.

Pacific Agreement on Closer Economic Relations (PACER) (18.08.2001). Online at: www.austlii.edu.au/cgibin/sinodisp/au/other/ dfat/nia/2002/11.html?query=^PACER.

Agreement Establishing the Pacific Islands Forum (08.11.2005). Online at: www.forumsec.org/_resources/article/files/ Forum%20Agreement%202005.pdf.

Asian Development Bank—Commonwealth Secretariat (eds.). *Toward A New Pacific Regionalism: Joint Report to the Pacific Islands Forum*. Manila: Asian Development Bank, 2005.

Crocombe, Ron. *The South Pacific*. Suva: University of the South Pacific, 2001.

Haas, Michael. *The Pacific Way: Regional Cooperation in the South Pacific*. New York: Praeger, 1989.

Holland, Martin. "'Imagined' Interregionalism: Europe's Relations with the African, Caribbean and Pacific States (ACP)." In Heiner Hänggi et al. (eds.), *Interregionalism and International Relations*. Abingdon and New York: Routledge, 2006: 254–271.

Howe, K.R., et al. (eds.). *Tides of History: The Pacific Islands in the Twentieth Century*. Honolulu: University of Hawaii Press, 1994.

Kelsey, Jane. *A People's Guide to PACER: The Implications for the Pacific Islands of the Pacific Agreement on Closer Economic Relations (PACER)*. Suva: Pacific Network on Globalisation, 2004.

Lal, Brij, and Kate Fortune (eds.). *The Pacific Islands: An Encyclopedia*. Honolulu: University of Hawaii Press, 2000.

Rolfe, Jim. "New Zealand and the South Pacific." *Revue Juridique Polynesienne* 1 (2001): 157–169.

Rolfe, Jim. "Peacekeeping the Pacific Way in Bougainville." *International Peacekeeping* 8, no. 4 (2001): 38–55.

Shibuya, Eric. "The Problem and Potential of the Pacific Islands Forum." In Jim Rolfe (ed.), *The Asia-Pacific: A Region in Transition*. Honolulu: Asia-Pacific Center for Security Studies, 2004: 102–115.

Smith, Rosaleen, et al. "Big Brother? Australia's Image in the South Pacific." *Australian Journal of International Affairs* 51, no. 1 (1997): 37–52.

ABOUT THE EDITOR

DR. LUDGER KÜHNHARDT has been Professor of Political Science and Director of the Center for European Integration Studies (ZEI) at the University of Bonn since 1997. After studying history, philosophy, and political science at Bonn, Geneva, Tokyo, and Harvard, and defending his dissertation (1983) and *Habilitation* thesis (1986) at the University of Bonn, he worked as a speechwriter for then German Federal President Richard von Weizsäcker from 1987 to 1989. He was Professor of Political Science at the University of Freiburg between 1991 and 1997, where he also served as Dean of his faculty. He has been Visiting Professor at the College of Europe, the University of Cape Town, the University of Jena, Dartmouth College, Stanford University, Seoul National University, and St Antony's College Oxford. He currently is Visiting Professor at the Catholic University of Milan (since 1997), the Diplomatic Academy Vienna (since 2002), and the Mediterranean Academy of Diplomatic Studies, Malta (since 2007). He has also worked as a Public Policy Fellow at the Woodrow Wilson International Center for Scholars in Washington, D.C. Kühnhardt has widespread experience in academic and political consultancy work. His books include *Die Flüchtlingsfrage als Weltordnungsproblem* (1984); *Die Universalität der Menschenrechte* (1987); *Stufen der Souveränität* (1992); *Europäische Union und föderale Idee* (1993); *Revolutionszeiten: Das Umbruchjahr 1989 im geschichtlichen Zusammenhang* (1994, also in Turkish); *Von der ewigen Suche nach Frieden* (1996); *Zukunftsdenker: Bewährte Ideen des politischen Denkens für das dritte Jahrtausend* (1999); *Atlantik-Brücke: Fünfzig Jahre deutsch-amerikanische Partnerschaft* (2002); *Constituting Europe: Identity, Institution-Building and the Search for a Global Role* (2003); *Erweiterung und Vertiefung* (2005); *European Union—The Second Founding: The Changing Rationale of European Integration* (2008; 2nd revised edition 2010); and *Crises in European Integration. Challenges and Responses, 1945–2005* (2009).